1,000,000 Books

are available to read at

www.ForgottenBooks.com

Read online
Download PDF
Purchase in print

ISBN 978-0-331-51842-9
PIBN 11082977

This book is a reproduction of an important historical work. Forgotten Books uses state-of-the-art technology to digitally reconstruct the work, preserving the original format whilst repairing imperfections present in the aged copy. In rare cases, an imperfection in the original, such as a blemish or missing page, may be replicated in our edition. We do, however, repair the vast majority of imperfections successfully; any imperfections that remain are intentionally left to preserve the state of such historical works.

Forgotten Books is a registered trademark of FB &c Ltd.
Copyright © 2018 FB &c Ltd.
FB &c Ltd, Dalton House, 60 Windsor Avenue, London, SW19 2RR.
Company number 08720141. Registered in England and Wales.

For support please visit www.forgottenbooks.com

1 MONTH OF FREE READING

at

www.ForgottenBooks.com

By purchasing this book you are eligible for one month membership to ForgottenBooks.com, giving you unlimited access to our entire collection of over 1,000,000 titles via our web site and mobile apps.

To claim your free month visit: www.forgottenbooks.com/free1082977

* Offer is valid for 45 days from date of purchase. Terms and conditions apply.

English
Français
Deutsche
Italiano
Español
Português

www.forgottenbooks.com

Mythology Photography **Fiction**
Fishing Christianity **Art** Cooking
Essays Buddhism Freemasonry
Medicine **Biology** Music **Ancient
Egypt** Evolution Carpentry Physics
Dance Geology **Mathematics** Fitness
Shakespeare **Folklore** Yoga Marketing
Confidence Immortality Biographies
Poetry **Psychology** Witchcraft
Electronics Chemistry History **Law**
Accounting **Philosophy** Anthropology
Alchemy Drama Quantum Mechanics
Atheism Sexual Health **Ancient History**
Entrepreneurship Languages Sport
Paleontology Needlework Islam
Metaphysics Investment Archaeology
Parenting Statistics Criminology
Motivational

AMERICAN AND MEXICAN COMMISSION

HERMAN STURM

VERSUS

THE REPUBLIC OF MEXICO

Claim No. 676.

INDIANAPOLIS:
J. G. DOUGHTY, PRINTER, 2D FLOOR, TILFORD'S BUILDING.
1872.

MAR 5 1910

AMERICAN AND MEXICAN COMMISSION.

THE CLAIM OF HERMAN STURM

VERSUS

THE REPUBLIC OF MEXICO.

No. 676.

Herman Sturm, the claimant in the above case, makes oath and says:

Sometime in the month of April, 1865, General José M. J. Carvajal, who represented himself to be the Governor of the Mexican States of Tamaulipas and San Luis Potosi, requested me to assist him and his Government in obtaining *materiel* of war, and other supplies in this country.

During several interviews, General Carvajal explained to me that he was the confidential agent of the Mexican Government, duly empowered by the same to negotiate a loan in this country, procure arms and munitions of war, and engage foreigners for the military service of that Republic.

He stated to me that his government was then at Paso-del Norté, in the State of Chihuahua, without resources of any kind, and that the few organized troops his Government had were poorly clad, and without arms and ammunition—so much so, that in some States the Liberal forces were compelled to fight the enemy with bows and arrows.

General Carvajal exhibited to me certain documents, written in Spanish, signed and certified to by the proper officers of the

Republican Government of Mexico, which documents he and Major-General Lewis Wallace, who was with him, assured me, gave to said Carvajal full authority to make contracts in the United States, for the purchase of arms, the negotiation of a loan, and for other purposes; and he requested me to accept the position of confidential agent of the Mexican Republic in the United States, to aid him in the fulfillment of his mission.

Being at that time in the city of Washington on business with the War Department for the State of Indiana, and being well acquainted, and on the most friendly terms with the Secretary—Edwin M. Stanton—I took occasion to ascertain from him, whether, as an officer and a citizen of the United States, I would be acting contrary to its laws and wishes if I should accept the proposals made to me by General Carvajal, and become the agent of the Republican Government of Mexico in the United States.

Secretary Stanton assured me, that he knew of no law that would prevent me, as a citizen of the United States, from giving aid and assistance, such as General Carvajal desired, to the Republican Government of Mexico; and that he did not think that the Government of the United States would have the least objection to my accepting the proposals of General Carvajal; and he also promised to aid me so far as he could.

I also communicated with Governor O. P. Morton, under whom I had served since the breaking out of the war in 1861, and was still serving as Commanding Officer of the Arsenal, and the Chief of Ordnance of the State of Indiana.

I communicated to Governor Morton the proposal made to me by General Carvajal, and the wishes of that gentleman, as well as the interview with Secretary Stanton, and requested him to allow me to resign my position for the purpose of giving assistance to the Mexican government, which permission after a while he granted.

On the first of May, 1865, General Carvajal and myself entered into a written agreement, by which, on certain conditions expressed therein, I was authorized to act for the Republican government of Mexico in the United States, as its confidential agent. (See Exhibit No. 1 on file in this case.)

After making this agreement General Carvajal directed me, in the presence of said General Wallace, to make arrangements for purchasing a large quantity of *materiel* of war, specified in a certain schedule which was subsequently approved by him; stating also that he had made arrangements for the money necessary to promptly pay for all these articles, as well as for their transportation to Mexico;

and that he expected me to have everything ready for shipment within three months from the first of May.

For my personal services and expenses during these three months, he promised to pay me not exceeding $20,000 nor less than $10,000. My agreement with General Carvajal was, at his request, to be held secret and confidential; but, as it was essential that I should have an authority of some kind from him, to exhibit to persons with whom dealings were to be had, he executed and delivered to me the instrument entitled "Power of Authority." (Exhibit No. 2.)

General Carvajal dated the "Power of Authority" *Soto La Marina, State of Tamaulipas*, in order, as he told me, to comply with certain suggestions of Mr Romero to him, touching the necessity of avoiding all questions in connection with the neutrality laws of the United States. It was very desirable to have, if possible, a certificate of the genuineness of General Carvajal's official signature and character, under the hand and seal of a Mexican representative, resident in the United States; for that purpose, the certificate of Juan N. Navarro, Consul General of the Mexican Republic, having an office in the city of New York, was appended to said "Power of Authority."

Subsequently, Mr. M. Romero, Envoy Extraordinary, &c , from the United Mexican States to the Government of the United States of America, certified the authority and official character of General Carvajal, in connection with the contract made by General Carvajal with a Mr. Daniel Woodhouse, of New York City; a copy of which certificate was afterwards furnished me by General Carvajal. (Exhibit No. 3.)

From General Carvajal I also received letters of direction and instruction, addressed to me as from Mexico, and relating particularly to the kinds and quantity of stores to be purchased, and arrangements for their shipment. (Exhibits 4, 5 and 6.)

After perfecting my agreement and instrument of authority as stated, I at once proceeded to execute the work entrusted to me by said Carvajal, and as a measure essential to success, engaged many agents, numbers of whom were late officers of the army of the United States, enlisted the sympathy of influential personal friends of mine, many of whom, as well as myself, visited the cities of New York, Cincinnati, Louisville, Ky., St. Louis, Mo., Indianapolis, Pittsburgh, Cleveland, Ohio, and other places, and earnestly endeavored, by means of the public press, personal efforts, and otherwise, to create public opinion in favor of the Republican Government of Mexico.

At the same time, assisted by my agents, I made all arrangements necessary for the purchase of the *materiel* of war specified by General

Carvajal, and its transportation to Mexico, together with several thousand Americans, late volunteers in the army of the United States, who had expressed themselves desirous of assisting the Liberal Government of Mexico, and had agreed to emigrate to that country for the purpose of taking military service after their arrival there, under said Generals Carvajal and Wallace.

Having accomplished this much, I informed General Carvajal of my readiness to proceed to Mexico, and desired of him the funds necessary to pay for the articles I had bought, and the expenses I had incurred incidentally. (Exhibit No. 7.) And on the 5th of August, 1865, in obedience to a telegram from him, I reported to him in person at the Union Place Hotel in New York City.

On my arrival there, I found General Carvajal surrounded by a large number of Mexican Officers, refugees from his country, and prisoners of war just returned from France; and a number of American, German, French and Hungarian gentlemen, whom the General had engaged, and who were depending on him for their subsistence, while waiting transportation to Mexico. I reported to General Carvajal my engagements for purchases, transportation, &c., in detail, and also the amount of expenditures properly chargeable to the secret service fund, advanced by me up to that time. These expenditures amounted to $19,725. And I also reported to him the amount due to me for personal expenses and services under the agreement with him of May 1st, ($10,000,) and an obligation I had contracted, by his direction, for a newspaper at Indianapolis, Ind., called the *Free Press*, ($20,000 in Mexican bonds.) (See Exhibit No. 8.) Said reports were satisfactory to and approved by General Carvajal.

On the 7th day of August General Carvajal handed me two drafts on a Company called the "European, West Virginia Land and Mining Company;" (Exhibits 9 and 10,) with which General Carvajal had made, as he informed me, a contract for the negotiation of a Mexican loan of fifty millions of dollars.

The first draft was for the sum of twenty thousand dollars of Mexican bonds; and it was given me for the purpose of defraying the liability contracted, as above stated, for the "*Free Press*." The second draft was for one million, five hundred thousand dollars, which I was instructed to use for the payment of bills contracted by General Carvajal and the numerous attachés he had around him; and for the payment of articles purchased by me under his instructions, and the amount due to me, as reported to him, under date of August 6th. General Carvajal also promised me, that within a few days, more money would be placed at my disposal to promptly settle all accounts, and enable me to quickly, but very secretly, transport to the Rio Grande the persons engaged, together with the munitions of war I had purchased for Mexico.

On presenting the draft to said Company, payment was refused, and I immediately reported the refusal to General Carvajal.

The non-payment of the drafts, and the subsequent failure of this Company to furnish General Carvajal with the money they had agreed to furnish, placed him in a most embarrassing position, as he had nothing whatever, with which to pay the various debts he had contracted for himself and his numerous dependants.

Under these circumstances, none of the agreements I had made for the purchase of munitions of war and their shipment to Mexico could be carried out; consequently my own position became very embarrassing. I informed General Carvajal of the fact, and requested him to release me from further service of this kind, until he had received the means necessary to carry out his project and the wishes of his government.

General Carvajal, however, urgently requested me not to forsake his government during this dark hour, and many Mexicans who were with him, and who held, and had held influential positions in that country, promised me faithfully that their Government and the Mexican people would gratefully remember and remunerate the services that had been, and might thereafter be rendered by me and the friends I had enlisted in the cause.

I agreed to continue my services; and as neither General Carvajal nor any other Mexican official in this country had the means, I advanced him money freely in order to avoid any excitement or exposure that might be injurious to the Mexican credit.

I also advanced for General Carvajal whatever money was necessary to amicably cancel the engagements that had been made up to that time. These additional advances, up to the 25th day of August, amounted to some $4,600.00.

As I was taken completely by surprise, and was utterly unprepared at the time, for such heavy cash expenditures, having arranged all my affairs at home, with a view to being absent at least two years; and as the necessity was urgent, I had to make a considerable sacrifice, and (in addition to paying out about $2,000 that I had with me) was actually compelled to borrow from several acquaintances various sums, aggregating $2,900, to enable me promptly, and without creating suspicion, to liquidate such obligations of General C. as would not admit of delay. I then returned to Indiana, to arrange my affairs to suit the altered condition of things, and the new obligations I had taken upon myself.

By referring to my agreement with General Carvajal, of May 1st, 1865, it will be seen that funds necessary to overcome difficulties, alluded to generally as "*all* difficulties," in connection with my undertaking, were to be placed at my disposal by him, as a "Secret Service Fund;" which, for the purposes specified, was to be used at my discretion.

The name and object of this fund sufficiently indicate that no detailed account of my disbursements against it was to be kept or reported. General Carvajal not only instructed me to that effect, but went further, and charged me to commit myself as little as possible in writing; stating that he was surrounded by French and Austrian spies, and other persons of doubtful affinities, who might interfere with his mission by vexatious legal proceedings.

Expenditures against the "Secret Service Fund," were, by his instructions, to be considered separate and distinct from expenditures made in the purchase and shipment of *materiel* of war, the former being confidential, and from their peculiar character, not properly matters of detailed account, while for the latter, I was to render, and did render, full reports, as my settlements with Mr. Romero will disclose.

Speaking generally of my outlays chargeable to the said Fund, I remark that, by looking back over the services of various kinds actually performed by me and my agents, and reflecting upon the costs such services would necessarily require of a person who would attempt them; and referring to such memoranda as were casually retained by me in the course of the business; such as my bank accounts, hotel bills, and amount of money drawn from the agent in charge of my private business in Indianapolis, I am satisfied that I expended of my own funds for the benefit of the Mexican Government, in the interval between the 1st of May and the 25th of August 1865, more than $32,000.00.

Having thus arranged the difficulties of General Carvajal in New York, I proceeded at once to Pittsburg, Cincinnati, Louisville and Indianapolis for the purpose of amicably canceling engagements I had made for the purchase of arms, transportation, &c., and on the 28th of August, I received several letters from General Carvajal, dated the 25th inst., enclosing a further agreement and instructions, urging me to redouble my efforts in behalf of the Mexican cause.

These letters, as well as the agreement, are on file, and marked respectively Exhibits Nos. 11, 12 and 13.

My arrangements in the West having been completed, I returned to New York, and, according to the directions of General Carvajal, in conjunction with Mr. J. N. Tifft, of the firm of J. W. Corlies & Co., with whom General Carvajal had made a new contract for the negotiation of a Mexican loan, I exerted myself to enlist the sympathy and active coöperation of my friends, many of whom were wealthy merchants and bankers.

Among the friends thus enlisted was the Hon. Robert Dale Owen, a gentleman of national reputation. I introduced him to General Carvajal, and Mr. Romero, the Mexican Minister; and for several months he engaged in the cause, writing pamphlets and editorials, which were generally read and with good effect.

On the 12th of September, 1865, I returned to General Carvajal, for cancellation, the two drafts he had previously given me, on the "European, West Virginia Land and Mining Co.," and received from him in lieu thereof two other drafts on Messrs. Corlies & Co., the newly appointed Financial Agents, who promised me that they should be paid from the first funds, that should come into their possession to the credit of the Mexican Government. The last named drafts are on file as Exhibits in this case, marked Nos. 14 and 15.

No payments were ever made to me in United States currency on said drafts, but afterwards, at various times, bonds were delivered to me on the order of Mr. Romero, to be used, and which were used by me, in making payments for munitions of war delivered, their shipment, and incidental expenses connected therewith, for all of which satisfactory detailed accounts were rendered by me to Mr. Romero at the time.

The receipts for said bonds, with the dates thereof, will be found endorsed on said draft.

I induced the Hon. Robert Dale Owen and other friends to accompany me to some of the leading bankers and moneyed men in New York City, in order to interest them in the Mexican cause, after which I proceeded to different Western cities to obtain active support for the Mexican Government by offering in exchange for money the bonds of the Republic of Mexico, at the rate of 60 per cent. of their par value; but the capitalists of the country had so little confidence in the stability of the Mexican Government and its good faith that I found it impossible to sell those bonds except to a very small amount. This small sale was reported to and accounted for to Messrs. J. W. Corlies & Co. On the 6th of November, 1865, I was introduced for the first time, to Senor M. Romero, the Minister of the Mexican Republic to the government of the United States, by General Carvajal, who was then residing at the house of Mr. Tifft, in East Seventeenth street, New York city. On the 8th of the same month I had a lengthy interview with Mr. Romero, during which that gentleman assured me of General Carvajal's authority, and expressed himself as exceedingly anxious for the success of his government. We discussed at length the unfortunate position of General Carvajal, and the precarious condition of Mexican affairs, and the best means of removing the difficulties that had presented themselves. (See Exhibit No. 16.)

In this dilemma I proposed to arouse the attention of the American people to the Mexican cause by appealing directly, or through intimate friends and attorneys engaged by me, to the Legislatures of different States then in session, urging the passage of resolutions against foreign intervention in Mexico, and in favor of giving the assistance of this government to the Mexican Republic.

In December of that year, the Legislature of the State of Indiana passed such a resolution, and similar resolutions were passed by the Legislatures of other States.

After this, I caused printed copies of these Legislative expressions to be distributed throughout the United States, in the form of circulars addressed to newspaper editors and prominent persons.

During these operations I also employed many agents, dispatching them to different parts of the country for the purpose of obtaining *materiel* of war and other necessary articles for Mexican bonds, and to form combinations of enthusiastic young men in favor of Mexico. I also urged General Carvajal, Mr. Romero, the financial Agents of Mexico, and others to appeal to the Congress of the United States for aid; and the Hon. Robert Dale Owen, as well as myself, had repeated interviews with the President of the United States, the Secretary of War, prominent Senators and Representatives, and other officials of the United States with reference to that subject.

On the 5th of January, 1866, (see Exhibit No. 17,)I was requested by General Carvajal to proceed to Washington as the Confidential Agent of the Mexican Government, for the purpose of asking of the Congress of the United States a loan of money to the Mexican Government, or a guaranty of the United States Government to a Mexican loan.

In conjunction with the Hon. Robert Dale Owen and Mr. J. N. Tifft, I remained at Washington City almost constantly until the latter part of June, 1866, faithfully and earnestly endeavoring, in conjunction with the Mexican Minister, Senor Romero, to obtain the aid sought by his government.

By the authority vested in me, I employed many agents and attorneys in Washington City and other places, to assist me in urging upon Congress the policy and necessity of giving financial and other aid to the Republic of Mexico, and also to impress upon business men, such as merchants, bankers, and manufacturers throughout the country, that the Mexican bonds issued by Gen'l Carvajal were valid, and that the Mexican government would faithfully fulfill any agreement or contract I, as its agent, might' make with them, and that said bonds would prove a profitable investment, at the rate they were offered for sale.

The employment of these agents became absolutely necessary in consequence of the many dissensions among the Mexicans themselves.

General Ortega, Chief Justice of the Supreme Court of Mexico, claiming to be the legitimate President of that country, had organized a strong party in this country in his favor, and endeavored in every way to thwart the efforts of General Carvajal and Senor Romero.

General Ochoa, a Commissioner of the Mexican Republic, had made a contract with prominent men in San Francisco for the negotiation of a loan of ten millions of dollars; and although Senor Romero declared the issue of such bonds to be without authority, many difficulties arose out of the fact, creating a distrust of all Mexican securities.

The arrival of Santa Anna in this country, caused new trouble and difficulties; and so fearful was the Mexican Minister at this time, that our efforts to obtain a guaranty from the United States, or to obtain other aid—either from the government or the citizens of the United States—might fail, that in a confidential interview he urged me to spare no pains or expense to accomplish the object sought, and offered to place at my disposal the sum of five millions of dollars of Mexican bonds to be used by me as a "secret service fund," (exclusive of that granted me by General Carvajal,) to enable me to overcome all difficulties, and requested me that in case doubts should arise in the minds of persons whom I wished to employ, as to the existence of a "secret service Fund," and my authority to dispose of the same, to refer all such parties to him for information on this subject. (See Exhibit No. 18.)

In accordance with this request of Mr. Romero, I did from time to time request persons who desired information on this subject to go to said Romero; and so far as I know, he did in every instance, state to them that I was acting under the proper authority from General Carvajal, and in full concert and harmony with him, Mr. Romero; that any agreement made with me, as the agent of the

Mexican government, would be faithfully carried out by that government. In addition to all this, Mr. Romero authorized me confidentially to settle the difficulties existing between General J. C. Fremont and the Mexican financial agent, Mr. J. N. Tifft, growing out of the issue of bonds in California by General Ochoa; and he agreed to furnish me with one million dollars of bonds, should I need them, to accomplish this object. *Neither of these sums, however, was ever placed in my hands.*

Myself and agents, as well as the Hon. Robert Dale Owen and many other friends were engaged daily, from early morning until late at night, visiting prominent officers of the government of the United States, Senators and members of Congress, and in many cases, receiving visits from them in return, at our parlors in Willard's Hotel, consulting with them in regard to the best mode of aiding Mexico, and urging upon them the necessity of doing something for that country, and as speedily as possible.

In consequence of the apparent liberality of the Mexican Minister, and his known anxiety to obtain aid, the money promised and the pledges made by him to me, and the absolute necessity, under the circumstances, of doing so, I did not hesitate to furnish the means to give entertainments, and social parties, etc., etc., for the purpose of bringing my friends, and being myself brought in contact with the prominent men of the country to whom we desired to appeal for aid.

Although I can not now distinctly recollect the many persons with whom I myself, the Hon. Robert Dale Owen, the financial agent, Mr. Tifft, and my own agents and attorneys, as well as Mr. Romero himself, were thus brought in contact, I am able to state, nevertheless, that among the prominent gentlemen who were thus constantly appealed to in behalf of the Mexican government, were the President of the United States, the Secretary of War, the General of the Army, and nearly every Senator and member of Congress of the United States.

Notwithstanding the cause of the Republic of Mexico was gaining strength, and obtaining new friends every day, Congress adjourned without passing a law guaranteeing the loan or furnishing any other assistance to Mexico.

In the meantime, however, failing to purchase for bonds, of regular arms dealers, I had succeeded in interesting several individuals and firms in New York city and Philadelphia, who expressed themselves willing to join together for the purpose of selling me a large amount of *materiel* of war for bonds, at prices that were equitable, and in many cases not more than half what the government of the United States, with all the money at its command, paid for similar articles during the late war in this country.

I also succceded in obtaining, from several of the most respectable business men in Philadelphia, two steamers to transport these goods and Mexicans then in this country, and such Americans as had engaged and were ready to go to Mexico to serve the cause there.

By authority from Mr. Romero, I also purchased a small gunboat, for which I induced the vendors to take Mexican bonds, at the rate of sixty cents on the dollar; but two of the guns intended for her I paid for in money.

This much accomplished, General Carvajal returned to Mexico to prepare for the arrival of the vessels and cargoes alluded to, leaving orders for his private Secretary, Col. W. F. Stocking, and his bookkeeper, W. G. Peckham, his surgeon, Dr. Hadden, and several others, to report to me to perform duties regarding which General Carvajal had given me private instructions.

A few days before the General's departure, which occurred on the 16th of May, 1866, said General, Mr. Romero, the Mexican Minister, General Trevino, Mr. Tifft, the financial agent, and myself, had several conferences at the Metropolitan Hotel, in the city of Washington, during which Senor Romero expressed himself as highly pleased with the result of my efforts. He, however, advised General Carvajal not to place too much confidence in the success of my onterprise, as he had been so often disappointed in negotiations he had at various times attempted in this country; and he did not believe it possible that merchants of this country would, in view of the situation of Mexico, furnish arms, etc., as I hoped. He, nevertheless, promised then and there, in the presence of these gentlemen, to assist me, to the utmost of his ability, in any efforts to serve his government. We all, at the same time, pledged ourselves to stand by and support each other, and act in concert in our endeavors to serve the government of Mexico, and especially to keep the utmost faith with every person with whom agreements on contracts had been or should be made.

In this way we proposed to elevate the credit of the Mexican government in the eyes of American citizens.

During interviews I had with General Carvajal, on the 15th of May, (see Exhibits Nos. 20 and 21), in New York city, he handed me a letter, (Exhibit No. 19), in which he approved of all arrangements then made, and instructed me to act in concert with Mr. Romero and General Wallace, in the making of new contracts. He also promised to send me copies of his authorizations from his Government, which documents I subsequently received. (See Exhibits Nos. 22, 23, 24 and 25.) On the day after these interviews with General Carvajal, I arrived in Washington City, and called on Mr. Romero, to whom I communicated my instructions from General C. (See Exhibit No. 26.)

On the 9th of July, 1866, I reported to Mr. Romero my readiness to forward the first cargo of munitions of war to Mexico. (See Exhibit No. 27.)

At my request, to guard against any annoyances, Mr. Romero accompanied me to the General of our army, through whom we obtained an order from the Secretary of the Treasury, permitting the steamers heretofore spoken of, to be cleared at the Custom House in New York. A copy of this order is on file, marked Exhibit No. 28.

On the twenty-sixth day of July, 1866, I dispatched the first steamer, "J. W. Everman," laden with arms and munitions of war, to Brazos, Texas, for General Carvajal; and according to the instructions of said General, I sent as passengers in said vessel, his officers and other Mexicans sent to me by Senor Romero; the ship and cargo being placed under the control of Col. W. F. Stocking, the private Secretary of General Carvajal.

Major General Lewis Wallace, who, for several weeks previous, had in every way assisted me in this enterprise, also took passage in said steamer, as instructed by General Carvajal.

I purposely made the departure of the Everman as public as possible. The United States Revenue Cutter escorted the vessel part of the way down the bay, and several of her officers, with many reporters of the press, were present, and partook of the collation which I had prepared on board for the occasion. I hired a band of music, and chartered a small steamer to bring invited guests back to the city. The sailing was noticed by the New York papers, and papers elsewhere, and with good effect on the public mind. Such a course was expensive; but I then thought, and yet think, that it tended to raise confidence in the goverment I was serving, and helped me to future contracts. It certainly convinced all persons interested, that the United States authorities were disposed to permit dealings of the kind I was engaged in.

A few days afterwards, I dispatched the steam gunboat Sheridan, heretofore mentioned, fully equipped, and sent out in her the officers appointed by General Carvajal to take command of her on her arrival in Mexico.

After the departure of this last vessel, I endeavored to the utmost of my ability to forward the third steamer, Suwance. laden with another cargo of arms, but I met with so many hindrances and delays through the machinations of Ortega and his party, and through General Santa Anna, who had actually established a sort of government on Staten Island, New York, with a Secretary of Foreign Affairs, a War and Treasury Department, etc.; and the agents of the French and Austrian governments in New York and Philadelphia, that the progress of this expedition was retarded very much.

With these difficulties came a much graver one, viz: About the middle of August, the parties in New York and Philadelphia, who had furnished me the steamer J. W. Everman and her cargo, and the Sheridan and Suwanee, received information from their agent at Galveston, Texas, that on the 12th of August, immediately after the cargo of the Everman had been landed in Matamoras, and taken possession of by the Mexican authorities there, the Mexican officers whom I had shipped as her passengers, combined with the troops in Matamoras, had revolted and deposed General Carvajal, and driven him from the city, and had also imprisoned General Wallace, Colonel Stocking, and the other Americans who had taken passage in her, as above stated.

They were further informed that the whole cargo of the Everman had been seized and was being plundered; also that no Mexican officer would receipt for the gunboat Sheridan, then arrived at Brazos.

I communicated this news at once to Mr. Romero, both by letter and in person; and as General Carvajal was deposed, and Matamoras in insurrection against the legitimate government, I consulted with Mr. Romero about a change in the original programme.

As several commissioners had arrived from different parts of Mexico, instructed to obtain aid in this country, Senor Romero requested me to send the Suwanee to another port of Mexico. He directed me also to obtain additional supplies, and transportation for the same.

In regard to future shipments, I requested of him special instructions in writing, which he subsequently gave me. (See Exhibits Nos. 45, 46, 47, 48, 49, 53, 54 and 55.)

The news from Matamoras, and also other places in Mexico, continuing to be even worse than at first anticipated, I was further and greatly embarrassed by the refusal of Messrs. J. W. Corlies & Co. to deliver me on the order of General Carvajal, (for $1,500,000,) the bonds required to make payments due, and shortly maturing, under my contracts.

Messrs. Corlies & Co. declined to deliver these bonds, unless Mr. Romero would furnish them the gold necessary to pay the interest due on them the 1st of October, 1866, as they were public guarantors of the interest up to that date.

I proceeded to Washington and informed Mr. Romero of this refusal, and, afterwards, I was partially relieved from the embarrassment mentioned, by his order and written directions for the delivery of bonds. I succeeded, however, in making various contracts for munitions with other parties to a very large amount.

By the written instructions of Mr. Romero, above referred to, all contracts made thereafter were to be approved by Mr. Navarro, the Consul General of Mexico in New York, or by Mr. Romero, himself.

I accordingly referred the parties who had agreed to sell me arms and munitions of war for Mexican bonds, to that official for his approval.

Said Consul General, verbally approved the contracts I sent to him, stating to the parties interested that the contracts were all right, and that I had proper authority to make them. He declined, however, to put that approval in writing, for the reasons, as he stated, that it was not necessary, and that he was not instructed to sign his name to any contract.

Mr. Romero, in the meantime, unfortunately absented himself from Washington on a pleasure trip to the West with the President of the United States.

I endeavored to reach him by telegraph; yet it was not until the 4th of September that I could obtain any reply from him; and although he then instructed me by telegraph to go to the Consul-General to obtain his approval, and that he would approve my contracts; and although I showed these telegrams, with letters, to the said Consul, he still declined to sign his name to the contracts in approval.

The utmost he would do was to verbally approve their correctness and validity, and he urged me not to wait, but to go ahead, as a written approval was a mere formality that would be settled on the return of Mr. Romero.

In my anxiety to serve the Mexican Government, believing that Mr. Romero on his return would fully approve my contracts in the manner I wished, I took upon myself the responsibility of guaranteeing the fulfillment of some of them.

In other instances, the amount being too large for me to become responsible for, knowing the immediate necessities of the Mexican Government, I urged the parties to fill their undertakings, at least so far that my inspectors might do their duty, and generally prepare the articles purchased for shipment, so as to lose no time.

Some of the parties agreed to this proposition; others refused to have anything further to do with the Mexican business.

Upon the return of Mr. Romero to Washington, about the 10th of September, he informed me by letter that he had instructed Dr. Navarro, the Consul General in New York, to approve my contracts in writing; yet the Consul refused to do so when called upon by the proper parties, on the ground that he had not as yet received Mr. Romero's instructions officially; whereupon, these parties, although more than five thousand stands of arms, their equipments, &c., had been inspected, boxed and made ready for shipment, (the expense of which I had paid,) refused to have anything further to do with the Mexican government. In this way several contracts fell through, amounting in total to more than $1,687,290.00.

In spite of these difficulties, as is fully shown by the correspondence between Mr. Romero and myself, on file in this case, I persevered in my efforts, and succeeded in obtaining a much larger amount of war material and shipping it in various vessels to Mexico.

As no arrangement had been made by Mr. Romero, looking toward the payment of interest on the bonds, the financial agent declined to guaranty said payment further than October 1st, 1866, and to induce parties from whom I wanted to purchase goods for bonds, to take them in payment, it became several times necessary to convince them that others had confidence in the stability and good faith of the Mexican Government.

To do this effectually I advanced, when buying of them for bonds, money with them, sufficient to cover the interest due in April and October, 1867. These coupons were retained by me, expecting of course that the Mexican Government would cheerfully repay me the amount advanced on them. The amount so paid out, as I have repeatedly stated to Mr. Romero was $19,950.00 in currency, but as it was an operation belonging to the secret service, and as I held the coupons, I made no special mention of it in my report to Mr. Romero, he knowing all about the matter.

As the manufacturers of gunpowder in this country generally declined to trust the Mexican Government, owing to their experience in the past, I appealed to Messrs. Dupont de Nemours & Co., manufacturers at Wilmington, Delaware, from whom I had purchased large quantities of powder during the late war, for the State of Indiana, to furnish me needed powder, and take in payment therefor the bonds of the Mexican Government at 60 cents on the dollar.

B

Through the influence of Messrs. Cattell & Co., Wm. J. Taylor, and other prominent gentlemen of Philadelphia, I succeeded in making an arrangement with Messrs. Dupont de Nemours & Co., by which they engaged to furnish me a large quantity of powder for Mexican bonds, provided two drafts amounting to about $9,000, duly accepted by a former minister of the Mexican Government at Washington, but remaining still unpaid, were also paid in the same manner.

As this proposition was so very fair, I at once accepted it, with the approval of Mr. Romero, who subsequently, in a letter, acknowledged the justness of the claim.

He stated, however, that he wished to inform his government of this transaction, assuring me at the same time, that it would certainly and gladly accept the proposal of Messrs. Dupont de Nemours & Co.

The latter part of January, 1867, some four months after the conclusion of this agreement, and after nearly all the powder had been shipped to Mexico, and I had repeatedly urged Mr. Romero to take upon himself the responsibility (as he could not hear from his government) of paying in bonds for the two drafts as agreed, Messrs. Dupont de Nemours & Co. declined to deliver the balance of the powder then urgently needed in Mexico, unless their contract was first complied with. Aware of the necessity of having this powder in Mexico, and anxious to preserve the good name and credit of the Mexican government, I, myself, settled the demands, Messrs. Dupont de Nemours & Co. had on account of these drafts, in full as agreed.

In this connection I may here state, that although the Mexican government, in this way, obtained one of the most necessary materials of war, it never did instruct its minister to comply with the agreement made with Messrs. Dupont de Nemours & Co.

About the commencement of the month of December, 1866, I informed Mr. Romero of the fact, that I had agreed to purchase for Mexican bonds a large quantity of arms and munitions from Mr. James T. Ames, of Massachusets, and other prominent and influential dealers in arms of the United States.

The affairs of his government having become more encouraging, Mr. Romero anticipated orders to discontinue such purchases in this country, and requested me, at an interview I had with him, and subsequently wrote me to the same effect, to select of the different contracting parties a few whose engagements he desired me to fulfill, and make some arrangements with the others by which, without prejudicing the interest of the government, it would not be required to take the articles. This was accomplished after considerable difficulty.

In the interview mentioned, Mr. Romero suggested, that if I could arrange it so that they or myself would send them to Mexico with a view of selling them on private account, he would give every facility to dispose of them, inasmuch as the goods were needed and would be paid for in cash by the Liberal authorities.

I accepted the suggestion, and entered into an arrangement with several prominent dealers in arms and their associates to send a large amount of munitions of war to Mexico on private account. As the Mexican government, some time in the month of February, 1867, had sent a commissioner, Col. E. A. Mexia, here, for the purpose of obtaining more supplies to be sent to Tampico, I chartered a steamer on my own account, and proposed to Mr. Romero to take to Mexico, free of charge, the said Commissioner and several Mexican officers who desired to return home, together with some sixty tons of munitions belonging to that government; provided the said government would give me every facility to dispose of such materials of war as I might send on private account, and require of me no duties or other charges on my cargo or the proceeds thereof.

This proposition, after being fully discussed by Mr. Romero, was gladly accepted by him. He promised to assist me in every way possible.

On the 31st of March, 1867, according to this programme, I dispatched the steamer General McCallum, with a large cargo of munitions of war furnished to me on the faith of my personal credit, and to account for which I am held directly responsible, and also a large quantity of military goods belonging to the Mexican government. At the same time Colonel Mexia and a number of Mexican officers took passage.

The vessel was under the charge of Colonel Stocking, formerly private secretary of General Carvajal, and my brother, R. C. Sturm.

Mr. Romero gave Mr. Stocking a letter of introduction, in Spanish, to General A. Gomez, the commandant of the Liberal forces at Tampico.

The steamer arrived at that port about the 15th of April, 1867. No sooner had she anchored than General Gomez sent an officer of the customs on board and held her in the port, refusing to allow the discharge of the cargo free of duty.

Several of the Mexican officers whom I had sent home in this vessel, as I learned subsequently, turned enemies and joined Gomez in his endeavors to defraud me and my friends.

Through the intervention of Captain Maxwell, of the United States steamer Yantic, the vessel was temporarily released; but was forced to proceed some seventy or eighty miles up the Panuco river, there to discharge the portion of the cargo belonging to the Mexican government.

Whilst on this compulsory trip, the steamer, owing to the tortuous course of the river, which was swift and narrow, was run ashore and sustained serious damages, for which I have settled and paid the owner the sum of $10,000.00.

For the delay in the return of the McCallum to New York and for expenses, caused by the interference of the Mexican authorities at Tampico, I have been sued in the United States Court, at Brooklyn, New York, and a judgment has been recovered against me for $11,888.67, which with costs and interest added amounts to $12,101.35. This judgment I have secured to the satisfaction of the plaintiffs in the case. (See copy of the record in this case and the affidavit of Norman L. Latson, marked Exhibit No. 409.)

On the return of the steamer to Tampico, Mr. Stocking and my brother desired to proceed to Alvarado, Mexico, as advised by Mr. Romero, for the purpose of selling the arms there; but General Gomez would not allow it, and forced the arms to be discharged at Tampico; allowing them, however, finally to be deposited in a store house under the protection of the United States Consul.

The powder, percussion caps, shot, and shell, he compelled Mr. Stocking and my brother to deposit in the *casamata* at Tampico.

General Gomez utterly denied them any privileges or facilities; he even pointed to Mr. Romero's letter of introduction to him, carried out by Mr. Stocking, as a reason for doing so. This letter is on file, marked No. 284.

He also stated that the vessel had cleared for Tampico, and that the government, and especially the port of Tampico, was entitled to all the duties thereon; that he had no guaranty that Mr. Stocking would go to any other Mexican port after he had gone to sea.

Subsequent to this last shipment, at the request of Mr. Romero, I sent in different vessels, the balance of the goods in my charge belonging to the Mexican government.

I also sent a large quantity of other munitions of war, which I had previously contracted for, on private account.

In every way possible, I assisted said government, until the invaders had left and it was in full possession of the whole country.

While thus engaged, I repeatedly called Mr. Romero's attention to the necessity of settling all accounts, yet outstanding, with those who had aided his country.

But he said that he had not obtained from his government any authority to that effect. He, some time in the month of July, informed me that he intended soon to return to Mexico; and, as I was cognizant of all the facts in the different cases, he desired me to proceed there with him, assuring me that, without doubt, his government would promptly settle all claims that had been contracted for through me.

Desiring, however, to make a settlement with me for my personal services, he requested me to state what amount I would take in bonds, or what arrangement could be made with which I would be satisfied. We had several interviews upon the subject. A number of propositions were discussed, and he stated to me that his government would be pleased to remunerate me, and the friends who had assisted me, in a handsome manner, by giving us valuable franchises or privileges for railroads, mining, and other enterprises.

He further stated that, considering the energy I had shown during my connection with his government, and the number of wealthy and influential friends whom I had in this country, it would not be difficult for me to carry out the project we had so often discussed, viz: to attract American enterprise and capital to the development of the resources of Mexico, as a means of bringing about a more friendly and intimate relation between the people of the United States and those of Mexico. I agreed with Mr. Romero to accompany him to Mexico, and offered him the most liberal terms of settlement, and proposed to confer with my friends about the matter. (See Exhibit No. 317.)

Upon consultation with my friends, I determined to investigate the subject thoroughly, and to leave the settlement of the accounts for my services, including those of my friends and agents to whom I was responsible, to the future, as I had previously suggested to Mr. Romero.

At a subsequent interview, I stated this conclusion to him; observing, however, that the amount of money that I had expended in cash for his government in various ways, was one hundred and fifty-seven thousand and five hundred dollars ($157,500). Of that amount, for expenses incidental to and immediately connected with the purchase of munitions of war, and their shipment to Mexico, and for salaries paid to clerks and officers who had remained with me, under General Carvajal's appointment, there was due me the sum of $47,978.57; the two drafts I had purchased from Messrs. Dupont & Co.

to save the credit of the Mexican government, amounted, with interest, to $9,642.91. As the vouchers and bills for the items here enumerated had been already furnished to Mr. Romero, in a report rendered to him on the 23d of August, I requested him to pay me this amount in cash, with interest.

For my services, and those of my friends and agents, as before stated, and for other expenses incurred by me, I proposed to accept some franchise or privileges that would be a fair remuneration, as I had offered him on July 12th.

Mr. Romero expressed himself highly pleased with this arrangement.

It was natural that Mr. Romero should desire to be well received at home. I myself wished to impress the Mexican authorities and people with the friendly feelings Americans, at that time, entertained for them.

With that object, I suggested to Mr. Romero the idea of inviting several prominent men of this country to accompany him home; and proposed, at my own expense, to charter a steamer to take him, his family, Secretary, and invited guests to Vera Cruz.

Mr. Romero gladly accepted this proposal, and invited several prominent men, among them Senator Morton and General Banks.

I chartered and fitted out a steamer for the purpose; but as the government of the United States subsequently tendered him a revenue cutter, Mr. Romero thought it best to accept this offer.

My proposition, being thus declined, in October, 1867, I proceeded on another vessel to Mexico.

On my arrival at the city of Mexico, I urged a speedy settlement of all accounts or claims that had originated through me.

Mr. Romero had been appointed by the Secretary of State of Mexico, to settle the accounts.

I soon found that however kindly Mr. Romero individually may have been disposed, his government did not share the feeling, and could not be brought to a fair settlement of the claims of any American who had rendered it assistance in its long struggle against European intervention.

The press of the country opened upon me in the most vindictive spirit, and spared not one of the American gentlemen in my company, all of whom had been and were true friends of Mexico.

To correct the erroneous statements in the newspapers, and the injurious impressions created thereby, Mr. Romero published a statement of my transactions with his government, (see Exhibit No. 335,) on file in this case, wherein he expressed himself fully satisfied with my conduct and the services I had rendered.

I remained at the Mexican Capital for more than three months vainly endeavoring to make a satisfactory settlement with the authorities.

The settlement I sought, covered the claims of all citizens of the United States, whom I had been instrumental in inducing to aid the Mexican Republic, as well as my own.

My cash expenditures as I had informed Mr. Romero, both verbally and in writing, were somewhat over one hundred and fifty thousand dollars. Of that amount I, at that time, requested reimbursement in cash, of the monies I had expended in connection with the purchase and shipment of arms and material of war; that is, money paid by me for inspection, boxing, drayage, labor, etc. It must be remembered that the goods were paid for in bonds furnished for the purpose; but for all incidental outlay, I advanced the money required.

I also asked repayment of the sums I had paid to clerks originally employed by General Carvajal, but, by his orders, subsequently retained in my employment.

For the amount of the two drafts of Dupont de Nemours & Co., which I had purchased, as before stated, to save the credit of the Mexican government, I also requested payment in cash.

For the balance, all I asked was an equitable fulfillment of the contracts the Mexican government had made with and through me.

Mr. Lerdo de Tejada, the Secretary of Foreign Affairs, directed the repayment to me of the monies advanced for shipment of arms, and payment for the two drafts and the salaries paid as before stated, for which I had furnished specific vouchers. For all other expenses incurred by me, and for my services he proposed to pay me only *eleven thousand dollars*, a sum of money that would not cover the expenses I had incurred during the first three months of my connection with his government.

All my agreements with General Carvajal were utterly ignored, and hardly listened to by Mr. Lerdo, the Secretary of Foreign Relations; for which reason, together with the excited state of the public mind in Mexico against American creditors of that government, I did not then and there, in writing explicitly demand a full settlement of my advances in money, and the amounts due me under the contracts for a secret service fund; but accepted Mr. Romero's suggestion to defer such settlement to a future and more favorable time.

On the 12th day of February, one day before my departure for the United States, Mr. Romero, during a lengthy and private conversation, urged me to accept Mr. Lerdo's proposition. (See Exhibit No. 349.)

He argued that, by not doing so, I might lose the chance of obtaining anything at that time, as Mr. Lerdo was determined not to change his offer.

I proposed to Mr. Lerdo, through Mr. Romero, to make his government a present of my own personal services; *provided*, his government would honorably settle the claims of the American citizens whom I had induced to serve and trust it.

This proposition was also refused; whereupon, I accepted the money offered me by Mr. Lerdo, on account, but not as complete payment or in final settlement, as will distinctly appear from the correspondence filed in this case, marked respectively, from No. 336 to No. 352.

After my return to the United States, I consulted with my friends and such of the creditors as I could meet, and urged the policy of bringing about a treaty, by which all our claims could be definitely settled.

In the month of June, 1868, Mr. Romero returned to this country, and during an interview he urged me, not to press this subject of a treaty, hoping, as he expressed it, that his government would shortly settle all the claims contracted with and by me.

Knowing, however, that the Mexican government was sending money to its agents here, for the purpose of purchasing its bonds at a low price, and that efforts were being made to depreciate the bonds as much as possible, instead of making provisions for paying the interest thereon, then long past due, I insisted on the making of a treaty for the settlement of the claims.

After fully explaining to Mr. Romero the advantages that would accrue to his government from such a treaty, he accepted the idea, and a treaty was accordingly made by Secretary Seward and Mr. Romero, and subsequently ratified. Afterwards, Mr. Romero wrote me a letter referring to the subject. (See Exhibit No. 360, on file in this case.)

In November, 1868, I again went to Mexico. The Mexican authorities had, in the meantime, purchased the greater portion of the cargo previously referred to as shipped by the steamer McCallum, and they had subsequently been guilty of such additional acts of bad faith, in connection with it, as left me no hope of settlement except by personal negotiation.

During this visit, as in the former, I endeavored to impress the authorities with a sense of duty toward their American creditors.

They paid me twenty-five hundred dollars on my account, but refused to settle my claims or those of others in my charge.

Unable to realize anything more from the Mexican government, or reduce the business with it to a satisfactory form, I anticipated a continuance at home of the cruel aspersions of my conduct and character, and constant harrassments by law suits, which would inevitably consume my means, and leave me no time to care for my private affairs, already in a suffering condition. I did not hesitate then to renew, through Mr. Romero, the Secretary of the Treasury, the offer made to his government on the occasion of my first visit, viz: that if the authorities would honorably settle the claims of all those whom I had induced to enter into transactions in aid of the government, I would release it from all claims due to me for my individual services and for the cash I had advanced for it, yet due me.

This offer will substantially appear in a letter to Mr. Romero, on file in this case, marked Exhibit No. 373.

During my stay in Mexico, I had several interviews with Mr. Romero, and availed myself of them to explain fully the disagreeable position in which I found myself placed. I reminded him that I had, in the course of my connection with his government, employed some seventy-five agents and attorneys in different parts of the United States—men of prominence and position, socially and politically—that he was acquainted with most of them, and knew the labor they had performed; and that I had contracted personal obligations to them, under the agreement to provide for and pay me a secret service fund.

I also told him that, since my first visit to Mexico, designing men had circulated rumors seriously compromising my reputation for truth and honor in connection with the faith and credit of his government; that the rumors were to the effect that his government had fully settled with me for my expenditures and all the services rendered by me and my agents and attorneys; that the cargo of the McCallum had been sold and paid for, and I had pocketed the proceeds of the sale.

I further told Mr. Romero, that it had generally become known, that money had been sent from Mexico to official agents of the government in New York, for the purpose, as was believed, of buying in its bonds at as low rate as possible; and it was charged that this speculation was authorized by his authorities; that instead of paying the interest, long over due, upon the bonds, agents, acting under direction of his department of the government, were actually endeavoring to depreciate their value to facilitate their purchase at the lowest possible rates; that many persons in the United States charged, and really believed, that I was an accessory to this scheme.

I also explained to him that, in consequence of this depreciation of the bonds, and the general bad faith that had characterized the dealings of his government with the claimants whom I represented, certain marine insurance companies, against which I and others associated with me had a claim for $163,000, on account of a cargo of arms, ($54,000.00 of which belonged to his government, and for which I, as agent, had become responsible,) lost in the Gulf of Mexico while on the way to Vera Cruz, had, as a defense to suits then pending, set up my connection with his government, and charged me with fraud. I urged Mr. Romero to explain all these things to Mr. Lerdo, that his associates in the conduct of affairs might be induced, out of consideration for their own interests, to promptly settle the claims about which, as above stated, I was so solicitous.

On the day before my departure from the city of Mexico, on this second visit, I ascertained through friends in that city, that a most outrageous attempt was being made to injure me and ruin my character in the estimation of the public.

An agent of the aforesaid Insurance companies, who had come to Mexico to obtain testimony against me, had taken advantage of the utter ignorance of the public generally, in regard to the true state of public affairs, and the intense feeling of discontent and opposition then prevalent in Mexico, against some of the gentlemen composing the cabinet of President Juarez; and using a certain letter of recommendation from the State Department of the United States, as also his personal acquaintance with the American Minister as a means to obtain credence; he cunningly arranged to have various false rumors circulated and even to have them published in the opposition press, to the effect: That in conjunction with some of the most prominent public men of the United States and Mexico, (Mr. Romero included,) I had swindled the Mexican Government out of large sums of money, by selling her, at enormous profits, old and worthless arms obtained from the United States Government; that we had divided this money between us; and that a steamer had been laden with boxes, filled with stones and had been sunk to obtain the insurance, etc., etc. In addition he actually attempted to bribe testimony to that effect. Fortunately this matter was found out in time to prevent mischief.

This incident (for the truth of which I refer to Mr. Romero, General Rosecranz, then United States Minister in Mexico, and Mr. Black, then United States Consul in Mexico,) determined me to make a last effort to bring my affairs with the Mexican Government to a close. I called on Mr. Romero, who was fully informed of the aforementioned plot, and begged him to intercede for me with his government, and to explain the disagreeable position in which, in consequence of the failure of his government to keep faith, I was placed; and I said to him (and subsequently wrote him to the same effect,) that I would relinquish every cent of my personal claims against his government, if it would settle with those I had induced to trust it, so that I might be relieved from embarrassment.

Although Mr. Romero promised to assist me to his utmost, all my efforts at settlement failed, and I returned home to struggle with my misfortunes as I best could.

To vindicate my conduct and character in the estimation of the many merchants and capitalists from whom I had purchased, and the agents and attorneys whom I had employed, who might not otherwise understand me, and who held me responsible for persuading them to put their trust in the Mexican government, I printed, after I returned to the United States, a pamphlet entitled "*The Republic of Mexico and its American Creditors.*" Upon learning the character of the work, Mr. Mariscal, Minister of Mexico resident in Washington, requested me, through my attorneys, Messrs. Johnston and Stanton, not to put it into further circulation. He promised, if I would withhold it, he would do all in his power to bring about a satisfactory settlement of my claims. I agreed, at his request, to accommodate him for fifty days. No such settlement has been made. The correspondence with Mr. Mariscal is herewith filed. See Exhibits marked 389, 390, 391 and 392.

By way of recapitulation I will state, that I was actively and constantly engaged, as the Agent of the Mexican government, from May 1st, 1865, until January 31st, 1868—a period of two years and nine months. In that time I made a large number of purchases for Mexico. The contracts made prior to August 25th, 1865, which covered all the *materiel* of war for forty thousand infantry, three thousand cavalry, fifteen batteries of artillery, and two thousand engineers, with one million of rations and a large amount of quartermaster, medical, and hospital supplies, were made on a cash basis, but the articles were never delivered, on account of the failure of the European and West Virginia Land and Mining Company, and amounted to over three million dollars.

My subsequent contracts for material of war, which was to be paid for in bonds, amounted to three million five hundred thousand dollars in United States money. The purchase of the Sheridan, and the charters of the steamers Everman, Suwanee and Vixen amounted to three hundred and twelve thousand, one hundred and ninety dollars, ($312,190.00.) In addition, various shipments were made on sailing vessels, the expenses of which I arranged should be paid by the Mexican authorities on arrival and delivery of the goods in Mexico.

The contract with Dewhurst & Emerson was fulfilled only to about the amount of $176,625, the firm having declined to furnish more until the goods they had delivered for transportation on the steamer Everman had been paid in bonds, according to the terms of sale.

To provide shipment for all of the said purchases, I chartered the following vessels:

Steamer J. W. Everman, of H. Simons, Philadelphia.
Steamer Suwanee, of E. G. Cattell, Philadelphia.
Steamer Vixen, of J. T. Wright, New York.
Steamer General McCallum, of N. L. Latson, New York.

In addition to said steamers, I secured transportation on sailing vessels for a large portion of the property.

The charter money of the steamers was paid in Mexican bonds, except the McCallum, for which I paid in cash. Besides the above I purchased of Henry Simons, of Philadelphia, the steamboat Sheridan, fully equipped, for $88,000, also payable in Mexican bonds.

I succeeded also in making various contracts to a large amount, with different parties, which fell through, partly in consequence of the unfortunate absence of Mr. Romero, and the refusal of Mr. Navarro to properly approve them, as above narrated, and partly on account of the failure to promptly furnish the bonds for payment. Of such contracts, I now remember the following:

One with Barton H. Jenks, of Philadelphia...............	$55,000 00
One with Fitch, Burbridge & Dunlap, New York........	714,750 00
One with A. K. Cory, New York.............................	411,000 00
One with Alfred W. Jones, New York...............about	330,000 00
One with D. Lafavour, New Jersey.................	176,540 00
	$1,687,290 00

I also purchased of Herman Boker & Co., and others in New York, goods to the amount of about $125,000, which, agreeably to the wishes of Mr. Romero, I took, as before stated, upon my own account, and sent to Mexico in the steamers General McCallum, and Wilmington, the brig Blonde, and schooner S. T. Keese.

The negotiations and contracts for the purchase of material of war prior to August, 1865, were conducted quietly, and without stating to the parties the name of the government for which I was acting, (save in a few instances) and as the articles were to be paid for in cash on delivery, my services and expenses in conducting these transactions were light, in comparison with what was required in the attempt to secure a guaranty of the loan mentioned, and in my subsequent efforts to make purchases of war material &c., and procure charters of vessels for Mexican bonds; as the failure of the "European and West Virginia Land and Mining Company" to furnish money; the failure of Congress to guaranty a loan; and the helpless condition of the liberal government of Mexico were well known and fully understood by business men, who invariably referred to these facts when I attempted to open negotiations with them.

In the face of these embarassing circumstances, and others herein stated, I sometimes almost despaired of being able to inspire prudent men with sufficient confidence in the stability, resources and good faith of the Mexican government, to induce them to part with their property on the terms I was enabled to offer them. I however persevered in the work, with the assistance of my numerous agents and attorneys, but with all my efforts and expenditures it was nearly a year before I was able to conclude the first contract for material of war for bonds.

In this connection it is proper to state that whilst persons of ability, character and influence were induced to assist me in my efforts, for certain stipulated portions of the "Secret Service Fund" of five hundred thousand dollars; many of them required, in addition thereto, that I should advance them from time to time, the money required to meet traveling and other necessary expenses incident to their engagement with me.

These advances were large, but from the circumstances attending them and the character of the service, receipts were not taken, or an account kept beyond a general memorandum of my outlays for expenses, other than those connected with the purchase and shipment of war material.

When I undertook to act as Agent of Mexico, the Chief Executive of that country, and his cabinet advisers, were in the corner of the most distant State of the Republic, without money, or credit, or army—facts well known to the people of the United States, and calculated to influence every intelligent and prudent man to whom I might address myself for services or aid in behalf of that government, and it is not too much to say, that without the money advanced by me, and the energy and zeal of myself, my agents, attorneys and friends, a box of arms could not have been purchased on the credit of that government in the United States. This allusion is not made in a spirit of unkindness toward the government or people of Mexico, who were served by me with fidelity, energy and enthusiasm during the best years of my life, and the painful facts stated have been mentioned solely for the purpose of illustrating the character and value of my services.

And deponent says further, that the foregoing statements of facts, so far as the same are within his personal knowledge, are true, and that as to facts derived from information of others, he verily believes them to be true; that the letters and documents filed by him in support of this claim, signed by General Carvajal, Mr. Romero, Mr. Lerdo de Tejada, and Mr. I. Mariscal, are the original documents, duly signed by them respectively, in manner and form as received by deponent from them; that the documents filed by him in support of said claim, purporting to have been written by deponent to the several parties addressed, are true copies of documents actually sent by him to the parties addressed, and as such retained by him in course of the transactions to which they allude; that the several memoranda of interviews filed by deponent in support of said claim, are correct memoranda of conversations actually had by and between the parties named therein, at the times and places therein given, and that they were taken either immediately, or within twenty-four hours, after the interviews occurred. And further deponent saith not.

H. STURM.

STATE OF INDIANA, } ss:
MARION COUNTY,

Before me, George H. Campbell, a Notary Public in and for said County and State, personally appeared the above named Herman Sturm, who subscribed and made oath to the foregoing affidavit, on this eighteenth (18th) day of January, in the year of our Lord eighteen hundred and seventy-two (1872).

IN WITNESS whereof, I have hereunto set my hand and affixed my Notarial Seal the day and year above written.

[SEAL.]

GEORGE H. CAMPBELL,
Notary Public.

AMERICAN AND MEXICAN COMMISSION.

[EXHIBITS.]

PAPERS AND DOCUMENTS

RELATING TO THE CLAIM OF

HERMAN STURM
vs.
REPUBLIC OF MEXICO.
} No. 676.

Agreement.

No. 1.]

"This agreement, made at Washington City, D. C., U. S. of America, this first day of May, 1865, between General Jose M. J. Carvajal, Governor of the States of Tamaulipas and San Luis Potosi, acting for the said States and the United States of Mexico, and General Herman Sturm of Indiana, witnesses: That said General Carvajal hereby engages said Sturm as Agent of the Mexican Republic, for the purchase and shipment of all material necessary for the prosecution of the war against the French; also as Secret Agent, to raise and transport emigrants from the U. States to Mexico; and generally to aid the cause of the Mexican Republic, by all means not in violation of the laws of the U. S. of America. Said General Carvajal agrees to pay to said General Sturm, for his said services and personal expenses in and about the same, while in the U. States, according to written orders, to be given him separately, and which are not to exceed, say, twenty thousand dollars, nor be less than ten thousand dollars in U. S. currency.

"At the close of the war, said Sturm is to have a position in the Ordnance Department, within the military command of the said General Carvajal, in Mexico, and be charged with the building of arsenals, and the manufacture of ordnance, and everything pertaining thereto, with the rank and pay of Brigadier-General in the Mexican army.

"General Sturm on his part agrees, for and in consideration of the above and other covenants and agreements to be kept and performed by the said General Carvajal and the Mexican Government, to resign his position as Brigadier-General and Chief of Ordnance of the State of Indiana, and give his whole time and attention to the interests of Mexico, placing himself, for the purpose, under the orders of the said Carvajal and the Supreme Government of the Republic of Mexico.

"To enable the said Sturm to carry out the plans which may be formed in this connection, he shall select such officers as may be necessary to him in the business; and to secure their services, the said Sturm is authorized to promise them, in case they emigrate to Mexico, positions and salaries equivalent to those last held by them in the service of the United States Government or the State service, or held by them at the time of their engagement.

"Said Carvajal also agrees to furnish, or to place at the disposal of said Sturm, all the funds necessary for the fulfillment of his contracts for arms, material, etc., as well as for the inspection and transportation of the same, and of the emigrants he may succeed in engaging, while they remain on duty in the United States, and until their arrival in Mexico. And the better to make the efforts of the said Sturm successful in overcoming *all* difficulties, the said Carvajal further agrees to place at the disposal of the said Sturm the necessary funds, when it shall be in his power so to do; the same to be in his hands a "Secret Service Fund," to be used at his discretion, to gain sympathy, opinion, and action in behalf of the Republic of Mexico, in the United States.

"It is further mutually agreed between the contracting parties, that this agreement shall be held strictly confidential, never to be shown or exposed unless specifically called for by General Carvajal, or the Mexican Government; or unless rendered necessary for the protection of said Sturm.

"In witness whereof, the parties hereto have interchangeably set their hands and seals, the day and year above written. [SEAL.]
  (Signed,)   "JOSE M. J. CARVAJAL,
Governor of the States of Tamaulipas and San Luis Potosi, and Agent for the Mexican Republic."
  (Signed,)   H. STURM. [SEAL.]

Power of Authority.

No. 2.]

"*To Whom it May Concern:*

"Being well assured that General Herman Sturm, of Indiana, has all the requisite qualifications to perform the duties hereinbelow specified, this is to certify, that the undersigned (having full authority so to do, by virtue of certain Supreme Orders, to me issued by Benito Juarez, Citizen President of the Republic of Mexico) has, this first day of March, A. D. 1865, appointed and commissioned the said Herman Sturm my lawful agent, for me, and in my name, place, and stead, to do the things following, to-wit:

First, "To contract for and purchase the Ordnance and Ordnance Stores contained in a printed invoice marked "A," and made a part of this instrument.

Second, "To contract for and purchase Quartermaster's Stores, including transportation, as per printed invoice herewith attached, and marked "A."

Third, "To contract for and purchase Commissary Stores, as per printed invoice herewith attached, and marked "A."

Fourth, "To purchase or charter six steamers, at least three of which shall be constructed or altered in such manner as to be able to ply on the coast of the Gulf of Mexico, and on the western rivers of the United States.

Fifth, "As incidental to the foregoing authorities, the said Herman Sturm is further empowered to appoint all subordinates, officers and agents, and contract with such boat captains and crews as may be necessary, in his opinion, to enable him to execute the objects contemplated; all of which are well known to him and to the undersigned, and Major-General Lew. Wallace of the U. S. Army.

Sixth, "All appointments, contracts, and shipments which the said Herman Sturm may make, under and by virtue of this instrument, shall, in my absence, be by and with the approval of the said Major-General Lew. Wallace.

Seventh, "Said Herman Sturm has full instructions and authority to arrange for the payment of such obligations as he may contract under the foregoing authority.

"SOTO LA MARINA,
STATE OF TAMAULIPAS, REPUBLIC OF MEXICO,
Dated March 1st, 1865.

(Signed,) "JOSE M. J. CARVAJAL, [SEAL.]
Governor of the States of Tamaulipas and San Luis Potosi, acting for said States and the U. S. of Mexico."

"The undersigned, Consul-General of the Mexican Republic in the United States of America:

"I do certify, that the signature authorizing the foregoing document, is that of General Jose M. J. Carvajal, of the Army of the Mexican Republic, Governor of the States of Tamaulipas and San Luis Potosi, and duly authorized Agent for the Constitutional Government of the Republic, under the Supreme Orders of the 8th and 12th of November, 1864, issued in accordance to law.

"Done under my hand and seal at my Consular Office, at the [CONSULAR] city of New York, this 5th day of June, 1865. [SEAL.]
(Signed,) "JUAN N. NAVARRO."

Certificate of M. Romero.

No. 3.]

LEGACION MEXICANA
EN LOS
ESTADOS UNIDOS
DE
AMERICA.

"The undersigned, Envoy Extraordinary and Minister Plenipotentiary from the United Mexican States to the Government of the U. S. of America, do hereby certify that General J. M. J. Carvajal, of the Mexican Army, is the Governor of the State of Tamaulipas of Mexico, appointed by the National Government of the Republic, and that he was authorized by his Government, under date of November 12, 1864, to make contracts for the purchase of arms and munitions of war and negotiate funds, under the terms and conditions and with power therein specified; *and that any contract or purchase that he will make in pursuance of and in accordance to said instruction, will bind the National Government of Mexico and the public faith of the country.*

"Done in the city of Washington, this 7th day of June, in the year 1865.
  (Signed,)   "M. ROMERO."

Carvajal to Sturm.

No. 4.]   HEADQUARTERS FORCES OF THE REPUBLIC IN TAMAULIPAS, SAN LUIS POTOSI, AND HUASTECAS, *Soto La Marina, March 11th, 1865.*

SPECIAL ORDERS No. —.]

General Herman Sturm is directed to proceed to the execution of the authority transmitted to him, dated March 1st, 1865. The better to execute the same, he will make all necessary arrangements for transportation of the material and supplies which he may succeed in purchasing, and in so doing he will exercise a sound discretion in forwarding them by *sea* or *land;* selecting that route which may prove under the circumstances the most secure and expeditious.

He is also instructed that a point, at or near Brownsville, Texas, is the place of delivery; the exact point, to be determined by the military situation in the State of Tamaulipas.

  (Signed)   JOSE M. J. CARVAJAL,
Govr. of Tamaulipas and San Luis Potosi acting for said States and the United States of Mexico.

Carvajal to Sturm.

No. 5.]   SAN CARLOS, TAMAULIPAS, *Republic of Mexico, July 4th, 1865.*

COL. H. STURM,
  Indianapolis, Ind.

COL.: You are hereby authorized and requested to buy for my Gov't the following articles, which you will ship according to instructions:

100 tons of Cannon powder.
100 do of Rifle   do.

The same to be packed in such a manner as to prevent damage from moisture or other accidents.

         Respectfully yours,
  (Signed)   JOSE M. J. CARVAJAL,
Govr. of Tamaulipas and San Luis Potosi, acting for said States and the United States of Mexico.

Carvajal to Sturm.

No. 6.]
SAN CARLOS, TAMAULIPAS,
Republic of Mexico,
July 4th, 1865.

COL. H. STURM,
    Indianapolis, Ind.:

You are hereby authorized and requested to buy for my Gov't the following articles, which you will ship according to instructions:

Fifteen Batteries of Field Artillery.
Two Batteries of Siege Artillery.
Carriages and Caissons for same complete. Also all implements, equipments and extra articles to meet accidents.
100,000 rounds assorted ammunition for Field Artillery.
20,000 rounds, &c., for Siege Artillery.

Respectfully yours,
    (Signed)   JOSE M. J. CARVAJAL,
Govr. of Tamaulipas and San Luis Potosi, acting for said States and the United States of Mexico.

Sturm to Carvajal.

No. 7.]   INDIANAPOLIS, July 28th, 1865.

SIR: I have the honor to report, that everything is attended to on this end of the line, and so far as we are concerned, you and Gen'l W. may leave at ten days' notice. Steamers have not yet been chartered, as the prices vary from day to day and there is no lack of them, so we can have them at two days' notice. Capt. Smith is here and will attend to that upon a telegraphic order. Col. B., I understand has fifteen hundred laborers ready near Memphis and I think they ought to be shipped first. The tools can all be concentrated in a few days, and I intend to forward them from Cairo, St. Louis; Evansville and Madison, Indiana. Everything is according to your wishes, and all that is required now is to commence moving. There are many things to be attended to in New York and I shall have to do that myself. For that purpose I propose to come on there, whenever you are ready. Be pleased to inform me of your further wishes in the matter.
    In great haste,
        Respectfully your Obt. Servt.,
            H. STURM.
To Gen'l J. M. J. C.

Sturm to Carvajal.

No. 8.]   NEW YORK, August 6th, 1865.

GEN'L: I have the honor to enclose herewith a statement of moneys required for the payment of the various contracts and purchases made by me, of which I have rendered you a complete list, as well as for various other expenses of which we spoke to-day, the part of which concerning me I have rendered you the vouchers for:

Total amount for armament as per statement	$3,287,000
For powder about	80,000
" medical stores	45,000
" transportation	650,000
	$4,062,000

Of the above everything is arranged for by me, *definitely*, and ready for shipment at short notice, except the Medical Stores, which are to be furnished by Dr. Bliss, who has not yet sent his bill, and the transportation.

In addition to the above there is required—

For cash advanced by me as per statement rendered last night, the sum of	$19,725
For personal expenses and services as per agreement	10,000
" payment of salaries, as estimated by you	26,500
" " of various bills, estimated by you	12,000
Total	$68,225

In addition there is due to me the sum of $20,000 for account of "Free Press," for which latter account, I would be pleased to take Mexican bonds in payment, as stated to you.

I am, Sir, Very Respectfully,

Your Obt. Servt.,

H. STURM.

To Gen'l J. M. J. CARVAJAL,
  Present.

Draft for $20,000.

No. 9.] NEW YORK, August 7th, 1865.

To the United States, European and West Virginia Land and Mining Company:

You are hereby directed to deliver to the order of General H. Sturm the sum of Twenty Thousand Dollars ($20,000) in Mexican Bonds.

$20,000. JOSE M. J. CARVAJAL,

Govr. of Tamaulipas and San Luis Potosi, acting for said States and the United States of Mexico.

NOTE. *Canceled.*—The contract having been canceled, another similar order has been drawn on Messrs. Corlies & Co., under date of Sept. 12th, 1865, for the same amount.

Draft for $1,500,000.

No. 10.] NEW YORK, August 7th, 1865.

To the United States, European and West Virginia Land and Mining Company:

You are hereby directed to pay to the order of General H. Sturm, the sum of One Million Five Hundred Thousand Dollars ($1,500,000) in United States Currency, out of the first disposable funds accruing from the sale of Mexican Bonds, and in case, at the time of the presentation of this order there shall not be sufficient funds in your possession to fill the same, you are then required to deliver to the said General H. Sturm, or to his order an equivalent in Mexican Bonds, of the whole of said sum or any fraction thereof that may be wanting to complete said sum, at the rate of Forty Dollars ($40) in gold, on the Hundred.
$1,500,000. JOSE M. J. CARVAJAL,
Govr. of Tamaulipas and San Luis Potosi, acting for said States and the United States of Mexico.

NOTE. *Canceled.*—The contract having been canceled another similar order has been drawn on Messrs. Corlies & Co. under date Sept. 12th, 1865, for same amount.

Carvajal to Sturm.

No. 11.] "NEW YORK CITY, August 25, 1865.
[Confidential.]

GEN. H. STURM,
Indianapolis, Indiana:

"*General:* I cannot longer conceal from myself and friends, that the so-called 'United States, European and West Virginia Land and Mining Company, is a fraud, and its agent, Woodhouse, a swindler. Accordingly I have thrown them off.

"My labors and hopes in that connection are, therefore, lost, the cause of my poor country retarded, and new embarrassments thrown around it. Yet I do not despair. In view of the arrangements made by you and General Wallace with other parties, I consider it only a duty to at once apprise you of the unfortunate and (to me personally) bitter disappointment, that you may take such action as may be necessary to satisfy and appease all with whom you have contracted, or may now be in negotiation.

"*It is of the highest importance that the good faith and name of my Government be not brought into contempt and ridicule by public exposures in the courts or newspapers.* This new aggravation makes my mission more difficult than ever. That mission, as you know, is to procure material assistance for my country, whose condition is gloomy beyond description.

"Two facts, alone, almost crush us: our enemy is the most powerful in the world, and actually holds our cities and the forts from which we chiefly derive our revenue; and the head of our Government, with his Cabinet, is in the corner of the most distant State of the Republic, without money, or credit, or army—facts well-known to the people of the United States, and calculated to influence every intelligent and prudent man to whom you may address yourself.

"My powers are very great—drawn, evidently, in view of the condition alluded to. They contemplate a necessity for extraordinary sacrifices, and seem to require them of me rather than fail in my task. The responsibility is terrible. If I make the sacrifices, will the necessity be appreciated by my people? I will trust them, and leave results to God. What are millions, so they purchase the independence of my country?

"I am not surprised that you report it difficult to find contracting parties. Certain preliminaries heretofore neglected must now be attended to: thus, the sympathy, voice and influence of the most prominent men in the country must be gained; the Press must be on our side; above all, we must enlist in the cause the most active and untiring agents, *and if they should at the same time be agents of the U. S. Government, so much the better.* I desire you to proceed to do this at once. General Wallace will advise and co-operate with you. The great advantage of our enemy is that he has money, and is spending it freely, while we have only promises to offer. The sole method of equalization is to use our promises on the most liberal scale. With this view, I have signed, and now send you, the annexed agreement, which is intended to be taken as incidental to the agreement heretofore delivered to you in Washington, under date of May 1, 1865.

"Your conduct has inspired me with faith that this great trust, in which my name and character and the credit of my Government and people are so deeply involved, will not be betrayed. If, after reading this letter and the agreement, you are in doubt as to their intent and meaning, come and see me in person: the nature of the business is of a kind that requires explanations to be exclusively verbal.

[Signed,]   "JOSE M. J. CARVAJAL."

Agreement for a Secret Service Fund.

No 12.]   "NEW YORK, August 25, 1865.

"*To whom it may concern:*

"WHEREAS, Acting in conformity to my authority, and instructions from my Government, under date of the 8th and 12th of November, 1864, the undersigned, Governor of the States of Tamaulipas and San Luis Potosi, and Agent and Commissioner for and in behalf of the General Government of Mexico, is about to contract with the house of J. W. Corlies & Co., of the City of New York, for the negotiation of a national loan of ($30,000,000), thirty million of dollars: In view of the funds expected to be raised or realized from the said contract and negotiations, and to enable General Herman Sturm, heretofore (to-wit, on the 1st of May, 1865,) by me duly appointed General Agent of my Government, with specified powers and duties, to successfully and speedily execute certain duties and offices mentioned in the letter of instructions to him directed and bearing even date herewith, the undersigned hereby undertakes and pledges himself officially and in the name of the Mexican Government, to pay to him the sum of Half a Million ($500,000) Dollars in United States currency, or its equivalent in bonds of the Mexican Republic at the regular rate; to be used by the said Gen. Sturm as a "Secret Service" fund, and to guaranty any promise, contract, or arrangement which he may have already, or may hereafter make, with any person or persons, in the effort to carry out the authority stated as heretofore given to him as General Agent, and so forth: provided, that such promises or contracts shall always be in conformity with my instructions given to him.

"It is also understood between the undersigned and the said General Sturm, that the Five Hundred Thousand Dollars, herein specified, are exclusive of any sum which may be used or placed at his disposal to buy arms, munitions, transportation, etc.; and that in the disposition of this half million of "Secret Service" fund, the said Sturm is to be at liberty to make engagements, either in his own name or that of my Government; and that for the disbursement of the said fund, or any part thereof, he shall not be held to account by my Government, or by any person acting under its authority,—except to furnish, on my order or that of my Government, his statement of the amounts contracted by him to be paid under this authority; without any obligation on his part to give any names where important parties aiding the cause of Mexico might be injured.

"And in the event that no funds should be realized from the sale of bonds about to be undertaken by Messrs. J. W. Corlies & Co., as above stated, or in the event of a failure to issue bonds of the Mexican Republic, the undersigned hereby agrees to and with the said Gen. Sturm, that the said Republic of Mexico shall owe and be indebted to, and liable to pay upon the demand of the said Sturm, or his legal representatives, the said sum of Half a Million ($500,000) of Dollars in United States currency, as an indemnity to him for his engagements made to and with other persons, as contemplated in the letter of secret instructions of this date, and to secure to all such persons whatever promises and undertakings he may be required to make to and with them: as to which, no account, of proofs or vouchers, shall be required by my Government in the final settlement with said Sturm further than his own statement, as above required.

"In witness whereof, I have hereunto set my official signature, at New York City, this 25th day of August, 1865.

[Signed,] "JOSE M. J. CARVAJAL,

"Governor of the States of Tamaulipas and San Luis Potosi, and Agent for the Mexican Republic."

Carvajal to Sturm.

No. 13.] "NEW YORK, August 25, 1865.

"GENERAL H. STURM,

Indianapolis, Indiana:

"SIR—I herewith return you the schedule of Ordnance, Quarter-master's and Commissary stores, which you, on the 1st of May last, submitted to me for approval. I have approved the same, and now desire you to proceed without delay to make the necessary contracts for such articles as are mentioned in this schedule; and in case you should be unable to obtain speedily the kind of articles mentioned in the schedule, you are hereby instructed to purchase, instead, such other kinds of a similar article as you may be able to obtain; leaving it to your judgment and discretion to get the best and most suitable for the purpose it is intended for—which is fully known to you.

"You are also authorized to make such arrangements in regard to payment for these articles—either in United States currency or in Mexican bonds, or both, according to the verbal instructions I have given you—as may in your opinion be most advantageous for my Government. In case payment is made in bonds, you are, under no consideration, to offer them at a lower rate than the minimum value of *sixty cents* on the dollar, in United States currency. A sufficient amount of money, or its equivalent in the bonds of the Republic of Mexico, (at the rate of sixty cents in currency for every dollar in bonds,) will be placed at your disposal whenever required by you for the purpose of promptly paying for all such articles as you may purchase under my instructions, and for meeting such other expenses as you may incur in the inspection, storage and transportation of articles purchased; and also to pay such agents, workmen, and other help as you may require in the prompt discharge of your duties.

[Signed,]   "JOSE M. J. CARVÁJAL,
"Governor of Tamaulipas and San Luis Potosi, acting for said States and the U. S. of Mexico."

Draft for $20,000.

No. 14.]   NEW YORK, September 12th, 1865.

JOHN W. CORLIES & COMPANY, and J. N. TIFFT, ESQ,
        Financial Agent of the Republic of Mexico:

You are hereby directed to deliver to the order of General H. Sturm the sum of Twenty Thousand Dollars in Mexican Bonds.

$20,000.   JOSE M. J. CARVAJAL,
Governor of Tamaulipas and San Luis Potosi, acting for said States and the U. S. of Mexico.

Draft of $1,500,000.

No. 15.]   NEW YORK, September 12th, 1865.

JOHN W. CORLIES & COMPANY and J. N. TIFFT, ESQ.,
        Financial Agent of the Republic of Mexico:

You are hereby directed to pay to the order of *General H. Sturm* the sum of *One Million Five Hundred Thousand Dollars* ($1,500,000) *in United States Currency*, out of the first disposable funds accruing from the sale of Mexican Bonds; and *in case*, at the time of the presentation of this order, there shall not be sufficient funds in your possession to fill the same, *you are then required* to deliver to the said *General H. Sturm*, or to his order, an *equivalent* in Mex-

ican Bonds of the whole of said sum, or any fraction thereof that may be wanting to complete said sum, at the rate of *sixty* (60) *cents on the dollar.*
$1,500,000.   JOSE M. J. CARVAJAL,
Governor of Tamaulipas and San Luis Potosi, acting for said States and the U. S. of Mexico.

(NOTE.—The following are the endorsements on above draft.)

NEW YORK, Aug. 22, 1866.

Received from John W. Corlies & Co., on the within draft, One Hundred Thousand Dollars in Mexican Bonds.
$100,000.   H. STURM.

: U. S. Rev. :
: 2c. Stamp. :

NEW YORK, Sept. 28, 1866.

Received from John W. Corlies & Co., on the within draft, One Hundred Thousand Dollars in Mexican Bonds.
$100,000.   H. STURM.

: U. S. Rev. :
: 2c. Stamp. :

NEW YORK, Oct. 8, 1866.

Received from John W. Corlies & Co., on the within draft, One Hundred Thousand Dollars in Mexican Bonds.
$100,000.   H. STURM.

: U. S. Rev. :
: 2c. Stamp. :

NEW YORK, Oct. 13, 1866.

Received from John W. Corlies & Co., on the within draft, Twenty Thousand Dollars in Mexican Bonds.
$20,000.   H. STURM.

: U. S. Rev. :
: 2c. Stamp. :

NEW YORK, Oct. 29, 1866.

Received from John W. Corlies & Co., on the within draft, Fifty Thousand Dollars in Mexican Bonds.
$50,000.   H. STURM.

: U. S. Rev. :
: 2c. Stamp. :

NEW YORK, Nov. 8, 1866.

Received from John W. Corlies & Co., on the within draft, One Hundred Thousand Dollars in Mexican Bonds.
$100,000. H. STURM.

[U. S. Rev. 2c. Stamp.]

Received, New York, Nov. 14, 1866, from John W. Corlies & Co., Two Hundred and Fifty Thousand Dollars in Mexican Bonds, on the within draft. (Coupons, Nov. 14, 1866.)
$250,000. H. STURM.

[U. S. Rev. 2c. Stamp.]

Received, New York, Nov. 24, 1866, from John W. Corlies & Co., One Hundred Thousand Dollars in Mexican Bonds, on the within draft. (Coupons, Nov. 24, 1866.)
$100,000. H. STURM.

[U. S. Rev. 2c. Stamp.]

Received, New York, Dec. 5, 1866, from John W. Corlies & Co., Two Hundred and Twenty Thousand Dollars in Mexican Bonds, on the within draft. (Coupons, Dec. 5, 1866.)
$220,000. H. STURM.

[U. S. Rev. 2c. Stamp.]

Received, New York, Jan. 4, 1867, from John W. Corlies & Co., One Hundred, Ninety-Six Thousand and Four Hundred Dollars in Mexican Bonds, on the within draft. (Coupons on $129,150, Nov. 24, 1866. Coupons on $67,250, Jan. 1, 1867.)
$196,400. H. STURM.

[U. S. Rev. 2c Stamp.]

Received, New York, January 8, 1867, from John W. Corlies & Co., Thirty-Three Thousand Five Hundred Dollars in Mexican Bonds, on the within draft. (Coupons, Jan. 8, 1867.)
$33,500. H. STURM.

[U. S. Rev. 2c. Stamp.]

Received, New York, March 14, 1867, from John W. Corlies & Co., Three Hundred and Eighty-Two Thousand, Four Hundred and Fifty Dollars in Mexican Bonds, on the within draft. (Coupons, March 14, 1867.)
$382,450. H. STURM.

:U. S. Rev.:
:2c. Stamp.:

Received, New York, April 8, 1867, from John W. Corlies & Co., Fifteen Thousand Eight Hundred and Fifty Dollars in Mexican Bonds, on the within draft. (Coupons, April 8, 1867.)
$15,850. H. STURM.

:U. S. Rev.:
:2c. Stamp.:

Received, New York, April 13, 1867, from John W. Corlies & Co., Eighty-Nine Thousand One Hundred Dollars in Mexican Bonds, on the within draft. (Coupons from Oct. 1, 1866.)
$89,100. H. STURM.

:U. S. Rev.:
:2c. Stamp :

Received, New York, July 9, 1867, from John W. Corlies & Co., One Hundred and Forty-Six Thousand, Six Hundred and Fifty Dollars in Mexican Bonds, on the within draft. (Coupons dated July 9, 1867.)
$146,650. H. STURM.

:U. S. Rev.:
:2c. Stamp.:

Memorandum of an Interview with Mr. Romero, the Mexican Minister, on the 8th of November, 1865, at No. 35 West Thirty-Third street.

No. 16.]

Mr. Romero visited General Carvajal this morning, and on leaving he requested me to accompany him to his residence. On the way there, Mr. Romero said, General Carvajal had told him of his engagements with me, and that he desired very much to know my views about the present situation and future prospects of said General. On our arrival at 35 West Thirty-Third street, Mr. Romero invited me to breakfast; but as I had already breakfasted, I declined. While eating breakfast, Mr. Romero said that I had been highly recommended to him, and in view of what General Carvajal, Mr. Zarco, and others had told him about the services I had rendered his country, he desired very much to become more familiar with me, as we should doubtless have some business together. After considerable conversation about the failure of the European and West Virginia Land and Mining Company, and the unfortunate position of General Carvajal, and the failure, so far, of realizing anything from the sale of Mexican Bonds; Mr. Romero said, that General Carvajal had received his authority and instructions direct from his Government, and reported direct to said Government, and that he (Romero) was not responsible for any of the acts of said General C. That he (R.) knew but little about military affairs; but as he had been the Minister of the Mexican Government for some time, and was familiar with Mexican affairs both at home and in this country, he wished to speak to me about a point or two and give me some advice. He wished it, however, understood that he had no desire or authority to interfere with any of General Carvajal's plans, and merely desired that all the Agents of the Government should work in concert to accomplish a good result. He next stated, that owing to General Carvajal's contract with Woodhouse & Co., many false and extravagant rumors had been set afloat as to the extravagance and imbecility of said General, which might tend to injure him and every person connected with him. He then said that General Carvajal had told him he had given me a draft on Messrs. Corlies & Co. for one million five hundred thousand dollars, and he wished to speak to me about it. As no money had yet been obtained from the sale of bonds, and it did not look as if there soon would be, he thought it better to cancel said draft and make some other and better arrangement for the purpose of carrying out General Carvajal's plans. He said if I should accept his idea, he would at once write to his Government about it; and he had no doubt money could be obtained from there direct, or, at any rate, I could obtain a better security than that draft.

In reply I stated to Mr. Romero that, as General Carvajal had fully communicated to him, his engagements with me, and as I thought I also fully understood the unfortunate position of Mexican affairs, I should be pleased to have a conference with him and Gen'l C , to consult together what was best to be done. I stated to him that on the first of August I had been ready to carry out all of Gen'l Carvajal's orders and plans entrusted to me, (and I explained to Mr. Romero some of the details of these plans,) and but for the failure of Gen'l C. to obtain the money, he would, so far as I was concerned, be in Mexico now, with an army fully equipped. I stated that I had first discovered the unsound condition of the Woodhouse concern, and although I had advanced large sums in my endeavor to collect and get ready for shipment so large an amount of munitions of war in so short a time, I had since the failure of said company not forsaken the cause of his country, but had furnished myself all funds absolutely needed, and should persist, if possible, to the end. I further said that if he and General C. could devise any plan that would be feasible, and promise immediate aid, I would cheerfully co-operate with them, giving them the benefit of my experience and the means I could command. I further said, *I would not like to cancel the said draft, until I had something else and better instead, as I had obligated myself to many friends and others engaged by me, upon the strength of the promises of Gen'l Carvajal to pay me in money or in Bonds.* Although the bonds might not be worth anything at present, I thought with perseverance they could be made so, at least I thought his Gov't good for them.

Mr. Romero thanked me for the expressions of faith I had just uttered in regard to the ultimate success of the cause of his country, and said he would write to his Gov't fully about me; but he thought it not advisable to interfere in the least, or appear to interfere, in the plans of General Carvajal. He expected to receive soon some instructions regarding this matter.

I then explained to Mr. Romero my plan of going West, where I was at home, and by means of the public press and through friends of the cause to create sympathy for the Mexican cause, assuring him that in the West the people generally, both Republicans and Democrats, were bitterly hostile to the establishment of an Empire on this continent.

Correct Copy.   H. STURM.

Carvajal to Sturm.

No. 17.]   "NEW YORK, January 5, 1866.

"*General:*

"As yet no money has been realized from the sale of Mexican Bonds, and my country being in the utmost need of money and means to defend itself against foreign aggression, it becomes necessary for us to invoke the aid of the American Government, either in the way of money or the loan of its credit, to enable us to obtain the necessary means from the citizens of the United States.

"I therefore request you to proceed to Washington, as Confidential Agent of my Government heretofore appointed, for the purpose of aiding Mr. J. N. Tifft, the Financial Agent of the Republic of Mexico, in obtaining from the Government of the United States either a direct loan of moneys, or a guaranty of a Mexican loan to the amount of—say from $40,000,000 to $50,000,000.

"Whatever expenses may be necessary for you to incur in accomplishing this object will be provided for.

                                        "JOSE M. J. CARVAJAL,
                                              "Major-General Mexican Army.

"General HERMAN STURM,
    "Confidential Agent of the Republic of Mexico."

Memorandum of an Interview between Mr. Romero and H. Sturm.

No. 18.]   *Sunday, April* 29, 1866.

Called on Senor Romero this morning, and stated to him that General Carvajal had informed me that morning that Mr. Romero was under the impression that, in assisting Mr. Tifft to obtain a guarantee to a Mexican Loan from the U. S., I was acting as agent or partner of Messrs. J. W. Corlies & Co. To avoid any misunderstanding about this matter, I reminded Mr. Romero of my interview with him of January 6th, and I again showed him my order from Gen'l C., dated January 5th. I stated to him distinctly that, although a friend of Messrs. Corlies & Co., I had no other interest common with them, except to serve his Gov't. That in all things, ever since my appointment in May, 1865, I had only acted as the agent of his Gov't, and had come to Washington only at the urgent request of Gen'l Carvajal, who had directed me to assist Mr. Tifft, as the order of January 5th plainly shows.

Mr. Romero replied, he had formed that opinion merely from some remarks made by Mr. Tifft, but would communicate this error to his Gov't at once, to which he had some time ago written and given his former impression. He said if he had known this before he would have communicated with me in regard to some important matters. He requested me to write a letter to him about this, and he would send it at once to his Gov't for information. After writing this letter on his table and delivering it to him, he requested me to call in the evening at four o'clock, as he would give me some advice. I replied I would do so, and should send Mr. Tifft to explain this matter also.

Called on Mr. Romero at four P. M. Met him in the parlor. He said Mr. Tifft had called and explained the matter. Mr. Romero then complimented me on my conduct and the prudent course I had pursued throughout, and said that hereafter he wished that he and I alone should manage the delicate business of obtaining a guarantee or other aid from the U. S. He said that an arrangement existed with Mr. Tifft about a secret service fund, and he had expected to pay the agents and attorneys employed by me out of said fund. For some time past many of the gentlemen engaged by me had requested him to have the bonds promised them in payment for their services deposited in some safe bank or place of deposit, to their credit, to avoid any difficulty in their delivery hereafter. This could not be done, as it would involve a double cost of printing, as the guaranteed bonds would be different. The gentlemen mentioned had, however, expressed their firm belief in my integrity and honor, and their satisfaction with my conduct. He had, therefore, thought it best to place at my disposal Five Million Dollars of Bonds, as a secret service fund, of which he would personally guarantee the payment to me in case of success of a Loan or a guarantee of a Loan by the U. S. Gov't. In reply, I thanked Mr. Romero for this proof of confidence, and said I did not wish to handle said bonds at all, or have anything to do with the custody or payment thereof, and advised him to select some good bank in Washington as the custodian of said fund. After some conversation, I told him all I desired was to have matters so arranged, that my agents would know that good faith would be kept with them; that in my endeavors to obtain munitions of war, etc., for Gen'l Carvajal during the last year, I had expended a large sum of money and had in addition, under my agreements with Gen'l C., obligated myself personally to others, and had advanced money freely for the payment of important political and secret services performed by agents and attorneys employed by me for that purpose, as well as in my efforts to extricate Gen'l C. from the unfortunate entanglements he had got into. I further stated I would cheerfully furnish further funds needed to accomplish success, but in connection with the financial business of obtaining a Loan from the U. S. I would much prefer to introduce to him direct my agents and attorneys, and he might arrange the manner of paying them their bonds or securing them their pay as should be most satisfactory to them. In this way I would not run the very probable risk of being charged with profiting myself out of the secret service fund.

Mr. Romero replied, that he feared no such result, and so far as his Gov't was concerned, he would fully explain this matter; but he thought, owing to the difficulty arising out of the Ochoa and Woodhouse bonds, his plan was the best and most feasible, and would inspire all the confidence needed.

After some further talk between us, we agreed that I should refer my agents and attorneys to Mr. Romero, and he would guaranty the fulfillment of my promises to them.

NOTE.—The above is a correct copy of the original notes taken by me of the above mentioned conversation.

H. STURM.

Carvajal to Sturm.

No. 19.] NEW YORK, May 15, 1866.

"GENERAL H. STURM:

"*General:* I am about to return to my Military Department. All your proceedings, contracts, etc., heretofore done conformably to your authorization, given by me, March 1st and August 25th, 1865, which have been approved by me, you are hereby directed to execute and carry out according to the spirit and letter of the said authorization: but whatever new engagements or contracts you may make in the future under said authorization, must be in concert with Major General Lew. Wallace and Senor M. Romero, Mexican Minister Resident, at Washington.

"Very respectfully,
[Signed,] "JOSE M. J. CARVAJAL,
"Major General Mexican Army."

Memorandum of an Interview between Gen. Carvajal, Gen. Wallace, Col. Stocking and myself, on the 15th day of May, 1866.

No. 20.]

General Carvajal instructed me to ship the goods bought of Merritt & Co., D. Smith and others, with the utmost speed on the two steamers engaged through Capt. Taylor, to Brazos. Ordered me to give the charge of the first cargo to Col. Stocking and send out in first steamers, Mr. Peckham, Gen. Wardwell, and the other officers if ready. Capt. Osborn is to proceed in gunboat, if I succeed in arranging this matter, together with his officers and men, but he is to have no command until the vessel is delivered to General Wallace or Colonel Stocking, or other officers appointed by General C., who are to deliver her to Capt. Osborn, somewhere on the coast of Mexico, in Mexican waters. General Wallace is to follow as soon as possible after the first shipment, in case he cannot be ready to go with the first cargo. All goods, according to an understanding with the parties, are to be delivered to me as Agent of Mexico, in New York City or Philadelphia, but nominally are to remain in their name until arrival on Mexican soil. In case I succeed in getting the gunboat, she is not to become Mexican property until delivered at Brazos. All goods are to be insured, and parties may charge the amount in their account. Gen. C. will pay in gold or specie, or in merchandise, on the capture of Matamoras, which he thinks can easily be taken. Gen. C. and Gen. Wallace fully approve of my contracts made with Messrs. Merritt & Co., Dewhurst, David Smith, and others; also about the two steamers from Taylor, and everything according to Schedule A, is to be sent as ordered, if possible. I shall provide six months supplies for gunboat, if I get her, and ship to Brazos. He will supply storage there. If the gunboat can get into Soto la Marina, that is to be the place for storing her supplies. I am ordered to send out Dr. Ramsay and his torpedo boats, and he instructs me to pay for them. Capt. Stone is to come out, if I should get a large gunboat; he is to be made the Commander of all naval matters. Gen. C. says, that in any other contract or purchases I may make, not approved by him, I must consult Mr. Romero and Gen. Wallace, and act in concert with them, and in case Gen. Wallace should go, then Mr. Romero is the only one to consult with. He promises to give me to-night a copy of the authorities he has from the Mexican Government, to protect me in case of accident. He also promises to state in writing that he has approved all my contracts so far.

Gen. C. called for Capt. Osborn and Mr. Peckham and told them that I had full power; they must report to me and obey all my orders. He said also that Mr. Tifft had promised him masonically, that he would faithfully carry out his agreements with him, and maintain his (Gen. C.'s) honor and credit, and that none of his agreements should be violated.

Literal copy of memorandum made by me in pencil in General Carvajal's room,

H. STURM.

Memorandum of Interview with Gen. Carvajal, Wallace, Col. Stocking, and Mr. J. N. Tifft, the Financial Agent of Mexico.

No. 21.]   *May* 15, 1866.

At 7½ P. M Mr. J. N. Tifft came into General Carvajal's room, and Gen. C. said he had some important matters to talk over with him in our presence. Gen. C. then explained our interview of the afternoon, and said to Mr. Tifft that he wanted a full and clear understanding about the payment of the obligation I had contracted; that he wanted the utmost good faith with every person, etc., etc. In reply, Mr. Tifft said that Gen. C. might rest assured he would do all in his power to aid him and his Government; he would not forget the interview with Mr. Romero, Gen. C. and myself at Metropolitan Hotel in Washington; that Mr. Romero had assured him also that everything should be done to carry out Gen. C.'s arrangements, and that the utmost good faith should be observed to all, and so soon as they could realize from the sale of bonds they would pay all drafts of Gen. Carvajal drawn on them, and would in every way assist Gen. Sturm to send arms, etc., to the aid of his country. Gen. Wallace then remarked, that if no money was realized from the sale of the bonds, then bonds ought to be punctually delivered on the order of Gen. Carvajal, and that I had been intrusted to make my contracts to that effect, to guard against the contingency that might arise in case bonds should not be sold for cash, or General C. should not succeed in taking Matamoras as soon as expected. Mr. Tifft said,

"*Certainly*, according to our contract the Mexican Government agrees to keep us supplied with one million dollars of bonds on hand, *duly signed*, all the time and to that extent we will always guarantee the delivery of bonds."

After some further conversation Mr. Tifft left the room, and Gen. C. said that he would send me a copy of all letters bearing upon the contract with Corlies & Co., and also copies of the contracts themselves, to protect all those interested, *in case of his death*, and to show that everything was fair and honorable on his part.

On going out, Mr. Tifft met Gen. Wallace, Col. Stocking, and myself in the next room, and reassured us that he would in every way assist and promote Gen. C.'s plans, and that at the last interview with Mr. Romero, the latter had said the same thing.

Literal copy of memorandum taken in Gen. Carvajal's room a few minutes after the occurrence of our interview.

H. STURM.

Carvajal to Sturm.

No. 22.] "NEW YORK, May 16, 1866.

"*General H. Sturm:* Herewith I transmit to you for your information, copies of my authority from the Republican Government of Mexico, dated 12th of November, 1864, translated into English, empowering me to contract a loan, buy arms, etc., etc., and admit foreign troops into the National service; also, another, dated 8th of November, 1864, naming me Governor and Military Commander of the State of Tamaulipas, with full and legislative powers.

"My authority as Governor of San Luis Potosi is also authenticated, but too lengthy and connected with other irrelevant matter, and is, moreover, unnecessary here.

"I also send you a copy of translation of modification of my powers subsequently by the Government, in favor of Senor M. Romero, Minister Plenipotentiary for my Republic at Washington City, requiring *his* approbation of any *future* contracts I might make. Respectfully, your friend and obt. servant,

"JOSE M. J. CARVAJAL,
Agent for Mexican Republic."

General Carvajal's Appointment and Powers as Governor of Tamaulipas.

No. 23.]

"DEPARTMENT OF WAR AND THE NAVY, REPUBLIC OF MEXICO. Sec. 1.

"The Citizen Minister of Foreign Relations and Government imparts to me, under date of to-day, the following: 'With this date, I say to the Citizen General J. M. J. Carvajal, what follows:

'Having received advices which produce the doubt as to whether the Citizen General Juan N. Cortinas has ceased to exercise the government and military command of the State of Tamaulipas, and desiring to avoid the great evils consequent upon the prolonged absence of the first civil and military authority of the said State, the Citizen President of the Republic has thought proper to direct, that if the Citizen General Cortinas should have actually relinquished the exercise of said duties, as soon as you receive this communication, you enter upon the discharge of the same, as Governor and Military Commander of the State aforesaid: being hereby amply authorized to dispose of all the military forces within the same, of whatever denomination; to organize and augment as far as possible the forces of the National Guards; to dispose of all revenues collected in the State, as well those properly belonging to the same, as those pertaining to the Federal Treasury, and to provide ways and means; to arbitrate and decree such other imposts as may be necessary in order to continue to uphold the cause of the independence and the institutions of the Republic.

'I have the honor to communicate it to you as relates to the appointment of Governor, and I transcribe the present to the Citizen Minister of War, that he may be pleased to transcribe it to you as far as relates to the appointment of the military command.'

"I transcribe it to you with the object aforesaid, and I transmit it to you as relates to the appointment of military command, and for the purposes attendant thereupon.

"Liberty and Independence.

"CHIHUAHUA, November 8, 1864.

 (Signed,)   "NEGRETE.

"*To the Citizen General J. M. J Carvajal.*"

"The foregoing is a true copy of translation of my authority as Governor and Military Commander of the State of Tamaulipas.

 (Signed,)   "JOSE M. J. CARVAJAL."

General Carvajal's authorization as Commissioner of Mexico to obtain Material aid and raise Funds in the United States.

No. 24.]

MINISTRY FOR FOREIGN RELATIONS AND INTERNAL GOVERNMENT; DEPARTMENT FOR FOREIGN RELATIONS, SECTION OF CHANCERY.

"Having taken into consideration what you formerly proposed at the City of Monterey, and what you now further propose through a commissioner, in reference to the fact that you can facilitate the advent of foreigners to augment the forces that are to sustain the cause of the Republic; procuring at the same time arms and munitions of war; and procuring likewise abroad the pecuniary resources which the realization of both these objects demand:—The Citizen President of the Republic, considering that, by the occupation of Tampico and that which may have been effected at the port of Matamoras, it is more expedient, under these circumstances, to admit foreigners in order to augment the National forces, having as one of their principal objects the recovery of those ports; and confiding in your ability and accredited patriotism,—has thought proper to direct in Cabinet Council, that you be authorized for the aforesaid objects under the following bases:

"*First*, That the number of foreigners you may engage for the service of the Republic shall be from one thousand to ten thousand, with the understanding that, by the mere act of entering into the service, they shall be considered as citizens of Mexico, according to the laws now in force, and shall remain in all respects subject to the laws of the Republic.

"*Second*, That the foreigners so engaged shall receive, during the term of service, the pay marked out for each class in the respective military tariffs of the Republic; having also a right, in conformity with the law of the 11th August of the present year, to receive the bounty allowed in the same, when their time of service shall have terminated, by having been disabled during the same, or by the actual termination of the foreign war.

"*Third*, That you may contract for the purchase, at ordinary prices, of as many as forty thousand rifles or muskets for infantry, and as many as three thousand of the divers arms for cavalry; as well as some batteries of rifled cannon and light or mountain artillery, and a proportional quantity of munitions of war.

"*Fourth*, That in contracting for the purchase of arms and munitions, you may assign and obligate for their payment *whatever may be necessary* of the revenues of the State of Tamaulipas—as well those properly belonging to the State as those of the Federation collected within the same,—and the products of the ports on its coast; allowing to the contractors, if it be necessary, an interest at the rate of six per cent. per annum, *more or less*, until such sums or loans shall have been paid; having a right also to consign said payment ('*pudiendo consignarlos*') the product of duties from customs, with a discount not exceeding the *maximum* of what is customary in said parties, according to the latest authorizations of the Government.

"*Fifth*, That under the same obligation and consignment of the public revenues, and with the same concession of interest and discount upon the duties from customs, according to what is expressed in the preceding bases, you may contract a loan in foreign countries to such an amount as you may consider necessary, according to the number of foreigners that may be engaged, as well for defraying the expenses of their transportation to the Republic, as for the payment of their salaries for the period of one or two years: provided, that the authority vested for contracting a loan shall have reference to that respecting the engagement of foreigners; that there may be a due proportion between the number of men engaged and the amount of the loan, in order to guard against the occurrence afterwards of serious difficulties for the maintenance of the forces composed of the former.

"*Sixth*, That the obligations you may contract in the name of the Republic and of its Government shall be upon condition, that when said arms and munitions shall have actually arrived upon the territory of Mexico, then, and not before, shall such obligations be considered as perfect and obligatory; and when such amounts of said loan shall have actually been received, shall such obligations be esteemed as perfect and binding on the Republic.

"*Seventh*, That the foreigners that you may admit to come and render their services shall be incorporated with the forces under your command; the whole of them remaining subject to your orders.

"*Eighth*, That in the capacity of Chief of said forces, you shall have all the authority necessary for organizing them, and for conferring upon the militia or upon foreigners volunteering to serve, military commissions up to the rank of Colonel, as required by the organization, conferring such degrees as National Guards, or as Auxiliaries of the Army; and also recognizing in said foreigners the degrees or rank they may have had in other countries; retaining or considering them, likewise, as belonging to the National Guards, or in the capacity of volunteers, or auxiliaries in the army—as you may direct at the time of recognizing the same.

"*Ninth*, That in all that relates to the command of those forces which you shall have subject to your orders, and to their operations in the field, you shall be subject only to the Supreme Government, reporting directly to the same as General-in-Chief of forces in active service; although maintaining—as regards the authority, civil and military, whose territories said forces may pass over, especially of the State of Tamaulipas, should you not be discharging the duties of Governor and Military Commander of the same—the necessary harmony, in conformity with what has been imparted to you in a separate communication.

"*Tenth*, That the period of one year, reckoning from this date, shall be the time in which you may, by virtue of the authorizations wherewith you are vested, contract for arms and munitions, as well as a loan, and admit foreigners into the service of the Republic, said especial authorizations now given you, relative to the three points above cited, ceasing to be in force after the expiration of one year: and I communicate it to you, recommending that you will be pleased to transmit timely reports of what you may transact in view of these authorizations.

"Liberty and Independence.
    (Signed,)   "LERDO DE TEJADA.
"CHIHUAHUA, November 12th, 1864.
"To the Citizen General J. M. J. Carvajal, Sota La Marina, or where he may be."

"The foregoing is a true copy of translation of my authority from Supreme Government, for the purpose therein contained.
    (Signed,)   "JOSE M. J. CARVAJAL."

"Certifico que la firma anterior del C. Jose M. J. Carvajal es la misma que acostumbra usar en todos sus negocios.
"NUEVA YORK, Mayo 16, de 1866.   [SEAL.]
    (Signed,)   "JUAN N. NAVARRO."

Senor Romero is directed to exercise certain Powers and Authority in the Execution of General Carvajal's Commission.

No. 25.]
    *   *   *   *   *   *   *

"The President has resolved that General Carvajal must proceed in concert with you, and that it is necessary that he may previously obtain your approval to what he may hereafter do in fulfillment of his authorization. With that purpose, besides your conforming yourself to the several instructions that I have communicated to you, or shall hereafter direct, you shall observe the following:

"*First.* You shall approve what General Carvajal may do in due fulfillment of his authority, if you deem it advantageous to the cause of the Republic—even should the act of said General seem more onerous than any other arrangement pending, if the latter have less probability of being realized without a very injurious delay.

"*Second.* It shall not be your duty to approve whatever General Carvajal might do in fulfillment of all his authorizations, or a part thereof, in case that there should arise any difficulties with regard to another secret project, which, in your judgment, could have a sufficient probability of being performed with greater advantage.

"*Third.* The Government relies on your patriotism, capacity, and discretion; and instructs you that, without omitting to try to procure the best, you may chose among those agreements which, in your judgment, may not be absolutely bad, that one which shall offer a greater security, or more probability of being the soonest carried out.

 * * * * * * * * * *

   (Signed,)   "LERDO DE TEJADA.
"CHIHUAHUA, July 13, 1865."

"I certify the foregoing to be a true translation of a part of an official dispatch from the Secretary of State of the Republic of Mexico, Senor Lerdo de Tejada, to General Jose M. J. Carvajal, transcribing the last instructions of the Mexican Government to its Minister Plenipotentiary, Senor M. Romero.
"NEW YORK, October 2, 1865.
   (Signed,)   "FRANCISCO ZARCO."

"A true copy of translation.
   (Signed,)   "CARVAJAL."

Memorandum of an Interview with Senor M. Romero on the Morning of May 16, 1866, in Washington City.

No. 26.]

Called upon Mr. Romero at ten A. M.; was admitted at once. I stated to Mr. Romero my instructions from General Carvajal and my hopes of success. He seemed dubious, but hoped all would turn out as I expected. He inquired about my contract with Mr. Gilson, Emerson, and others. I told him I felt sure of success. I stated General Carvajal's anxiety to have arms, etc., shipped at once, and told him that I hoped within a month to be able to send the first cargo. I also stated to Mr. Romero the amount of purchases and contracts and conditions. He told me, when speaking about delivery of goods, that he wished I would arrange it so that in every contract a clause should be inserted, that the goods should be considered the property of the vendors until delivered on Mexican soil, to guard against accidents that might arise. I told him that would be almost impossible, unless the Government would give security for payment in cash on delivery in Mexico; but I would endeavor to do as he wished. He told me he did not wish that clause to be an obstacle to getting arms. I then related to him fully my plans, with which he was much pleased. He evidently does not believe in our success. He asked me if General Carvajal had left. I said I thought he would leave to-day for New Orleans. I stated that General Carvajal had told me to report to him what I was doing, and he said, in reply, that he would assist me all he could. He said he would write to his Government about my efforts, and would probably soon have some instructions that would enable him to do more than he could at present. He had made some efforts himself to get arms, but had not yet heard definitely the result of his arrangements.

Literal copy of memorandum made by me on my return to Willard's Hotel at noon.

H. STURM.

Memorandum of an Interview with Mr. Romero and General Grant, on the 9th of July, 1866, at the City of Washington.

No. 27.]

Called on Mr. Romero at eleven A. M. Stated to him that I was ready to send the first cargo of arms to Matamoras; that I had chartered two steamers from Mr. Cattell and Mr. Simons, in Philadelphia, to convey the goods to Brazos, Texas, at which Mr. Romero was much pleased. I requested him to go with me to General Grant, to arrange matters so that I should have no trouble in Texas. He requested me to call at Headquarters of General G. at one P. M., and he would be there.

Called at Headquarters at one P. M. precisely. Mr. Romero was detained some time. On his arrival we saw General Grant, who said he would get us an order from the Treasury Department to clear the goods from New York, and would also give me a letter to General Sheridan, so I shall have no trouble in Texas. We spoke about purchasing the gunboat Sheridan, to which Mr. Romero assents. General Grant recommends sending out some torpedoes, and Mr. Romero requests me to get some, if I can get some one that knows how to use them.

Four P. M. received telegram from Captain Taylor that gunboat Sheridan can be had for $88,000 U. S. currency. Mr. Romero requests me to buy her, payable in bonds. I so telegraph Taylor.

Literal transcript of memorandum made same day at Willard's Hotel.

H. STURM.

McCulloch to Sturm.

No. 28.]

TREASURY DEPARTMENT, July 10, 1866.

Sir: Your letter of this date is received, requesting permission to ship from New York to Brownsville, Texas, *in transitu*, for a foreign market, certain ordnance and ordnance stores, as specified in an invoice inclosed therewith.

In reply, you are respectfully informed that the matter has been duly considered, and in accordance with the determination arrived at on the subject, you are hereby permitted to ship the said articles as requested by you, of which permission the Collector at New York has been duly notified.

I am, very respectfully,
(Signed,) H. McCULLOCH,
Secretary of the Treasury.
H. STURM, ESQ.,
Care of W. H. Gilson, Esq., 64 Courtlandt street, New York.

Memorandum.

No. 29.]

July 11, 1865. Called at the Financial Agency, 57 Broadway, at eleven A. M.' with Mr. Gilson, Capt. Taylor, Mr. Dewhurst, and Mr. Emerson, Sr. I stated to J. N. Tifft that the gentlemen desired some information from him about the draft from General Carvajal for $1,500,000, and asked him to answer the following questions:

1st. "Is this draft of September 12th, 1865, signed by General Carvajal? and do you recognize it as valid?"

Mr. Tifft replied: "That draft is drawn and signed by General Carvajal, and is good and valid, and will be so regarded by us."

2d. "Have you bonds now on hand, or will you have them on hand, to deliver to these gentlemen in case General Carvajal does not pay them in gold or merchandise, as he has personally promised them?"

To this Mr. Tifft replied, that the Mexican Government, in their contract with him, had agreed to keep him supplied at all times with $1,000,000 of bonds; and to that amount he would bind himself to pay the draft.

Capt. Taylor then said to Mr. Tifft: "This is a very large risk we are taking, and there is a general distrust about the honesty of the Mexican Government. Do you think they will keep good faith?"

Mr. Tifft replied: "I have not the least doubt about it; in fact I know they will. They can not afford to be dishonest toward you; and even if they should attempt it, we will make them pay you, so far as our contract with them can compel them; and I know General Carvajal will do all he can to pay you in cash, as he has promised."

Literal copy of memorandum made by me at the time of the occurrence of above interview.

H. STURM.

Wallace to Sturm.

No. 30.] CRAWFORDSVILLE, IND., July 11, 1866.
GEN. H. STURM,
New York City:

The contract for arms, munitions, etc., and the arrangements perfected by you for their transportation and delivery to the Mexican authorities, reported by you

July 8th inst. as having been made with W. H. Gilson and his house, are within the authority given you on March 1st, 1865, by Gen. J. M. J. Carvajal, and the same are hereby approved.

                 LEW. WALLACE,
     Mil. Agent for Gen. J. M. J. Carvajal and his Government.

Sturm to Romero.

No. 31.]   57 BROADWAY, NEW YORK, July 14, 1866.

Senor M. ROMERO, Mexican Minister, etc.,
    Washington, D. C.

Senor: I have delayed writing you in order to give you the details of my arrangements here. I have now the honor to report that my affairs are progressing rapidly, and I trust will be carried out to your entire satisfaction. I have completed my contract for the steamer, and it is duly signed and sealed, with parties who are perfectly responsible. The steamer will leave on Sunday night for this city, arriving here on Monday next, when we shall at once proceed to place our merchandise on board. I have made very comfortable provision for your officers, and desire that all that are going shall report to me at 32 *Dey street*, (office of Corlies & Co.,) at 11 o'clock on Thursday next. I have room for fifteen officers. I have been somewhat disappointed in one quarter, about a portion of the arms, but am now closing with other parties who are perfectly responsible. The disappointment was occasioned by the demand for the articles made by agents of the Austrian and Prussian Governments, who are buying here. Everything is being pushed with the greatest possible dispatch, and every contract I have made is in perfect accordance with your directions and instructions in the matter.

I shall be able to obtain *more* than I stated to you, but shall of course make the same arrangements and contract upon the same terms as stated to you, and shall take *all* I can get, believing that it may be better to close present offers than to trust to the future.

     I have the honor to be,
       Very respectfully,
         Your Obt. Servt.,
           H. STURM,
          Agt. for the Republic of Mexico.

Romero to Sturm.

No. 32.]   WASHINGTON, July 15, 1866.

General H. STURM,
   New York.

General: I have received your letter of yesterday. I request the officers who are waiting transportation for Brownsville to report to you on the place and time appointed.

I am glad to hear that matters are going on well, and expect to have a more detailed account of your operations.

Respectfully,
M. ROMERO.

Sturm to Romero.

No. 33.] NEW YORK, July 27, 1866.

Senor M. ROMERO, Mexican Minister, etc.

Sir: Yesterday noon, at 12:30 M., the steamer J. W. Everman sailed with the enclosed list of stores aboard. She cleared for Brownsville, Texas, there to be delivered to such officers as may be appointed for the purpose by the General commanding the forces in Mexico, opposite Brownsville. The goods are all new (except some of the cartridge boxes). Copies of the contracts, bills, etc., will be forwarded to you as soon as I am able to get them ready. I am nearly exhausted with my constant labors, not having but three and one-half hours' rest during the last forty-eight hours. Mr. Fuentes went out with me to see her safely out to sea. Everything is well provided for. The steamer Sheridan will leave on Tuesday or Wednesday next. I am preparing her now.

I am, Sir, Yours Truly,
H. STURM.
Agent for the Republic of Mexico.

Romero to Sturm.

No. 34.] WASHINGTON, July 28, 1866.

General H. STURM,
New York.

Sir: I have just received your favor of yesterday, by which I am informed that on Thursday last the steamer "Everman" left New York for Brazos, with a cargo of arms and munitions for the Mexican forces on the Rio Grande.

I am very glad to have this news that I communicate to-day to my Government.

I expect to receive, as soon as your convenience will allow it, the copies of the contracts and bills that you promised to send me.

I am, Gen., Very Respectfully,
Your Obt. Servt.,
M. ROMERO.

Romero to Sturm.

No. 35.]   WASHINGTON, July 31, 1866.

General H. STURM,
  New York.

Dear Sir: Col. Jose Licastro will present you a card of mine, and I request you to have him embarked for the Rio Grande on next ship, by paying his passage in the manner agreed—just as the other officers should have gone. Do not give him any money, but merely facilitate his passage to-morrow or on next occasion.

Respectfully, Your Obt. Servt.,

M. ROMERO.

NOTE.—The above letter shows evidently that Romero was cognizant of the charter of steamers.
H. S.

Romero to Sturm.

No. 36.]   WASHINGTON, Aug. 1, 1866.

General H. STURM.

My Dear Sir: I was sorry to see what the "World" published the day before yesterday.

Will that do any harm?

Please forward me the copies of your contracts and bills, as I have to send them home.

I enclose to you, for your own action, a letter that I have just received.

Respectfully Yours,

M. ROMERO.

Sturm to Romero.

No. 37.]   PHILADELPHIA, August 2, 1866.

Senor. M. ROMERO,
  Mexican Minister, etc.

Sir: Your letter of July 31st has been duly received, and as soon as No. two can get ready, I will notify you at once, and see to it that your officers are provided for. I am as busy as it is possible for me to be, getting the Sheridan ready for sea. She will leave on Saturday morning. I think I have had her put in the best order from stem to stern, and have no doubt will do excellent *Tug-boat* service. I sent you a copy of the agreement for this boat. I am entirely alone, and have to be constantly about, so that I get no chance to write and copy those other papers for your use, but expect to be able to do this in a few days. I think I shall conclude a contract to-morrow for six field batteries, with plenty ammunition. If so, I shall have to come to Washington with the steamer for the purpose of loading some of the stores, at the arsenal there: in that case I shall see you in person, and my papers can be copied while there.

I am, Sir,

Your Obt. Servt.,

H. STURM.

Sturm to Romero.

No. 38.] NEW YORK, August 7, 1866.

SENOR M. ROMERO,
Mexican Minister, etc.

Sir: I have the honor to herewith enclose copies of contract with W. H. Gilson, and of charter party for steamer Everman; also copies of bills for goods shipped on board that steamer to Brownsville. Texas. I am now arranging for another shipment of arms, etc.. particularly artillery, and have no doubt will be able to do so by next week. I also will be able to take out some twenty passengers, in case you have any to send. I shall, however, inform you in time, when she is likely to sail.

I am meeting everywhere with the most annoying hindrances, by parties representing themselves as Agents authorized to buy for General Escobedo and other Mexican officers, who are trying to buy arms, etc., offering cash payments in Mexico, etc., thereby increasing the price and the difficulty to obtain anything for bonds. I shall, however, persist until I have succeeded in sending enough for ten thousand men, and will do so, although the terms are more onerous than at first contemplated. There are plenty of parties who offer for cash, and some at low prices, but *none* will take bonds, and are even making it their business to discourage parties from taking bonds in payment; and the goods of some parties (offered by them) are not all like sample, and even old and worthless, which, of course, I cannot take. I have, during the first shipment, rejected over 5,000 Enfield rifles, and over 20,000 equipments, which parties tried to palm off. Everything I sent is good and new, with the exception of 820 rifles and a few equipments, which were not quite new, but I had to take them to avoid delay, and they are really as good as new.

Please inform me whether, to your knowledge, there are any Agents here authorized by your Government to buy, so that an arrangement may be made whereby competition is avoided. If any parties have goods to send for the *Mexican Government*, I can have them transported without risk or further cash outlay to your Government.

I remain, yours truly,

H. STURM.

Romero to Sturm.

No. 39.] WASHINGTON, August 8, 1866.

GENERAL H. STURM,
>   New York.

Dear Sir: Your letter of yesterday concerning some of the papers I have been expecting to receive, came to hand this morning. Do you want any of those papers returned? Please send me the balance of them as soon as you can, as I have to forward them home.

I notice what you say about your steps to make further purchases, and the difficulties under which you have to labor. Your letter will be submitted to the Mexican Government.

I know of nobody sent to New York, or any where else in this country, by General Escobedo, or any other officer of the Mexican army, with or without funds to purchase arms and munitions. I am sure I would know about it should any agent have been sent.

I am, sir, very respectfully, your obedient servant,

. M. ROMERO.

Romero to Sturm.

No. 40.] WASHINGTON, Aug. 12, 1866.

General H. STURM,
>   New York.

Dear Sir: Mr. Campbell offers me for sale 1,600 breech-loading carbines, that he made for the Government. I have seen a sample of them, and it seems to me to be a good substantial arm.

He asks $50 a piece in Mexican Bonds at 60 per cent. They will be inspected and accepted at Hamilton, Ohio, and he will furnish the necessary means to forward them to Mexico.

These carbines were sold to the Government at $25 a piece, and Mr. Campbell would take $20 a piece in cash.

Will you give me your opinion about the following points:

1st. What would be a fair price for these carbines in Mexican Bonds at sixty per centum?

2d. Have you any way to send them to the Rio Grande if they are delivered to us in New York?

3d. Could you go to inspect and receive them at Campbell,* Ohio? Should you go Mr. Hamilton† would pay your expenses.

Please answer me this letter at your earliest convenience.

Respectfully,

M. ROMERO.

---

* Should read "Hamilton, Ohio."   † Should read "Mr. Campbell."   H. S.

Sturm to Romero.

No. 41.] NEW YORK CITY, August 14, 1866.

Senor M. ROMERO,
    Mexican Minister, etc.

Sir: In answer to your letter of August 12th, received yesterday, in regard to Mr. Campbell's carbines, I have the honor to state that I am well acquainted with the arm, and if Mr. Campbell would sell them at twenty-five dollars, or thirty dollars at most, taking Mexican Bonds at sixty cents, I would suggest that they be bought; provided that, say 300,000 rounds of ammunition for the same could be furnished with them, at twenty dollars per thousand, on same conditions.

In this case I will inspect, or cause to be inspected, by a competent officer, said carbines, at Hamilton, Ohio, as proposed, and I can send them to the Rio Grande if they are delivered at New York.

    I am, Sir, Very Respectfully,
        Your Obt. Servt.,
            H. STURM.

P. S. I leave again for Philadelphia to-night to inspect some army wagons purchased, and to look after loading them. The steamer will leave next week for Brazos.

            H. S.

Sturm to Romero.

No. 42.] PHILADELPHIA, August 15, 1866.

Senor M. ROMERO,
    Mexican Minister, etc.

Sir: Enclosed please find an offer from Mr. Jenks of this city for two batteries of field artillery, rifled guns, also harness, forges, tools, etc., all perfectly complete and *quite new*, and in excellent order; these batteries are the best in use by our Government. The exact amount for ammunition I can not now state. The total sum for the batteries, ammunition and all, will probably be seventy thousand dollars.

Mr. Jenks desires, however, to have these bonds delivered to him at once (when the goods are delivered) and hold them as collateral, so that if the Government can not pay cash, he can then hold these bonds as his property in payment as agreed.

Mr. Jenks, like a great many OTHERS who hear all kinds of stories, is afraid that there might be some trouble within sixty days, and Corlies & Co , might not deliver the bonds, etc. I do not see why this should not be done, as it is of the utmost importance that some artillery be sent to Mexico as soon as possible. In my opinion it does not make any difference *to your Government* whether the bonds are delivered now or in sixty days, and I can not get these goods otherwise. If you consent to this arrangement, be pleased *to telegraph to me to-*

morrow to 64 Courtlandt street, New York, that you approve of this arrangement.

We are securing in Mr. Jenks one of the first men of the country, who of course will be financially interested in the success of your Government. All he desires is, to be quite secure.

I am sir, very respectfully,
Your obd't servant,
H. STURM.

Be pleased to return me the enclosed offer if you approve of it.

Romero to Sturm.

No. 43.]   WASHINGTON, August 17, 1866.

Gen. H. STURM,
    New York.

Dear Sir: I only had this morning your letter dated at Philadelphia, on the 15th inst. If the proposal about the guns made to you by Mr. Barton H. Jenks is acceptable on all other accounts, I would not insist about the delivery of the bonds sixty days after the receipt of the goods at Matamoras, has been received, but would accept their proposition.

I am sir, very respectfully,
Your obt. servant,
M. ROMERO.

Romero to Sturm.

No. 44.]   [Telegram.]

WASHINGTON, August 17, 1866.

Gen. STURM,
    64 Courtlandt street.

I wrote to you by this mail. I will be here to-morrow.

M. ROMERO.

Memorandum of an interview between General Sturm and Mr. Romero.

No. 45.]   WASHINGTON, Aug. 18, 1866.

Arrived in Washington 7 A. M.

Saw Mr. Romero at his house at 10:30 A. M. I referred him to my letter of the 15th from Philadelphia, and said that Mr. Jenks was one of the most prominent manufacturers of that city, and I was anxious to close the contract with him at once, and as a difficulty had presented itself, I had concluded to call in person to arrange this matter. I said I had presented General Carvajal's draft for $1,500,000 to Messrs. Corlies & Co., the financial agents, and requested them to pay me $100,000 of bonds on said draft, but to my great surprise they had declined to deliver the bonds. I said that both Mr. Tifft and Mr. Corlies stated to me, they had guaranteed the interest on all bonds issued by them until Oct. 1st, 1866, and they had not sold sufficient bonds to cover the interest of the bonds they had already issued, and that if I wanted bonds before the 1st of October, either he (Mr. Romero) or myself must deposit with them money sufficient to pay the interest on all bonds I should draw from them to that date. I then said to Mr. Romero that it was of the utmost importance that some arrangement be made by which I could have bonds at once. I stated that I could not afford to furnish means to advance the interest, and thought that was the business of the financial agents. I said I had expended already a large amount of money, to help General Carvajal and his Government, and was compelled to husband my means to defray expenses incidental to and absolutely necessary in obtaining and purchasing munitions of war. I said that all the incidental expenses had to be paid in cash; that I could not pay clerks, inspectors, laborers, draymen, and the various other agents that I needed to manufacture credit for his Government, in bonds, and I begged him to make an immediate arrangement with Mr. Tifft regarding this matter, and suggested, in case it could not otherwise be done, to have the interest coupons cut off up to Oct. 1st, 1866.

Mr. Romero promised to attend to this at once, and that he would order the financial agents to deliver me $100,000 of bonds I had asked for. I then asked Mr. Romero to give me some definite written instructions in regard to purchases I might make hereafter, under him, such as I had received from General Carvajal, so as to avoid misunderstanding, especially as he was not familiar with this business, and I begged him to be as prompt as possible, as now is our time to take advantage of past labor. I told him that in case the Mexican Government should meet with reverses, it would be more difficult to obtain goods for bonds, and I explained to Mr. Romero how difficult it had been for me to obtain what goods I had already purchased. Mr. Romero promised to attend to all this immediately and requested me to call again in the evening.

Second Interview.

Saw Mr. Romero again at 4:30 P. M., and had a lengthy interview with him. Mr. Romero stated to me his great satisfaction at my success. He said that some Commissioners from the Mexican Government had arrived to obtain supplies in this country, for portions of the Mexican Army, other than that under the command of General Carvajal, and he asked me if I would be willing to endeavor to obtain supplies for them, same as I had done for General Carvajal. I said I should do, or try to do, whatever he might direct. He then said after I had sent the next cargo to General Carvajal, I should first fit out an expedition to assist General Diaz, and for that purpose he would to-morrow send me the instructions I had asked for. He said that he would also send the Commissioners to me. He says I shall not supply them from anything I have purchased for General Carvajal, as he does not wish to interfere with his plans or arrangements, but that I shall endeavor to make separate and additional arrangements to supply his Commissioners. I said I would try to do so, and if he would make the necessary arrangements, so that I could have the bonds promptly, as I needed them, I had no doubt I would shortly expedite his Commissioners with a large supply of material of war.

I told Mr. Romero that Captain Wright had offered to charter me his steamer (the Vixen) for an expedition to Mexico, and I would, if possible, take her at once. Mr. Romero requested me to do so if I think the terms equitable, and told me not to buy anything unless I have first a steamer to transport the goods, as trouble may be caused if the Mexican Government should have a quantity of goods on hand in this country that could not be forwarded at once. I told Mr. Romero that I would endeavor to arrange it so that the goods would remain the property of the vendor until delivered to me on board of the steamer, but I told him that it would be almost impossible for me to obtain from one or two individuals or firms the variety of goods required by his Commissioners in quantities sufficient to make a cargo, but that I would be compelled to pick up the goods in small quantities, wherever I might get them, until I had collected a lot sufficient for a cargo.

To avoid the trouble anticipated by Mr. Romero, I suggested the propriety and advantage of having a steamer of our own, and proposed to purchase one if he would furnish me sufficient bonds for that purpose. I said I would furnish what money might be necessary to pay all expenses of running her that could not be paid for in bonds, and I told Mr. Romero that in this way a great saving could be effected to the Government, that in about a year the vessel would have paid for herself, besides the advantage of having her under our own control. Mr. Romero says he will consider this matter and send his instructions to-morrow.

Literal copy of Memorandum made by me August 18, 1866.   H. STURM.

Romero to Sturm.

No. 46.]   WASHINGTON, Aug. 19, 1866.

General H. STURM,
    New York.

Dear Sir: Senor Don Justo Benitez, bearer of this letter, is the Commissioner of General Porfirio Diaz, Commander-in-Chief of the Eastern Military Division of the Mexican Republic. Senor Benitez will inform you what is needed in that Division which he represents, and what is the best way to send it there, and what will be the best place to send the goods to.

You may place entire reliance in his judgment and information.

I am, Very Respectfully,
    Your Obt. Servt.,
        M. ROMERO.

Romero to Sturm.

NO. 47.] WASHINGTON, August 19, 1866.

General H. STURM,
    New York.

Dear Sir: General P. de Baranda, bearer of this letter, is the gentleman I spoke to you yesterday as the Commissioner of Alexandro Garcia, Second in Command of the Eastern Military Division of the Mexican Republic. He will inform you what is needed in his Division, what is the best way to send it there, and where it ought to be sent.

    I am, General, Very Respectfully,
        Your Obt. Servt.,
            M. ROMERO.

Romero to Sturm.

No. 48.] WASHINGTON, August 19, 1866.

GEN. H. STURM,
    New York.

Dear Sir: I enclose to you, as agreed upon yesterday, an order to Messrs. John W. Corlies & Co. to deliver to you $100,000 in Mexican Bonds.

Enclosed you will find your instructions. Please ask Mr. Mariscal or Mr. Fuentes to translate them for you. I am instructed to write all official letters in Spanish.

I also enclose General Carvajal's order.

    In great haste, respectfully yours,   M. ROMERO.

Romero to Sturm.

No. 49.]

MEXICAN LEGATION
   IN THE   [Translation.]
U. S. OF AMERICA.

                                WASHINGTON, August 19, 1866.

After duly considering what you stated to me in the two interviews which we held yesterday in relation to the need you feel of having a sum of Mexican Bonds to your credit, to make the purchases of articles of war which you propose to send to the Republic, in conformity with your instructions, since many of the vendors are not willing to accept the terms you have offered them of giving them the bonds sixty days after the notice has been received of the arrival out of their goods, and since, at times, the delay of a single day in the delivery might impede the conclusion of advantageous contracts, as in the case of that of Mr. Jenks, which you referred to, I have come to the conclusion to order that one hundred thousand dollars in bonds be delivered to you on account of the million and a half dollars that General Carvajal ordered to be given to you under date 12th September, 1865, which draft you showed me yesterday.

You will find herein enclosed an order to Messrs. John W. Corlies & Co., holders of the bonds, that they may deliver you the sum aforesaid. When you may have disposed of said sum, I shall give you another equal sum, which course I think shall avoid many of those difficulties you have so far encountered to make your contracts.

In setting at your disposal the sum referred to, I think it fit to state in writing the instructions which I had previously given you verbally, adding some others which my experience of what has happened suggests as necessary, and to which you shall bind yourself in the purchases you are to make. Said instructions are thus:

1st. You shall not buy anything which you have no means of transporting to the Republic, as no goods would be of any use to us if they were to remain in this country.

2d. You shall offer for such purchases as you may make, only bonds of those signed by General Carvajal, giving them at sixty per centum, nothing less, and when the goods may be bought at market prices.

3d. You shall endeavor, to your utmost possibility, to insert in the contracts you may enter into, the following clause:

"The shipment shall be made for the port of * * * * * in the name of the vendors, as their own property, who shall provide for the transport and the rest that may be necessary till the goods reach their destination and be delivered to a loyal Mexican officer, in which case, and no sooner, should they become property of the Mexican Government."

4th. In your purchases you shall give preference to the arms, of all classes, in the following order:

    I. Guns, rifled or unrifled.
    II. Carbines.
    III. Pistols.
    IV. Sabres.
    V. Light Mountain Artillery.
    VI. Field Artillery.

5th. You shall endeavor that each remittance may be accompanied with the greatest possible amount of ammunition suitable to the arms that be then remitted; and in case they may not be attainable, you shall send at least the powder and lead necessary to make said ammunition, and the greatest possible number of caps, which are extremely scarce all over the country.

6th. You may buy army clothes, or stuff to make it, provided you may get it here at lower prices than could be obtained in the place of the Republic where they are bound to. As a general rule, I tell you that our soldiers are almost entirely clad with cotton or light linen goods.

7th. The same rule you will observe as to provisions. The base for the feeding of the Mexican soldier is Indian corn, and this is scarce only sometimes along the frontier. It abounds in the interior, and freight would raise it to a fabulous price if sent from here.

8th. You shall pay especial attention to avoid the purchase of articles which may be considered necessary for the United States Army, but which in our army would be luxury, such as camp tents, shoes, stockings, coffee, etc., etc., etc.

9th. Before signing each contract, you shall send a copy of it for my approval.

10th. You shall pay preferential attention to fitting out a cargo of arms and ammunition for the "East Army Corps." General Baranda and Mr. Benitez, Commissioners from Generals Garcia and Diaz, shall inform you of what is most needed in those States, and where to send the vessel carrying such goods.

11th. When you shall have disposed of the bonds now placed at your disposal, you shall forward me the account thereof, with the proper vouchers, that I may order to your credit another sum.

12th. You shall not buy any other ship without express orders from the Mexican Government.

Such are the instructions which I deem sufficient for the present, and which I shall extend when I deem it convenient.

I renew to you the assurances of my distinguished consideration.

M. ROMERO.

To General HERMAN STURM, New York.

Stocking to Sturm.

[Received August 21.]

[No. 50.] BROWNSVILLE, August 13, 1866.

My Dear General:

I have sad news for you. A revolution yesterday deposed General Carvajal, and placed Canales in power as Governor. Our goods were all on the wharf, or partly drawn by General C. We Americans were arrested, and in much personal danger for some time, but were finally allowed by Canales to come to this place with our baggage. While under arrest, General Wallace wrote a note to the American Consul, telling him that all those stores landed from the boats were the property of American citizens, and that he must protect them. Immediately upon my release, I went to the Consul and had a long conversation with him before a witness. I told him the goods were mine, had not been delivered to any authority, and asked him at once to take steps to protect them. He wrote a letter at once to Gen. Canales, protesting as I desired. After having crossed to this side, I returned to Matamoras twice. The first time while there I had three interviews with Gen. Canales. *I told him that the goods were mine*, and I had already claimed the protection of the U. S. flag for them, and that in case of loss I should hold him responsible; that I represented parties who were able to protect their rights, and that *he* must be responsible to the U. S. authorities, who would certainly ask and expect to receive from him my rights. At this time I again saw the American Consul and asked him to place the U. S. flag over the goods upon the wharf. *Gen. Canales assured me that he would respect any arrangement made with Gen. C., and that he would either pay for, or return the goods.* I then asked him to assist the Consul, under whose protection I had placed them, by giving him a guard. He said there was already a guard over them. In the evening I went back and saw the Consul again, and asked him to advise me if anything else was necessary to be done. He said no, I had done everything I could. To-day I shall renew my efforts and try to get possession of the goods.

Will write you soon; mail just leaving; Carvajal and all are safe *here*. He killed the officer who tried to arrest him. All well.

Yours truly,
W. F. STOCKING.

Sturm to Stocking.

No. 51.]

NEW YORK, August 22, 1866.

My Dear Sir.

Your letter, dated Brownsville, August 13, informing me that you have claimed the protection of the American Consul for goods, etc., was received yesterday, and I hasten to reply to it so you'll receive it in time. I am glad you acted as you did, as it is of importance that these goods are not used against Juarez or Carvajal, *but under no circumstances do anything without the written order from Gen. Carvajal,* and *above all, get a full receipt from him for everything,* as this is the only way to insure prompt payment to the parties who sold the goods. You say Canales assured you that he would carry out any arrangement made with Gen. C., and would pay for these goods or return them. *Unless General Carvajal orders you to do this,* have nothing to do with Canales. He has placed himself in antagonism to the lawful authority, *and the arms, etc., sent out by me are the property of the Mexican Government,* and I have no right to sell them to any one, much less to a person who has usurped authority, and who, I verily believe, is in league with Ortega and others, and is, at all events, inimical to his Government.

If the arms are taken by force, or kept by Canales in such a way that you can not remove them, you must take written affidavits of this fact, signed and attested by the American Consul and other American officers of prominence, *but above all* by General Carvajal, who is the only lawful authority there, and who, although at present removed, is still recognized by the Government as such.

I write by this same mail to General Carvajal informing him that I shall soon send him more, and would have done so before now had not the news of this revolution been received here and been commented upon by the papers, and I also urge him to at once send me the receipts in duplicate for everything. This is absolutely necessary, for I understand that I can not get any bonds to pay the parties without the receipts being filed by me.

Senor Romero was exceedingly glad that everything went off so well, although the papers did say something about the *Filibusters*, as they called *you*, and he is aiding me all he can.

The Sheridan has by this time arrived. You have the papers I sent out by her. The guns and everything are ready for her, and will be sent out next week by the Suwanee. Tell this to General Carvajal, and also to Osborn.

Yours in haste,
H. STURM.

Sturm to Carvajal.

No. 52.] "NEW YORK, August 22, 1866.

My Dear General:

From Mr. Stocking I have learned that a revolution has temporarily deposed you. Nothing could possibly have occurred more damaging to the cause than this. If the French had captured Matamoras, it would have been a great deal better, for then it would have given strength to the feeling of sympathy for your cause; but that a Mexican officer, and of your reputation at that, and at the very time when aid sent from here to Mexico arrives, should act as you have done, has created quite a feeling of distrust here in the minds of some of Mexico's best friends. Under the circumstances, do not lose a moment in sending me duplicate receipts for everything I have sent to you, so that when the time for payment arrives I can at least deliver the promised bonds at once, to the parties from whom I purchased these goods. If this is not done, and it becomes known that there is delay or uncertainty in regard to the payment, it will be ascribed to want of good faith, etc., and it will be utterly useless for me to spend any more time and money in the attempt to aid you and your Government. I speak thus frankly with you, because no one can appreciate the difficulties encountered in purchasing anything for your Government at the present time, and without cash, so well as I, and I know you appreciate these efforts of mine, and will of course not blame me, if I explain to you freely the true condition.

The steamer Sheridan must by this time have arrived. In a few days I send another steamer with goods, and in her I send you two additional large guns, (20 pound rifled,) with a complete outfit, also rations, etc., for your gunboat. Use her well, and give the French "Hail Columbia" before long.

Hope to hear from you soon.

I am, yours truly,
H. STURM.

Romero is doing all he can to aid me and you, and hopes I may succeed in purchasing and sending out more goods.

To General JOSE M. J. CARVAJAL, Brownsville, Texas.

Sturm to Romero.

No. 53.] NEW YORK, August 22, 1866.

His Excellency, Senor M. ROMERO,
Mexican Minister, etc.

Sir: I have the honor to acknowledge the receipt of your esteemed letter of the 19th inst., enclosing order on John W. Corlies & Co·, for one hundred thousand ($100,000) dollars, in Mexican Bonds, and containing certain instructions for my guidance in future operations.

I have this day presented the order to Messrs. J. W. C. & Co., and they have duly honored the same.

In relation to the instructions contained in your letter, I deem it necessary to make some observations and request some changes, as without such changes, I believe it certain that my power to benefit your Government will be much impaired if not entirely destroyed.

I most heartily approve of the general principles and ideas of those instructions, and should be perfectly content to abide by them were it practicable to do so, and so far as it may be practicable, shall certainly do so; but in some cases it will be absolutely necessary that I should depart from them.

First, then, in relation to your 3d point of instructions, I would state that I find it to be an impossibility to purchase from any one person a sufficient quantity to load a ship, wherefore I am compelled to buy from *various parties* such articles and in such quantities as they may have for sale, and I am able to get; and, hence, it is impossible to arrange with them for the delivery of the goods at any Mexican port, there being no regular conveyance, and, besides, if by dint of such argument and persuasion as I am able to use, I succeed in making a purchase for Mexican Bonds, scarcely any of the venders are wiiling to be held responsible for the goods after their inspection and delivery to me at the ports ot New York, Philadelphia, etc. One of the principal reasons given for this is, that as we are not able to designate a specific officer, at a specific port, to accept the same on the part of the Mexican Government, a serious risk might be incurred by them of delivering the goods to some party or parties, who would not be duly authorized by the Government to receive them, or even should we designate some particular person for this purpose, such person might not be on hand on the arrival of the goods, thereby causing the venders loss of time and money. They further argue, that the Mexican Government having an agent here for the purchase of these goods, that agent ought to accept the goods here on the part of the Government, and ship them to the proper officers, whom he certainly should best know to be the proper person to receive them; further, that they do not wish to assume all the risk, and that nothing could be more fair than that the Government should assume the risk of capture, as they are taking risk enough in selling their goods for bonds, which are not at the present time salable, and have no market value.

Even if I partially convince them that there is but little if any risk of capture, they very naturally inquire then, why the Government hesitates to accept the responsibility.

A further objection lies in the fact, that the goods must be cleared in my name, as the U. S. Government will not allow articles of this kind to be shipped to States lately in rebellion in such quantities unless fully satisfied that they are not intended to the injury of this Government.

In regard to the 9th point of your instructions, I would say, that the very thing which I desire to avoid is delay, and my principal reason for desiring the bonds to be placed subject to my order was, that I might close an advantageous arrangement the very moment I should be able to secure it, whence it will be very likely to occur that it would be impossible for me to send a copy of an agreement before signature, without one of the principal dangers which I wished to avoid, when I desired the bonds placed to my credit. Of course, I shall be pleased to send you such copies beforehand, when I can do so without risk, and in every case as soon after signature as possible.

I would, therefore, in view of all these circumstances, and bearing in mind the necessity that your Government should obtain these supplies on the best terms and at the earliest moment possible, request that you authorize me to proceed in the manner I may find necessary and best, governing myself only so far as may be practicable by the instructions in your letter under consideration, and departing from such instructions in the points herein mentioned, when in my opinion the exigencies of the case shall seem to require such a course.

It seems certain, that I shall be obliged in nearly every case to make arrangements for transportation separate and distinct from those of purchase, and with different parties, but I do not consider that the Mexican Government runs any risk in this, as the supplies will, in every instance, be shipped in an American vessel, under the American flag, by an American citizen, unless specifically ordered otherwise by you.

Requesting the earliest reply which may be convenient, I have the honor to remain,

Very respectfully,
Your obedient servant,

H. STURM.

Romero to Sturm.

[Translation.]

No. 54. WASHINGTON, Aug. 23, 1866.

MEXICAN LEGATION IN THE U. S. OF AMERICA.

I have received the note that you addressed to me under the date of yesterday, wherein you acknowledge the receipt of mine of the 19th instant, and informing me that the draft I sent you, drawn on Messrs. John W. Corlies & Co. for one hundred thousand dollars in bonds to your order, had been presented and paid.

In reference to the instructions I communicated to you in my aforesaid note you state that in general they meet your most complete approbation and that you will comply with them as far as possible; but that some of the points of said instructions impede your making advantageous purchases, and on that ground you solicit that I may alter them as you deem it necessary. Such points are confined to what is contained in the clauses 3d and 9th of said instructions. I proceed to speak about them in the same order you refer to them.

All you state in regard to clause 3d of my aforesaid instructions seems to me quite reasonable, but I do not deem it sufficient to either omit or alter it. In the first place I did not make it a binding condition that you should put the stipulation therein mentioned in all contracts that you may enter into, *but that you should earnestly endeavor to do it to your utmost possibility:* granting so to your discretion a most ample freedom. You will recollect that I handed you said clause in writing the first time that I communicated verbally to you the bases under which I wished your purchases should be made. I drew said clause from a draft of a contract that I signed with Gen. Sullivan, who deemed it equitable, and in proposing it I have but complied with the wishes of my Government, it having been recommended to me in the most especial manner that such goods as may be sent to the Republic go on the account and risk of their seller. *If I obtained it without difficulty in that contract, it does not seem to me that it will be impossible for you to realize it in any case.

The 9th clause of said instructions has also been suggested by my Government, who, with the object of preventing abuses that might be committed in making purchases, desires that I should intervene in them all. I do not think I could give any greater proof of my confidence in you than that which I gave to you in placing at your disposal a considerable amount of money in bonds. I have also sufficient confidence in you to feel sure that in all your purchases you will act with your characteristic good faith and honesty; but as I do not deem it convenient to depart from the orders of my Government, or set a precedent that might afterwards be alleged as a reason for soliciting the same proofs of confidence, I do not consider myself authorized to release you from that requisite. Wishing, however, to facilitate purchases you are authorized to make, I consent to alter that clause in the following terms:

9th. Before signing each contract a copy thereof shall be submitted to me for my approval. When, in your judgment, it would not be possible to wait the time necessary to comply with said requisite, without serious disadvantage to the interests of the Mexican Government you may obtain, instead of my own approbation, that of the Mexican Consul at New York, or in case he should be absent that of such person as he may designate. In case the purchase should have to be made at any other place but New York you might proceed thereto accompanied by said Mexican Consul in said port, or by such person as he may designate.

I think that this addition shall remove all difficulties that you have indicated.

I am, Your Obt. Servt.,

M. ROMERO.

To General H. STURM,
New York.

Romero to Sturm.

No. 55.]   WASHINGTON, Aug. 24, 1866.

General H. STURM,
New York.

Dear Sir: I received yesterday your letter of the 22d inst. I suppose the translation of my letter to you of the 19th instant was not very correct, at least in instruction No. 3, as you will see by reading my official reply to your said letter. I did not ask you to insert in *all* contracts that stipulation; but to do so as far as it was possible in your judgment.

---

*NOTE. General Sullivan never complied with his contract.   H S.

It would be very desirable to send arms and ammunition to the Pacific coast. There are several States on that coast which are entirely unprovided and where arms would be of the greatest use. Any amount of arms of any kind would be very valuable.

Gov. J. J. Baz knows very well that coast and the officers who have their headquarters there. I have requested him therefore to see you, and inform you what is needed and what is the best way of sending it, and where.

Should you be able to make a shipment there I would be delighted.

In a great hurry, Yours,

M. ROMERO.

Sturm to Romero.

No. 56.] NEW YORK, August 25, 1866.

Senor M. ROMERO,
Mexican Minister, etc.

Sir: Your letter of yesterday was duly received. I am having the same translated by Mr. Fuentes. I regret not to have had the same on yesterday. The news from the Rio Grande is very bad. I enclose a dispatch from Mr. Thompson, (Agent for Mr. Gilson.)

Two other parties have received dispatches from there, and according to them the bonds of the Republic are *repudiated* entirely, as are all of General Carvajal's actions; besides, nobody is willing to receipt for the goods now there, or pay for them in cash, goods, or give any other order of payment for them. This places me, and all of us, in a very bad position, although I tell them that this is a contract with the General Government, and that Carvajal was duly authorized as the Commissioner and Agent of the Government, and therefore all his contracts are binding on the Government, and the Government will see to it that the parties interested are properly protected.

The steamer Suwanee is ready, coaled and provisioned, and also partially loaded with goods; besides, I have concluded partial arrangements for supplies to go to Minititlan. Now, I would respectfully, but urgently, request you to send me a letter, which I am authorized to show *to parties concerned,* wherein you say to me that any contract made by me, under authority from General Carvajal and with your approval, is binding on the Government of Mexico and will be duly carried out, and the interests of the parties concerned will be protected.

Please do this *at once,* and in such terms as to leave no doubt in the minds of men who are willing to aid your country, but do not fully understand the political status of the same.

The worst is, that neither Carvajal, or anybody else, will receipt for the goods now there; but each party seems to repudiate the actions of the other, without regard to consequences.

Should you come here next week, I should be happy to see you for a few minutes.

Yours truly, etc.,

H. STURM.

Romero to Sturm.

No. 57.] WASHINGTON, August 26, 1866.

General H. STURM,
    New York.

Dear Sir: Your letter of yesterday, informing me of the advices you had from the Rio Grande, has just been received. I regret very much that events have occurred there which are calculated to disturb the confidence that merchants, who are willing to sell you articles of war for the Mexican Government, ought to have in our ability to fulfill our contracts. I look upon the late occurrences at Matamoras as of a very transitory nature, and which will be remedied as soon as the Mexican Government will be able to come to Monterey, which I have no doubt will soon be done.

I think it is unnecessary for me to tell you that you may inform all interested parties that any contract that you have entered into, or you may enter into hereafter, as Agent of General Carvajal for the purchase of supplies, and which has been approved or will be approved by me, will be binding on the Mexican Government, and will be faithfully carried out on our part, as we do not mean to bind ourselves to anything that we are not sure we have the ability to fulfill.

    I am, sir, very respectfully,
        Your obedient servant,
                M. ROMERO.

Romero to Sturm.

No. 58.] WASHINGTON, August 27, 1866.

General H. STURM,
    New York.

Dear Sir: Governor J. J. Baz, from Mexico, will hand you this letter. He is very well acquainted with the southern part of Mexico, bordering on the Pacific, and especially with the States of Michoacan and Guerrero. He enjoys the confidence of Generals Alvarez and Regules, commanding said States. I have asked him to consult with you about sending a cargo of arms and ammunition to the Pacific. I spoke to you on this subject in one of my previous letters. You may rely on his advice, as he knows what is needed there, what is the best way of sending it to Mexico, and which would be the port of destination. I hope you may be able to send there a large cargo, notwithstanding the recent difficulties.

    I am, General, very respectfully,
        Your obedient servant,
                M. ROMERO.

Sturm to Romero.

[Telegram.]

No. 59.] NEW YORK, September 3, 1866.

To Senor M. ROMERO,
Mexican Minister, with President's party, Cleveland, Ohio.

Have made several advantageous arrangements. Please authorize Mr. Navarro to sign.

H. STURM.

Romero to Sturm.

No. 60.] KENNARD HOUSE,
CLEVELAND, OHIO,
September 4, 1866.

General H. STURM,
New York.

Dear Sir: Your telegram of yesterday was duly received. As I was so much engaged before I left Washington, I could not communicate officially to Dr. Navarro the instruction I gave you about the participation that he might have in your purchases.

I beg you to show to him the two letters of instructions that I gave you in August last, and that will be all that is required.

Respectfully, M. ROMERO.

Romero to Sturm.

No. 61.] CHICAGO, ILL., September 7, 1866.

GEN. H. STURM,
New York.

Dear Sir: I will leave this evening for Washington, and expect to be there early next week.

In great haste, respectfully,

M. ROMERO.

Sturm to Romero.

No. 62.] NEW YORK CITY, September 10, 1866.

SENOR M. ROMERO,
Mexican Minister, etc.

Sir: Your letter from Chicago was received by me this morning. I am exceedingly glad that you have returned, for I deem it of the utmost importance to your Government that certain contracts and acts of mine be at once approved or disapproved by you.

During your absence, and a few days before, I have negotiated with various parties for supplies to be furnished for the benefit of your Government. Generals Baranda and Senor Benitez have furnished me with a list of stores, to be supplied to them as stated in your letter to me, dated August 19; in accordance therewith I had concluded, as far as it was in my power, contracts for medical stores and surgical instruments, clothing, blankets, ammunition, field artillery, etc. Unfortunately, however, owing to the fact that Mr. Navarro did not feel himself authorized to approve my contracts (although I showed him your instructions to me of August last, as well as your letter dated Cleveland, September 4) without written instructions from you.

The contracts partially made, fell through, because the parties had somehow or other been influenced against doing so, or had become discouraged on account of news received, not favorable to the cause.

I find that Mr. Woodhouse is still engaged in thwarting our efforts by representing that his bonds are valid, and, as I have ascertained to-day from Judge Burnett, of this city, by showing what he pretends to be your approval of his contract, and by offering his bonds at 15 and 20 cents on the dollar. Mr. Gould, and others interested in the Ochoa Bonds, are also interfering, by causing distrust in the legitimate bonds.

Besides, the fact that General Carvajal has been removed from command, as stated in the newspapers, has shaken the confidence of a great many people.

You can readily appreciate the difficulties under which I labor, all of which, however, will not deter or prevent me from continuing to make advantageous contracts for your Government (on more favorable terms than the United States did during the war) if it can be so arranged, that my contracts, made in accordance with your views and wishes, can be at once officially approved as binding on the General Government of the Republic of Mexico, without first allowing parties willing to make contracts to be influenced by parties who either are inimical to the Republican cause, or have some other selfish motive at heart.

I would therefore respectfully suggest that you at once send full instructions to Mr. Navarro to approve my contracts either himself, or in his absence, by his deputy.

Having two steamers ready to convey our goods to where you desire they should be sent, and deeming it of utmost necessity and advantage to your Government, I have assumed the responsibility of closing the following contracts without first waiting for your approval, as you instructed me to do, viz.: Contract with Quintard, Sawyer & Ward, for twelve hundred (1,200) tons of coal to supply our gunboat Sheridan, and for other purposes.

Contract with P. W. Lawrie & Co. for two hundred and fifty thousand (250,000) rations for said gunboat and other steamers.

Contract with Fitch, Burbridge & Dunlap for seven hundred and fourteen thousand, seven hundred and fifty dollars ($714,750) of arms and ammunitions.

Copies of these contracts are herewith enclosed, and you will see they are free from objections, except so far as clause 3 of your instructions is concerned. But it was impossible to obtain the consent of the parties to that clause being inserted, on the ground that they would be unable to know who might be in command, or properly authorized to receipt for the goods on their arrival, and they might be put to great expense and loss in consequence.

I hope it is hardly necessary for me to assure you that in taking this responsibility, under the circumstances, I had no intention or desire to disobey your instructions, but acted from the best motives, firmly believing that upon your return you would fully approve what I have done.

Mr. Fitch, who lives in Chicago, and who took his contract with him contrary to my advice, for the purpose of obtaining your approval to the same there, on yesterday telegraphed to his partners here not to furnish anything, or do anything under this contract until you had approved the same.

There is, however, a clause in this contract, as you will see, which compels them to deliver the goods at such time as I may order, and in consequence, not desiring to lose any time, and keep the steamers and my inspectors waiting, I have insisted on their complying with this clause, assuring them that your approval would certainly be obtained, and I have to-day inspected 3,000 rifles, all new, and several other stores.

I should be pleased, however, to have a telegam from you to-morrow stating that Fitch's contract is approved, as it would save me a great deal of time and trouble, and I am very anxious to send these two steamers for General Baranda and Governor Baz by next week, if possible.

In conclusion, allow me to say that I desire very much (if it meets your views) that Corlies & Co. be instructed to deliver to me the necessary amount of bonds to comply with my contracts, when the goods are delivered on board ship, as agreed. I understand from Messrs. Corlies & Co. that it will be necessary for you to instruct Mr. Fuentes to sign some bonds for that purpose.

Hoping to receive further instructions from you, I remain,

Very respectfully,
Your obedient servant,
H. STURM.

Romero to Sturm.

[Translation.]

No. 63.] WASHINGTON, September 10, 1866.

MEXICAN LEGATION IN THE U. S. OF AMERICA.

I enclose herewith, in pursuance of instructions received, a copy of a note that Senor Lerdo de Tejada, Minister of Foreign Affairs of the Mexican Republic, addressed to me from Chihuahua, under No. 366, dated the 6th of August last, communicating that the President has ordered that General Carvajal be impeached for the capitulation that he celebrated with Don Thomas Mejia the 27th of June ult., in virtue whereof said General has ceased, not only to hold the position of Governor and Military Commandant of the State of Tamaulipas, but likewise the commission and authorizations which had been previously confided to him, and which gave occasion for his coming to this country.

I enclose to you a copy of No. 23 of the *Periodico Oficial*, referred to in the note, of which I enclose a copy.

Yours respectfully, M. ROMERO.

To General H. STURM,
No. 32 Dey street, New York.

P. S.—In view of the state of affairs on the frontier, and in view of the near approach to it of the Supreme Government of the Republic, you will suspend your purchases and remissions of the material of war for that place until the Government communicates its precise instructions relative to this particular.

M. ROMERO.

Lerdo de Tejuda to Romero.

[Translation. Received Sept. 10, 1866.]

No. 64.]

CHIHUAHUA, August 6, 1866,
DEPARTMENT OF FOREIGN AFFAIRS,
SECTION OF AMERICA,
NUMBER 366.

COMMISSIONS AND AUTHORIZATIONS OF GEN. CARVAJAL. CAPITULATION OF MATAMORAS.

I enclose you herewith a copy of No. 23 of the *Periodico Oficial* of the Supreme Government, of this date, in which has been published the capitulation which General Jose M. J. Carvajal and his commissioner, Don Juan J de la Garza, wished to celebrate on the 22d of June last, with Don Thomas Mejia, that he might evacuate the city of Matamoras; the communications of Generals M. Escobedo and S. Tapia, relating to said capitulation, and the Government's orders issued through the office of the Secretary of War, declaring null and void said capitulation and ordering that General Carvajal and Don Juan J. de la Garza be submitted to trial.

In consequence of this resolution, the President has ordered that I tell you that General Carvajal ceases not only to hold the capacity of Governor and Military Commandant of the State of Tamaulipas, but also ceases in the commission and authorizations that had been previously confided to him, and which gave occasion for his going to that country where he entered into agreements that you know of.

You will be pleased, therefore, to make the resolution known to such parties as General Carvajal may have left something pending with, in regard to public business.

In conformity to the other resolutions which I have communicated to you at the proper time, everything that General Carvajal might have done in fulfillment of his commission and authorizations, should be submitted for your approval, but now, and in virtue of this new resolution, and as he is no longer able to interfere in what may be done, you alone should interfere in what may have been left unfinished in accordance with the authorizations and instructions which you have from this Government.

If anything should occur hereafter, I will take care to communicate it to you in due season.

LERDO DE TEJADA,
Minister, etc., etc.

To Citizen M. ROMERO,
Envoy Extraordinary and Minister Plenipotentiary of the Mexican Republic in Washington, D. C.

True copy.
Washington, September 10, 1866.

C. ROMERO,
Attachee to the Legation.

Romero to Sturm.

No. 65.] WASHINGTON, September 11, 1866.

General H. STURM,
New York.

Dear Sir: I received this morning your telegraphic dispatch of this date. In the enclosed letter you will find the answer to your question.

General Tapia has been appointed by the Mexican Government to succeed General Carvajal as Governor of Tamaulipas. He will therefore be the proper party to receive the goods.

A gentleman by the name of Mr. Fitch met me at Detroit and followed me to Chicago, asking my approval to a contract which he handed to me. I answered to him that while I was traveling I could transact no business, but that I would soon be here and would then act on the premises.

If you will send me your report with the contract, I will take it into consideration.

I am in great haste.

Your obedient servant,

M. ROMERO.

Romero to Sturm.

[Translation.]

No. 66.] WASHINGTON, September 11, 1866.

MEXICAN LEGATION IN THE U. S. OF AMERICA.

I send under this date, to New York, to the Consul-General of the Republic, my instructions that he revise and approve, as the case may be, such contracts as you may hereafter enter into in behalf of the Mexican Government, and this very day, in a separate note, I state to you that you should stop all purchases or remittances of goods for Matamoras till orders be received from said Government, which is to come shortly to a place nearer to that port.

As to the three contracts which you sent me with your official note of the 10th inst., I tell you that I approve in all its parts the one you signed on the 31st of August, with Messrs. George A. Fitch, Oscar H. Burbridge and John F. Dunlap, of the City of New York, for the purchase of 20,000 Enfield Rifles, and other arms, ammunition, and military equipments, referred to therein, to the amount of $714,750.

The conditions I set to my approval are:

1st. That said goods shall be particularly for the States of the Eastern and Southern Lines of the Republic, to which effect you shall agree as to their remittance and distribution with Mr. John J. Baz, General P. Baranda and M. Justo Benitez.

2d. That said goods shall be speedily sent to such points as the above gentlemen shall designate.

As regards the other two contracts, one for the purchase of coal and the other of rations, as they refer to goods intended for Matamoras, I can not approve them till I receive instructions from my Government.

I renew to you my distinguished consideration,

M. ROMERO.

To General H. STURM, New York.

Sturm to Romero.

No. 67.] NEW YORK, September 12, 1866.

Senor M. ROMERO,
    Mexican Minister, etc.

Sir: Your letter of September 11th, enclosing your communication in Spanish, dated Washington, September 10th, and the copy of note of Senor Lerdo de Tejada, dated Chihuahua, August 6, 1866, has been received by me; and, in reply, I have the honor to say that I shall act in accordance with the instructions contained therein.

I am, Sir, respectfully,
    Your obedient servant,

H. STURM.

Romero to Sturm.

[Translation.]

No. 68.] WASHINGTON, Sept. 12, 1866.

MEXICAN LEGATION
  IN THE
U. S. OF AMERICA.

I return to you the papers you forwarded to me in relation to some torpedoes, the construction of which was ordered by General Carvajal, stating to you that when said General submitted to my inspection the contract that he had signed for their construction, I answered him in an official note that I approved of it only as to the construction of one of said torpedoes, which was at that time near its completion. I am therefore disposed to carry on said contract as to that torpedo alone.

As to the claim it is pretended to raise on account of the delay alleged, I can not recognize any right or foundation for it, since no timely notice has been given me about any of the torpedoes being ready for delivery to my Government, and it was only to me that parties should apply with that object.

I remain, yours respectfully,

M. ROMERO.

General H. STURM,
New York.

Romero to Sturm.

No. 69.] WASHINGTON, Sept. 12, 1866.

General H. STURM,
New York.

My Dear Sir: After I wrote you my letter of yesterday General Schofield handed me your official letter of the 10th instant.

I thought of answering it to-day; but I have been so unwell that it has been impossible for me to do so.

I will try to have it answered to-morrow.

I send to-day his instructions to Dr. Navarro.

Respectfully,

M. ROMERO.

Romero to Sturm.

No. 70.] WASHINGTON, Sept. 13, 1866.

[Translation.]

MEXICAN LEGATION IN THE U. S. OF AMERICA.

In reply to your note dated the 11th inst., wherein you are pleased to inquire from me to whom the goods purchased by you for the Mexican Government, and which are now in Brownsville, should be delivered, I must say that the proper party to whom said goods should be delivered is Gen. Santiago Tapia, Governor and Military Commandant of the State of Tamaulipas, appointed by the Supreme Government.

I renew to you the assurances of my distinguished consideration.

M. ROMERO.

To General H. STURM,
New York.

Romero to Sturm.

No. 71.] WASHINGTON, Sept. 13, 1866.

General H. STURM,
    New York.

My Dear Sir: I send you my official letters in answer to your several communications.

I think it will be better to keep in abeyance the two contracts about coal and rations until we hear from home. In the meanwhile the Sheridan will have wood and provisions enough for all purposes.

    In great haste,
        Yours respectfully,
            M. ROMERO.

Romero to Sturm.

No. 72.] WASHINGTON, Sept. 19, 1866.

General H. STURM,
    New York City.

Dear Sir: I enclose to you a list of stores which Mr. Baz has sent me, stating those are the goods wanted for the State of Michoacan. If you can make those purchases according to my instructions, and send the articles in conformity with Mr. Baz's suggestions, you are authorized to do it.

These goods will be bought besides those referred to in your last contract approved by me, in case the latter are not sufficient to cover the demands of the three gentlemen I have referred you to, viz: General Baranda, Mr. Benitez, and Mr. Baz. My object is to provide the States represented by these gentlemen, with your last contract and if this is not sufficient, with an additional one.

    Yours sincerely,
        M. ROMERO.

Romero to Sturm.

No. 73.] WASHINGTON, Sept. 20, 1866.

GENERAL H. STURM,
    New York.

Dear Sir: Yours of yesterday has been received and its contents duly noticed by me. When you have transmitted to me the detailed information you promise about matters on the frontier, I may possibly suggest something for the security of the Mexican interests. In the meantime I repeat to you that when Gen. Tapia will have assumed the commandment of Matamoras, all will be right.

    Yours sincerely,
        M. ROMERO.

Sturm to Romero.

No. 74.] NEW YORK, September 21, 1866.
SEÑOR M. ROMERO,
        Mexican Minister, etc.

Sir: I enclose herewith, for your perusal and use, a copy of a letter from Dr. Hadden, a physician and surgeon of very high standing in Jersey City. Dr. Hadden went on the Everman as surgeon with the intention of joining the Liberal Army, as promised him by General Carvajal. He was present at Matamoras during the revolt there, and being most of the time with Generals Carvajal and Canales, as also with Mr. Stocking, is, of course, fully competent to give an account of what occurred there.

I requested him to write a statement of the occurrences there, and have made him certify it by an affidavit, as also by the affidavit of Mr. Daniels, who was also present. I did not deem it necessary to go to the expense of obtaining other affidavits, as they can be had at any time if desired. They all agree in the main, except that some of the parties are not so fully cognizant of all the facts as those two gentlemen.

The reason why I have acted thus is, that it might be of importance to you to have such a document to send to your Government.

All parties sent out by me, in charge of the goods, as also Captain Smith, the agent of the Associated Press in Galveston, who *was present* during the revolt in Matamoras, and Major Wood, Quartermaster of the Liberal Army under General Carvajal, agree in one thing, that Mr. Stocking acted heroically in protecting the goods, and that there is an intense feeling of hatred toward us on the part of certain merchants there who have made considerable money out of the traffic in arms, etc. and who have more sympathy with the Imperialists than with your Government.

I intended to come on to Washington to-night, but can not do so, as I am overwhelmed with labor, contradicting injurious statements and re-assuring parties here that all will be right, etc., etc.; and to-morrow being your mail day I have concluded to leave to-morrow night, and will see you on Sunday morning and return that same night.

I am sir, very respectfully,
Your obd't servant,
H. STURM.

Copy of Dr. Hadden's Statement.

No. 75.] NEW YORK, September 20, 1866.
BRIG. GEN. H. STURM,

Dear Sir: At your request I proceed to make to you a statement of certain circumstances of which I was a witness during my recent trip to the Rio Grande.

I was the Surgeon of the steamer J. W. Everman, (expecting to join the Liberal Army in the same capacity,) which left New York on the 26th day of July,

1866, for Brazos Santiago, Texas, with a cargo of munitions of war and medical stores intended for the Government of the Republic of Mexico.

We arrived at Brazos on the 7th day of August, and on the 8th orders were received from General J. M. J. Carvajal, Commandant of Matamoras, and Military Governor of the State of Tamaulipas, to forward the cargo at once to Matamoras. The steamer Tamaulipas No. 2 came alongside on the 9th, and took on board our entire cargo. She arrived at Matamoras and commenced discharging the cargo on the night of Saturday, August 11th; and the goods were all landed before 12 A. M. of the next day, and so far as possible they were conveyed as fast as landed, by orders of Gen. Carvajal, to the Government store houses, and guarded by Mexican soldiers.

I was at the quarters of General Carvajal early on this Sunday morning, in company with Gen. Lew. Wallace and others, until after breakfast, when I went down to the landing in company with a Captain Morrison, of the Mexican army, to look to the medical stores.

At this time I found, the arms, powder, and medical stores, some of the ammunition, and all the surgical instruments had already been conveyed to the Government store houses, and the balance of the cargo lying at the landing under guard of Mexican soldiers. I returned to Gen. Carvajal's quarters some time before noon, and on my arrival there I found everybody in a state of excitement; and Gen. Lew. Wallace informed me that Gen. Carvajal had just gone out of the window and fled to Brownsville, his life being in danger on account of the revolt just then taking place. A few minutes afterward the place was surrounded by the revolutionists, consisting entirely of soldiers, who immediately arrested all the Americans, taking possession of everything; among the rest, of a box containing $30,000 in gold. We were, however, soon released, and told that Gen. Carvajal had been deposed, and that Gen. Servando Canales had been proclaimed Governor and Military Commander in his place. All the arms and stores that had been delivered as aforesaid at Matamoras by Gen. Carvajal's orders, were at once seized by the revolutionists.

Toward evening the city was threatened with an attack from Cortinas, who, it was said, had promised all men belonging to his band, or who would join him, that he would give them twenty-four hours pillage of the city, after it should have been captured. Everything in the city was confusion; citizens and others arming to defend themselves.

The legitimate authorities of the Mexican Government having been driven from the city, Mr. Wilbur F. Stocking (who, up to this time of their landing at Matamoras, had sole charge of the goods) was urged and importuned by prominent men to claim these goods as private property, and have them placed under protection of the American Consul. Mr. Stocking, under the circumstances, feeling that the arms might fall into the hands of parties who might use them to the injury of the very Government they were intended to benefit, at once acted on these suggestions, and claimed the protection of the American Consul for such portion as were then lying at the landing, and had a portion of them taken to the American storehouse.

On this day, Monday, August 13th, the firm of King, Kennedy & Co. protested to the American Consul, that they claimed these goods, having, as they said, a claim upon them for a private debt due from Gen. Carvajal, and also freight charges on the same from Brazos Santiago, to Matamoras. In this way the goods were detained for several days, but finally released. During all this time a great portion of them was exposed to the heavy rain that fell during those few days, and no one was allowed to protect them. Permission was at last obtained to remove them to Brownsville, as well as those yet remaining in the storehouse, but on their removal it was found that a large portion had been distributed to, or taken by the officers and soldiers during the revolt. The amount so taken I can not state exactly, any further than that all the surgical instruments and a large portion of the medical stores were missing. I have seen officers and privates having revolvers, sabres, and other arms in their possession which I knew to have been a portion of the cargo of the J. W. Everman.

Mr. Wilbur F. Stocking made every effort in his power, even at the risk of his life, to protect the interests of the Mexican Government by saving as much of the cargo as he possibly could; but from the moment that Gen. Carvajal left, everything was in utter confusion, the revolutionists having full sway, and not only plundering, but actually threatening the lives of those who in any way attempted to interfere with them.

A very disgraceful part of the affair, in addition was, that merchants and others, both in Matamoras and Brownsville, combined to take every advantage, and to rob the Government by trumping up charges and claims upon the goods on account of private debts which they claim to be due them from Gen. Carvajal, and by throwing every imaginable difficulty in the way to prevent the friends of the Government from saving anything. The principal cause for this, as I have learned and fully believe, is that those men, for years, have had the monopoly of supplying, at exorbitant rates, arms and ammunition to the people there, both Liberalists and Imperialists, and they naturally fear that if the Government of Mexico should adopt a systematic cause for obtaining its supplies, a large portion of their nefarious but lucrative trade would be taken away from them.

As an instance of this, I will simply mention that a certain party in Brownsville offered me a large percentage if I would aid in disposing of a large quantity of damaged powder to the Mexican Government; and you may expect that in the future these men will endeavor by all means, no matter how unscrupulous, to prevent, if possible, the Liberal Government obtaining any supplies, except through them, only at exorbitant rates and for specie.

After seeing the goods, which Mr. Stocking succeeded in saving, safely stored at Brownsville, I returned to Brazos, from whence, after a passage of eighteen days, calling at Galveston and Key West for coal and provisions, I yesterday arrived in New York.

(Affidavit attached.)   J. W. HADDEN.

Signed and endorsed also by

Mr. A. H. DANIELS.

Copy of Mr. W. C. Peckham's Statement.

No. 76.]   NEW YORK, September 22, 1866.

General H. STURM.

Dear Sir: In relation to the recent shipment of arms and ammunition to the Republic of Mexico, I have to state that the cargo per steamer J. W. Everman, arived safe at Brazos, and was re-shipped by order of General Carvajal on board the river steamer "Tamanlipas No. 2," for Matamoras.

We arrived at Matamoras on the morning of Saturday, August 11th, leaving the steamer at Brownsville. In company with General Wallace and Mr. Wilbur F. Stocking, I immediately visited General Carvajal, who, on being shown a copy of the manifest, ask where the steamer was with the goods; on being told, at Brownsville, he said, "But I ordered them here."

The steamer "Tamaulipas No. 2" crossed the river either that day or early the next morning, and discharged her cargo.

At about 11 o'clock on Sunday, the 12th of August, I went down on board the steamer, and was told by Mr. Forsyth, the clerk, that the cargo was nearly all out, the landing at the time being covered with goods, which were being taken away in vans by the Government as fast as possible. I returned then to Green's Hotel, and a very short time after being called to the window by an unusual noise in the street, witnessed the surrounding of General Carvajal's headquarters, and the arrest of my companions. I soon learned, as the result of the revolt of the troops, that General Carvajal had fled to Texas, and that Col. Canales had been proclaimed Governor, and the goods of course in the hands of the insurrectionists. This was a source of great anxiety to Mr. Stocking, in whose company I was daily and almost hourly during my stay in Mexico, and I learned from him the additional fact, that certain parties, who have the monopoly of trade in arm's there, had made unlawful claims against the cargo, for other than freight charges, to an enormous amount, and Mr. Stocking was advised by influential citizens, both of Brownsville and Matamoras, in order to save the goods, and to prevent them from falling into the hands of Cortinas, to take them to the Texas side of the river. Acting upon this suggestion, he tried every means in his power to carry it out, but it was not until Wednesday, the 18th inst., that he was able to obtain permission from Col. Canales and take them over, at which time Cortinas was reported by scouts to be within twelve miles of Matamoras, marching upon the city, and that his troops had been enlisted with the promise of twenty-four hours pillage after the city should be taken; and the risk to the goods was considered so great that they were crossed at night on flat-boats.

During the time the goods were in the hands of the insurrectionists, they were exposed to rain, without adequate covering, as I learned from an officer in the quartermaster's department, and damaged accordingly, and a very large amount of the goods stolen, such as surgical instruments, sabres, pistols, cartridges, revolvers, etc.; as I know of my own personal knowledge, having tallied the goods at different times. The goods got over, being stored at Brownsville.

Mr. Stocking remained to protect them.

WILLIAM C. PECKHAM.

CITY AND COUNTY NEW YORK, ss:

William C. Peckham, the subscriber of the foregoing letter, to me known personally, on being sworn, deposes and says, that the statements contained in the foregoing letter are in all respects true.

WILLIAM C. PECKHAM.

Sworn and subscribed before me this 22d day of September, 1866.

JEROME BUCK, Notary Public.

Sturm to Stocking.*

No. 77.] NEW YORK, September 19, 1866.

WILBUR F. STOCKING, Esq.,
  Brazos Santiago, Texas.

Dear Sir: The steamer Everman has returned, and from her passengers, as also from your message, through Mr. Peckham, and from your letter of the 6th inst. to Mr. Tifft, I have learned quite full particulars in relation to all that has transpired in regard to the arms, munitions, etc., which were sent out in your charge.

You have acted in good faith, and in what at the time seemed to you the best judgment throughout the recent operations there; and all who were present bear witness to your noble efforts and almost self sacrifice to protect the interests of the Government; but you seem to have forgotton or have ignored the fact, that the goods taken out by the Everman were and are the property of the Mexican Government, having been inspected and accepted by me, as an officer of said Government, at the port New York.

Under the circumstances, therefore, it is important that the goods should be placed in the hands and subject to the control of the Government at the earliest possible moment; and to this end, you are hereby instructed to cause them to be delivered, as soon as possible, to General Tapia, or in his absence, to such other officer of the Mexican Government as may be in command at Matamoras, taking his receipt for the same.

Yours truly,

H. STURM.
Agent for the Republic of Mexico.

*Copy of a letter handed to Mr. Romero, September 24, 1866.

Fitch, Burbridge & Dunlap to Sturm.*

No. 78.] NEW YORK, September 19, 1866.

General:

Your letter of the 15th inst. requiring the delivery of 10,000 Enfield rifles by the 22d, assigning as a reason therefor, the delay of your steamers at a great expense, takes us somewhat by surprise, and would have been earlier replied to but that we were absent from the city. We have now to state, that owing to circumstances over which we have no control, we are unable to furnish the arms as required. It is our desire to act with entire frankness with you, and hasten to lay before you some of the reasons for our failure to comply with your request and our agreement. At the date of the signing of the contract some three weeks ago, it was understood distinctly, by all of us, that Mr. Romero would officially recognize and confirm the contract, as the Minister of the Republic of Mexico, and we so stated to our moneyed friends we had here in New York, and through whom we expected aid and assistance to effectuate a contract of such magnitude, involving so large a sum of money. Our pecuniary arrangements were based and predicated upon that important fact, and the sum of one hundred and fifty thousand dollars was arranged for in good faith. At the time of the signing of the contract, the Consul-General, for some reason or other, declined approving it, saying he had no authority to do so. This seemed strange to us at the time. Our Mr. Fitch, in Chicago, saw Mr. Romero and tried to obtain his approval there; but he did not do so because he was on a pleasure trip, and did not wish to transact any business, but promised to attend to it on his return to the Capital. We were compelled to await his convenience, though loth to lose the time. On his return to Washington City, being called upon by us, he orally confirmed and substantiated your authority, and stated that what you did was all right and would doubtless meet the approval of the Government; and that the Consul-General was the proper person to approve, over his official seal and signature, such commercial transactions. On our return to New York you informed us that the Minister approved the contract, and instructed or *would instruct* the Consul-General within a day or two to sign it, and that the matter was all right. In the meanwhile rumor was rife, and we learned through private sources, that all *your* acts being derived and obtained from General Carvajal, would be abrogated and annulled in consequence of his removal, and eventually be disapproved by President Juarez. These rumors and delays threw an air of doubt and suspicion over the whole transaction, which not only seriously embarrassed, but finally were fatal to our money arrangements. With regret we state our inability to comply with our agreement, and our inability to move further in the matter. It has cost us a great waste of time and trouble, and we have beside expended over three thousand dollars in having the arms prepared and made ready for shipment.

If, as we suggested at the time, you could have given us our pay as agreed for and stipulated in the contract, (namely in *bonds*,) it would have obviated all difficulties; as we could have made satisfactory arrangements, and at once, by depositing these bonds, together with other paper, with our banker, and there would have been no necessity for the approval, which necessitated and caused the delays. The parties with whom we were arranging our money matters seemed disposed to think your authority to make contracts without Minister Romero's official approval, inadequate to insure the issue of the bonds.

Thus you perceive, through the unfortunate delays that have surrounded this transaction, together with the confused, false, and exaggerated reports and rumors concerning Mexican affairs generally, the whole matter terminates in this, to us, disastrous and unsatisfactory manner, and we fear, with much inconvenience and trouble to yourself. We have endeavored to show by a plain recapitulation of the facts, some of the causes that have rendered futile our earnest and honest endeavors to faithfully perform and discharge our part of the contract.

For your promptitude in furnishing us with information necessary for us to know, and for your uniform urbanity and deportment toward us, we beg to express our grateful thanks.

Wishing success to the cause you so ably represent, and with great respect,

We remain, General, with great consideration,

Your most obedient servants,

GEO. A. FITCH.
O. H. BURBRIDGE.
J. F. DUNLAP.

General H. Sturm, New York.

*Copy of a letter handed to Mr. Romero, September 24, 1866.

Memorandum of an Interview between Mr. Romero and General Sturm.

No. 79.] *Sunday, Sept. 23.*

Saw Mr. Romero at his house this morning, and stated to him something must be done to expedite matters and facilitate my labors, as otherwise it would be impossible for me to keep up any longer against the odds presented. I told him that I had tried my best to induce the Mexican Consul (Dr. Navarro) to approve in writing various contracts I had made during Mr. Romero's absence from Washington, but that the Consul had stated to me he had no authority to sign his name to any contract. I said to Mr. Romero that a mere verbal approval was not regarded as sufficient by contracting parties. I further said that the delay in obtaining bonds, had caused me the loss of the contract with Mr. Jenks, of Philadelphia; and in consequence of the Consul's refusal to approve or disapprove contracts, distrust had been created, and the contract with Messrs. Burbridge, Fitch, and Dunlap had also fallen through the day before. I then said that it cost me considerable outlay before I could induce any party to trust his Government, and I thought it hard that in consequence of the delays mentioned I should lose not only the time and labor spent, but also the benefit of moneys expended by me in efforts to make contracts; and I sincerely hoped he would consider this matter and immediately make a different arrangement. I called Mr. Romero's attention to the fact that the unfortunate affair at Matamoras had injured the credit of the Mexican Government very seriously; and I urged him to lose no time to counteract the evil influences of this affair, by promptly settling with the parties who had furnished the goods and vessel for the first expedition.

Mr. Romero stated in reply that he had no instructions from his Government about this, and could not therefore take the responsibility of delivering the bonds on said shipment, especially as he had understood that General Escobedo and others had paid for a great portion of said cargo in specie; but he would pay the bonds for such portions of the cargo as should be delivered to a loyal Mexican officer and not paid for in specie. He then said that General Carvajal, as he had informed me a long time ago, had received his instructions from the Mexican Government direct, and as he (Romero) had never received positive instructions to interfere in General Carvajal's contracts, he had always thought it best not to interfere at all, except to give advice, and that he therefore was not responsible for anything in connection with General Carvajal's engagements; but he had no doubt that the Mexican Government would very shortly instruct him to arrange this matter to the satisfaction of all parties concerned. He desired me to say so to Messrs. Dewhurst & Emerson, and the other parties concerned; and said he would by next mail call the attention of his Government to the necessity of settling and paying for the cargo and charter of the steamer Everman. He then said I shall have no fault to find with anything I might do under his authority, and he would instruct Dr. Navarro fully, and would also make provision for the prompt delivery of bonds. He said, however, in reply to a question from me, that he could not, in the absence of instructions from his Government, order the payment of any bonds on General Carvajal's drafts, but he would order bonds to be delivered on said drafts, to pay for articles I might purchase under his own instructions.

Monday, September 24th, at 11 *o'clock A. M.* Saw Mr. Romero again and repeated my request that he should take the responsibility to settle for the charter and cargo of the Everman: he declined to do so, and requested me to be patient and all would be right shortly. I then called his attention to the fact that, owing to the trouble at Matamoras and the other vexations I had mentioned, the expeditions of Mr. Benitez, General Baranda, and Governor Baz, had been delayed, and that the charter of the Suwanee would shortly expire; and I asked him if I should renew this charter.

He said he wished me to do so if possible. I said I would telegraph to the parties.

4 P. M. I saw Mr. Romero and showed him the dispatch received from Mr. Cattell, in Philadelphia, saying that he would extend the charter of the Suwanee. Mr. Romero expressed himself satisfied, and said he hoped I would do my utmost to expedite the supplying of the three commissioners he had sent to me with as large a cargo of arms as possible.

I took this occasion to remind Mr. Romero of the many difficulties besetting me, in my efforts to assist his Government, and called his attention to the fact that, although I could get some goods for Mexican Bonds, all other expenses had to be paid for in cash; and I had numerous agents, mostly friends of mine, at work in different parts of the country, to keep this Mexican business before the people; and that all sorts of efforts were made to raise the credit and standing of his Government in the estimation of the American public: all of which cost considerable outlay of money, for which I had to provide, as his Government had not the means.

I called Mr. Romero's attention to the policy and the advantages of a regular system of purchasing, and requested of him authority to purchase in whatever quantities I might be able, a certain specified quantity of material of war; to collect the same in a storehouse hired for the purpose; and thence ship to Mexico, as might be required. And I pointed out to him the great saving in time and money, as well as labor, that would accrue to me and to his Government, in consequence of such a system. He requested me to put this proposition in writing as concisely as possible; and he would give it his careful consideration. Before leaving, he assured me that he would render to his Government a full account of the difficulties encountered by me and the valuable services I was rendering to his country.

NOTE.—The above is a literal copy of a memorandum made by me on September 23d and 24th.
H. STURM.

Sturm to Romero.

No. 80.] WASHINGTON, September 24, 1866.

Senor M. ROMERO,
　　Mexican Minister, etc.

Sir: I would respectfully state to you, that since the recent difficulties at Matamoras have become known here, it is almost impossible to make contracts of amount with parties in this country. Nearly all my arrangements heretofore made (except direct purchases) have fallen through; the parties refusing to deliver the goods, being fearful of a similar occurrence, and that they may not obtain their pay (bonds) promptly in consequence.

Under these circumstances, and knowing full well that your Government needs almost all kinds of military stores and supplies, and as soon as possible, I would respectfully submit to your consideration the following proposition, viz:

That you authorize me to purchase in open market, or at private sale, whenever it is possible for me to obtain the same,—

All Ordnance and Ordnance Stores, Quartermaster's and Commissary and Hospital Stores, necessary to arm, equip, and supply according to the United States Army and Ordnance Regulations:—

1st. (30,000) Thirty thousand Infantry.
2d. (6,000) Six thousand Cavalry.
3d. (15) Fifteen batteries of Light Field Artillery.
4th. Say (100) one hundred pieces Heavy Artillery for fortifications and siege purposes, with all their equipments and necessary supplies.

All these articles, or so much of them as I am able to obtain under present circumstances, will be selected by me according to the U. S. Regulations, and at lowest possible rates, and not exceeding the prices heretofore paid by the U. S. Government for the same articles; are to be paid for in bonds on their delivery at the storehouse, and will be shipped at such times and to such places only as you may direct; and I will report to you every two weeks, or oftener if desired, the exact quantity on hand, with a statement of the purchases and disbursements.

It would, in my opinion, be wise to supply your Government, at the present time, with all it can obtain in this way, until you hear further from the Government in regard to this matter; for even if the French should withdraw, it will be necessary for your Government to have a large supply to strengthen itself, and to overcome any opposition that might show itself from other quarters than foreign countries, and to maintain the supremacy of law and order; and in this way, also, the Government has absolute control over all the supplies, and avoids the difficulties (as the United States experienced to its cost during the first two years of the late Rebellion) of being at the mercy of a few men, whose only aim is to obtain all the gold they can get, and who have no real sympathies with it, but would as soon sell to its enemies; and I also would not be annoyed and troubled by parties refusing to complete contracts they have negotiated, on account of bad news received, etc., etc.

I am, Sir,
Very respectfully,
H. STURM.

Romero to Sturm.

[The following was received at New York, September 25th, 1866.]

No. 81.]   WASHINGTON, September 21, 1866.

General H. STURM,
New York.

Dear Sir: Mr. Campbell is disposed to sell, for the Mexican Republic, certain arms, the particulars of which will be communicated to you by General Baranda.

I hope you will conclude a contract with Mr. Campbell, in accordance with my general instructions, and think it practicable, because said gentleman seems ready to grant some fair terms.

Very truly, yours,
M. ROMERO.

Sturm to Romero.

No. 82.] NEW YORK, September 25, 1866.

Senor M. ROMERO,
 Mexican Minister, etc.

Sir: After carefully considering all the circumstances of the case in connection with what you told me yesterday, as well as what Mr. Campbell has told me to-day, I have come to the conclusion to close the contract with Mr. Campbell for the carbines, etc., at the prices he asks. He desired me, however, to insert a clause in the contract about exchanging the bonds he may receive under this contract for any other bonds of the Republic hereafter to be issued, or that may be guaranteed by the United States. This, of course, I am only partially authorized to do; but as he wanted it, and as the contract must be approved by you before it is valid, (Mr. Campbell preferring that you should approve it instead of Dr. Navarro,) you will, of course, decide this matter yourself.

I am, Sir,
Very respectfully,
H. STURM.

Romero to Sturm.

No. 83.] WASHINGTON, September 25, 1866.

My Dear General:

I am so much engaged to-day with different matters that I am unable to attend the subject of your letter of yesterday. I will do so to-morrow.

The news from Matamoras are worse than I anticipated.

In great hurry,
Yours truly,
M. ROMERO.

Sturm to Romero.

No. 84.] NEW YORK, September 26, 1866.

Senor M. ROMERO,
    Mexican Minister, etc.

Dear Sir: Your letter of yesterday received this afternoon. I am very, very sorry that the accounts from Matamoras are true. I hoped all last night and to-day that it might be a canard; but as it is true, I think the best thing we can do is to act promptly, and thereby overcome the disaster. There certainly is some movement on foot, on the part of Ortega and other enemies of your Government, to overthrow the same, and I would therefore urge that every effort be made *at once* to obtain arms, etc., before further sad news, or the particulars of the same, are received here. *I will do all I can*, and am quite confident that in a short time all will be right and your Government triumphant.

Be pleased, therefore, to arrange with Corlies & Co., so that I may be able to obtain such bonds as I need, to pay *at once* for articles, etc., purchased, and also for the payment of *one-half* of Dr. Ramsey's draft. In this way we will soon have a *political* and *monetary* strength here in favor of the legitimate Government, and also have practical aid in the shape of supplies, which your Government so much needs.

I am, Sir, very respectfully,
    Your obedient servant,
        H. STURM.

Romero to Sturm.

[Translation.]

No. 85.] WASHINGTON, September 27, 1866.

MEXICAN LEGATION
    IN THE
U. S. OF AMERICA.

With your letter of day before yesterday, I received to-day the contract which you closed on the same date with Mr. A. C. Campbell for the purchase of 1,500 carbines and 100 cases of ammunition; said contract has been approved by me on account of the special circumstances attached thereto.

Enclosed you will find an order for $100,000 in bonds, drawn on Messrs. John W. Corlies & Co., and with said funds you will pay the value of the purchased goods.

Yours respectfully,
        M. ROMERO.

To General H. STURM, New York.

Romero to Sturm.

No. 86.] WASHINGTON, September 27, 1866.

General H. STURM,
    New York.

Dear Sir: I have approved the contract you signed with Mr. Campbell on the 25th instant. I send you a draft for $100,000 in bonds, with a view that you will have funds enough to make the payment. Mr. Campbell desires to have his bonds deposited, and I have designated Mr. Fuentes as depositor. I beg of you, therefore, that as soon as you receive this letter, you will have $108,000 in bonds deposited at Mr. Fuentes' to Mr. Campbell's order.
    I am, very respectfully,
        Your obedient servant,
            M. ROMERO.

Sturm to Romero.

No. 87.] NEW YORK CITY, Sept. 28, 1866.

Senor M. ROMERO,
    Mexican Minister, etc.

Sir: I have the honor to acknowledge the receipt of your letter of yesterday, in which you instruct me to place in the hands of Mr. Fuentes the sum of one hundred and eight thousand ($108,000) dollars, Mexican Bonds, to the order of Mr. A. C. Campbell. I also received your order on Corlies & Co. for one hundred thousand ($100,000) dollars, Mexican Bonds, which I have this day presented to them, and it has been duly honored. To-morrow morning I shall deliver the bonds to Mr. Fuentes and take his receipt for the same. I have given orders to Mr. Campbell to ship the arms, etc., at once to this place; which he has promised to do.

To-morrow I shall send you vouchers for bonds expended, and as I have but little left, I would again urge the necessity of arranging with Corlies & Co., so that I may not be hindered in making purchases, etc.
    I am, Sir, very respectfully,
        Your obedient servant,
            H. STURM.

Sturm to Romero.

No. 88.] NEW YORK, Sept. 29, 1866.

SENOR M. ROMERO,
    Mexican Minister, etc.

Sir: I have the honor to state that I have this day delivered to Mr. Fuentes the sum of one hundred and eight thousand ($108,000) dollars in Mexican Bonds, to be deposited by him to the order of Mr. A. C. Campbell, as requested by you in your letter of the 27th inst.

As soon as the goods contracted for with Mr. Campbell are received by me, I will notify Mr. Fuentes of the fact.

I am, Sir, very respectfully,
Your obedient servant,
H. STURM.

Sturm to Romero.

No. 89.] NEW YORK, Sept. 29, 1866.

Senor M. ROMERO,
Mexican Minister, etc.

Sir: I have the honor to state that I have purchased (approved by Dr. Navarro) of the American Arms Co., Philadelphia, (2,260) two thousand two hundred and sixty carbines, at thirty-four dollars and fifty cents ($34.50), United States currency, each. The total amount, with boxes, amounts to one hundred and thirty thousand four hundred and fifty ($130,450) dollars in Mexican Bonds, which are to be delivered next week. The carbines have been inspected, and are entirely new and excellent.

I am, Sir, very respectfully,
Your obedient servant,
H. STURM.

Romero to Sturm.

No. 90.] WASHINGTON, Sept. 30, 1866.

My Dear Sir:

The reason I have not sent to you the instructions you asked, has been that I have been expecting to hear from home before doing so. I expected last evening my mail from Chihuahua, which did not come. I suppose it will be here this evening. In this case I will send you to-morrow, without fail, my instructions.

In great hurry,
Respectfully,
M. ROMERO.

Sturm to Romero.

No. 91.]   NEW YORK, Oct. 2, 1866.

Senor M. ROMERO,
    Mexican Minister, etc.

Sir: Enclosed please find the following bills of purchases made by me, properly receipted, and paid by me out of the funds at my disposal:

Wm. J. Taylor, supplies	$13,193	
Henry Simons, "	13,757	
	$26,950, or in Mexican Bonds,	$44,900
In addition to the above I have (in the absence of other funds) sent for the use of Mr. Stocking to enable him (in case he can use them) to pay necessary expenses, Mexican Bonds to the amount of		20,000
Paid for coaling steamer for Gen. Baranda's expedition		10,000
Paid according to instructions to Mr. Fuentes		108,000
		$182,900
Received from Corlies & Co., $200,000. Balance		17,100
		$200,000

I am, Sir, Very Respectfully,
            Your Obt. Servt.,
                H. STURM.

Sturm to Romero.

No. 92.]   NEW YORK, October 2, 1866.

Senor M. ROMERO,
    Mexican Minister, etc.

Sir: Captain Tuttle, the master of the steamer Everman, reports to me today, that the steamer is discharged of her cargo, and waiting further orders. He also reports that the freight and passage money, amounting to four thousand three hundred and thirty-two dollars and twenty-three ($4,332.23) cents, realized on her return trip, has according to the instructions given him by the owners of the steamer, been disbursed by him for wages, etc., although I gave him instructions to collect the money for, and deliver the same to me as soon as collected.

I enclose herewith copy of my instructions to him; also of his reports.

Be pleased to communicate to me at once, whether I shall order said steamer to return to Philadelphia and be discharged from further service of the Government, or whether it is desirable to hold her for further use.

I am, Sir, Very Respectfully,
            Your Obt. Servt.,
                H. STURM

Sturm to Romero.

No. 93.] NEW YORK, October 2, 1866.

Senor M. ROMERO,
    Mexican Minister, etc.

Sir: Your letter of September 30th, in which you state that on account of your expecting your mail from Chihuahua, you have delayed giving me any instructions, has been received.

I would respectfully state to you that I deem it of utmost importance that the bill of the American Arms Co., of Philadelphia, be paid as agreed, as soon as I receive the goods. They are being loaded now, and I expect the bill of lading to-morrow or next day, when I ought to be in position to deliver to them their bonds.

I can not understand why I do not hear from Matamoras or Brownsville, and am afraid that the troubles there are very bad. I enclose herewith some articles from the evening papers of yesterday. They are calculated to do injury, and I also fear that Santa Anna is really doing something not calculated to help the Government. I know positively that he enlists officers and men; issues commissions, and pays from one to two months' salary in advance.

To fully test this matter, I have directed a certain officer, whose name for good reasons I do not mention in this letter, to try and enlist and obtain his commission, etc. If he succeeds, I shall be able to show you some proof of what Santa is doing. I have given this officer, who is truly loyal to the Government, my word that I will communicate this to you at once, as also the reasons which prompt me to do so, so that he may not be blamed by the Government for this act undertaken only to serve its interests.

Some parties seem to think this is only a "Herald" sensation, etc , but I have good reason to think otherwise, as I have been reliably informed that arms, etc., have been purchased, etc.

The steamers at Staten Island are being watched by United States officials in our interests, and can not get away without our knowing it in time. Matamoras is the place of destination, although Corpus Christi is the first place of rendezvous, of these parties.

The class of men surrounding and enlisted by Santa Anna, is of the *notorious* and *determined* kind, and can do no real good to any party; but are amply able to do a great deal of mischief.

Be pleased to communicate to me your opinion of this affair.

I am, Sir,
            Truly your Obt. Servt.,
                        H. STURM.

Romero to Sturm.

[Translation.]

No. 94.] WASHINGTON, October 2, 1866.

MEXICAN LEGATION IN THE U. S. OF AMERICA.

I have received your note of the 24th of September last, wherein you ask of me power to buy for the Mexican Republic all ordnance stores, quartermaster, commissary, hospital, and medical stores necessary to arm, equip, and provide, according to the ordnance regulations of the U. S. Army, 36,000 infantry, 6,000 cavalry, 15 batteries of light artillery, and you say, for instance, 100 pieces of heavy artillery for siege and fortification purposes, with all accoutrements and appurtenances necessary. As I am not acquainted with the military laws of the United States, I want to know, before I answer the main part of your question, which are the goods you refer to. For that purpose, it would be well that you send me a detailed statement of all the articles you refer to, and which are necessary, according to the respective laws of the U. S. for an army corps of the strength you mention. It may be that many of said goods are not necessary on account of the peculiar circumstances of the Mexican army; and this is the reason why I ask you for the above-mentioned statement.

I repeat to you the assurances of my most distinguished consideration.

M. ROMERO.

To General H. STURM, New York.

Romero to Sturm.

[Translation.]

No. 95.] WASHINGTON, October 2, 1866.

MEXICAN LEGATION IN THE U. S. OF AMERICA.

Through your note of the 29th of last month, I am informed that you have purchased, with Consul Navarro's approval, 2,260 carbines, for the price of $34.50 each in U. S. currency; the whole invoice, together with the cases, amounting to $132,450 in Mexican Bonds, which you are bound to deliver next week. That you may pay that sum, I enclose herewith another order on Messrs. Corlies & Co., that they may deliver you $100,000 in bonds, which, together with the balance of the bonds in your possession, will enable you to cover the above said payment.

I repeat to you the assurances of my distinguished consideration.

M. ROMERO.

To General H. STURM, New York.

Romero to Sturm.

No. 96.] WASHINGTON, October 2, 1866.

My Dear General:

I send you my answer to your letter of the 24th ultimo. Please inform me as erarly as possible of what I ask you there.

Please send me a letter asking me to pay to Dr. Ramsay for his torpedo, and I will send the order to Corlies & Co.

Send me, if possible, a copy of General Carvajal's draft to Dr. R.

In great hurry,

M. ROMERO.

Sturm to Romero.

No. 97.] NEW YORK, October 3, 1866.

Senor. M. ROMERO,
  Mexican Minister, etc.

Sir: I have the honor to acknowledge the receipt of your letter of yesterday in relation to the authority I asked of you in my letter of September 24th, and in answer would state, that I will make out a detailed statement of the articles referred to in that letter, and will remit the same to you as soon as possible.

I am, Sir, very respectfully,
  Your obedient servant,

H. STURM.

Sturm to Romero.

No. 98.] NEW YORK, October 3, 1866.

SENOR M. ROMERO,
  Mexican Minister, etc.

Sir: I would respectfully ask that you instruct Messrs. Corlies & Co. to pay to Dr. Ramsay the sum of seven thousand five hundred ($7,500) dollars in Mexican Bonds, at sixty (60) cents on the dollar, on account of a draft given for fifteen thousand ($15,000) dollars to Dr. Ramsay by General Carvajal in payment for two torpedo boats. As Dr. Ramsay has only one of the boats now ready, the above sum will cover the amount for one boat only.

A copy of this draft I sent to you on September 10th, and the papers relating to Dr. Ramsay's matter have not been returned to me as yet.

I am, sir, very respectfully,
  Your obedient servant,

M. ROMERO.

Sturm to Romero.

No. 99.] NEW YORK, October 3, 1866.

Senor M. ROMERO,
    Mexican Minister, etc.

Sir: I have the honor to acknowledge the receipt of your communications (in Spanish) of yesterday, as also the letter to Messrs. Corlies & Co., wherein you instruct them to place at my disposal one hundred thousand ($100,000) dollars in bonds, and in answer, I would state that Mr. Tifft told me he would communicate with you in regard to having some bonds signed, there not being a sufficient amount signed to fill the order, and that it would therefore not be filled at present.

From my communications of yesterday you will have seen that I have really a balance on hand of only seventeen thousand and one hundred ($17,100) dollars; this with the addition of the present order for one hundred thousand ($100,000) dollars, still leaves a deficit of over thirteen thousand (13,000) dollars, for the purpose of paying for the carbines.

Be pleased therefore to place an additional amount at my disposal, as I ought to have some spare funds on hand to meet contingencies.

I am, Sir, very respectfully,
    Your obedient servant,
        H. STURM.

Romero to Sturm.

[Translation.]

No. 100.] WASHINGTON, October 3, 1866.

MEXICAN LEGATION IN THE U. S. OF AMERICA.

I have received your note of yesterday wherein you enclose accounts and vouchers of Wm. Taylor and Mr. Henry Simons for goods bought by you from them for the Mexican Republic. The first for the amount of $13,193, and the second for $13,757, the aggregate of both sums being in Mexican bonds at 60 per cent., $44,900; besides this amount you state to me that you have disposed of $20,000 of said bonds, which you have remitted to Mr. Stocking for expenses, which makes the aggregate which you have spent $182,900 at par, and remaining in your hands $17,100. as you have received $200,000 from Messrs. Corlies & Co.

I will tell you, in answer, that as the $20,000 in bonds were not remitted to Mr. Stocking with my knowledge, I shall consider them in your hands in order that, when you render the account of the expenses incurred by Mr. Stocking, you may be credited with the sums which should be allowed according to the nature of the said expenses.

As to the amount of $10,000 for coals for General Baranda's expedition, I beg you to inform me if said coal was already purchased, or when, and under what circumstances the purchase was made.

I repeat to you the assurances of my most distinguished consideration.

M. ROMERO.

General H. Sturm,
  New York.

Romero to Sturm.

No. 101.]   Washington, October 3, 1866.

Gen. H. Sturm,
  New York.

Dear Sir: Your two letters of yesterday have just been received. I am very much obliged to you for the important information they convey.

I sent to you yesterday the necessary amount to pay for the Philadelphia carbines.

I will answer you later your two letters of yesterday's date.

Please inform me of all you know about Santa Anna's movements. I return you a letter belonging to you.

In great haste,
  Respectfully yours,
    M. ROMERO.

Romero to Sturm.

[Translation.]

No. 102.]   Washington, October 3, 1866.

Mexican Legation
 in the
U. S. of America.

I am in receipt of your note of yesterday wherein you communicate to me that the Captain of the steamer Everman reports to you that he has unloaded at that port and awaits your orders, as also that the amount of freight and passages on the return voyage, say $4,333.23 was spent by him as wages, etc., against instructions you had given him, and of which you enclose me a copy. I have not received this copy; only two dispatches addressed to you by the Captain.

You ask me whether you should order said steamer back to Philadelphia, discharging her from the service of the Government, or if you should retain her in said service.

Should the Everman be ready to start in four days loaded with goods in charge of General Baranda, it will be well that you retain her for that purpose, but should said goods not be ready, or if for any other reason it is not possible that said sailing take place within the time named, you must put an end to said steamer's contract, trying to get either the same or other steamer when the time comes.

I renew to you the assurances of my most distinguished consideration.

    M. ROMERO.

To General H. Sturm,

Sturm to Romero.

No. 103.] NEW YORK, October 4, 1866.

Senor M. ROMERO,
  Mexican Minister, etc.

Sir: Your letter of yesterday was duly received and contents noted. I have the honor to state, that this afternoon the officers (I sent two of them separate and unknown to each other) that I sent to Santa Anna reported to me in substance the same thing, viz.:

That Santa Anna has really organized a Government at Staten Island with Narphegy as Minister of Foreign Affairs, General Perzl as Secretary of War, and Santa Anna's father-in-law (so they state) as Minister of Finance. The officers were received, and as I surmised, their offer was accepted, and on Saturday next they shall receive their commissions, and two months' pay in advance. Santa Anna himself spoke to them (through M. Narphegy) and stated that he had ample means to pay his troops regularly, etc., but urges them to be cautious and do nothing that might injure the cause, as he expected to have dispatches from Washington to-morrow, when a definite plan of action would be determined upon.

To one of the officers sent to him by me, and who has but just returned from Matamoras, and knows, of course, all about affairs there, he was very attentive, asked all about the city, its forts, the number of guns, etc. He was particularly anxious about General Ford, who commands the forts at Matamoras, and wished to know if my man knew him well. On being told that he did, Santa Anna inquired, as it was very important that Ford should be secured over to "our side," if my man would perhaps arrange this matter with Ford. He then explained to him that he intended to take 2,000 men and take Matamoras first, but nothing definite would be done until he heard from Washington, as he intended to arrange with certain parties about an emigration scheme, and in this way it might all be done without interfering with the neutrality of the United States.

On Saturday or Monday I will know more, but there is no doubt of his being actively engaged in planning a conspiracy to overthrow your Government. He exacts from all, that they call him President, and the others all have their titles. General Sweeny, Roberts, and others are constantly about or near him, and I believe that Clay Crawford furnishes a part of the funds now being used by him.

Would it not be well to inform General Grant of this at once? as it would be of great injury if the parties should be allowed to get Matamoras in any way, and they mean to do this certain. I also believe it would be well to at once take steps to so arrange matters with Ford (who I have good reason to believe is still faithful to the Government) or in some other way at Matamoras, so as to interfere with the designs of these parties.

Santa Anna has bought 2,000 rifles and other articles, and pretends to be acting in perfect concert with Mr. Seward.

As soon as I learn more I will notify you.

                Yours truly,
                   H. STURM.

Sturm to Romero.

No. 104.] NEW YORK, October 5, 1866.

Senor M. ROMERO,
    Mexican Minister, etc.

In answer to your letter of yesterday in relation to my disbursements, etc., I have the honor to state that of *course* I expect to be charged with the twenty thousand ($20,000) dollars bonds given to Mr. Stocking, until I account for their expenditure.

The coal was purchased by me for General Baranda's expedition, it being absolutely necessary, and I will send you a receipt for the same as soon as I can see the Captain of the vessel.

This expedition would have started some time ago, had it not been on account of interferences and difficulties with which you are perfectly familiar.

    I am Sir,
        Very respectfully,
            Your obedient servant,
                H. STURM.

Sturm to Romero.

No. 105.] NEW YORK, October 5, 1866.

Senor M. ROMERO,
    Mexican Minister, etc.

Sir: Your letter in relation to the steamer Everman has been received. I herewith enclose a copy of my order to Captain Tuttle, master of said steamer. This copy must have been left out of my letter at the time of closing the same.

As I have a very fast steamer for the use of General Baranda, much more suitable to that purpose than the Everman, and as I can not, under present circumstances, be ready for said expedition in four days, I shall order said steamer to be returned to Philadelphia, and discharge her from the Government service according to contract.

    I am Sir, very respectfully,
        Your obedient servant,
            H. STURM.

Sturm to Romero.

No. 106.] NEW YORK, October 5, 1866.

Senor M. ROMERO,
    Mexican Minister, etc.

Dear Sir: Enclosed I send two official letters in answer to those received from you to-day. As your letters are in Spanish, Mr. Fuentes read them to me, and will translate the same into English.

I have been extremely busy for the last few days, and in the hurry of closing my mails I must have neglected to send the copy of order to Tuttle.

I sent you that statement of disbursements the other day, not for the purpose of settlement, but merely to show you how I had disposed of the funds in my charge, and that I had not sufficient on hand for other purposes.

You are aware that it sometimes becomes necessary for an officer, in my position, to expend funds for which (although he is still responsible) he can not produce vouchers until some time after. I shall always give such a statement, to enable you to see how I act, and as soon as I obtain my vouchers I shall remit them, when you will please place the same to my credit.

I also inform you that I expect to close a purchase for twenty or thirty thousand Enfield rifles (splendid and new guns) in a few days, the parties asking twenty ($20) for them, but I will get them for the old price. In this case it is absolutely necessary that arrangements are made in time to have bonds ready, as I understand from Mr. Tifft that there are not sufficient printed or signed; the one hundred dollar bonds are too small, and it takes too long to get them ready,

I have the honor to be,
Very respectfully,
Your obedient servant,
H. STURM.

Romero to Sturm.

No. 107.] WASHINGTON, October 5, 1866.

My Dear Sir:

I received this morning you two letters of yesterday; one of them I took to Gen. Grant. As he was not in his office I left it for his perusal.

I send you the draft for $7,500 in bonds to the order of Dr. Ramsay.

I attach very little importance to Gen. Santa Anna's movements, although they are calculated to do a great deal of harm to the Mexican cause here. I do not suppose they can do any harm at home. I do not believe Santa Anna can send either men or supplies to Mexico, and all this will end in more law suits against him. Under such circumstances I do not think it very wise to spend our means in ascertaining what he is about. I will write to you more fully about it.

I do not think it proper to mention your name, as agent to make purchases, in the official notice from the Legation on the subject.

In great hurry,
M. ROMERO.

Romero to Sturm.

[Translation.]

No. 108.] WASHINGTON, October 5, 1866.

MEXICAN LEGATION IN THE U. S. OF AMERICA.

In answer to your note of the 3d inst. wherein you ask me for an order that Messrs. John W. Corlies & Co. may deliver to Mr. Ramsay $7,500 in bonds at 60 per cent. of their par value, for the purpose of covering the amount of one torpedo, ordered by Gen. Carvajal, I enclose herewith the order that you wish, and beg of you that you see it paid at once in bonds, and receive the torpedo that it may be sent, as soon as possible, where it may be useful to the Mexican Republic.

I repeat to you the assurances of my most distinguished consideration.

M. ROMERO.

To General H. STURM,
New York.

Sturm to Romero.

No. 109.] NEW YORK, October 6, 1866.

Senor M. ROMERO,
Mexican Minister, etc.

Sir: I have the honor to herewith transmit a copy of instructions, to Mr. Simons, owner of the steamer J. W. Everman, informing him that said steamer is discharged from further service.

I am, Sir, very respectfully,
Your obedient servant,
H. STURM.

Sturm to Romero.

No. 110.] NEW YORK, October 6, 1806.

SENOR M. ROMERO,
Mexican Minister, etc.

I have the honor to acknowledge the receipt of your communication of yesterday, enclosing:

1st. Instructions for me in regard to Dr. Ramsay's torpedo boat, and

2d. An order on J. W. Corlies & Co., to pay Dr. Ramsey seven thousand five hundred ($7,500) dollars on his draft.

The instructions given me will be complied with, and the order on J. W. Corlies & Co. I have delivered to them, and they will pay the same as soon as I notify them that said boat has been received by me.

I have the honor to be, Sir,
Very respectfully,
Your obedient servant,
H. STURM.

Sturm to Romero.

No. III.] NEW YORK, October 6, 1866.

Senor M. ROMERO,
    Mexican Minister, etc.

Sir: I have the honor to state that I have received from the American Arms Co. (2280) two thousand two hundred and eighty carbines, and (114) one hundred and fourteen packing boxes, as per bill of lading herewith enclosed, all in excellent condition.

As you will see, there are (20) twenty more carbines and (1) one more packing box than first mentioned.

The sum total due said company for the arms, etc., is:

2280 carbines, at $34.50	$78,660.00
114 boxes, at $2.75	313.50
	$78,973.00

Or, in Mexican Bonds, $131,600.00

As soon as they are paid for, I shall remit you a receipt in full for said goods. You will see, however, that I have not funds enough to pay this amount, and I wish you would give additional instructions to Messrs. Corlies & Co., so as to pay for them on Monday next.

    I am, Sir, respectfully,
        Your obedient servant,
            H. STURM.

Sturm to Romero.

No. 112.] NEW YORK, October 6, 1866.

Senor M. ROMERO,
    Mexican Minister, etc.

Dear Sir: I notice what you say in regard to Santa Anna, and while I agree with you that in the end he will not be able to do any harm to the Government *at home,* I yet fear that temporarily he will do mischief *here,* particularly if he should succeed in getting off to Matamoras, which I know to be his intention. I am very glad that you informed General G., for he is the best friend we have had, and will do all he can to prevent this.

I expect on Monday next, (provided this meets your views,) to make a contract with the New York Mail Steamship Co., for passage at fixed rates, between here and New Orleans, for such officers as you may desire to send to Mexico, payment to be made in bonds. As Dr. Navarro has no authority to approve such a contract, it would be desirable that you give him this authority. If it is possible for me to do so, I shall remit the contract *to you* for approval. In this way you will be enabled at any time to send men to Mexico at fixed rates, and it will of course save you some trouble and inconvenience.

What you say in regard to the card published by Mr. Mariscal meets my wishes exactly, although it was quite important that the public should know there is but one agent purchasing for your Government, and he, under your instructions and with your approval.

I have the honor to be, very respectfully,

Your obedient servant,

H. STURM.

Romero to Sturm.

No. 113.] WASHINGTON, October 6, 1866.

General H. STURM,

Dear Sir: I have received your three communications of yesterday, answering the last of mine. I shall request Mr. Tifft to have ready as many bonds as you may want for the contracts you are about to conclude.

Very sincerely yours,

M. ROMERO.

Romero to Sturm.

[Translation.]

No. 114.] WASHINGTON, Oct. 8, 1866.

MEXICAN LEGATION IN THE U. S. OF AMERICA.

I have received four notes from you under date 6th inst. In the first you acknowledge the receipt of the one I addressed to you on the 5th with regard to the torpedo built by Dr. Ramsay.

In the second you enclosed a copy of instructions you have given to Mr. Simons, owner of the steamer Evverman, advising him that the charter of said vessel is ended, according to the terms I gave you.

In the third, you state to me you have received from the Philadelphia Arms Co. 2280 carbines packed in 114 cases, being twenty (20) more carbines than you had previously reported, all of which are already on board the steamer Suwanee, according to the shipping receipt, dated on the 5th inst., at Philadelphia, which you enclose to me.

In the fourth note, receipt of which I herein acknowledge, you state to me you are in hopes of making a contract for the sending, at fixed rates, all officers that should sail from that port to New Orleans.

I have to answer to this last note, and do it at once, telling you not to enter into any contract for passages which you refer to, since there will be only very few Mexican officers whose traveling expenses from New York to New Orleans should be paid.

I renew to you the assurances of my most distinguished consideration,

M. ROMERO.

To GEN. H. STURM,
  New York.

Romero to Sturm.

NO. 115.] WASHINGTON, October 9, 1866.

General H. STURM.

Dear Sir: Messrs. Quintard, Sawyer & Ward, after having asked me in reference to the notice published by the Legation, if you are an authorized agent for contracts, and in view of my answer that you are so, but your contracts subject to my revision for approval, ask now if your contract with them has been approved by me, or will be so when sent to this Legation.

Before giving my answer to them, I think it proper to inform you of their movements, and have to inquire of you whether the contract alluded to is the one for General Baranda's expedition or any other.

Sincerely yours,

M. ROMERO.

Sturm to Romero.

No. 116.] NEW YORK, October 10, 1866.

Senor M. ROMERO,
    Mexican Minister, etc.

Sir: I have the honor to acknowledge the receipt of your letters of the 6th and 8th inst. As you suggest in your letter of the 8th, I shall do nothing further in regard to the proposed arrangement for passage, but wish to state that I thought it would be of great convenience to you to have an arrangement made whereby you could send parties home at any time, without trouble, and without paying *cash*.

I yesterday telegraphed you for half a million of bonds, to enable us to pay for (20,000) twenty thousand Enfield rifles, etc. The parties are willing to give me the best security for the fulfillment of their contract, which, upon examination, I find to be just as represented, but they demand of me that I shall put up fifty thousand dollars of bonds as security on my part. This I cannot do as I have not even bonds enough to pay the American Arms Co., and it is necessary, therefore, to hasten this matter, or I may be again disappointed in obtaining these supplies.

I am doing all I can, but with Ortega (about whom I shall write fully as soon as my health improves) doing all he can to injure your Government, by representing to parties willing to help your Government, that the bonds will be repudiated; and also Santa Anna and his friends against me; It is very hard work to purchase anything.

I have been quite unwell for the past three days, and you must excuse my not writing more fully at present.

I am, Sir, very respectfully,
    Your obedient servant,

H. STURM.

Sturm to Romero.

No. 117.] NEW YORK, October 10, 1866.

Senor M. ROMERO,
    Mexican Minister, etc.

Dear Sir: Your note of yesterday in regard to Quintard, Sawyer & Ward, has just been received, and as it is already late, I have but time to to say that this is all right, the coal paid for by the Government being for General Baranda and Governor Baz. I will write more fully to you, but wish, in the meantime, that you inform the gentlemen accordingly as soon as you can, as they seem to have some doubts about my authority in consequence of that card published.

    I am, Sir, very respectfully,
        Your obedient servant,
            H. STURM.

Sturm to Romero.

No. 118.] NEW YORK, October 11, 1866.

Senor M. ROMERO,
    Mexican Minister, etc.

Sir: I have the honor to herewith transmit to you the bill of the American Arms Company, of Philadelphia, properly receipted by the President and Treasurer of said company, for one hundred and thirty-one thousand six hundred ($131,600) dollars, Mexican Bonds, that being the amount due said company for carbines furnished according to contract.

You are aware that I did not have sufficient funds to pay the whole of this amount, and I was therefore obliged to give them my due bill for the balance, and I should be obliged if you would instruct Messrs. Corlies & Co. to deliver me an additional amount, so that I may be able to pay the balance due as soon as may be.

    I am, Sir, very respectfully,
        Your obedient servant,
            H. STURM.

Sturm to Romero.

No. 119.] NEW YORK, October 12, 1866.

Senor M. ROMERO,
    Mexican Minister, etc.

Sir: I have the honor to state, that I have completed partial arrangements (that is, so far as I am able) for twenty thousand (20,000) Enfield rifles, five thousand (5,000) suits of clothing, surgical instruments, and other supplies, but fear that, owing to my inability to secure to the parties the delivery of the bonds, some of those arrangements may fall through. You can not possibly imagine the difficult position I am placed in, for want of funds. Messrs. Corlies & Co., although anxious to aid me, do not feel at liberty to go my security for the delivery of the bonds, as they have no bonds on hand, and have no instructions from you to deliver me any. It is, therefore, absolutely necessary, if I shall purchase successfully, that such arrangements be made with Corlies & Co. at once, that I can control sufficient bonds to pay for all articles purchased under your orders, and I therefore respectfully call your attention to this matter, hoping that you will arrange it at your earliest convenience.

You are aware that I have persistently and faithfully labored to obtain such supplies as your Government urgently needs, and can well imagine how mortifying it is to me to find, when I have succeeded, after weeks of labor, to interest parties sufficiently to sell goods to me, that the purchase is lost on account of my inability to promptly pay the parties, or to give them the proper security.

General Baranda, Mr. Baz and Benitez, with whom I work in perfect concert, are anxious to return home. Transportation and a portion of the stores have been ready for some time, and the balance of the goods needed I can not (on account of the persistent efforts of Ortega and others to injure the credit of your Government) at present obtain, unless I have bonds at command to give as security or as payment at once.

Hoping to hear from you soon in regard to this matter, I remain,
Very respectfully,
Your obedient servant,
H. STURM.

Sturm to Romero.

[Confidential.]

No. 120.]   NEW YORK, October 12, 1866.

Senor M. ROMERO.

Dear Sir: A *very wealthy and prominent gentleman* of this city, and a particular friend of General Grant, (his name I will give you verbally) told me a few days ago, during a conversation I had with him about purchases, that he and several other gentleman had, on the strength of a private letter and request from General Grant, made up a fund of over one hundred and fifty thousand dollars, to be used for the purpose of sending supplies to President Juarez.

General Ortega, who somehow was, or became, acquainted with the persons connected with this matter and their object, told them, however, not to do any thing of the kind; called Juarez a usurper, and stated that the bonds were worthless, and would certainly be repudiated, etc. This, of course, had the effect to break up the whole arrangement. Ortega has since persistently done the same thing, and loses no opportunity to injure the credit of the Government.

Mr. Ames, of Massachusetts, with whom I have been negotiating for some time for a large amount of supplies, yesterday called on me and stated again (as on a former occasion) that a certain General offers Ochoa bonds in Boston and elsewhere for five cents on the dollar, thereby injuring the credit of our bonds.

I give you these facts (as promised in one of my former letters) merely to show you how persistently some parties endeavor to prevent supplies from being purchased for and sent to the aid of the Government.

I am fully aware that we can not prevent this; but we can, undoubtedly, overcome the difficulty by energetic and prompt action on our part.

I am, Sir,
Yours truly,
H. STURM.

Romero to Sturm.

[Translation.]

No. 121.]

WASHINGTON, October 12, 1866.

MEXICAN LEGATION
IN THE
U. S. OF AMERICA.

I have received two notes of yours—one dated on the 10th, the other on the 11th inst. In the first you refer to the contract for coal, which you had contracted for with Messrs. Quintard & Ward. In the second, you state that you are contracting for 20,000 Enfield rifles, and need at once the sum of $50,000 in bonds, to be given as security; and with the third you enclose the amount and vouchers of the Philadelphia Arms Co. for the 2,280 carbines which you bought of them for the Mexican Republic.

I answer this day to Messrs. Quintard, Sawyer & Ward, that their contract with you may be approved by Consul Navarro, who is empowered to do so in my name. Until said Mr. Navarro does not advise me of having approved said contract, or that relating to the Enfield rifles, which you tell me you are in treaty for, it will not be possible for me to send you an order for the delivery of the bonds that you may need for either of them.

As regards the bonds that you want for delivery to the Philadelphia Arms Co., as they refer to a contract already closed and approved, I have no objection to give at once the order for their delivery to you.

I accompany, for the purpose, an order for $20,000 in bonds, with which you will be amply able to cover your engagements with the above mentioned company.

I repeat to you the assurances of my most distinguished consideration.

M. ROMERO.

To General H. STURM, New York.

Sturm to Romero.

No. 122.]　　　　　　　　　　　　　　NEW YORK, October 13, 1866.

Senor. M. ROMERO,
　　Mexican Minister, etc.

Sir: I have the honor to acknowledge the receipt of an order on John W. Corlies & Co. for twenty thousand ($20,000) dollars in Mexican Bonds. This order has been presented by me, and has been duly honored.

I shall at once remit the amount still due the American Arms Co., and place the balance to the credit of the Government.

　　　　I am, Sir, very respectfully,
　　　　　　Your obedient servant,

　　　　　　　　　　　　　　　H. STURM.

Sturm to Romero.

No. 123.]　　　　　　　　　　　　　　NEW YORK, October 13, 1866.

Senor M. ROMERO,
　　Mexican Minister, etc.

Sir: In relation to the contract with Mr. Lawrie & Co., which I also made during your absence from Washington, as mentioned in my letter of September 18th, and which you desired me to hold in abeyance until you heard from your Government, I wish to ask you, whether you think it likely that these articles will be needed by the Government or not. If you do not think it advisable to use the *whole amount* for the Government, I shall take *only so much* as I necessarily need for General Baranda's expedition, and arrange for the balance in such a way that the contract be kept; but the Government pays only for what is actually needed at present. The articles contracted for, have at present such a price that I can dispose of the balance at once to advantage.

Hoping to hear from you in regard to this matter,
　　　　I remain, very respectfully,
　　　　　　Your obedient servant,

　　　　　　　　　　　　　　　H. STURM.

Sturm to Romero.

No. 124.]　　　　　　　　　　　　　　NEW YORK, October 13, 1866.

Senor M. ROMERO,
　　Mexican Minister, etc.

I have the honor to acknowledge the receipt of your letter of yesterday; the same has been translated to me by Mr. Fuentes.

There seems to be a misunderstanding in regard to both points mentioned in this letter. In the first place, as regards the contract with Quintard, Sawyer & Ward, permit me to call your attention to my letter of September 10th, and your answer thereto of September 11th. In my letter of that date I stated that, on account of your absence from Washington, and want of power on the part of Dr. Navarro to approve my contracts, and because it was necessary for the purpose of carrying out my arrangements, *I had taken* the responsibility of making these contracts: one with Messrs. Fitch, Burbridge & Dunlap; the other with Quintard, Sawyer & Ward, for (1200) twelve hundred tons of coal for the Sheridan and other purposes; and the third one with P. W. Lawrie & Co., for (250,000) two hundred and fifty thousand rations for same purpose; and I stated to you the reason why I had done so, and hoped you would approve said contracts.

In your answer of the 11th of September and afterwards, you say that you approve Fitch's contract, but can not approve of the other two for coal and rations, as they are designed for Matamoras, and you desired me to hold the same in abeyance until you could hear from your Government.

Understanding fully that, as far as regards General Baranda's and Governor Baz's expedition, you authorized me to do what might be necessary, I have put aboard General Baranda's steamer (400) four hundred tons of coal, and the same I have charged to the account of the Government in the statement I forwarded to you on October 2d.

As, according to the contract, I was compelled to take the coal in thirty days, it being an article fluctuating in price, and as you had disapproved of my buying said coal for the Sheridan, I have paid Messrs. Quintard, Sawyer & Ward for the balance, eighteen thousand ($18,000) dollars in bonds out of my own funds (due me from General Carvajal), which you had the kindness to instruct Mr. Tifft to deliver to me. I felt in duty bound to do this, as I had taken the responsibility, and as it would have injured my character, as well as the interests of the Government, if I had stated to Messrs. Quintard, Sawyer & Ward that their contract would not be carried out.

You seem to understand, however, that this is a new contract and has not been paid, and that funds are desired to pay for them; whereas you will now see that they already have received their bonds, according to the terms of the contract.

I shall be pecuniarily the loser by this operation, but I rather preferred to do this than to have Messrs. Quintard, Sawyer & Ward, who cheerfully sold the coal when I asked them, believe that there was any intention to impose on them; particularly as I know that sooner or later we shall need more coal of them for the service of the Government. Dr. Navarro understands the matter fully, and will arrange everything satisfactorily with the gentlemen when they call

As regards the fifty thousand ($50,000) dollars bonds asked on account of the rifles, I wish to say that the contract will not be signed by the parties unless I give them good security for ultimate payment, or I deposit with some good responsible house, in this city, the above mentioned sum. If I ask parties to secure me for the fulfillment of their contracts, they demand the same of me, and I find it useless to spend my time making contracts with anybody, which afterwards, for one reason or another, are not carried out by the parties.

It would indeed, be the best way for us to pay bonds at once, and make a direct purchase; as most parties, while the contract is being written, signed, approved, etc., allow themselves to be frightened by some parties and ultimately back out of their arrangements; as there is hardly anybody who will sign a written document, which binds him to do anything, without taking time to consider and consult his lawyer or friends.

This has been my sad experience so far, and will continue to be as long as the host of enemies here are busy to defeat us. If, however, on the other hand, I can ask a person to deliver his goods at once, and pay him as soon as delivered, he will in most cases, not consult with anybody outside, and there is not the chance of outside interference.

Dr. Navarro has promised me to day that he will also write to you, and explain these things fully to you.

I am, Sir, very respectfully,
Your obedient servant,
H. STURM.

Romero to Sturm.

[No. 125.]   WASHINGTON, October 14, 1866.

Dear Sir:

I received yesterday your two letters of the 12th inst. I had nothing from you this morning. Dr. Navarro writes to me stating that you wish to have deposited with Mr. Fuentes, some bonds to make the purchase of the Enfield rifles. I enclosed to you to-day an order for $50,000 in bonds, which I beg of you to deposit them at Mr. Fuentes' and use them only for the purchase of said rifles.

I hope this will settle satisfactorily all your difficulties.

In great hurry,
Respectfully yours,
M. ROMERO.

Romero to Sturm.

[Translation.]

[No. 126.]   WASHINGTON, October 14, 1866.

MEXICAN LEGATION IN THE U. S. OF AMERICA.

As you have directly stated to me, and also through the Mexican Consul General in New York, that you are about making a contract for the purchase of 20,000 Enfield rifles which you might successfully carry out provided a deposit of $50,000 in bonds is made in a safe place, I have come to the determination of putting at your disposal said sum for the above object. To that effect I enclose you a draft to your order on Messrs. Corlies & Co., for $50,000 in bonds, and I request you that when you receive them you deposit them with Messrs. Fuentes & Co., that they may be delivered to the sellers of the rifles together with the balance of their value, as soon as the contract relating thereto is approved by me or by the Mexican Consul General in that city, according to my previous instructions to you.

Very respectfully yours,
M. ROMERO.

To General H. STURM,
New York.

Sturm to Romero.

No. 127.] NEW YORK, October 15, 1866.

Senor M. ROMERO,
Mexican Minister, etc.

Sir: I have the honor to acknowledge the receipt of your letter of yesterday, enclosing order for fifty thousand ($50,000) dollars, bonds. Immediately upon receipt of the letter, 11 o'clock this A. M., I tried to see the parties about the rifles, but found them absent from the city; and as you direct me to use this money only for the rifles, I have not as yet presented the order, but shall do so as soon as the parties return.

I am sir, very respectfully,
Your obd't servant,
H. STURM.

Sturm to Romero.

No. 128.] NEW YORK, October 15, 1866.

Senor M. ROMERO,
Mexican Minister, etc.

Dear Sir: I have not received one line from Brownsville since the Everman returned, and feel quite anxious about matters there. Have you heard anything either directly or indirectly about the arms, etc., sent out there? Mr. Stocking was quite ill when the Everman left Brazos, and I fear that something may have occurred to him.

Be pleased to let me know what you think of the state of affairs there, as the 28th of October is near at hand, and the parties from whom I purchased the goods are almost daily inquiring of me, but I can not, of course, give them any satisfaction.

Enclosed herewith please find a letter which fell into my hands to-day.

I am, Sir,
Very respectfully,
H. STURM.

Romero to Sturm.

No. 129.] WASHINGTON, October 15, 1866.

General H. STURM,
New York.

Dear Sir: Reserving to answer what you state in your two letters of the 13th instant about contracts with Messrs. Quintard, Sawyer & Ward, and with Lawrie & Co., when I receive information from Dr. Navarro, I merely acknowledge the receipt of said letters.

I mailed yesterday a communication to you enclosing an order to Messrs. J.W. Corlies & Co. for $50,000 in bonds.

I remain sincerely,

Your obedient servant,

M. ROMERO.

Sturm to Romero.

No. 130.] NEW YORK, October 16, 1866.

Senor M. ROMERO,
Mexican Minister, etc.

Sir: I have the honor to acknowledge the receipt of your letter of yesterday.

Messrs. Dupont de Nemours & Co., of Wilmington, Delaware, are willing to sell to the Government a large quantity of gunpowder, and take bonds at (60c.) sixty cents in payment, provided an old claim of theirs, amounting, as they say, to some eight thousand dollars, can be paid in the same way.

I shall probably go to Philadelphia to-morrow, and after seeing Mr. Dupont, I will communicate to you the particulars.

I am, Sir, respectfully,

Your obedient servant,

H. STURM.

Romero to Sturm.

No. 131.] WASHINGTON, Oct. 17, 1866.

General H. STURM,
New York.

Dear Sir: In answer to your letter of yesterday, I have to state that Messrs. Dupont de Nemours & Co., of Philadelphia, actually have some old claim, as they represent; but I do not know its amount, nor do I remember the circumstances thereof. Let them produce their titles or papers, and we might conclude a contract under the general terms they propose.

Yours sincerely,

M. ROMERO.

Romero to Sturm.

No. 132.] WASHINGTON, October 18, 1866.

General H. STURM.
New York.

Dear Sir: Your interesting letter of yesterday has just been received. I will transmit its contents to my Government by this mail.

I heard yesterday morning from Monterey. In a letter dated the 22d ultimo, I am informed that Gen. Escobedo was negotiating to purchase the whole cargo of the Everman, and that he very likely would get it, paying for it in gold. Under such circumstances you can very readily see that I can not pay any part of said cargo until I know positively what disposition has been made of it.

In great hurry, I am truly,
Your obedient servant,
M. ROMERO.

Mr. Mariscal will introduce to you a gentleman. Hear what he has to say, and see what you can do with him.

Mariscal to Sturm.

No. 133.] WASHINGTON, October 18, 1866.

General H. STURM,
New York.

Dear Sir: I beg to introduce M. C. A. Bochert, who is about going to New York, and wants to treat some business with you.

IGNO. MARISCAL.

Sturm to Romero.

No. 134.] NEW YORK, October 19, 1866.

SENOR M. ROMERO,
Mexican Minister, etc.

Sir: I have the honor to acknowledge the receipt of your two letters of the 17th and 18th inst.; and would also inform you that I have just returned from Philadelphia. Mr. Dupont *has agreed to sell me* what powder I need for General Baranda and others, without waiting for the settlement of the old claim.

I stated to him that, in the meantime, you would have an opportunity to examine into and consider the proposition for settling the old claim.

I enclose herewith the papers relating to the old claim; and if it can be arranged, it will help us in getting for bonds, any time, what powder may needed for the Government.

The powder is to be paid for in bonds as fast as delivered, and there is no contract necessary. I shall remit you Mr. Dupont's proposition in writing as soon as I receive it.

Hoping to hear from you soon,
I remain, respectfully.
Your obedient servant,
H. STURM.

Sturm to Romero.

No. 135.] NEW YORK, October 20, 1866.

SENOR M. ROMERO,
   Mexican Minister, etc.

Sir: I have the honor to enclose herewith the proposition of Messrs. Dupont & Co. Be pleased to communicate to me your views in regard to this matter.

I also enclose a note, received this day, about the twenty thousand (20,000) Enfield rifles. I knew yesterday that ten thousand (10,000) of these arms had been sold *for cash* to parties who are connected with other movements; and I take the liberty to repeat here, that unless an arrangement can be made whereby the bonds can be immediately delivered, either as payment in full or as security, it will be difficult to obtain articles that are constantly in demand.

I have also been asked several times, by Messrs. Lawrie & Co., about the delivery of the rations, and would respectfully ask you to decide whether these goods shall be taken or not. If you conclude to take them, they can be delivered at some time in the future; but it ought to be decided at once whether the Government desires the goods or not. I am quite satisfied that it will make no difference if you should consider it advisable not to take the goods.

The order on J. W. Corlies & Co., for fifty thousand ($50,000) dollars (bonds), that you sent to me the other day, is still in my hands, subject to any instructions you may give in regard to the same.

I am, Sir, very respectfully,
   Your obedient servant,
      H. STURM.

Romero to Sturm.

[Translation.]

No. 136.] NEW YORK, October 22, 1866.

MEXICAN LEGATION
   IN THE
U. S. OF AMERICA.

I have received your communications of the 19th and 20th inst, with enclosed proposal made to you by Messrs. Dupont de Nemours & Co about the sale of powder to the Mexican Government, together with the copies of the documents that said gentlemen have handed to you in reference to their old claim against said Government.

In your first note you assured me that said gentlemen did not make it a particular condition, for selling the powder for bonds, that their former credit shall paid them at once; and so it appears they say at least in relation to two hundred barrels of said powder, which they seem willing to give at once for bonds while the documents relating to that claim are being examined. With this understanding, I will at once consult with my Government for the immediate payment of the bill presented by Messrs. Dupont de Nemours & Co., and meanwhile you remain at liberty to buy from them the two hundred barrels of powder they offer, if you think the powder to be reasonable under the circumstances and under the previous approbation of the terms by Consul Navarro.

In the second communication, to which I answer you also, you tell me that Messrs. Lawrie & Co. make frequent questions as to whether they are to deliver the rations that they contracted for with you, and you beg of me an immediate reply. This point is already resolved by me since when you sent me your contract for rations, I stated that I did not approve of it, and I only approved one of the three contracts which you then sent me together.

I renew to you the assurances of my distinguished consideration.

M. ROMERO.

To General H. STURM. New York.

Romero to Kemble and Warner.

[Copy.]

No. 137.] WASHINGTON, October 22, 1866.

Messrs. KEMBLE & WARNER,
    New York City.

Gentlemen: I have received your letter of 16th inst., containing statement of account of Messrs. E. J. Dupont de Nemours & Co. against the Supreme Government of Mexico on a certain purchase of your powder by Carlos Butterfield, under date of July 7, 1859. General H. Sturm will inform you of my action in reference to said claim.

I am, gentlemen, respectfully,
    Your obedient servant,

M. ROMERO.

Romero to McDonald.

No. 138.] WASHINGTON, October 23, 1866.

Mr. JOHN McDONALD.

Sir: In answer to your letter of yesterday, proposing the sale of some Enfield rifles, I would refer you to General H. Sturm, who is authorized by me to make such contracts for the Mexican Government, with the approval of the Mexican Consul at New York, duly instructed on the premises.

You can find General Sturm at No. 32 Dey street, office of Messrs. John W. Corlies & Co.

Very respectfully yours,

M. ROMERO.

Sturm to Romero.

No. 139.] NEW YORK, October 25, 1866.

Senor M. ROMERO,
    Mexican Minister, etc.

Sir: I have just closed a contract with Mr. Cory, of this city, for (20,000) twenty thousand new Springfield rifles, and (25,000) twenty-five thousand new Enfield rifles, at sixteen dollars and fifty ($16.50) cents each; (10,000) ten thousand carbines, Sharp's pattern, Starr's make, at twenty-one dollars and seventy-five (21.75) cents each; and (10,000) ten thousand infantry accoutrements, for four dollars and fifty ($4.50) cents each.

They are to deliver at once, and bonds must be delivered as soon as goods are delivered. Dr. Navarro has just approved and signed the agreement.

Be pleased therefore to arrange for the bonds. Dr. Navarro will write you tomorrow, after I have given him a copy of the agreement.

    Yours truly, in haste,

        H. STURM.

Romero to Sturm.

No. 140.] WASHINGTON, Oct. 26, 1866.

General H. STURM,

Dear Sir: I have received your communication of yesterday, informing me of the contract you have just closed with Mr. Cory, of that city. As soon as I shall receive Dr. Navarro's report on said contract, and you will let me know the quantity of bonds you need for it, I will send you an order that you may get as many bonds as necessary to meet the present exigencies.

    I am, dear Sir, yours very truly,

        M. ROMERO.

Sturm to Romero.

No. 141.] NEW YORK, October 28, 1866.

Senor M. ROMERO,
    Mexican Minister, etc.

Sir: I have the honor to herewith enclose for your information, a communication from Mr. Stocking, dated Brownsville, October 9th, 1866.

Will you please return the same to me after you have examined it, and oblige,

    Yours truly,

        H. STURM.

Romero to Sturm.

No. 142.] WASHINGTON, October 30, 1866.

General H. STURM,

Dear Sir: I wish you to tell me how much in bonds you need to pay any immediate and actual delivery of goods in connection with your agreement with Mr. Cory. The whole amount would be two millions; but you know that so many are not ready, and I have to furnish you with them in proportion as you can use them.

So I will send you an order for as many bonds as can be ready, and you are in want of for a payment, originated with actual delivery of articles or any security exacted.

Very truly,
Your obedient servant,
M. ROMERO.

Romero to Sturm.

[Translation.]

No. 143.] WASHINGTON, October 30, 1866.

MEXICAN LEGATION
IN THE
U. S. OF AMERICA.

I return to you the letter of Mr. Stocking, dated the 9th inst., which you had the kindness to remit to me for my perusal, with your communication of day before yesteaday.

According to trustworthy information which I have received this day from Brownsville, Mr. Stocking has in his possesrion but one thousand more guns, he having disposed of all the arms in various ways.

I reiterate to you the assurances of my most distinguished consideration,
M. ROMERO.

Sturm to Romero.

No. 144.] NEW YORK, November 3, 1866.

Senor M. ROMERO,
Mexican Minister etc.

Sir: I have the honor to acknowledge the receipt of your letter of October 30th, enclosing the letter of Mr. Stocking, that I sent to you, also your letter asking me what amount of bonds and how soon they will be needed. In answer to this second letter, allow me to say, that it would be very desirable to have two (2) millions of bonds ready, and in the hands of Dr. Navarro, Mr. Fuentes, or any other person you may select, so that they may be ready at a moment when needed to pay for purchases, or as security.

This is all important, for I could have had arms before to-day, if I could have controlled a sufficient amount of bonds at once. You are aware that, as long as no payment has actually been made, it is in the power of the contracting parties, *if they change their minds*, which they often do, to back out of their contract; and it is under existing circumstances difficult to compel parties to comply with a contract they are not willing to carry out.

I am, Sir, very respectfully,
Your obedient servant,
H. STURM.

Romero to Sturm.

No. 145.] WASHINGTON, November 5, 1866.

MEXICAN LEGATION IN THE U. S. OF AMERICA.

I answer your note of the 5th inst., in which you state that it would be desirable that two million dollars in bonds be deposited with Messrs. Navarro or Fuentes, to your order, to make purchases at any moment; but as it is not possible to get this sum ready at once, I enclose you herein an order that Messrs. J. W. Corlies & Co. may deliver you $100,000 in said bonds, requesting you to deposit them with Messrs. Fuentes & Co., as also the bonds you may have remaining on hand, to use them as they may be needed, and exclusively for the purchase of the goods which you may receive, in conformity to the contract signed by you with Mr. Cary, on the 25th October last, and which Consul Navarro approved on the same date.

I repeat to you the assurances of my most distinguished consideration.

M. ROMERO.

To General HERMAN STURM,
New York.

Sturm to Romero.

No 146.] NEW YORK, November, 6, 1866.

Senor M. ROMERO,
Minister, etc.

Dear Sir: I am now arranging and looking for General Baranda's expedition. This morning I sent to Dr. Navarro the contract for charter of the steamer, but to my surprise he does not feel authorized to approve any contract except for arms, etc. He will send the contract to you for approval. Be pleased to approve it and return it as soon as possible, as my intention was to send Gen. Baranda on Thursday or Friday morning. I have tried the vessel and engines twice, and I am pleased and completely satisfied with everything, and so is General Baranda.

More than this I am quite cheerful to say, because I have received already over two thousand guns, etc., and everything looks better.

Gov. Baz I expect to start next week, and then I shall come to see you in person.

Yours truly,
H. STURM.

P. S. Mr. Campbell telegraphed me that his arms had been sent, and are now in New York. I have answered his telegram requesting him to inform me by what road they come and to whom consigned.

Yours truly,
H. S.

Romero to Sturm.

No 147.] WASHINGTON, November 6, 1866.

Gen. H. STURM,
    New York.

Your confidential letter of the 3d inst. has been received and its contents noticed.

Do not credit the rumors you speak about. I am sorry to hear what you state about Gen. Carvajal. You will find an official letter in answer to your note of the 3d.

Respectfully,
M. ROMERO.

Sturm to Romero.

No. 148.] NEW YORK, November 7, 1866.

Senor M. ROMERO,
    Mexican Minister, etc.

Sir: I have the honor to herewith enclose for your information, a letter from Mr. Stocking at Brownsville, dated October 21, 1866.

I am, Sir, very respectfully,
Your obedient servant,
H. STURM.

Sturm to Romero.

No. 149.] NEW YORK, November 7, 1866.

Senor M. ROMERO,
    Mexican Mnister, etc.

Sir: I have the honor to acknowledge the receipt of your letter of November 5th, which came to hand this morning, enclosing an order on J. W. Corlies & Co. for $100,000 in bonds.

I have now loaded 2,500 Enfield rifles, with accoutrements, also Prussian caps, sabres, etc., and to-morrow shall load more, perhaps *all*, (for General Baranda.) These arms I have bought of Messrs. Schuyler, Hartley & Graham, well-known here, and I am glad to be able to say that these gentlemen have undertaken to furnish us goods. Mr. Cory although his references are very good indeed, has not fulfilled his engagements, and assigns various reasons for it, which I have not time to mention this evening, and I can not wait on him and let an opportunity to obtain arms from other parties slip by, and thereby keep General Baranda and ship waiting.

Messrs. Schuyler, Hartley & Graham propose to furnish the arms, etc., for Baranda and Governor Baz; but as soon as they have delivered me a lot of goods, I have their bill for that lot at once approved by Dr. Navarro, and pay them the bonds *after* such approval. In this way these bills, amounting to $120,000 in bonds, have already been approved; but it is very necessary to have more bonds *at once* to pay for the articles as they are delivered, as these gentlemen do only a straight cash business.

Be pleased, therefore, to arrange for bonds as in your opinion may be best, so that no delay may occur.

I do not deem it best to notify Mr. Cory at present, that his contract is abrogated until I have obtained all I need for present emergencies from Messrs. Schuyler, Hartley & Graham.

Gen. Baranda and myself have determined to have the vessel sail on Saturday morning next.

In haste, I am yours,
Very Respectfully,
H. STURM.

Romero to Sturm.

No. 150.]
WASHINGTON, November 7, 1866.

My Dear General:

I received your letter yesterday, and in answer, have to say that I send to-day instructions to Mr. Navarro, about the chartering of the steamer.

In great hurry.

I am your obedient servant,
M. ROMERO.

Sturm to Romero.

No. 151.]
NEW YORK, November 8, 1866.

Senor M. ROMERO,
Mexican Minister, etc.

Dear Sir: Your letter of yesterday has been received. Dr. Navarro also received your letter, and he informs me that you exact the following points before signing the charter.

1st. That the price paid be equitable.
2d. That payment shall commence from the day of loading the goods.
3d. That no more than three days shall be occupied in loading the vessel.

In answer to the first point, Dr. Navarro will inform you that the price is very reasonable.

In regard to the second and third points, allow me to state, that for over four weeks I have kept the owners of the vessel busy getting her ready in *such a way* that every precaution is taken against accident, etc. They have gone to an expense of $16,500 in overhauling machinery, etc; and I agreed that, if on the trial trip the *vessel* was to my satisfaction, and to the satisfaction of General Baranda, then I would agree to charter her, and pay for her from the day she was ready for me. This was all done by them on the 15th day of October. She is in every respect what I desire, and I can only say, that the whole arrangement is very advantageous and reasonable in my opinion.

It is utterly impossible for any one to load a vessel in such a short space of time, as you mention, and particularly under the circumstances under which I have to labor.

Hoping that after you consider all these points the arrangement will meet your approval I remain,

Respectfully,
Your obedient servant,

H. STURM.

Romero to Sturm.

[Translation.]

No. 152.]

MEXICAN LEGATION
IN THE
U. S. OF AMERICA.

WASHINGTON, November 8, 1866.

I have received your note of yesterday, in which you announce to me that you have already shipped 2,500 Enfield rifles, with accoutrements, besides percussion caps, etc., and that you expected to ship more goods to-day—perhaps all that General Baranda is to take out. You tell me that you have made a contract for these goods with Messrs. Schuyler, Hartley & Graham, and that Consul Navarro has already approved said gentlemen's bill to the amount of $120,000 in bonds; but as you need a larger amount of these to deliver them as you receive the goods, you should wish that I made arrangements to procure them for you at once. I shall do so as far as possible, and to the extent consistent with the interests of my Government, subject to various considerations. Meanwhile, I should like that you get ready the invoice that General Baranda is to take out, in order that the vessel may sail from that port next Saturday, as you announce to me.

With regard to Mr. Cory's contract, I think it would be well that if, at the expiration of the thirty days agreed upon, he has not delivered the goods, both you and Consul Navarro serve on him the official announcement that said contract is of no effect for the future; at all events, such articles as you may have got from Messrs. Schuyler, Hartley & Graham should be discounted from those you may receive of him.

I repeat to you the assurances of my most distinguished consideration.

M. ROMERO.

To General H. STURM, New York.

Romero to Sturm.

No. 153.] WASHINGTON, November 8, 1866.

My Dear General:

I have read the letter that Mr. Stocking addressed to you from Brownsville on the 26th ultimo. It is interesting.

I forwarded to him, by this mail, copies of several pamphlets of interest on Mexican affairs.

I am, General, very respectfully,
Your obedient servant,

M. ROMERO.

Romero to Sturm.

No. 154.] WASHINGTON, November 9, 1866.

General H. STURM,
New York.

Dear Sir: In answer to your letter of yesterday, with regard to the steamer Vixen, I have to say, that I send Dr. Navarro a communication reminding him that he is fully authorized to approve your contracts according to his own judgment, although I express my opinion (since I have been consulted on the charter) that if three days for the loading may be a short term, the one commencing on the 15th ultimo, to finish until the ship be ready, is a too long and indefinite one.

Nevertheless, Dr. Navarro will act on this matter freely, according to circumstances, following his own prudent inspiration and the general spirit of my instructions, without consulting me again on that point.

Very truly, yours,

M. ROMERO.

Sturm to Romero.

No. 155.] NEW YORK, November 10, 1866.

Senor M. ROMERO,
Mexican Minister, etc.

Sir: I have the honor to acknowledge the receipt of your letter of yesterday, and also of day before yesterday.

I shall be ready to sail at midnight. I have paid one hundred and fifty-nine thousand ($159,000) dollars. Each bill was approved by Dr. Navarro before I paid the same. It is *necessary now* that I should have at least $250,000 (bonds) more at my disposal by Monday next. If you will give the order, I can arrange with Corlies & Co. to certify my drafts.

In great haste,
Yours truly,

H. STURM.

Romero to Sturm.

No. 156.] WASHINGTON, November 11, 1866.

General H. STURM,
New York.

Dear Sir: Your favor of yesterday is at hand. I am glad to hear that the steamer was going to leave yesterday.

I am sorry I can not send to you to-day the bonds you need to make the payments. This being Sunday, the members of the Legation do not come to the office to have the orders ready. To-morrow morning I will send you a draft on Messrs. Corlies & Co. In the meanwhile, you can show this letter to the interested parties.

You will oblige me by sending to me, as early as possible, an account of all that was sent on board the steamer Vixen, so that I will be able to communicate it to my Government.

In great hurry,
Respectfully,

M. ROMERO.

Romero to Sturm.

[Translation.]

No. 157.] WASHINGTON, November 11, 1866.

MEXICAN LEGATION IN THE U. S. OF AMERICA.

I have received your note of yesterday, wherein you announce to me that the steamer Vixen was to sail from that port in the evening, and that you had already delivered $159,000 in bonds, which amount is all you had at hand, and needed about $250,000 more for to-morrow.

In answer, I enclose you an order that Messrs. J. W. Corlies & Co. may deliver you $250,000 in said bonds, which you shall spend exclusively in payment of such goods as may have been forwarded by the Vixen.

I renew to you the assurances of my most distinguished consideration,

M. ROMERO.

To General H. STURM, New York.

NOTE—The above letter, although dated November 11th, was not received until November 14th.

Sturm to Romero.

[Translation.]

No. 158.] , NEW YORK, November 14, 1866.

Senor M. ROMERO,
    Mexican Minister, etc.

Sir: I have the honor to acknowledge the receipt of your communication of November 11th, enclosing an order on John W. Corlies & Co. for $250,000 in bonds. I have presented the same; but as only $100,000 are signed, I could only draw that amount.

Be pleased to instruct Mr. Fuentes to sign some more bonds, so that I may not meet with the same difficulties in equipping Governor Baz as I did in General Baranda's case. I wish you would arrange it so that I may obtain, speedily, all articles needed by Governor Baz, and he can leave next week without fail. If you give the necessary instructions to Messrs. Corlies & Co. to have the bonds ready, I can arrange matters so that any checks certified by Corlies will be accepted, in certain cases, until bonds are ready; but in some cases I will be compelled to deliver the bonds at once, or lose the purchase.

I am, Sir, in great haste,
    Your obedient servant,

H. STURM.

Sturm to Romero.

No. 159.] NEW YORK, November 14, 1866.

SENOR M. ROMERO,
    Mexican Minister, etc.

Sir: I have the honor to state that the steamer Vixen left New York on Sunday morning with a cargo of arms and munitions, the invoice of which I herewith enclose.

General Baranda, Mr. Benitez, together with some of their staff, went as passengers in her.

My brother, Mr. Robert C. Sturm, accompanied by two trusty men, accompanied the General and cargo as my agent. His instructions are to proceed to the place designated by General Baranda, and there to deliver to him all the stores aboard, and return at once to New York, unless otherwise directed by General Baranda, and in every respect to obey the orders of this said General. I accompanied the vessel as far as the Delaware breakwater (where the Vixen loaded her powder), and returned last night to this place. The Vixen is in first-rate order and made a splendid run, over ten miles an hour, although a heavy sea was against her; and in three or four days, when some of her coal is burned out, she will be able to run from 15—18 miles an hour, and can of course outrun any vessel now in the Gulf.

I enclose herewith a copy of the invoice, also a receipt from Schuyler, Hartley & Graham for $250,000 bonds, which I paid to them. A portion of this is already on Governor Baz's account. I also enclose three bills from Schuyler, Hartley & Graham, giving in detail the amount furnished *by them* for General Baranda's expedition; also one bill for instruments inspected and approved by Dr. Navarro. The balance of the bills I shall remit to you as soon as I have paid them.

I have the honor to be, Sir,
Very respectfully,
Your obedient servant,
H. STURM.

Sturm to Romero.

No. 160.] NEW YORK, November 15, 1866.

Senor M. ROMERO,
  Mexican Minister, etc.

Dear Sir: Since returning I have been constantly at work to get ready for Governor Baz. I have up to this day bought of Schuyler, Hartley & Graham (10,000) Enfield rifles and accoutrements, (3,000) sabres, with proportioned ammunition for carbines, also revolvers, five millions percussion caps, and various other necessary articles. Their bill amounts to $941,000 in bonds.

Most all the bonds you sent me, I have used for Schuyler, Hartley & Graham so far, as their articles are the most necessary and bonds are required by them at once. The account now stands about thus:

Messrs. Schuyler & Co furnished me for General Baranda goods to the amount of...	$87,185	
Now ready..	564,600	
Total amount...	$651,785	
Or in bonds say..		$1,086,000
I have paid them, Nov. 14th...............................	$250,000	
Nov. 15th...	30,000	
Have promised them to-morrow............................	120,000	
Total..		400,000
Leaves balance still due...................................		$686,000

Will you please to send me another order for bonds? Mr. Fuentes will probably have signed the balance of my order by to-morrow, and as soon as I deliver them to Messrs. Schuyler, Hartley & Graham, 1 will send their receipts to you, and as I pay them more I will remit the receipt for them in the same way, and shall remit the itemized bills to you, also receipted when paid.

In great haste,

I am, Sir,

Yours truly,

H. STURM.

Romero to Sturm.

[Translation.]

No. 161.]

WASHINGTON, November 16, 1866.

MEXICAN LEGATION IN THE U. S. OF AMERICA.

I have received your note of the 14th inst., wherein you announce the sailing of the Vixen from that port, and enclose invoice of the goods she takes on board, together with the receipt from Messrs. Schuyler, Hartley & Graham for $250,000 in bonds.

You tell me besides that you enclose *three* bills from said gentlemen with the approbation note of Mr. Navarro, but in reality you have sent *four*, *two* of which I send you back, as they have not said approbatory note, without which I can not take them into consideration. As soon as this requisite is performed send them to me, together with the others yet wanting in relation to the cargo of the Vixen.

Please tell me why the carbines which you bought from the Philadelphia American Arms Co. are not among the goods sent out by the Vixen.

I have just received a telegram from General Baranda, dated to-day at Norfolk, wherein he communicates to me that said steamer had to call at said port, where she would lay four or five days for repairs. This indicates that she was not in very good order.

I repeat to you the assurances of my most distinguished consideration.

M. ROMERO.

General H. STURM,
New York.

Mariscal to Sturm.

No. 162.]

WASHINGTON, November 16, 1866.

General H. STURM.
New York.

Dear General: Mr. Romero is very much indisposed, and is scarcely able to talk business and sign. Nevertheless he has noticed the contents of your **two** letters, dated respectively on the 14th and 15th instants.

He says that Mr. Fuentes will sign as many bonds as necessary for the payment of the orders he issues on Messrs. Corlies & Co.

In your letter of the 15th you say that up to that day you had bought of Schuyler & Co. 10,000 Enfield rifles, 3,000 carbines, and 10,000 accoutrements. Mr. Romero remembers that Governor Baz has never asked more than 5,000 arms, and so he does not understand how you have got much more than that when it is only for him (Governor Baz) you are to make purchases. Please explain this to Mr. Romero.

As for the statement of account contained in your letter, we do not understand it yet; but it is doubtless because we do not see all the bills of Schuyler & Co. So please send all these bills, and then send a new statement comprising only what was sent by the Vixen, reserving other purchases for another account.

I am, dear General,
Yours very sincerely,
IGNO. MARISCAL.

Sturm to Romero.

No. 163.] NEW YORK, November 17, 1866.

Senor M. ROMERO,
Mexican Minister, etc.

Sir: I have the honor to acknowledge the receipt of your letter of yesterday, but have not time to answer in full to-day. I have only to say that the carbines of the American Arms Co. are destined for Governor Baz, and not for General Baranda; also, that I have not purchased any more rifles of Schuyler, Hartley & Graham, than are necessary to fill both orders for Governor Baz and General Baranda, and Mr. Benitez. I will, however, explain this in a tabular statement by Monday next.

One thing I wish to say here, however, viz.: That if I have an opportunity to buy articles that are absolutely necessary, as for instance, percussion caps, revolvers, sabres, etc., I ought certainly to purchase them, to a certain limit, for if I do not do so when they are offered, I may not have an opportunity again for some time to obtain them.

Dr. Navarro has approved the charter party, and he informs me that after inquiring of principal parties, he has satisfied himself that my contract is equitable and reasonable.

I am, Sir, very respectfully yours,
H. STURM.

P. S. I enclose herewith a receipt from Schuyler, Hartley & Graham, for one hundred thousand dollars, which I paid them on account; also, a statement of articles purchased for Governor Baz's account. Of the percussion caps, I think I had better retain one-half for other portions of the country.

Yours truly,
H. STURM.

American and Mexican Commission—No. 676.

Sturm to Romero.

No. 164.] NEW YORK, November 17, 1866.

SENOR M. ROMERO,
Mexican Minister, etc.

Sir: In your letter of yesterday you say, that General Baranda telegraphed you, that the Vixen had put into Norfolk for repairs, which probably would occupy four or five days, and *that this would indicate that she was not in good condition.*

Allow me to say, that the Vixen is first-class, the machinery excellent, everything being tested and tried several times before sailing, and the Government Inspector's certificate, at this city, will show you at any time that this is so; but you know that I have no control over the sea and storm.

I herewith enclose to you a few extracts from newspapers, showing you that it was a fearful gale, and that even Government men-of-war, were compelled to put into harbor, and many other first-class ships of much larger size, were damaged seriously. The captain of the Moro Castle reports it the worst storm he ever passed through; and the fact that the Vixen did not suffer more than she did speaks well for her and her captain; and I know that in the whole City of New York, there is not another ship so well adapted for the purpose she is intended for, and so safe.

P. S. I already wrote you this morning on the subject, stating that probably I would go down to Norfolk myself, but this I find to be impossible, as it would seriously interfere with Governor Baz's matter. and I have therefore dispatched Major Bridgeford, my agent, to see to it that she is repaired at once. He will be there by to-morrow, and I think the vessel will not be delayed much.

I am, Sir, respectfully,
Your obedient servant,
H. STURM.

Sturm to Romero.

[Private.]

No. 165.] NEW YORK, November 17, 1866.

Senor M. ROMERO,

Dear Sir: In another letter I told you, that the fearful storm since Monday compelled the Vixen to go into Norfolk, and that I am going down there to look after her, if I possibly can arrange matters so that they do not interfere with Governor Baz's expedition, etc.

The charter for this vessel is not approved yet by Dr. Navarro. I saw him yesterday, and after reading to me your letter to him on the subject, he told me that probably he would approve the charter to-day. *I know* that he is confident that the terms are reasonable, under the circumstances, and that at least no one else, that we know of, is willing to furnish us a vessel on anything like these terms, but still he feels as though he was taking an immense responsibility in the matter. If you could be here for one or two days only, to see for yourself how difficult it is to do anything; if you could hear all *I have* to hear, and then follow me in my endeavors to help your country and Government, by overcoming opposition and persuading parties, and defending the justice of the cause, and the interest of your Government against the powerful combinations that have been for some time formed against your Government, I feel that you would at once conclude, that energetic and prompt action is necessary to insure complete defeat to the opposition; and you would also see, that although certain terms and arrangements may appear at first sight to be onerous to your Government, yet it is absolutely necessary to comply with them to save and help the Government.

I have felt hurt to see that, while I am straining every nerve, (neglecting private interests, wife, family, and everything that is dear to me,) working from morning until late at night, to serve you and your Government, I shall be obliged to be encompassed by so much red tape and delay. You can not expect that I shall be able to do things any faster or on better terms, than the Government of the U. S. did during the war; yet if you will examine carefully every bill, you will see that the terms are very much less than our Government paid for similar articles.

You exact from me, in the first place, to have the necessary transportation for the articles purchased. I have urged you some time ago, to allow me to purchase one or two steamers, so that we may have them under our control. They can run under American register, and *I will see to it* that they are managed and provided; and then the expense of charter, etc., can be dispensed with.

It is impossible for me, under existing circumstances, to load and forward a vessel any faster than an ordinary merchant does. There are so many delays, disappointments, etc., and I have not the force that our Government had at its command, but must do all with bonds that have but little credit; and, yet, I have not by far the same power and discretion at my commond, that the U. S. Government granted to its officers, who had cash at their disposal and plenty of men. I am not working for *mere pay*, nor have I entered into this matter as a speculation. I have not made one cent as yet, but have borrowed from friends what I need to carry us through, and can get more if necessary, expecting only to earn the approval of your Government and yourself, leaving it entirely to your Government to decide what my reward shall be.

But I am compelled to say to you now that unless some arrangements can be made, whereby you and I can do things more expeditiously and with less trouble to myself, I shall be compelled to resign my position. My health and family are objects as dear to me as your Government, and taking all things into consideration, I think that your Government may well grant me the same power and facilities, which the U. S. Government grants to officers, who hold as responsible a position as I have done lately. Believe me, my dear friend, that I do not write this in a moment of passion, etc., but I have carefully weighed everything, and although there is nothing that I should regret as much as this step, yet I can not act otherwise. You are master of your profession, and I think I am well posted in regard to my duties; and as I know that you are *truly* and *firmly* a friend of your Government, but can not of course understand all that is necessary in regard to military matters, and all the difficulties in consequence, it is absolutely necessary for you and I to make some arrangements whereby we can aid your Government in the shortest and most direct way; and as two true friends of a government in need, take upon ourselves certain responsibilities and duties, which only can be appreciated by parties here in this country. If the instructions from your Government are such, however, as to preclude such an arrangement, I shall not be able to continue any longer my efforts, than may be necessary to expedite Government Baz, and settle all accounts.

I expect to send Governor Baz, next Saturday certain, having bought nearly all he needs in the arms line; and I wish you would communicate to me as soon as possible to what place you design me to send him.

I am, Sir, yours truly,

H. STURM.

Sturm to Romero.

No. 166.] NEW YORK, November 17, 1866.

Senor M. ROMERO,
Mexican Minister, etc.

Sir: I have the honor to state to you that I yesterday evening received a dispatch, stating that the steamer Vixen was compelled to put into Norfolk, Va., owing to machinery being disabled during the storm of the 14th inst. I am very sorry for this, but it can not be helped, and I intend to go to Norfolk this afternoon if possible, or in case I can not go myself, I shall send a trusty man.

I am, Sir, yours truly,

H. STURM.

Sturm to Romero.

No. 167.] NEW YORK, November 18, 1866.

Senor M. ROMERO,
Mexican Minister, etc.

Sir: As to-day is Sunday and I have some little time, I have thought it well to write to you and propose a plan, which if it meets your approval, is effective, and will save a great deal of trouble and annoyance to yourself and myself, and afford great help and assistance and a great saving to the Government. The reasons which prompt me to propose this at once are, first, because I *know*, and have known for some time, of the combinations formed by prominent parties, and interests inimical to the Government, which have for their object the defeat of President Juarez and elevation to power of Ortega. Who those parties are, and what their influence, you know well, but I am confident that unless we place a barrier in their way at once, they will do a great deal of harm. I informed Mr. Tifft some time ago that when Congress meets again there will be hard fighting to do, and although the United States Government at present seems favorable to President Juarez, yet there is no certainty of it remaining so, but on the contrary *there is a possibility* that large railroad and other interests may be so able to influence the administration that after all a compromise may be made at once detrimental to President Juarez, and in my opinion injurious to Mexico, and certainly to *yourself*. Whether these are mere idle speculations and chimerical ideas of mine, or whether they are true, you certainly are able to judge for yourself. I assume they are true, and I have good reason for believing them so, and urge therefore that no time be lost, while the bonds have some credit and goods can be had for them, to purchase a certain definite quantity of war material, to be determined by yourself and myself, to be collected and kept on hand here, and transported to such places in Mexico at such times as you may determine. To do this effectively and save time and money, authorize me to get storeroom and a certain place which I can control, to load our vessels, so that I may not be compelled again to wait nine days, as in the case of the Vixen, before I can find a wharf for the ship. I would further urge that, instead of being compelled to hire vessels for each trip, etc., one or two vessels be chartered for a long term, or best of all, be bought outright, said vessels to run under American *register*, name and *ownership* which is known only to yourself and myself. If you agree to this proposition and allow me to go ahead, I assure you that in my judgment you will be doing one of the greatest services to the Government, whereby you strengthen it and weaken its enemies, for with every bond placed in the hands of citizens of this country, you are gaining a vote in favor of the legitimate Government and against its enemies, while at the same time you place at the disposal of the Government the very articles it so much needs, and without which it can not maintain itself.

Gen. Baranda and Don Benitez urged me, before leaving to send some clothing, stating that they are very much needed. The same thing I have heard from other persons just from Mexico. You know winter is before us, and your poor soldiers, ill provided as they are, will bless you and remember you for providing them with the means to keep themselves at least tolerably comfortable. It is utterly useless, as long as the bonds have no market value, to attempt to fill an order specifying certain definite articles in anything like a reasonable time, and then without great trouble and vexation; but if you allow me to form a general depot here, I can buy for instance to-day a quantity of rifles, to-morrow this or that article, and I can buy them here, there, and everywhere, wherever and whenever I have an opportunity to buy, and then I can work systematically, take my time and report every week the exact quantity on hand, and you can order me at any time to send whatever you want of such articles as I have, to any place you may desire. This is the only reasonable and proper way of supplying your Government, and will insure success and prompt assistance, and I urge you to consider this at once, for you may rest assured that, although just now through my determined efforts I have succeeded, in spite of all opposition and troubles, of which you know nothing, in obtaining some goods; there will be an effort made by our enemies, in a very short time, to shake the confidence of the people in regard to the bonds, and if I had not been able to send the Vixen so very slyly, and were it known very generally that I really do obtain a large amount of goods, it would have been done already.

By enlisting the Ames' family and others, whose names I can not write here, we secure a powerful element of New England, and effectually block or interfere with General F. * * Ochoa and others.

Be pleased to answer this at your earliest convenience, and if the plan suggested meets your approval, I will make a complete statement of articles to be bought; but it would be well if you come here for, say one day only.

I am, Sir, very respectfully,
Your obedient servant,
H. STURM.

Romero to Sturm.

No. 168.] WASHINGTON, November 19, 1866.

General H. STURM,
New York.

Dear Sir: I received yesterday your favor of the 17th instant, and this morning the one of yesterday. Although I do not feel well yet, I will to-day answer you both of them, as far as I can.

I am fully aware of your energy and activity, and am persuaded that without you we could not have sent any arms or ammunition home. I am also satisfied of your integrity, and, as proof of this, have placed large amounts of money at your disposal. But I have not been disposed to second every thought and plan of yours, for fear that success will not crown our efforts: as, so far, I am acting under my own responsibility, having no instructions from my Government authorizing me to send arms or supplies. I have been expecting to hear by every mail on this subject, but, so far, I have got nothing. By last mail I heard that General Wallace was at Chihuahua, and that he gave some information about the cargo of the Everman. I hope that will be the occasion of my Government to send me instructions on this important subject. This explains why I have sometimes inclined to postpone matters, and, at others, unwilling to do certain things.

About things that I was willing to have done, I never hesitated or delayed them with red tape. There were several directions from my Government that I had to comply with, and I tried to do so. In the case of the steamer Vixen, for instance, I did not know that she had been chartered, nor why she had not been loaded.

To approve the contract that Dr. Navarro sent me, required some information that I could not obtain here. I empowered Dr. Navarro to ascertain about the facts, and act in accordance with his judgment and equity. If he delayed approving the contract, I had nothing to do with it. My official language to him about you has been such that you certainly cannot take any exceptions at.

When I see success, like the sailing of the Vixen, I rejoice as much as you do. I have just received your telegram, of this morning, about the repairs of the Vixen. I am glad that she will sail on the 21st.

I am not prepared to approve the plan you suggest in your letter of yesterday. If, as I expect, I receive this week my instructions on the subject, I will be prepared to give at once a definite answer.

Governor Baz was here yesterday. He left this morning. We have changed the place where he is going to land with his expedition, as he will inform you. Please send him, if possible, during this week.

In great haste,
I am, dear Sir,
Your obedient servant,
M. ROMERO.

Romero to Sturm.

No. 169.] WASHINGTON, November 20, 1866.

GEN. H. STURM,
New York.

Dear Sir: This letter will be handed to you by Senor Don F. Ferrer, a commissioner from the Governor of the State of Puebla, for the purpose of taking arms and ammunition to that State. He brought some funds with him, and has made some partial purchases.

Please facilitate to him what he wants to complete his cargo.

I am, Sir, very respectfully,
Your obedient servant,
M. ROMERO.

Sturm to Romero.

[Telegram.]

No. 170.] NEW YORK, November 22, 1866.

Senor M. ROMERO,
Mexican Minister, etc.,
Washington, D. C.

Can you send me an order to-day for one hundred thousand dollars? Please answer.
H. STURM.

Sturm to Romero.

No. 171.] NEW YORK, November 22, 1866.

Senor M. ROMERO,
Mexican Minister, etc.

Sir: I have on board Governor Baz's steamer the 2,280 carbines of the American Arms Co., and the two guns and implements for the Sheridan; also the wagons which I purchased some time ago in Philadelphia. Governor Baz's order for carbines is only 1,000, and the other articles are not on his order.

Shall I send all with him, or retain a part of this, and what? Also, shall I send the torpedo boat if I have room enough? Please answer me in regard to this matter.

I enclose you a list of the articles which I purchased some time ago, copies of which bills you already have, to enable you to see what I already have on hand.

I am, Sir,
Respectfully yours,
H. STURM.

Sturm to Romero.

No. 172.]   NEW YORK, November 22, 1866.

Senor M. ROMERO,
Mexican Minister, etc.

Sir: Mr. Ferrer called this morning with a letter of introduction from you, in which you ask me to assist him. Mr. Ferrer has already purchased 5,000 rifles, some powder and lead for cash, but desired me to purchase a battery of artillery for him. I have tried everything to obtain the same for bonds, but the parties who have the battery refuse to take the bonds at any price, and I have just informed Mr. Ferrer that it will be impossible for me to get a battery for him in time for this shipment.

I am ready to start Governor Baz on Sunday morning, but Mr. Ferrer informs me that his arms can not be here until Monday, and if I shall take his arms I will have to delay Governor Baz's expedition until next week. *Shall I do this,* or shall I send Mr. Ferrer at some later time.

Please telegraph me *at once* about this in the following manner, viz.: Do not wait, or you better wait, and in either case I will understand your telegram.

I have room enough for your arms in case you decide that I shall wait for him.

Yours truly,
H. STURM.

Sturm to Romero.

No. 173.]   NEW YORK, November 22, 1866.

Senor M. ROMERO,
Mexican Minister, etc.

Dear Sir: I send you to-day a tabular statement of bonds received and expended since I made you a statement in my letter of October 2d, also a statement of purchases made and partially paid, showing the balance due. You will see that I have but a few bonds left, and the parties want bonds and must have them or it will interfere seriously with me. I only pay after goods are inspected and accepted, and only with approval of Dr. Navarro.

You must bear with me just now if I do not send statement in detail. I am doing the work of two men in reality, and my head swims from over work.

In haste, your truly,

H. STURM.

Romero to Sturm.

[Translation.]

No. 174.] WASHINGTON, November 23, 1866.

MEXICAN LEGATION IN THE U. S. OF AMERICA. According to the request you made of me in your letter of the 20th inst., and the telegraphic dispatch you sent me to-day, I remit you an order so that Messrs. John W. Corlies & Co. will deliver you one hundred thousand dollars in bonds, so that you may employ them in payment of the goods which Sr. D. Juan Jose Baz will take out.

I repeat to you the assurances of my most distinguished consideration.

M. ROMERO.

To General H. STURM,
New York.

Sturm to Romero.

No. 175.] NEW YORK, November 23, 1866.

Senor M. ROMERO,
Mexican Minister, etc.

Sir: I have the honor to acknowledge the receipt of your letter of yesterday enclosing an order on John W. Corlies & Co. for $100,000 in bonds.

I send you to-day, enclosed in this letter, a receipt from Schuyler, Hartley & Graham for said amount. Be pleased to send another order as soon as may be.

I have not heard from you in regard to waiting for Mr. Ferrer, and am now loading his goods that are ready, in connection with those for Governor Baz.

The Vixen left Norfolk on Wednesday evening (November 21) at nine o'clock.

I am, Sir, yours truly,

H. STURM.

Romero to Sturm.

NO. 176.] WASHINGTON, November 23, 1866.

General H. STURM,
New York.

Dear Sir: I have received your two letters of yesterday, and hasten to send you this reply.

,If all the carbines are already on Gov. Baz's steamer, and he wished to take them all, let him do so.

As for Mr. Ferrer, let Gov. Baz determine what he wants. If he likes to stay until Monday, let him remain, but no longer.

In great hurry,

,I am, dear Sir,

Your obedient servant,

M. ROMERO.

Romero to Sturm.

No. 177.] WASHINGTON, November 25, 1866.

General H. STURM,
New York.

Dear General: The haste with which your letter of the 22d inst. relative to shipment in Gov. Baz's steamer caused the omission of my answer on the torpedo. Now I hasten to tell you that in case it is time to remedy it, you should not send the torpedo, but keep it until it can be properly sent to Matamoras.

If it is already on board and can not be removed without much expense and trouble, then never mind—let it go.

I have received your communication of the 23d inst. covering receipt of Schuyler & Co. for draft of $100,000 in bonds.

Yours truly,

M. ROMERO.

Sturm to Romero.

No. 178.] NEW YORK, November 28, 1866.

Senor M. ROMERO,
Mexican Minister, etc.

Sir: I have the honor to state that yesterday noon the steamer Suwanee left this port for *Brazos, Texas*, with Governor Baz and staff as passengers on board, and an assorted cargo as per inclosed invoice. In addition to this invoice I have also shipped the goods belonging to Mr. Ferrer. The invoices were compared by Governor Baz before leaving.

I have been so prostrated since yesterday that I could not remit invoice before now.

I am, Sir, very respectfully,

Your obedient servant,

H. STURM.

Romero to Sturm.

[Translation.]

No. 179.] WASHINGTON, November 29, 1866.

MEXICAN LEGATION IN THE U. S. OF AMERICA.

I have received your note of yesterday wherein you are pleased to announce to me the sailing of the steamer Suwanee, and enclose to me the invoice of goods she takes on board. In answer I must tell you that appreciating to their full value your efforts to send this last remittance which was on hand, and as there remains no Commissioner here who would take charge of the remittance of goods to any determined point of the Mexican Republic, and as I am expecting instructions from the Government as to the means of sending to Matamoras and other points, you will be pleased to suspend for the present all purchases or business directed to provide for the Mexican Government war material until I give you further advice, which will perhaps be very soon, if I soon receive the answer I am awaiting.

Please send me as soon as you can a general account of all the purchases you have made, detailing what yet remains to be paid.

I repeat to you the assurances of my most attentive consideration.

M. ROMERO.

General H. STURM,
New York.

Memorandum of an Interview with Mr. Romero.

No. 180.] *Sunday, Dec. 2d, 1866.*

Arrived at Willard's Hotel 7:30 A. M. Saw Mr. Romero at half past ten. I told Mr. Romero I had come over to personally confer with him in regard to his letter of Nov. 29th, which I had received yesterday; and not fully understanding his meaning, I wished him to explain why he had written to me "to stop purchases now," when he knew from letters, and verbal messages sent to him by his Secretary of Legation, that I had made many engagements, with different parties, to carry out his orders for purchases directed to be made for Mr. Benitez, General Baranda, and Governor Baz.

In reply, Mr. Romero said that as these commissioners had sailed for Mexico, and there was no other person here to take the balance of the goods to Mexico, he desired me to stop for the present, but to hold the contracts I had made in abeyance; so that without making the Government liable to purchase the goods in case it should not need them, we might yet get them in case of necessity.

I replied that this was not the way business could be done for account of the Mexican Government in this country. I said: a firm, individual, or Government like the United States Government, having unlimited credit, could always command and control parties who were dealing in articles required by a Government, or individuals; but that his Government had really not a particle of credit, and the little it had obtained had been virtually manufactured at great trouble and expense, through myself and friends, and agents employed for the purpose.

I told Mr. Romero that although he knew fully the difficulties I had to encounter in my efforts to get anything on Mexican credit, and that but a short time ago he had himself considered it impossible to get anything for Mexican bonds, he yet had no idea of, and could not conceive the means and stratagems I was compelled, as the agent of his Government, to employ for the purpose of inducing parties to credit his Government.

I told Mr. Romero frankly that the position I had occupied so far as agent of his Government, had been an extremely unpleasant and disagreeable one, and that the duties imposed upon me were more onerous and laborious than those performed by any two, or even three, officers under the Government of the United States.

I said I wished him to remember all the circumstances surrounding this business; and that his Government had not, and could not, furnish a dollar toward defraying the most necessary expenses incidental to the shipping of the arms, after I had succeeded in obtainig them for bonds, let alone all the other expenses incurred by me in paying agents, etc., engaged in manufacturing credit for his country.

I also desired him to remember that he had offered to certain parties large sums of bonds for the purpose of obtaining their assistance, and had actually paid out a large amount of bonds for that purpose, without realizing much therefrom; but that so far I had not received a cent from his Government, either in shape of money or bonds, but everything had been provided for by me in the firm belief that his Government would appreciate the services I was rendering, and repay me for all my trouble and expenses; but that it was absolutely necessary that my efforts should be seconded by his Government or himself, and that above everything else, I desired promptness, and decisive action, and faithful performance of contracts and promises made. I reminded Mr. Romero that he had sent to me his Commissioners, and had requested me to purchase for them a large amount of material of war specified in schedules furnished me by them, and sanctioned by him. Owing to the bad faith shown to the parties who had furnished the steamer Everman and her cargo, his refusal to pay them even in bonds, as agreed, and his inability to hear from his Government about this matter, these gentlemen, as he knew, had declined to do anything more until the first cargo had been paid for as agreed. Thereupon I had made numerous new contracts with other parties, all of which I had reported to him at the time. That it was fully understood between us that Dr. Navarro should approve all contracts I might make under his (Mr. Romero's) authority; but that all these contracts had fallen through, and the time, labor, and expense incurred by me in bringing them about had been lost, partly in consequence of his (Mr. Romero's) absence from Washington while on the trip with the President to the West, but chiefly in consequence of the refusal of Dr. Navarro to approve in writing, as I had requested and believed it necessary it should be done, the contracts I had presented for his approval, although I had shown him Mr. Romero's letters and telegrams; and in consequence of my inability to pay the bonds promptly on delivery of goods, or to give security for their delivery except such as I might furnish myself through the assistance of my friends.

I told him I had requested him some time ago to make an arrangement by which the Financial Agents would be enabled to furnish me the bonds promptly as required, or to give security for the fulfillment of contracts I might make under his direction; but this had not been done, and parties with whom I was contracting or laboring for assistance to his country, thought it strange, and that there must be something wrong because of the refusal of Messrs. Corlies & Co. to take any responsibility, especially as they had all the bonds in their hands.

I said to Mr. Romero: "To fill the orders of his Commissioners I had made contracts with Schuyler, Hartley & Graham and others, who had already delivered their goods on board the Vixen and Suwanee; and I had made arrangements that could not be violated, with other parties, to supply the balance of the orders he had previously given me; among them Mr. Ames, Mr. Gaylord, and others, of Massachusetts; and Herman Boker & Co., Schuyler, Hartley & Graham, and others, of New York City.

I requested Mr. Romero to come to a definite understanding with me now, in regard to what should be done, as I could not afford to be placed in a false and ridiculous position toward these gentlemen. I also urged him, as he could not hear from his Government; and to uphold the credit and fair name and reputation his Government had recently acquired, to take upon himself the responsibility to deliver the bonds due on the charter and cargo of the Everman, and the purchase money of the Sheridan.

Mr. Romero replied to me, saying: "He would send a full report of my doings and services to his Government, and he expected every moment to hear from there. That there had been many statements concerning the cargo of the Everman; that the same had been paid for in specie by Mexican officers, or had been sold by Mr. Stocking; and until he had a detailed account of all this he could not take any responsibility in the matter, as the contract was not made by any order of his.

He said he was fully aware of the difficulties under which I labored, and would assist me all he could, but he did not think it possible that a better arrangement could be made with Messrs. Corlies & Co. in regard to the delivery of bonds, but would ask instructions from his Government. In regard to the stopping of purchases requested in his letter of the 29th, he would say to me that he did not wish to create any ill-feeling or misunderstanding betweeen myself and the parties with whom I had been negotiating; but he wished me not to keep any goods on hand as the property of the Mexican Government, as long as there was no Commissioner here who would take the goods away. All the purchases he had ordered me to make had been made without any special instructions from his Government, and although he was willing to take some responsibility, he would not take the risk, he would incur by keeping goods on hand any length of time, and he thought as I had succeeded so far, I would not find it very difficult to buy goods at some future time, when they should be wanted, from other parties.

I told him I was not so sure of that; at least I did not wish to lose the time, labor, and expense incurred in obtaining what I now had on hand, or had contracted for. I again repeated to Mr. Romero what I had before said to him about the difficulties encountered in obtaining credit for Mexican Bonds, and the cash expenses incident thereto, and told him that, had I known at the commencement of my agency, the true position of affairs, I should have hesitated to accept the trust; but having done so I intended to carry out in good faith my part.

I explained to Mr. Romero that the manner in which his Government tried to do business was suicidal and impolitic; while trying to do business in a sm-

way, thinking it doubtless economical, the Government had actually to pay double prices when compelled to purchase in time of necessity, as the delay and expense caused by disappointments, as had repeatedly happened before, would more than outweigh the original cost of the goods. And I urged Mr. Romero to allow me to collect, as I had before requested of him, the material of war necessary for a certain number of men; so it would be on hand and ready to be shipped at a moment's notice. Besides this advantage, I told him there was another, viz: I could obtain better, and more carefully select, all articles when not pressed for time; and could also obtain them cheaper.

Mr. Romero replied that although he had no definite instructions from his Government, he would carefully consider the proposition, as he saw the policy of it, and asked me to make it to him in writing, so that he might forward it to his Government.

Dec 3. Called on Mr. Romero, and handed him two letters of this date; one requesting $600,000 of bonds, the other containing in writing the proposition spoken of yesterday.

Mr. Romero said he would think over the matter, and write me to-morrow about the proposition I had made, and would also send me all the bonds he could. Mr. Romero said to me, as I had purchased or agreed to purchase the balance of the goods required by Governor Baz and the other Commissioners, he would take the responsibility of paying for them in bonds, if the contracts could not be canceled without causing ill feeling, or could not be kept in abeyance until another Commissioner should arrive, or he could hear from his Government about their delivery in Mexico.

Mr. Romero suggests to me a plan of selling these goods to the Liberal officers in Mexico. He says that they pay for arms there, very high prices, and all in gold or silver; that arms are much needed there, and if I can induce the parties from whom I have purchased, to take them to Mexico for sale, I can have a chance of making money, as most of the officers know of me and will gladly buy of me rather than anybody else. He says he will give me every assistance in his power, and if I succeed in arranging this it would relieve him of the responsibility of these arms.

I told Mr. Romero I would try to arrange this if possible, if he thought that the undertaking would be profitable.

I told Mr. Romero that I had been repeatedly spoken to, by some parties desirous of establishing a steamship line between New York, New Orleans and Mexico, and asked him if he could give me any assistance in such an undertaking by giving certain privileges in Mexican ports, or contracts to carry the mail, etc. If an advantageous arrangement could be made I would try to establish a line of steamers to Mexico.

Mr. Romero requested me to write him on the subject, and he would facilitate as much as possible my projects.

Sturm to Romero.

No. 181.] WASHINGTON, December 3, 1866.

Senor. M. ROMERO,
Mexican Minister, etc.

Sir: I would respectfully ask you to place at my disposal an order on John W. Corlies & Co. for the sum of $500,000 in bonds to enable me to pay for certain articles purchased heretofore, and to pay for others that I *may* purchase hereafter.

In addition I would ask you to give me another order on a *separate account* for $100,000 bonds, to enable me to pay expenses heretofore incurred for clerk hire, inspection, drayage, and other incidental expenses.

The reason why I ask for this latter order on a separate account, is that in this way I am enabled to account to you separately for expenses incurred for purchases, and for those incurred for necessary labor, etc.

I am, Sir, very respectfully,
Your obedient servant,
H. STURM.

Sturm to Romero.

No. 182.] WASHINGTON, December 3, 1866.

Senor M. ROMERO,
Mexican Minister, etc.

Sir: In consequence of the fact that the United States may, perhaps, guarantee a Mexican loan at the present session of Congress, and on account of the determined efforts made by the friends of your Government, quite a number of the influential men of this country have concluded to sell to the Government of Mexico, arms and munitions of war indispensably necessary for its defense, support, and preservation.

I do not believe that the Government of the United States will guarantee a loan just now; and knowing full well that as soon as this fact becomes known to the public, it will be impossible to obtain any further supplies of this kind for bonds, I would respectfully ask of you the authority to take advantage of this present good feeling, and to purchase at once a certain amount of war material for the Government, as well as power to store the same and arrange for its transportation to Mexico—the exact point of disembarkation to be determined by you hereafter, viz:

Rifles, equipments, clothing, and ammunition for 20,000 infantry.

Carbines, revolvers, equipments, clothing, and ammunition for 3,000 cavalry.

Fifteeen batteries of light artillery and equipments, implements and ammunition.

Engineers' tools and instruments for 3,000 men.

One hundred pieces of artillery, complete, with ammunition, etc., for fortifications and sea coast defense.

I may not be able to obtain all the above-mentioned articles, but if you give me the authority to purchase them now, I shall be able to obtain a great portion of them at the price of the Government of the United States, and shall make every effort to get all I can possibly obtain; and in this way the Government will be for some time provided, and be able to obtain these goods *just now*, and at very reasonable prices; whereas, as before stated, it will, in my opinion, be almost impossible to obtain anything hereafter, except for cash, and at the same time we necessarily secure a great amount of influence of prominent persons of this country in favor of the present Government of Mexico, because they are the holders of the bonds.

In addition to the above, I would suggest that you authorize me to purchase two steamers, capable to run and carry cargoes between New York and Mexico. By doing this we have the control of the shipment of goods entirely in our possession, and will, in the course of six or seven months, have paid for said steamers out of the saving of the charter money.

Hoping to hear from you at once in regard to this matter,

I remain, Sir, very respectfully,
Your obedient servant,
H. STURM.

Romero to Sturm.

No. 183.] WASHINGTON, December 4, 1866.

General H. STURM.

Dear General: In answer to your letter of yesterday, asking me to authorize you for the purchase, with bonds, of arms and equipments for 20,000 infantry, 3,000 cavalry, batteries, etc., I have to state that although feeling the weight of your arguments, for the reasons explained to you I do not think it proper to take such step until I receive from my Government the instructions I expect.

But, in the meantime, you might give me a statement of what you have been offered by the Ames family, or what you could purchase of them, and I would authorize you to enter into negotiations with said family.

Very sincerely yours,
M. ROMERO.

Romero to Sturm.

[Translation.]

No. 184.] NEW YORK, December 4, 1866.

MEXICAN LEGATION IN THE U. S. OF AMERICA.

In answer to your communication dated yesterday, in which you ask me for an order of $500,000 in bonds to pay the sums yet due for the goods you have bought, I will tell you, that I do not consider it necessary to remit that part corresponding to the goods sent on board the Everman, as that quantity ought not to be paid until we know that those goods have been duly delivered.

In order to enable you to pay the money that you owe yet for the other goods, according to contracts approved, and according to the note which you presented to me, I enclose you an order on Messrs. J. W. Corlies & Co. for the sum of $220,000 in bonds.

I renew to you the assurances of my distinguished consideration.

M. ROMERO.

To General H. STURM, New York.

Sturm to Romero.

No. 185.]   NEW YORK, December 5, 1866.

Senor M. ROMERO,
    Mexican Minister, etc.

Sir: I have the honor to acknowledge the receipt of your letter of yesterday, enclosing an order on John W. Corlies & Co. for $220,000 in bonds. I am sorry they are not signed, for Messrs. Schuyler, Hartley & Graham ought to have them to-day, but hope they can be ready for delivery to-morrow.

I am, Sir, very respectfully,
    Your obedient servant,
        H. STURM.

Romero to Sturm.

No. 186.]   WASHINGTON, December 7, 1866.

General H. STURM,
    New York.

Dear Sir: I have been very sorry and very much mortified to hear that the Suwanee was sunk on the 3d instant and all her cargo lost.

This disagreeable incident has decided me to stop all further purchases of goods for the Mexican Government. You are aware that, so far, the first remittance has been of no avail to the Mexican Government. It looks as an attempt to sell twice, goods which have already been sold to us.

The impression produced by General Wallace and Mr. Stocking's proceedings and representations has not been calculated to inspire much confidence to the Mexican Goverament. The second remittance had scarcely left, when the steamer which carried the goods met with an accident, and I would not be surprised if she, too, is lost. The third remittance has been a death loss.

Under such condition of things I can not authorize the purchase of anything else until I receive the instructions from my Government that I am waiting for. What is the use of our purchasing, at high prices, needed articles, if we can not get them to Mexico.

I suppose you heard, last evening, from the Suwanee.

In great haste,
    I am, Sir, very respectfully,
        Your obedient servant,
            M. ROMERO.

Sturm to Romero.

No. 187.] NEW YORK, December 8, 1866.

Senor M. ROMERO,
    Mexican Minister, etc.

Sir: I have the honor to acknowledge the receipt of your letter of yesterday, and in reply, allow me to say that I returned this morning from Boston, Springfield and Chicopee, where I had been to inspect some sabres and equipments manufactured for us by Mr. Ames, to complete General Baranda's order. The guns, etc , I have done nothing with at present.

On my return, I was completely thunderstruck to hear of the loss of the Suwanee, and you may rest assured I feel this disaster as keenly as yourself, but shall refrain at present from any comments on this subject; but I do wish to say to you, and of which I am sure you bear me witness, that I can not possibly be blamed for any disaster that has occurred.

In July last, I succeeded, after a year's hard and persistent labor and struggle, in obtaining for your Government, with its bonds that had no market value, a cargo of arms and a vessel to transport them to Matamoras. The arms arrived safely, and were delivered at that place, when an unforeseen accident threw everything into confusion, and caused difficulties for which neither you nor I can be held responsible. I have on my part communicated to you all the facts as they were given me, as well as all correspondence which I have received on the subject.

In November I again sent another steamer, the Vixen, with a cargo of arms. She met with an ordinary accident, that occurs almost every week to some steamers of the first class; it was promptly repaired, and the vessel has sailed again, with my brothers in her, to look after the cargo, etc. Now another cargo has been sent through my agency and efforts, on a vessel which I had caused to be thoroughly examined in July last, when I first engaged her, by a very responsible and well known steamboat man of Philadelphia, whose certificate of her seaworthiness is in my possession. In addition to this, I was shown the certificate of the Government Inspector, of Philadelphia, a copy of which I shall obtain as soon as possible. On her arrival here and before sending her out, I have had her re-examined, and nothing has been neglected on my part to insure success, or to guard the interests of the Government. The parties from whom I chartered said vessel are perfectly responsible, and bear a very high reputation ; and they have stated to me that she was complete and seaworthy. They had so much confidence in her and her captain, that they have not even an insurance on her, and are therefore themselves heavy losers. This steamer foundered in a gale, out of my reach or control, and until I hear particulars from those in her, I can not say where the blame lies, but I am quite confident it does not rest with me. Whatever mistakes, as stated in your letter, General Wallace or others may have made, I am not responsible for. I have done everything in the promptest and best manner possible; and in the case of the Everman, according to instructions given by General Carvajal, and I am in hopes that the Government will soon understand the true state of the case.

As soon as I can obtain the copy of the Government Inspector's certificate, and other facts, I shall remit the same to you.

I enclose herewith a letter which I found in the office this morning, from Mr. Cattell. Be pleased to return the same to me after noting its contents.

I am, Sir, very respectfully,
Your obedient servant,
H. STURM

Sturm to Romero.

No. 188.] NEW YORK, December 10, 1866.

Senor. M. ROMERO,
Mexican Minister, etc.

Sir: Referring to my letter of the 8th inst., I now enclose you a copy of the Government Inspector's certificate, signed by the said inspectors, and certifying that on the 27th of July last, when I engaged the Suwanee, *she was in all respects staunch, seaworthy, and in good condition for navigation;* and they declare it to be their deliberate conviction, that the said steamer may be employed upon the waters between Philadelphia and New Orleans without peril to life from any imperfections, or from age or use.

In addition to this, I enclose the certificate of Captain Wm. J. Taylor of Philadelphia, dated July 28th, in which he declares that she is in the most complete order and suitable for any voyage, and is in all respects a first-class steamer. Captain Taylor was an entirely disinterested person, of very extensive experience in ocean steam navigation, and himself the owner of several steamers, whom I engaged on behalf of the Mexican Government, to inspect the steamer.

This will afford proof that, so far as human precautions could be taken to prevent the sad accident that has happened, nothing has been neglected; and that it is impossible justly to attach any blame either to you or to myself, for what happened by the act of God, during a furious hurricane, not uncommon at this season off the southern coast.

But there is still greater proof that the vessel is trustworthy, to be found in the fact that the owners, who must have known her well, and had so much at stake, did not insure the vessel at all, so that she is a dead loss to them.

The goods might, it is true have been insured, but Governments are not in the habit of insuring under such circumstances. The house of Schuyler, Hartley & Graham, of New York, the largest exporters of arms and military goods in the United States, who have shipped in the last few years goods for various South American Governments, to the amount of several millions, stated to me that they never, in a single instance, were instructed to insure, and never did insure a single cargo. Add to this, that in the United States military regulations there is a positive prohibition to all officers against insurance.

Under these circumstances, I did not consider myself at liberty to effect insurance upon these goods, having no instructions so to do; nor had I any money to pay the necessary premium, which would have been at least fifteen thousand dollars cash, though perhaps that might have been arranged.

I shall send you the particulars of the shipwreck at the earliest period that I can procure them.

All men and all governments are liable to just such accidents as that which has overtaken us. We met with many such of a far graver character, at the commencement of our war, but the only effect upon our people and Government was, to cause them to increase their exertions to repair the loss, and to go forward with renewed energy in the struggle we were engaged in.

Ought not Mexico, under the pressure of this misfortune, to do the same thing? Will she not obtain the respect of the world by showing that temporary reverses do not diminish her courage, and that her spirit rises superior to ill-fortune?

I feel assured that your Government, which has never lost heart during all the misfortunes of the last five years, will cordially approve your course, if you see fit, instead of slackening your exertions and ceasing from further purchases of arms and other supplies, to go on perseveringly so as to repair in the future the losses of the past; and I think you ought to pursue that course.

The necessity for military supplies is imperative, and will, I am sure, cause your Government fully to approve any steps you may authorize to send on further supplies. If you consider it most prudent they may be insured.

If you decide to go on, you may rest assured that no exertions on my part shall be spared, and no precautions neglected, to insure better fortune in the future than has been our lot heretofore.

In the end perseverance wins the day.

I am sir, very respectfully,
Your obd't servant,
H. STURM.

Sturm to Romero.

No. 189.]   NEW YORK, December 10, 1866.

Senor M. ROMERO,
Mexican Minister, etc.

Sir: I have the honor to transmit herewith a receipt from Messrs. Schuyler, Hartley & Graham, for $150,000 bonds, which I paid to them on December 5th, 1866.

I am, Sir, respectfully,
Your obedient servant,
H. STURM.

Romero to Sturm.

No. 190.]   WASHINGTON, December 12, 1866.

General H. STURM.

Dear Sir: I have received your two letters dated, one the 8th and the other the 10th inst., with enclosures.

I return to you the enclosed letter of Mr. Cattell, as you request.

I will inform the Government of all the particulars, that they may form a correct idea of the disaster met by the Suwanee.

As for the reflections you make on the impossibility of preventing such calamity, allow me to tell you that I have not charged you with any fault in that connection, and I am convinced of the earnestness of your efforts to render useful services to my Government.

The suspension of purchases was decided by me, as you can notice, previously to the disaster of the Suwanee, and from different motives, which I explained to you in my communication.

Respectfully,
Your obedient servant,
M. ROMERO.

Sturm to Romero.

[Private.]

No. 191.] NEW YORK, December 13, 1866.

Senor M. ROMERO,

Dear Sir: Your letter of yesterday enclosing Mr. Cattell's letter has been received. I certainly did not mean to intimate, in my letter to you, as if I felt that you blamed me for the terrible calamity that has befallen us, or that you had, on this account alone, concluded to stop further supplies; but I felt this loss so deeply that, having been the principal and responsible agent in getting the ship, I naturally stated what I did in my letter; and to show to you, who had extended to me so much confidence, that I had exercised due diligence, etc., I enclosed the certificates for the purpose of enabling you to judge how I had acted, as well as to lay them before the Government; but I felt then, and do now, that my duty was, to *at once* repair the loss, and fit out again Gov. Baz to enable him to proceed again without delay, as delay, in my judgment, may prove disadvantageous, if not, perhaps, disastrous to the Government. The greater the difficulty and trouble, the more ready and willing I am to work and aid you. *Rely on this.* I will never be conquered by adversity, but shall always try to show the same pertinacity and energy that has been shown by President Juarez during this struggle.

I know of a great many schemes and complications on foot to defeat you and your Government, some of which I have mentioned to you, and only yesterday an officer of Maximilian arrived here with one hundred and twenty thousand dollars in *gold* to purchase arms for your enemies. I have my men watching him now, and shall interfere with him if possible. If I had only the *tacit* consent of yours, I would at once buy and arm a little vessel and capture this cargo, and *sink it if necessary.*

At all events I know there will be more fighting to do, and to make success certain you must have more arms, etc., and the sooner the better.

Yours truly,
H. STURM.

Romero to Sturm.

No. 192.] WASHINGTON, December 17, 1866.

General H. STURM,

Dear Sir: I have received your favor of the 16th enclosing Mr. W. L. Hanscom's proposal for the construction of monitors for the Mexican Government.

In answer I have to say that I will forward said proposal to my Government, and that I have had some arrangement in that connection for future contingencies with said Mr. Hanscom, of whom I entertain a high opinion.

I remain, dear Sir,
Your obedient servant,

M. ROMERO.

Romero to Sturm.

No. 193.] WASHINGTON, December 17, 1866.

General H. STURM,

Dear Sir: I have to acknowledge the receipt of your letters, dated the 13th and 15th instant, with the enclosed proposal of Mr. W. L. Hanscom. As I have officially told you, all purchases and contracts whatever are to be suspended until I receive new instructions from the Government. This conclusion I had come to is now strengthened by a letter which I have just received from the Secretary of War, saying to me that I should stop all contracts. Although this is an unofficial letter, it makes me think that I may at any moment receive an official dispatch to the same purpose, and causes me to confirm my determination on the subject.

When I see you I will explain to you fully all in this connection, and you will be convinced, I hope, that it is necessary to wait until the Government, being in Monterey, may decide upon the resumption of contracts.

I am, dear Sir,
Sincerely yours,

M. ROMERO.

I send you my answer about Mr. Hanscom's letter.

Sturm to Romero.

No. 194.] NEW YORK, December 18, 1866.

Senor M. ROMERO,
Mexican Minister, etc.

Sir: Your letter of yesterday in which you say that the Secretary of War has suggested to you to stop all further purchases, has been received. Under these circumstances there is of course no further need for my services here, and

I propose to leave for home at as early a day as possible, as I have been away, and have not seen my family for a year.

You are aware that I have on hand a certain amount of goods that have been purchased by your order, and that some contracts or arrangements are still unsettled, as for instance the charter for Everman and Sheridan, and others, as well as my cash expenses. I will now at once set about to make a statement of the amount still due on old purchases, as well as my cash account; also of the articles on hand, and I would be obliged to you if you would direct me to whom I shall deliver these goods now on hand in this city.

2d. I wish, that so far as lays in your power, all the old contracts be settled and paid for while I am here to aid you in this matter.

3d. I wish you would be kind enough to place at my disposal a certain amount of bonds, *as my own property*, for services rendered your Government.

I think you will see at once that it is important to you that all these matters are arranged before my going away from here, as it will be exceedingly difficult, or at least troublesome to you to correspond about all these things hereafter, although some arrangements, as for instance the Vixen, can not be settled until the contract is fulfilled, but in those cases you can call on me at any time, if it should be necessary to do so, and I will be glad to aid you.

On the whole I think that the Government has come to a very *unwise* and *suicidal* conclusion in stopping now from obtaining the advantages that are just about being derived from the labors of the last eighteen months, and you may rest assured that if the Guarantee Bill does not pass, or you do not succeed in obtaining money in some way, it will be impossible to obtain any goods for your bonds, besides you lose the opportunity of getting a strong and powerful influence in your favor, in the cheapest and most substantial way, that would be able to help you materially in defeating your enemies.

I am, Sir, very respectfully,
Your obedient servant,
H. STURM.

Romero to Sturm.

No. 195.]   WASHINGTON, December 19, 1866.

General H. STURM,
New York.

Dear Sir: I have just received your favor of the 18th instant. The Secretary of War, in a private letter, dated at Chihuahua on the 19th of November, tells me that the President had decided to stop all purchases here, and he thought I should receive instructions on the subject from the Department of State.

This instruction did not come, and I suppose I will have them to-morrow or next day. When I have them I will officially notify you of the fact.

In the meanwhile it will be convenient that you should prepare a statement of all articles you have purchased and are to be sent, and a list of all liabilities not yet paid. I will try to have all this settled before you go home.

As for the compensation for your services, I beg of you to say to me confidentially how much you think you are entitled to in bonds.

I am aware of what you remark about the difficulty of making further purchases when the guaranty does not pass, but I must act under my instructions.

I am, Sir, very truly,
Your obedient servant,
M. ROMERO.

Sturm to Romero.

No. 196.]   NEW YORK, December 23, 1866.

SEÑOR M. ROMERO,
Mexican Minister, etc.

Sir: Governor Baz and Mr. Fuentes called on me this morning, and from their conversation with me, it seems that either Governor Baz did not understand me correctly when he asked me, what I had on hand, or else you do not fully understand what I have done and how far I have gone in the matter of purchases, etc. To explain this as short as possible, allow me to say, that Gen. Baranda, Mr. Benitez, and Governor Baz have ordered of me a certain amount of goods. I could not, at the time of their leaving, send with them all they have ordered, but only a portion. I was instructed to send the balance the next time. Of course I had made my arrangements for *all* they ordered, and a portion of the balance is now on hand, and another portion is arranged for, but not yet fully inspected and delivered.

In addition to this, you authorized me, during an interview on the 5th inst., to purchase from Mr Ames some sabres and equipments and carbines, and I at once left for Boston (and Philadelphia, whither I went to see Messrs. Simons & Cattell) to inspect these goods. The articles offered by Mr. Ames you did not decide upon, but asked me for a statement, that you might, perhaps, authorize the purchase. With this I have, however, done nothing, as your letters, on my return from Boston, instructed me not to do anything more until orders from your Government should arrive. All the articles now on hand, or to be delivered yet, have been purchased under previous orders; and no new arrangement has been made by me since receiving your instructions to stop. I write this to you to-day, so that you may not be under the apprehension that I have gone further in this matter than I was authorized.

I regret, however, exceedingly, that I could not buy the articles of Mr. Ames, as the amount is but small, and think it very important to enlist those Eastern manufacturers largely; but of that I will speak with you when I see you.

You will please bear in mind, however, the fact that I have made several contracts for arms that are now void entirely, as the parties have refused to complete them, and that you now really do not get near as many arms as were expected; and it is very probable that the Government believes, that for instance, the contract with Mr. Fitch and with Mr. Cory will be filled, and judge from this that the Government will soon be in possession of a large quantity of arms, and therefore does not think it necessary to purchase more; whereas, you are aware, these contracts are all void and useless and of no benefit to the Government.

I shall try my best to see you on Tuesday morning, if possible; but as I am closing my accounts here entirely up to the present time, I can not get away until I finish it, as I do not intend to return to this city after seeing you, but shall go to Indiana direct from Washington; and as my clerk is going home too, it may be, therefore, that I do not leave here before Tuesday night.

I am, Sir, very respectfully,
Your obedient servant,
H. STURM.

Sturm to Romero.

No. 197.] NEW YORK, December 23, 1866.

Senor M. ROMERO,
Mexican Mnister, etc.

Sir: I have the honor to enclose herewith a letter received this morning from Mr. Simons, in relation to his claim for the Everman and the Sheridan. I also enclose a copy of my answer to him.

I am now preparing all the statements you ask of me, so as to enable you to settle such of them as are due.

I am, Sir, very respectfully,
Your obedient servant,
H. STURM.

P. S. I have received from Brazos a receipt for a portion of the goods sent there, signed by Mr. Saavedra, agent for General Escobedo. I shall remit the same with the other accounts.

H. STURM.

Sturm to Romero.

No. 198.] WASHINGTON, December 27, 1866.

Senor M. ROMERO,
Mexican Minister, etc.

Sir: Referring to your letter of December 23d, I have now the honor to state that a portion of the cargo of the steamer Everman has been delivered to Mr. Saavedra, agent for the Mexican Government at Matamoras; and from information received, I believe that the balance of the goods on hand will be or have already been delivered to General Escobedo. Under these circumstances, I think it advisable and important that the claim of Mr. Simons, for the Everman be settled as soon as possible, and would request you, therefore, to send me an order for one hundred and thirty-four thousand seven hundred and fifty ($134,750) dollars, Mexican Bonds, the coupons to date from October 1, 1866.

The above amount is what is still due to Mr. Simons for the charter of the Everman, after deducting the $4,332.23, collected by him for freight and passage money.

I am, Sir, very respectfully,
Your obedient servant,
H. STURM.

Sturm to Romero.

No. 199.]   WASHINGTON, December 27, 1866.

Senor M. ROMERO,
    Mexican Minister, etc.

Sir: I have the honor to herewith enclose a receipt, signed by Senor Manuel M. Saavedra, as agent of the Republic of Mexico, for a portion of the goods sent by steamer Everman, in July, 1866, to the port of Matamoras, Mexico.

According to enclosed receipt, there is due Messrs. Hall & Ruckell, for medical stores, the sum of seventeen hundred and seventy-nine ($1779) dollars; to David Smith, the sum of twenty-nine thousand eight hundred and sixty-seven dollars and thirty-three cents ($29,867.33); and to Messrs. Merritt Wolcott & Co., and Dewhurst & Emerson, the sum of forty-five thousand nine hundred and thirty-four dollars and twenty cents ($45,934.20). The sum total amounting to seventy-seven thousand five hundred and two dollars and thirty-two cents, in currency of the United States, or in Mexican Bonds, at the rate of sixty cents on the dollar, amounting to *one hundred and twenty-nine thousand one hundred and fifty dollars.*

I would, therefore, respectfully ask you to give me an order for that amount of bonds, the coupons to date from October 1st, 1866, so that I may enabled to pay those parties above mentioned, the amounts severally due them.

In haste, I am yours,
Very Respectfully,
H. STURM.

Romero to Sturm.

No. 200.]   WASHINGTON, December 28, 1866.

General H. STURM,
    New York.

I received to-day my mail from Minatitlan. Gen. Baranda reports the Vixen very slow. Please discharge her as soon as possible, and send to me the account of her charter.

I am, Sir,
Very respectfully,
Your obedient servant,
M. ROMERO.

Sturm to Romero.

No. 201.]   NEW YORK, December 29, 1866.

Senor M. ROMERO,
    Mexican Minister, etc.

Dear Sir : Your letter of yesterday asking me to discharge the Vixen has been received.

I wrote you last night in a hurry stating that I would settle this matter at once before going to Washington.

The statement of Gen. Baranda that the Vixen is slow is not exactly correct, but from the statements of my brother I learn that there was every disposition on the part of the Captain to delay and make a long trip. Now, as I wrote you yesterday, I will settle this matter to-day, and I am determined to deduct for the time the Vixen was lying at Norfolk repairing; also for the eighteen hours she was delayed at the Bahamas shifting coal, and eighteen hours at Cape San Antonio, where she went on account of stress of weather, as the Captain *calls it.*

I expect Mr. J. T. Wright at 11 o'clock, when I will settle with him, *on this basis alone,* otherwise I shall not approve his account. I have notified him already that the Vixen is discharged from 12 M. *this day,* and have sent my Steward aboard to give him an inventory of the provisions that are left, which I shall take care of for further use; also of the engineer's stores left, all of which are the property of the Government. Under these circumstances it will be night before I get through with my work, if I get through at all to-day, so I can not come to see you before to-morrow night.

I am, Sir, very respectfully,
                  Your obedient servant,
                          H. STURM.

Romero to Sturm.

No. 202.]   WASHINGTON, December 29, 1866.

MEXICAN LEGATION.   I received your communication of date of the 27th inst. in which you enclose to me a receipt signed by C. Manuel Saavedra (commissioned by Gen. Escobeda) on the 25th of November last for a certain quantity of goods carried to Matamoras by the steamer Everman, and declaring their amount according to the respective contracts, to be $77,502.33 in U. S. currency, or $129,150 in Mexican Bonds, asking me to send an order for this remittance with the object of paying the respective contractors.

IN THE
U. S. OF AMERICA.

In answer, I will say that in a separate note I have remitted to you an order, according to which there will be delivered the sum of bonds mentioned; also the amount necessary to pay the charter of the steamer Vixen.

I repeat to you the assurances of my distinguished consideration.
                              M. ROMERO.

To General H. STURM.
    New York.

Memorandum of an Interview with Senor Romero.

No. 203.] December 31, 1866.

Called on Mr. Romero at 10 A. M. I told him that a portion of the cargo of the Everman had been delivered to Mr. Saavedra. I begged him to pay for the charter and cargo of the Everman now. Mr. Romero said he could not do it until he heard from his Government. He also declined to pay Messrs. Dupont & Co., for the same reason. He wished to give me some bonds, and wished to know of me if he could settle with me in that way, and how much I should require. I replied, that the bonds had no market value beyond what I had given them; and I explained to him that in several instances I had advanced the interest on the coupons for the purpose of giving confidence to parties I was dealing with; and, in addition, I had advanced every dollar needed in the purchase and shipment of arms, and also for political services; and that the promise of his Government to pay me was as good as the promise to pay the bonds; and I would wait until the war was over, and then we could come to a settlement in full.

I told Mr. Romero I had arranged with several parties to send arms, etc., to Mexico, to be sold there to the Liberal authorities for cash, with the understanding that Mr. Romero and the Mexican Government provides us all protection and freedom from all charges. I said, if this is done he need not pay in bonds for that part of the goods some time since bought by me to be sent to Mexico, but the arms from Mr. Ames and his friends, and a few other parties ought to be bought and paid for. I said to Mr. Romero that I would get a steamer or sailing vessel to take the goods to Mexico, and I would take out the goods belonging to the Government free of all charge in consideration of the privileges given us by his Government. Mr. Romero assents to this and will write his Government about it, and may order some of the goods to Mexico very soon. He wishes me to request of him, in writing an order for bonds to pay for the charter of the steamer Vixen. Mr. Romero had a long conversation with me about my remuneration, and says he will write to his Government fully about all I have done for them, and will see full justice done to everybody, but wants some little time to bring this about, and wishes me to say so to Dewhurst and Simons.

Sturm to Romero.

No. 204.] WASHINGTON, December 31, 1866.

Senor M. ROMERO,
    Mexican Minister, etc.

Sir: I have the honor to herewith submit the enclosed bill of John T. Wright, for the charter of the steamer Vixen, which bill, as corrected after deducting the nine and three-fourths' days the said steamer was unnecessarily detained on the voyage, amounts to $40,350 U. S. currency, or $67,250 Mexican bonds.

I would respectfully ask you to give me an order for that amount of bonds, so that I may be able to pay said bill.

    I am, Sir, very respectfully,
        Your obedient servant,
            H. STURM.

Romero to Sturm.

[Translation.]

No. 205.] WASHINGTON, December 31, 1866.

MEXICAN LEGATION IN THE U. S. OF AMERICA.

I received your communication of to-day enclosing the account of John T. Wright, Jr., for the charter of the steamer Vixen, as corrected by you, said Wright having accepted the correction, amounting to $40,350 in U. S. currency, or $67,250 in bonds, at 60 per cent. You request me to send you an order for delivery of said bonds, to cover said accounts. In answer, I enclose you an order on Messrs. John W. Corlies & Co., for $196,400 in Mexican Bonds, to the end that you may cover the sum mentioned; and the remaining sum of $129,150, also due in bonds for the goods received by M. Saavedra, in Brownsville, on the 24th of November last.

I repeat to you the assurances of my most distinguished consideration.

M. ROMERO.

To General HERMAN STURM,
New York.

Romero to Sturm.

No. 206.] WASHINGTON CITY, D. C., January 3, 1867.

General H. STURM,
New York.

Dear Sir: I enclose to you the official letters you desire.

I have concluded not to sell the tents that you have at hand. We can make a better disposition of them.

In great haste,
Respectfully yours,

M. ROMERO.

Romero to Sturm.

[Translation.]

No. 207.] WASHINGTON, January 3, 1867.

MEXICAN LEGATION IN THE U. S. OF AMERICA.

I have received your communication, under date of 27th December last, in which you ask me for $134,750 in Mexican Bonds to pay for the charter of the steamer Everman. As this amount corresponds to more than three months, at the rate of $950 per day, according to the terms of the contract, and as it does not appear to me that during all this time said steamer has been used in the service of the Mexican Government, nor has been detained at all by any competent authority, it is not possible for me to consent, at the present moment, to pay that which you indicate to me. I have no objection to pay at once so much as corresponds to one month's ·charter of the Everman; but respecting that which is left, I hope to receive official information that I now ask for from Matamoras, and also other vouchers which you will render to me to prove that said steamer was detained all the time referred to by order of a party legitimately authorized to do it.

Please tell me at once, in answer, if Mr. Simons wishes to receive at once the one month's charter, which I am ready to pay; in which case I shall send you an order, that the corresponding bonds may be delivered to you.

I reiterate to you the assurances of my most distinguished consideration,

M. ROMERO.

To General H. STURM,
    New York.

Sturm to Romero.

No. 208.]   NEW YORK, January 4, 1867.

Señor M. ROMERO,
    Mexican Minister, etc.

Sir: I have the honor to acknowledge the receipt of your two letters of December 29th and 31st, 1866, enclosing an order on Messrs. John W. Corlies & Co. for one hundred and ninety-six thousand four hundred dollars ($196,400), Mexican Bonds, for the purpose of paying for the goods receipted for by Mr. Saavedra on the 24th of November last, and also for the charter money due to Mr. Wright on account of the steamer Vixen.

The above mentioned order has been presented by me this day to Messrs. John W. Corlies & Co., and has been duly accepted, and the above amount of bonds will be properly accounted for by me as follows, viz:

Dewhurst & Emerson	$76,550 00
David Smith	49,750 00
Hall & Ruckel	2,850 00
	$129,150 00
J. T. Wright, Jr., charter of Vixen	67,250 00
	$196,400 00

        I am, Sir,
            Your obedient servant,

H. STURM.

Sturm to Romero.

No. 209.] NEW YORK, January 4, 1867.

Senor M. ROMERO,
 Mexican Minister, etc.

Sir: Your note of yesterday, requesting me not to sell the tents, has been received and will be complied with.

I am, Sir, very respectfully,
 Your obedient servant,

H. STURM.

Sturm to Romero.

No. 210.] NEW YORK, January 5, 1867.

SENOR M. ROMERO,
 Mexican Minister, etc.

Dear Sir: I send you by this mail my official answer to your letter of January 3d, in regard to the steamer Everman. I am very sorry that you have taken this view of the matter, and thereby place me in the attitude of an attorney for the owners of said ship, which I do not like at all. If you had told me on last Monday, while I was with you, that you entertained any doubt about the propriety of paying the amount claimed, I could have explained all the points mentioned in my letter of to-day. You know that we can not hold the owners of the steamer responsible for any delay or loss caused by Mexican officials themselves, and it is highly detrimental to the credit of the Government and its people to raise such difficulties as these, and it does more to injure the good cause than anything else.

I fully understand your anxiety to protect the interests of your Government in every way, and no one appreciates your efforts or zeal in this direction more than I do, but still I must confess that I think that you sometimes go too far.

I honestly believe that, not only in this case, but also in the case of the Sheridan, the owners have a righteous claim for damages caused by detention, which was not through any neglect on their part, as it is strictly our duty, or the duty of the Government, to provide a proper officer duly authorized to receive the goods on their arrival. This is, in my opinion, a part of the contract.

The greatest difficulty that I have experienced, during my labors of the past eighteen months in behalf of your Government, has been the feeling of distrust entertained by the people of this country in regard to the honesty of the Mexican officials, and the faithful and prompt fulfillment of contracts made with the Government; and I have labored hard to convince those men from whom we have purchased anything, that they will be fairly dealt with. You fully understand all these difficulties caused by former Governments and officials, and you know that the present Government, no matter how honest its intentions, has to labor under and overcome them; and I beg you therefore to carefully consider all the facts of the case and to at once settle these accounts.

I enclose herewith two letters received from Mr. Simons in regard to his claims, since the one I sent you the other day. I dislike to send you such letters, and always try to get along without troubling you with the numerous complaints of which I am the innocent victim; but in this case I consider it my duty to send them to you, as I am fearful of trouble unless this matter is settled, and I have therefore not as yet communicated to Mr. Simons your views of this case, deeming it to be to the interests of the Government to wait until I can hear from you again.

I am, Sir,
Your obedient servant,
H. STURM.

Sturm to Romero.

No. 211.] NEW YORK, January 5, 1867.

Senor M. ROMERO,
Mexican Minister, etc.

Sir: I have the honor to acknowledge the receipt of your letter of Jan. 3d, in which you say that you can not just now pay the amount of the charter party of the steamer Everman, as it does not appear to you that she has been in the service of the Mexican Government all the time for which payment is claimed, or that she has been detained by competent authority.

In answer allow me to state that the said steamer was sent to Brazos Santiago, Texas, consigned to General Carvajal, with positive orders to report to, and *subject only* to the orders of said General, or in his absence, to such other officer of the Mexican Government as might be *duly* in command at Matamoras. At the time of the arrival of the Everman, General Carvajal had competent authority, but in consequence of the revolt of the 12th of August, and the subsequent flight of General Carvajal, there was no person *in authority* there, willing or competent to order the steamer to return home, and she therefore remained at Brazos several weeks, *waiting orders*, until my agent (Mr. Stocking) fearing (as has since proved to be the case) that before some officer duly authorized by the Government would arrive, a long time might elapse, and that thereby a large loss would accrue to the Government, took upon himself the responsibility to order said vessel to return to this port.

Under these circumstances, I can not see that any blame can be attached either to the Captain or the owners of the vessel, and it is my conviction that it is proper and just to consider her as having been in the service of the Government during the time she was detained, and that therefore this time ought to be paid for, as agreed upon in the charter.

I am, Sir, very respectfully,
Your obedient servant,
H. STURM.

Sturm to Romero.

No. 212.] NEW YORK, January 5, 1867.

Senor M. ROMERO,
    Mexican Minister, etc.

Sir: I have the honor to herewith transmit the bill of Messrs. Dupont de Nemours & Co. for powder delivered to me, amounting to $12,424.43. This powder I have received, and it is now stored in the magazine near this city, subject to the orders of the Government. The claim of Messrs. Dupont & Co. now amounts to as follows:

Bill of powder sent in the Vixen and Suwanee as per statement to you Dec. 24, 1866	$7,669 00
Bill of powder now on hand	12,424 43
	$20,093 43

or, in Mexican Bonds at 60c., $33,489.65, or rather $33,500.

Be pleased to send me an order for the above amount of bonds, so that I may pay the same, and return you a receipt for said amount. Mr. Dupont also inquires whether his old claim, copy of which I sent you Oct. 19th and 20th may be paid yet.

    I am, Sir, very respectfully,
        Your obedient servant,
                H. STURM.

Romero to Sturm.

[Translation.]

No. 213.] WASHINGTON, January 6, 1867.

MEXICAN LEGATION IN THE U. S. OF AMERICA.

Mr. Lerdo de Tejada, Minister of Foreign Affairs of the Mexican Republic, in his note No. 541, of the 5th December last, communicates to me certain instructions from the President, that I may make no further purchase of arms and ammunition for bonds, and that I should withdraw any authorization which I might have given to any party to that effect.

Said order binds me to confirm my previous orders which, in anticipation of these instructions I had given you, not to enter into any new contract to that effect; but as I must honor such contracts as in accordance with your instructions you may have already perfected or so far carried through, that it would not be possible to ignore them without serious damage, I entreat you to tell me in answer which goods you have already definitely purchased, and which are those goods you have contracted for in terms that can not be rescinded and which it will not be possible to drop without damage, the amount of which you will oblige me by stating.

I renew to you the assurances of my most distinguished consideration,
                                M. ROMERO.

To General H. STURM,
    New York.

Romero to Sturm.

[Translation.]

No. 214.] WASHINGTON, January 6, 1867.

MEXICAN LEGATION IN THE U. S. OF AMERICA.

I have your communication of yesterday in which you enclose the account of Messrs. Dupont de Nemours & Co., and in answer, I remit to you an order on Messrs. J. W. Corlies & Co., for $33,500 in Mexican Bonds, that you may settle the accounts expressed therein.

You may say to Messrs. Dupont de Nemours & Co., that I have not yet received the decision of my Government in regard to the payment of their old account, in the manner which they desire.

I repeat to you the assurances of my most distinguished consideration.

M. ROMERO.

To General H. STURM, New York.

Romero to Sturm.

No. 215.] WASHINGTON, January 8, 1867.

General H. STURM,
  New York.

Dear Sir: In my official letter of this date I ask you for the list of the goods you have on hand, and those already contracted for, when the negotiation can not be abandoned without inconvenience. My idea is that while obeying the instructions from my Government to afford the speedy acquisition of 10,000 muskets with their accoutrements, which I understand you have contracted for, and the powder and percussion caps, I have authorized you to get all the balance of the list you left with me in your last visit to Washington, should be omitted if possible.

I am, very respectfully,
  Your obedient servant,
   M. ROMERO.

N. B. The reference of the Senor to an official letter of January 8th, 1867, is an error. He evidently means one written January 6th, 1867. H. STURM.

Romero to Sturm.

[Translation.]

No. 216.] WASHINGTON, January 9, 1867.

MEXICAN LEGATION IN THE U. S. OF AMERICA.

In answer to your note of the 5th inst., in reference to the charter of the steamer Everman, I must say that it strikes me that said steamer has been delayed more than three months in her coming back. After she had been unloaded it was evident that she was not wanted for any other purpose, and the absence of General Carvajal, or any other Government official who should receive the goods, was an obstacle merely to Mr. Stocking's formal delivery of said goods; but it was in no way an obstacle to the coming back of the steamer, contracted to carry said goods to the Rio Grande, which had then been done.

On said grounds, I asked you for information, and have asked from Matamoras about the circumstances of the steamer's detention. As long as I do not receive all the information, I can not assume the responsibility to pay a charter for so lengthy a time, and the amount of which is almost equal to the value calculated for the vessel itself, when, according to my judgment, it has been altogether unnecessary to detain her so long.

I repeat to you that I am disposed to pay at once one month's charter, withholding my determination as to the balance, till I ascertain who is the party responsible for the extraordinary detention of the Everman.

I remain, very respectfully,
Your obedient servant,
M. ROMERO.

To General H. STURM,
New York.

Romero to Sturm.

No. 217.] WASHINGTON, January 9, 1867.

Gen. H. STURM,

Dear Sir: I answer your letter of the 5th inst. In my official communication of to-day you will see the reason why I do not think it was necessary at all to detain the Everman, when its cargo was landed and under Mr. Stocking's care. I am very sorry that you take such an opposite view of the case, that you even believe the owners have a righteous claim for damages, besides the full charter money they claim, I suppose.

As soon as I receive the full information I want, all will be settled in an equitable manner.

As for the Sheridan, it is inevitable to wait for the official report of her having been duly received; as soon as we have it, the payment will ensue

I return to you Mr. Simons' letters.

I am, dear Sir, yours very sincerely,

N. B. The foregoing had no signature. H. STURM.

Sturm to Romero.

No. 218.] NEW YORK, January 10, 1867.

Senor M. ROMERO,
Mexican Minister, etc.

Sir: I have the honor to acknowledge the receipt of your letter, dated Washington, January 6th, enclosing an order on Messrs. John W. Corlies & Co., for $33,500, Mexican Bonds, for the purpose of paying Messrs. Dupont de Nemours & Co., the amount of their claim for powder furnished to the Mexican Government. As soon as said order is accepted by Messrs. Corlies & Co., I will pay said amount to Messrs. Dupont & Co., and return you the proper voucher.

I shall state to Messrs. Dupont & Co. what you say in your letter in regard to their old claim.

I am, Sir, very respectfully,
Your obedient servant,
H. STURM.

Sturm to Romero.

No. 219.]

TAYLOR'S HOTEL,
JERSEY CITY, N. Y., January 14, 1867.

Senor M. ROMERO,
Mexican Minister, etc.

Sir: At the request of General Sturm, I have the honor to state that he has received your communications of the 6th and 9th inst., and that he will answer the same as soon as he is enabled to do so. He also desires me to state that he has paid to Mr. David Smith and to Messrs. Dewhurst & Emerson, the amount of bonds you remitted him, and has notified Messrs. Hall & Ruckel and Dupont de Nemours & Co., that he is ready to pay them.

He has also settled with and paid Mr. John T. Wright, Jr., for the charter of the steamer Vixen, after having sold to him the provisions and stores left over from the expedition, for which he has received, upon appraisement made, the sum of five thousand six hundred and fifty dollars in Mexican Bonds, and fifteen hundred dollars in cash, which latter amount he says, he is to be charged with. The proper vouchers will be sent to you at an early date.

The General has been quite prostrated by serious illness the last four days; but feels better to-day, and hopes to be out again and able to attend to business in a day or two.

I am, Sir, very respectfully,
Your obedient servant,
J. R. McCOMB,
For Gen. H. STURM.

Romero to Sturm.

[Translation.]

No. 220.]

WASHINGTON, January 18, 1867.

MEXICAN LEGATION.
IN THE
U. S. OF AMERICA.

Mr. Manuel Saavedra writes me from Matamoras, under date of the 4th inst., that Gen. Escobedo received the goods that were at Brownsville in charge of Mr. Stocking, (a receipt whereof said gentleman signed, as you are aware) having said gentleman paid five thousand dollars gold, that said amount be credited to the Government on the account you shall produce here, since he refused altogether to approve the bill of charges that was presented to him, as he deemed it exorbitant.

Mr. Saavedra tells me at the same time that Gen. Escobedo had also received some arms that were at Roma, and that he had paid for them another sum, but he was not aware of the details of said transaction. I therefore communicate this information to you that you may ask Mr. Stocking for the vouchers relating thereto.

M. ROMERO.

I repeat to you the assurances of my most distinguished consideration.
To General H. STURM,
    New York.

Sturm to Romero.

No. 221.]   NEW YORK, January 19 1867.

Senor M. ROMERO,
    Mexican Minister etc.

I have been quite ill for the last ten days, and yesterday for the first time I was out of my hotel. I do not feel quite so well to-day, but hope to be able on Monday to attend to outside business. Since I saw you in Washington the last day of the old year, I have been able, in conjunction with my brothers and other friends, to raise the necessary means to obtain a vessel for myself. My original intention, as you will recollect, was to either buy or hire a sailing vessel, but upon careful reflection, considering the circumstances, dangers, and delays incident to a sailing vessel, I have deemed it more prudent and safe, in a business view, to engage a steamer.

The steamer I have is small (225 tons) but fast, and well suited for the purpose, from New Orleans and along the Mexican coast. I was not able to purchase her at the present time, and furnish, equip, and run her a length of time. I have therefore made a contract very advantageous to myself, according to which, upon my paying in advance the money required for wages of the crew for the time of which she is chartered, the owners have agreed to furnish everything that may be necessary to run said vessel for three hundred and forty days, and have placed her under my absolute control, giving me the power to select and appoint my own officers and crew, thereby relieving me from all the trouble and annoyances heretofore attending chartered vessels.

I am now ready to carry out the project I laid before you the other day, and although fully aware of the pecuniary responsibility of the undertaking, I feel quite hopeful and confident that I can make it advantageous to the Government and myself by transporting all material required by the Government, and at the same time carrying such private freight as I may be enabled to obtain through Mexican friends, or as I may be able to procure for myself.

I shall run this vessel between New Orleans and Mexican ports in possession of the Liberals, so as to establish a regular line of communication. I shall be ready to send this vessel on her first voyage on or about the 5th of February and whatever goods there may be to ship from New York, I shall have no difficulty in sending to New Orleans for trans-shipment.

I would now ask you to furnish me with such letters to the proper officers in Mexican ports as will assist this enterprise, and also, if you deem it expedient, that you will inform the Government of this movement.

I shall take the first opportunity to see you and make full and permanent arrangements for the future.

My desire is, if I can obtain the necessary means, to run two vessels constantly, instead of one, although for the first few months I feel assured it will be unprofitable. I hope the facilities this will give to Mexican citizens to obtain supplies, will after a while, establish a trade that will remunerate me for my outlay and risk.

The vessel has comfortable accommodations for thirty cabin passengers, which may help to pay expenses.

I am, Sir, Very Respectfully,
Your obedient servant.
H. STURM.

Sturm to Romero.

No. 222.]   NEW YORK, January 19, 1867.

Senor M. ROMERO,
Mexican Minister, etc.

I have the honor to state that I have settled with Capt. Wright for the charter of the steamer Vixen. You are aware that some of the stores furnished by me to said vessel were left over, after her discharge. My first intention was to reserve these stores for a future occasion, but found it impossible (owing to their being somewhat damaged and partially used) to obtain anything like a reasonable price for them. I therefore had the stores appraised by a competent person, and have deducted nearly their full value as per original cost, from the amount of charter money due Capt. Wright, in my settlement with him.

This arrangement was made in consequence of his written refusal to deliver up these stores on my order, he claiming that all stores that were left over from the voyage became the property of the ship.

This action on his part has caused much trouble and some expense, and as there is nothing in the charter party that can possibly be construed, entitling the ship to any of the stores, I therefore adopted the most advantageous way (for the Government) to settle this difficulty by charging the ship with said stores, after an appraisement was made.

Enclosed please find the account of John T. Wright, jr., fully receipted for by him, by which you will see that after deducting for detention and provisions sold him, there was a balance due him of $61,600, Mexican Bonds, which I have paid him.

In addition to this I have sold Mr. Wright such of the engineer's stores as were left over, for which he has paid me the sum of ($1,500) fifteen hundred dollars currency, their actual value. This amount you will please charge me with. I herewith enclose you the necessary vouchers.

Hoping my action in the premises will meet your approval,

I remain, Sir,
Your very obedient servant,
H. STURM.

Sturm to Romero.

No. 223.] NEW YORK, January 19, 1867.

Senor M. ROMERO,
Mexican Minister, etc.

Sir: I have the honor to enclose herewith receipts of Merritt, Walcott & Co., Dewhurst & Emerson for seventy-six thousand, five hundred and fifty dollars, Mexican Bonds, and also receipt of David Smith for fifty-nine thousand, seven hundred and fifty dollars, Mexican Bonds.

These amounts were paid the several parties on account of goods sent by them to Matamoras, and receipted for on the 24th of November last by Senor Manuel Saavedra.

I am, Sir,
Respectfully yours,
Your obedient servant,
H. STURM.

Sturm to Romero.

No. 224.] NEW YORK, January 19, 1867.

Senor M. ROMERO,
Mexican Minister at Washington, D. C.

Sir: I have the honor to state that I am in receipt of a letter from Messrs. Dupont de Nemours & Co. in answer to my letter advising them of my readiness to pay them the amount of bonds due them for powder delivered. Mr. Dupont, in his letter, declines to receive the bonds unless he at the same time can receive the amount due him on his old claims, (copies of which I transmitted you in my letter of October 19, 1866) without waiting for a reply from the Mexican Government.

Mr. Dupont has attached all the powder I now have on hand in the magazine near this city, and will not deliver it unless his claim is settled. Under these circumstances, and as I am very anxious to send this powder at first opportunity, I would respectfully ask you, in case you do not feel at liberty to settle this old claim of his until you have heard from the Government, to place at my disposal some bonds, charging the same to me on my private account, and I will pay this old claim myself, and wait the action of the Government.

The reason why I am so very anxious about this matter is: *first*, because Mr. Dupont has been very liberal and quite willing to furnish me with what powder I needed for Gen, Baranda and others, without first waiting for a settlement of his old claim. *Secondly*, Because Mr. Dupont is a very influential and prominent man, and can, and no doubt will, do a great deal of good for our cause

Be pleased to let me hear from you in regard to this matter.

I remain,
Yours very truly,
H. STURM.

Romero to Sturm.

[Translation.]

No. 225.]   WASHINGTON, January 21, 1867.

MEXICAN LEGATION IN THE U. S. OF AMERICA.

I have received your communication dated the 19th inst. enclosing two receipts from Mr. Wright, one for the price of the steamer Vixen, and the other for $1,500, the price of certain engineer's stores that you sold to him. I am acquainted also that in consequence of the difficulties raised by Mr. Wright to give back the goods that remained on board after the unloading of said steamer, you resolved to deduct from the price of freight the value of said goods, after they had been valued by an expert, which in consequence reduced the amount to $61,600 in bonds, which you delivered to him as the balance of his account.

As to the $1,500 received by you for the engineer's stores, I charge that to your account as you indicate to me.

I repeat to you the assurances of my most attentive consideration.
M. ROMERO.

General H. STURM,
New York.

Romero to Sturm.

[Translation.]

No. 226.]   WASHINGTON, January 21, 1867.

MEXICAN LEGATION IN THE U. S. OF AMERICA.

I have received your communication of the date of the 19th inst., in which you enclose me two receipts, one from Mr. David Smith for forty-nine thousand, seven hundred and fifty ($49,750) dollars, and the other from Messrs. Merritt, Walcott & Co., and Dewhurst & Emerson for seventy-six thousand, five hundred and fifty ($76,550) dollars, both of these accounts, as you say to me, are for the goods sent to Matamoras, and which were receipted for on the 24th of November last by Senor Don Manuel Saavedra.

I repeat to you the assurances of my most distinguished consideration.
M. ROMERO.

General H. STURM.
New York.

Sturm to Romero.

No. 227.] NEW YORK, January 22, 1867.

Senor M. ROMERO,
    Mexican Minister, etc.
        Washington, D. C.

Sir: I have the honor to acknowledge the receipt of your two letters of the 6th and 9th inst., in the former of which, you asked me for a list of stores purchased, and so far contracted for, and that should paid; in the last letter you gave me your opinion in regard to the charter of the steamer Everman.

In answer, allow me to state my exceeding regret, owing to sickness, my inability sooner to reply to these letters.

Enclosed I send you a statement of such articles as I have positively purchased, and have already in my possession. All these articles came through Mr. Ames and other friends, (excepting the coats and tents, which are from Schuyler, Hartley & Graham, and have already been paid for,) and before receiving them were thoroughly inspected, and new and of excellent quality. The amount still due and unpaid is $227,559, exclusive of boxes, for which, I wish you would send me an order, so that I can settle this amount with Mr. Ames and friends; and at the same time authorize Mr. Navarro to approve this account.

In regard to the other goods mentioned in the list furnished you December 31, I have to say, that I can do as you may direct in the matter, as I can avoid taking these goods without difficulty. No new contracts or purchases have been made by me.

In regard to the steamer Everman, I shall carry out the instructions in your letter.

I am ready now, as soon as the bills for goods are settled, to ship them at once from here to New Orleans, and thence to such places on the coast of Mexico as you may designate.

    I am Sir, very respectfully,
        Your obedient servant,
                H. STURM.

Sturm to Romero.

No. 228.] NEW YORK, January 22, 1867.

SENOR M. ROMERO,
    Mexican Minister, etc.
        Washington, D. C.

Sir: I have the honor to acknowledge the receipt of your letter of the 18th inst., in which you advise me that General Escobedo has paid to Mr. Stocking $5,000 in gold, to be credited to the Government.

In answer, I wish to say, I will attend to this matter as soon as Mr. Stocking, who is now on his way to this city, arrives.

    I am, Sir, very respectfully,
        Your obedient servant,
                H. STURM.

American and Mexican Commission—No. 676.

Romero to Sturm.

No. 229.]   WASHINGTON, January 22, 1867.

GEN. H. STURM,
   New York.

Dear General: I am in receipt of your favor of the 19th inst., in which you explain your scheme about some steamers to be run from New York and New Orleans to the Mexican ports in possession of the Liberals.

As you announce that you will come and see me before the 5th of February, I reserve to talk with you on your plan, for that opportunity.

I am very glad that you have recovered, and hoping you will in future enjoy better health, remain,
            Dear General,
                  Yours truly,
                        M. ROMERO.

Romero to Sturm.

[Translation.]

No. 230.]   WASHINGTON, January 22, 1867.

MEXICAN LEGATION IN THE U. S. OF AMERICA.

I have received yours of the 19th inst., with the communication concerning Messrs. Dupont de Nemours & Co., in which they refuse to deliver the powder which you have contracted for, unwilling to receive its price, until their old credit against the Mexican Government is settled. With pleasure, I would immediately place at your disposal the bonds necessary to cover this old credit, but I have sent an account of the affair to my Government, and I hope to receive a reply in answer from it every day. If this should not be received when we need the powder, I will give to you on my own responsibility, the bonds which you require to settle the old credit.

I repeat to you the assurances of my attentive consideration,
                        M. ROMERO.

General H. STURM.
   New York.

Sturm to Romero.

No. 231.]   NEW YORK, January 23, 1867.

SENOR M. ROMERO,
   Mexican Minister, etc.
      Washington, D. C.

Sir: I have the honor to state that I have received your two letters of the 21st inst., in which you acknowledge the receipt of the vouchers of Merritt, Walcott

& Co., $76,550; David Smith, $49,750; also vouchers of J. T. Wright, $61,600; and that you have charged me with the $1,500 cash that I received from Mr. Wright.

I am, Sir, very respectfully,
Your obedient servant,
H. STURM.

Sturm to Romero.

No. 232.]

NEW YORK, January 25, 1867.

Senor M. ROMERO,
Mexican Minister, etc.

Dear Sir: I am in receipt of your communication of the 22d inst., in reference to the old claim of Messrs. Dupont de Nemours & Co. In reply thereto, I would respectfully say, as I am very desirous to retain the good will of our friends, that in the absence of instructions, I will endeavor to conciliate the settlement by making personal arrangements for the present, as will meet with their approval.

From your private and kind note to me, I see that you expect to see me in your city about the 5th of February; This I think is hardly possible, for the reason that my time is so much occupied in perfecting arrangements in endeavoring to dispatch my vessel on her first trip on the 5th proximo, and forwarding the goods for the Government. Mr. Stocking also is expected here daily, and I must see him, to close out all that old transaction. As no further purchases will be made for the Government after the goods now on hand have been sent to Mexico, it is of course not necessary for me to remain here, and it is therefore best to close up every transaction that I have made for the Government, which I shall try to do as far as possible.

Will you be kind enough now, to give me your idea about my proposition, and also to communicate to me whether you have as yet determined to what point the goods now on hand shall be sent. The sooner we send the clothing to Mexico, the more serviceable it will be to the troops, as now is the coldest season, and the most need for them there.

I am so much better now that I can attend to all my outside business again, but shall take care for a few days yet.

I saw Messrs. Schuyler, Hartley & Graham to-day; they have the rifles ready for us they say, but it would be well for you to instruct me as soon as possible what to do, as I have no doubt (as mentioned in my letter of the 22d inst.) that I can readily avoid taking them if you desire it, without causing very bad feeling.

Yours truly,
H. STURM.

Romero to Sturm.

[Translation.]

No. 233.]

WASHINGTON, January 25, 1867.

MEXICAN LEGATION IN THE U. S. OF AMERICA.

I have received your telegram of to-day, stating that "one million of Woodhouse's bonds were offered at almost nothing" and that you had seen them. Such being the case, please send at once a copy of one of said bonds, with full description of them, and all the details you can get about their printing, negotiation, and everything conducive to the investigation of the fraud.

I seize this opportunity to renew to you the assurances of my consideration.

M. ROMERO.

General H. STURM,
New York.

Sturm to Romero.

No. 234.]

NEW YORK, January 28, 1867.

Senor M. ROMERO,
Mexican Minister, etc.

Sir: Your letter of the 25th inst., wherein you ask me to send you one of the fraudulent bonds, was not received until to-day.

Owing to the publication of Mr. Mariscal's card, all these bonds, it seems, have been suddenly and mysteriously withdrawn from the market, so that I have been unable to obtain one for you to-day, but shall try to do so to-morrow. There is, however, one of these bonds in the hands of Corlies & Co., who will, no doubt, send it to you after the return of Mr. Tifft.

I understand that Mr. Woodhouse is very bitter against you for thus interfering with him, and now threatens openly to have nothing more to do with the Juarez Government, but will throw all his immense wealth and influence (???) in favor of Ortega or Maximilian, he does not yet know which.

I am, Sir, yours truly,

H. STURM.

Romero to Sturm.

No. 235.]

WASHINGTON, February 1, 1867.

General H. STURM,
New York.

Dear Sir: I have received yours of the 25th ultimo. Since you say that it is hardly possible for you to come on the 5th, as you had previously announced, you had better write out your proposition about the steamer, showing what you want to do, and what you desire me to do in your behalf; so that there is an official statement of your plan, to which I will answer, letting you know what I can do in the premises.

I do not think it necessary, under the circumstances, to take the rifles from Messrs. Schuyler & Co. So you should try and avoid taking them, as you suggest, without causing any bad feeling.

Yours sincerely,

M ROMERO.

Sturm to Romero.

[Private.]

No. 236.] JERSEY CITY, February 4, 1867.

Senor M. ROMERO.

Dear Sir: I have received your letter of the 1st inst., in which you desire to me to write you fully about the proposition in regard to running some steamer to Mexico, in order that you submit the proposition to your Government.

Before writing you officially in regard to this matter, I would prefer to give you an outline of what I propose to do, and what I desire in compensation for the risk accompanying the enterprise. It is my purpose to run one or more steamers between the United States and such ports in the Republic of Mexico as may be in possession of the Liberal Government, for the purpose of facilitating the Government in obtaining supplies of material of war and other articles necessary to its support and maintenance, at regular periods, and also at fixed reasonable rates of transportation; and also for the purpose of maintaining regular mail communication, and facilities for the transmittal of dispatches and the transportation of its officers.

Under present circumstances, considering the situation of affairs in Mexico, this undertaking, on my part, is a precarious one, as I well understand: still I desire to make the effort, and with proper assistance from yourself and your Government, I believe I can establish and maintain regular communication between the two Republics. This arrangement, as you will perceive, must result in much benefit to the Republic of Mexico.

In order that this arrangement may be made practicable and reasonably profitable, it is necessary that certain special privileges and facilities may be extended to me by the Government of Mexico, as, for instance, the privilege of retaining, for my own use, such portion of the carrying capacity of the vessels as may not be required and used for the transportation of goods belonging to the Government; and that I may be permitted to carry such goods, as I may take for my own private account, into the Republic free of all duties; and that all moneys or merchandise, which I may receive in payment for said goods, shall also be free from all duties. Also, that my steamers may be allowed to enter and clear, from any Mexican ports, free of custom house and port charges. These privileges and facilities to be extended for a specified time, to be agreed upon.

I regret that I am not able to personally see you, but Mr. Ames is here, and to-morrow I have an interview with Messrs. Cattell & Simons, and at the same time I am waiting the movements of General Crawford, who, as I now feel confident, is plotting mischief in connection with General Santa Anna, and I can not leave here at present without (as I believe) injury to the good cause; but I have requested Mr. Stocking, who is bearer of this letter, and who has my confidence in everything, to explain to you more fully my views. Be kind enough, therefore, to tell him what facilities I can obtain, should I undertake the above proposed enterprise, and on what conditions you think these facilities could equitably be granted.

Mr. Stocking will also explain to you all that has occurred at Matamoras during the past six months.

    I am, Sir, very respectfully,
      Your obedient servant,
           H. STURM.

Romero to Sturm.

No. 237.]   WASHINGTON, February 7, 1867.

General H. STURM,
  New York.

Dear Sir: I am very sorry to hear that Mr. Simons and Mr. Cattell, from Philadelphia, have been dissatisfied with me, and even have thought that I was not acting in good faith towards them. I thought you had explained matters to them in such way as to dispel any doubts that they might have about my good faith.

To-day Mr. Cattell brought me two bills for the charter of the Suwanee, and, to my surprise, they are both approved by you. One of them is for sixty days of a charter of the steamer, and the other for fifty-six days. When you spoke to me about the charter of the Suwanee, you left in my mind the impression that you had just chartered the steamer. I ask you to-day, officially, explanations on this subject, and I will be very much obliged to you if, at your earliest convenience, you send me a statement of the case; besides, sending to me your report in writing.

I think it would be policy that, at your earliest convenience, you should visit this city to speak about this and other subjects.

I have not received yet Mr. Stocking's report, and will be obliged to you if you send it me as soon as possible.

    In great hurry,
      Respectfully,
           M. ROMERO.

Romero to Sturm.

[Translation.]

No. 238.] WASHINGTON, February 8, 1867.

MEXICAN LEGATION IN THE U. S. OF AMERICA.

Mr. Elijah G. Cattell, of Philadelphia, has presented to me a contract for a charter of the steamer Suwanee for sixty days, signed by you on the 11th day of July, 1866, and renewed on the 26th day of September following for ninety days. Mr. Cattell at the same time presented me two accounts for the charter of said steamer for the sixty days on the first contract, and fifty-six days for the second, dated 1st of October and 21st of November last, which accounts both have your approval at the bottom.

Lastly, Mr. Cattell presented me a copy of the powers which General Carvajal intended to confer upon you, so that you might purchase certain articles in this country.

General Carvajal, as well as myself, stated to you at different times that the Government of Mexico had made known to him that it was an indispensable requirement in order that the acts of said General be valid and obligatory, they must first have my approval, without which they would have no value. In approving the commission conferred on you by said General Carvajal, I imposed various restrictions, contained in the instructions which I gave you on the 19th of August, 1866, in which, according to clause 9, I state to you expressly, "that the contracts which you make in the name of the Mexican Government should be approved by me in person." In view of the statements which you gave to me, that I might withdraw that condition, I altered it, on the 23d of August of the same year, in the manner following: "When you believe that there would be time lost in obtaining my approval you can solicit that of the Consul General of the United States of Mexico, resident in your city, and that his acts would have the same effect as mine."

All the contracts that you have made in the name of the Mexican Government, and which have been submitted under said instructions, have been and will be respected by me, but those which you have made separate from these conditions can not be considered as valid.

The contract for the charter of the steamer Suwanee is one which appears to me as being made under the second case. You made the same without my cognizance or approbation, and at a time when it appears there was no necessity for said vessel, since said vessel laid idle without being used for one hundred and sixteen days. When she was used, it was only for the purpose of losing her with her cargo on board.

I remember that in a conversation which you had with me, shortly before the departure of the Suwanee, you told me the vessel was chartered only a few days before, but that Mr. Cattell had arranged with you to charge for said vessel only from the day of her sailing, or a little before. After this I can not understand why you signed the accounts of said vessel for one hundred and sixteen days, and approved this account without considering this circumstance. For the purpose of deciding what ought to be done in this case, it is necessary that you furnish me information how this occurred, and I beg you therefore to remit the same as soon as possible.

I repeat to you the assurances of my most distinguished consideration.

M. ROMERO.

General H. STURM,
New York.

Romero to Sturm.

No. 239.] WASHINGTON, February 9, 1867.

General H. STURM,
New York.

My Dear Sir: In answer to your letter of the 4th inst. I have to state that I lack powers to grant any exemption of duties or port charges; so that it would be necessary to apply to the Government for such grant as you contemplate in connection with your scheme.

Nevertheless, in the first trip, and possibly in some other single voyage, we might arrange that the price of transportation of the goods belonging to the Government should be paid or compensated with the duties of other merchandise on your account or the port charges for the vessel.

I am, dear General,
Yours very sincerely,
M. ROMERO.

Romero to Sturm.

[Translation.]

No. 240.] WASHINGTON, February 10, 1867.

MEXICAN LEGATION IN THE U. S. OF AMERICA.

I have received to-day your note of yesterday, with which you forwarded to me the report rendered to you on the 8th inst., by Mr. Wilbur F. Stocking, about the manner in which he disposed of the cargo of arms and war ammunition sent to Matamoras, on board the steamer Everman.

The rebellion, which unhappily broke out in Matamoras on the 12th of August last, impeded the safe delivery of said cargo into the hands of the Mexican authorities, and the incident which interposed made Mr. Stocking assume responsibilities of a nature, which it does not come into my province to determine about.

When the Everman left New York you acted under instructions, which you had from General Carvajal, and which, as you are aware, required my approval to make them binding on the Mexican Government. If the cargo had arrived safely, and had not been paid for by General Carvajal, I would not have hesitated in making here the payment in bonds, in accordance with the relative contracts, as I have already done with regard to the arms that were delivered to Mr. Saavedra, commissioner of General Escobedo; but what has transpired gives a different aspect to this matter, which I don't believe it to be my duty to assume the responsibility of determining anything about. Mr. Stocking went to Matamoras as your special commissioner, and proceeded with regard to the cargo with the same independence as if it had been his private property. The result has been undoubtedly better for Mexico than if the whole cargo had been left in the hands of Don Servando Canales, but whether it was impossible to attain a yet better result, is something which can only be determined by data, which I have not, and which the Government of the Republic may easily acquire.

In virtue of these considerations, I can not come to the conclusion to pay for the goods that were not delivered to the Mexican authorities, until I know the resolution of my Government on this point.

Meanwhile, I will pay for the goods that Mr. Stocking delivered to Mr. Laing, commissioner of General Viesca, Governor of the State of Coahuila, when you send me the receipt of them, together with the proper vouchers as to the authority intrusted to Mr. Laing by General Viesca.

I repeat to you the assurances of my consideration,

M. ROMERO.

To General H. STURM,
New York.

N. B. The foregoing letter was received by me February 14th. Senor M. Romero made a mistake in the date of it, as my letter, to which it was sent in reply, was not mailed in New York until the evening of the 10th inst., consequently it could not have reached him until the following day, the 11th inst. H. STURM.

Sturm to Romero.

No. 241.] JERSEY CITY, February 11, 1867.

Senor M. ROMERO,
Mexican Minister, etc.

Sir: I have the honor to acknowledge the receipt of your letter of the 8th inst. in which you ask for an explanation why I signed the two certificates for the charter of the Suwanee, and in which you state that you are not aware of this charter; that it has been made without authority, and is therefore invalid.

In reply, allow me to state that I did this for the following reasons:

1st, Because Mr. Simons demanded them of me at once, at that very time, and I could not refuse, as it was a positive fact, which the owners could have proved at any time without such certificate, as they had the original charter party in their possession.

2d. Because, after a consultation with Mr. Tifft, it was concluded that such a certificate could not affect the rights or position of the Government so far as any claims are concerned which the Government might have against the parties, or which they might have against the Government. I signed it to date November 21st, 1866, this being the day on which Messrs. Cattell & Simons agreed with me to execute a new charter, according to which they promised to relinquish (considering that the vessel to that time had been awaiting orders) ninety days of their claim. I so stated to you in Washington on the 3d day of November last, also subsequently to Dr. Navarro. As I was compelled to go to Boston and did not return until after the sinking of the Suwanee, this agreement was not put in writing. I can not see, however, how you can be under the impression that the contract for the Suwanee was made without your cognizance (as I understand from your official letter.) By referring to my letters of August 2d, 7th, 14th, and 25th; September 10th, and subsequent ones, you will see that I stated that the vessel was ready and partially loaded, and I was expecting to send her off from week to week, but was delayed by reason of unforseen difficulties, and particularly on account of the revolt at Matamoras. I also, on the 8th day of August sent you, with other papers, a copy of the charter of the Suwanee. Subsequently, on the 24th day of September, while in Washington, I asked you whether it would not be best, considering that it was intended to send out two more expeditions, to retain the steamer for a longer term, if Mr. Cattell was willing, as it would be difficult to obtain a steamer for bonds, under the then existing state of public feeling. In reply you said you thought it would, and I at once telegraphed to Mr. Cattell asking him, "Will you extend charter three months." I received a reply to this on the same day in the following words:

"Have no objection to extend charter three months.
"E. G. CATTELL."

I reported this to you on the same day before leaving Washington, and you expressed yourself pleased. I presume that in the multiplicity of your duties these details for the moment have escaped your memory.

Under the existing circumstances I would suggest that a speedy and amicable settlement of this matter would be best for the interests of all parties concerned.

It is, however, impossible for me, in the present state of my health, to come to Washington. I will, however, execute any wish you may have in the matter, as I can have Messrs. Simon & Cattell come here at any time.

In regard to the other points contained in your letter above referred to, I will reply at the earliest possible moment that my health will permit.

I am, Sir, very respectfully,
Your obedient servant,
H. STURM

[1st Copy enclosed in No. 241.]

PHILADELPHIA, November 21, 1866.

The Republic of Mexico,
By Gen. Herman Sturm, Agent,
To Elijah G. Cattell, Dr.

To fifty-six (56) days' service of steamer Suwanee from 26th Sept., 1866, 12 o'clock noon, to the 21st November, 1866, at 12 o'clock noon, as per charter party between Elijah G. Cattell and Gen. H. Sturm, agent of the Republic of Mexico, at the rate of eight hundred ($800) dollars per day.. $44,800.

The above amount is correct as per charter party made on the 11th day of July, 1866.

PHILADELPHIA, Nov. 24, 1866.

H. STURM, Agent.
For the Republic of Mexico.

(Given Feb. 4, 1867, to Mr. Simons.)

[2d Copy enclosed in No. 241.]

PHILADELPHIA, October 1, 1866.

The Republic of Mexico,
By Gen. Herman Sturm, Agent,
To Elijah G. Cattell, Dr.

To sixty days' service of steamer Suwanee from 28th July, 1866, 12 o'clock noon, to 26th Sept., 1866, 12 o'clock noon, as per charter party between Elijah G. Cattell, and Gen. Herman Sturm, agent of the Republic of Mexico, at the rate of $800 per day...................................... $48,000.
Certificate of service of W. J. Taylor appended hereto.

I hereby certify that the above account is correct and just, as per charter party made on the 11th day of July, 1866.

PHILADELPHIA, October 1, 1866.

H. STURM, Agent.
For the Republic of Mexico.

(Given Feb. 4 to Mr. Simons.)

Sturm to Romero.

No. 242.] JERSEY CITY, February 11, 1867.

Senor. M. ROMERO,
Mexican Minister, etc.

Sir: Mr. Ames has just notified me that he will be here either to-morrow or the next day, and is anxious to have his accounts settled for the goods that I have purchased of him and his friends. A list of these goods I remitted you on the 22d day of January.

I would respectfully ask you to instruct Dr. Navarro to approve the Ames' accounts. The goods, as you are aware, have been in my possession since December, and I am myself very anxious to get all these old accounts settled.

I am, Sir,
Very respectfully,
Your obedient servant,
H. STURM.

Sturm to Romero.

No. 243.]   JERSEY CITY, February 12, 1867.

Senor M. ROMERO,
   Mexican Minister, etc.

Dear Sir: I yesterday replied to your questions in regard to the reasons why I signed the certificates for the Suwanee. I regret exceedingly that I did not notify you at once of having given these certificates, but it is done, and what harm can they do? It certainly was in accordance with the facts in the case, and although the owners agreed to make a new charter, they afterwards refused to do so, and whatever claim the Government may have against them can certainly not be injured by these certificates. I am very sorry that the accounts for the Everman have not been settled, for if they had been, there would have been no reason for these gentlemen to feel angry, and consequently this matter would not have been pressed on us as it is.

Mr. Simons and Mr. Cattell both wrote to me, saying you told them you had written to Dr. Navarro about their claims, and that they must be approved by him. I saw the Doctor to-day, but he has not yet received instructions from you in regard to this matter.

Be pleased now to write to me as soon as possible, what you think ought to be done, and I will do everything I can in this matter.

There is one thing about this whole matter that I do not like; and that is, that you take the ground (if I understand you correctly) that all the first arrangements required your *written* approval, or that of Dr. Navarro, as well as those made after the 19th of August, or after I was officially notified that General Carvajal had ceased to be Governor of Tamaulipas. I never understood this so; on the contrary I have always believed that whatever I did upon a consultation with you and with your knowledge and consent, was right. If this is not so, I think you ought to have informed me of this *distinctly*, and ought also to have signed the first contracts made by me under General Carvajal's positive instructions.

You are fully aware that my whole soul was wrapped up in the success of your Government. You know that I saved Carvajal and the Government from the hands of that scoundrel Woodhouse, and that my efforts have always been directed to introduce good honest men to him, thereby saved him from disgrace in this country, and the Government certainly a great deal of trouble and expense; and I have also spent my own means to assist the officers of your Government in this country, when they had but few friends, until I have no more to give, and have gone into debt on account of it, believing always in the success of your Government; and such a terrible misunderstanding in regard to my position and authority ought therefore not to exist, and the sooner it is settled the better it will be for all of us.

Be kind enough, therefore, to write to me whether you have in your possession a copy of the powers conferred on me by General Carvajal, and if you have not I will remit to you a copy at once. General Carvajal assured me (so did Mr. Zarco and others) that a copy had been forwarded to the Government, and as it is now nearly two years (during which time I have left family and honorable and lucrative position) since I first undertook to assist the Government, it is high time that I have my position distinctly defined.

Feeling assured that you will see the justice of this, and hoping to hear from you soon,

I remain in the most friendly spirit,

Yours truly,

H. STURM.

Romero to Sturm.

[Translation.]

No. 244.] WASHINGTON, February 12, 1867.

MEXICAN LEGATION.
IN THE
U. S. OF AMERICA.

I have received the communication which you directed to me, under date of yesterday, in answer to mine of the 8th inst., in which I ask for information about the charter of the steamer Suwanee, which was presented to Mr. Cattell. You tell me that under the date of the 8th of August you sent to me the contract of the charter of the said steamer, and that there must be some mistake in the matter. In the communication of the 7th of August (numbered 8), you admit to me the charter of the Everman, but not the one of the Suwanee, which contract can not be found in the archives of this Legation; was totally unknown to me, and I had not seen it until Mr. Cattell presented the same to me.

I remember that at different times you told me that you could obtain, at any hour that it might be necessary, a steamer in Philadelphia; but I understood that you had the facility to close a contract for a charter whenever said steamer should become necessary; and I never could imagine, nor did you tell me clearly, that you had celebrated a contract for a charter in order to hold said vessel in Philadelphia for entire months.

My desire to save my Government from unnecessary expense, which you should have understood, could not allow you to believe that I would sanction the payment of $800 dollars per day for a vessel while it was not in the service, and during whole months.

In business of this kind, it is impossible to proceed without sufficient data. In order that I should approve the contract of the Suwanee, I should have seen the contract; but I was totally ignorant of it until a little while ago. What I have said to you in familiar conversation, under the supposition that this was not the state of affairs, can not be taken as approbation of a fact totally different.

I reiterate to you the assurances of my consideration.

M. ROMERO.

To General H. STURM. New York.

Romero to Sturm.

No. 245.] WASHINGTON, February 14, 1867.

General H. STURM,
  New York.

Dear Sir: Your favor of the 12th inst. was received yesterday. It would be very difficult to explain to you in a letter all the reports about which there seems to be a misunderstanding between us; and the best plan is, in my opinion, that you should come here as soon as your health will permit it.

I have no copies of the orders given to you by General Carvajal, and you will oblige me by giving me copies of them.

I asked, on the 8th instant, Consul Navarro's report of the charter of the Suwanee, and on the 10th instant I received his answer. I have nothing further to say to him on the subject.

With a view to have this matter settled, I have asked professional advice from a very distinguished lawyer of this city, and in two or three days I expect to have his written opinion. In the meantime neither Mr. Cattell, nor Mr. Simons, nor Senator Cattell have come to press me for an answer to their claims.

I have had no time to take up your letter in regard to Mr. Ames' goods, but will do so in two or three days.

In great haste,
  I am, Sir, very respectfully,
    Your obedient servant,
      M. ROMERO.

Romero to Sturm.

No. 246.] WASHINGTON, February 16, 1867.

General H. STURM,
  New York.

Dear Sir: Dr. Navarro tells me, with yesterday's date, that you stated to him that the charter of the Everman amounts to $80,857.79, and not to $173,190, as you had stated. He further says, that you will explain this to me should I ask for an explanation. I will like to have any explanation you can give, under the circumstances.

Mr. Tifft informed me, this morning, that you had a sick child, which might cause you to go to Indiana. I really hope he will recover; and you will be able to come to Washington.

In great haste,
  I am respectfully yours,
      M. ROMERO.

Sturm to Romero.

No. 247.] JERSEY CITY, N. J., February 16, 1867.

SENOR M. ROMERO,
    Mexican Minister, etc.

Sir: I have the honor to acknowledge the receipt of your letter, dated February 10th, in which you acknowledge the receipt of Mr. Stocking's report; and in which you communicate to me that you can not assume the responsibility of paying for the goods which I purchased under the authority given me by General Carvajal, and which, with your approbation, I sent to Matamoras, until you can hear from your Government in regard to this matter, except so far as those goods are concerned which were actually receipted for by the Mexican authorities.

In answer, allow me to state that I have communicated your determination in this matter to the parties who sold these goods to the Government, and who, since the return of Mr. Stocking became known to them, have pressed me daily and almost hourly for a settlement of their claims. They insist that the goods sold by them were delivered, according to the terms of their contract, to General Carvajal, and that the Government ought to be responsible for any loss or damage caused by a disaffection and revolt of Mexican officers, over which they had no control; and they also insist that they are in no wise responsible for whatever Mr. Stocking may have done in the matter, he being an agent for the Government.

I enclose herewith a communication received from Mr. Gilson in regard to this matter, also copy of letter received from them February 8th, and my answer thereto. With other parties interested, I have had only verbal communications.

I have the honor, Sir, to be very respectfully,
    Your obedient servant,
        H. STURM.

Sturm to Romero.

No. 248.] JERSEY CITY, N. J., February 16, 1867.

Senor M. ROMERO,

Dear Sir: Your note of yesterday and the one of the 11th inst. received. I told Dr. Navarro this, that the amount due for the charter of the Everman, (as stated in your letter to him $134,750) was only $80,857 currency, or in *bonds at sixty cents*, was equivalent to $134,750. The total amount due to Mr. Simons for Everman, Sheridan, etc., being $173,190 currency. I called his attention to this difference, as from your letter he seemed to have the idea that it was $134,750 currency.

It is true that my child is very sick, but I can not go home now, much as I desire it, until our matters are definitely settled.

I would come on to see you, but I am troubled with a disease of the kidneys, and lately have been much worse, so I am afraid to undertake the trip to Washington, but will try to do so soon. Should you, however, have occasion to visit this city, I would be very glad to see you, and in *one hour* we could determine what to do. One thing, however, ought to be done at once, that is, to settle with Mr. Ames and his friends, as soon as you conveniently can do it.

I notice that you write to me that you intend to do so in a few days, but it ought to be recollected that I have had the goods since December last, and these gentlemen do not understand why their accounts can not at least be approved, since I have stated to them they would be. Dr. Navarro of course could not do so without positive instructions from you, and therefore I write to you on the subject; and also because this is another transaction which I have entered into in consequence of a personal understanding with you, but without your written orders. I am having copies made of the powers conferred on me by General Carvajal, and shall send them to you; but I must confess that I have been very much astonished to hear from you that General Carvajal neglected to furnish you with such before his return to Mexico, particularly as he informed you that he had given me a draft on the house of Corlies & Co. for two million five hundred thousand dollars in bonds, for the purpose of purchasing certain supplies, and defraying the necessary expenses incurred to send them to Mexico.

Yours truly,
H. STURM.

Romero to Sturm.

No. 249.]   WASHINGTON, February 18, 1867.

General H. STURM,
New York City.

Dear Sir: I beg to introduce Col. Enrique A. Mexia, just arrived from Mexico, as a Commissioner from General D. Paron, Commander of the Northern Line of Vera Cruz State. I will write you some instructions relative to Col. Mejia's mission. In the meantime he will confer with you.

Very sincerely yours,
M. ROMERO.

Romero to Sturm.

No. 250.]   WASHINGTON, February 18, 1867.

General H. STURM,
New York.

Dear Sir: General Baranda writes to me, under date of Tlacotalpam, January 19th, 1867, that on delivering the cargo of the Vixen to a Commissioner of the State of Oaxaca, one box, containing musket wipers, was missing; and he thinks it was left in New York on account of the hurry of the loading. Please inform me if such case was left, or what you know about it.

I am, dear Sir,
Sincerely yours,
M. ROMERO.

P. S. General Baranda says the missing box was marked with No. 8.

Sturm to Romero.

No. 251.] JERSEY CITY, February 20, 1867.

Senor M. ROMERO.

Dear Sir: Your letter of yesterday came to hand to-day. There was left behind, of the goods delivered for General Baranda's expedition, the following articles: One box of carbines and twenty-five boxes of ammunition. The latter were left because the Erie Railroad Company could not deliver the same until two days after the time the vessel sailed, and as your instructions were to send the vessel at once, I promised General Baranda to send them as soon as possible.

All these articles have been taken care of by me, and are now safely stored and subject to your orders. The clothing for General Baranda is also stored and waiting orders. The General must, however, be mistaken as to the box of wipers, as the box now here is marked 8.

I think now that I will be able to come this week to Washington to see you.

I am, Sir, yours truly,

H. STURM.

Sturm to Romero.

No. 252.] JERSEY CITY, N. J., February 20, 1867.

Senor M. ROMERO,
    Mexican Minister, etc.

Sir: I have the honor to herewith enclose copies of the powers conferred on me by General Jose M. J. Carvajal, dated respectively March 1st, 1865; March 11th, 1865; July 4th, 1865 (two orders); August 25th, 1865; January 5th, 1866, and May 15th, 1866. In addition to these, General Carvajal, in May, 1866, furnished me with copies of the powers conferred upon him by the General Government, duly approved as correct by the Consul General, Juan N. Navarro, under date of May 16th, 1866. He also gave me at the same time a copy of the certificate given him by you.

I also enclose for your information copies of two letters, sent by me to Mr. Stocking and General Carvajal under date of August 22d, 1866.

Very respectfully,
    Your obedient servant,

H. STURM.

Romero to Sturm.

No. 253.] WASHINGTON, February 21, 1867.

General H. STURM,
    New York City.

Dear General: I have just received your two letters of yesterday, one enclosing powers of General Carvajal, and the other informing me of the goods that were left behind after General Baranda's expedition. Besides the copies you have sent, please forward to me those of the instructions given by the Government to General Carvajal, with the certificate of Dr. Navarro, and also mine.

Very sincerely yours,

M. ROMERO.

Memorandum of an Interview with Senor Romero.

No. 254.] February 24, 1866.

Saw Mr. Romero at 11 A. M. Begged him to pay Dupont & Co. as promised. He declined to do this, and also to pay Messrs. Simons, Cattell, and others interested in first shipments. He said he had nothing to do with Carvajal's transactions, and had consulted Mr. Cushing about the matter. As soon as he should have his opinion or hear from his Government he would inform me. I told Mr. Romero I had a steamer in view to take the goods I had relieved him from, to Mexico, and asked his opinion as to the best place to ship them to. He thought Tampico or Alvarado would be good places, and if I should ship to either place he would give me letters there to assist my agents, and if I should take out some Government goods free, I should be relieved from all duties on my ship or cargo.

I made another attempt to convince Mr. Romero of the propriety of paying Dupont & Co., but he said if he had not written his Government about it he would pay, but now he would not until he heard from home.

Sturm to Romero.

No. 255.] WASHINGTON, February 24, 1867.

Senor M. ROMERO,
Mexican Minister etc.

Sir: I have the honor herewith to transmit the bill of Messrs. Dupont de Nemours & Co., amounting to thirty-three thousand five hundred dollars in Mexican Bonds. Said bill is properly receipted for by Mr. T. L. Kneeland, the agent of Messrs. Dupont & Co., to whom I delivered the above stated amount of bonds, in accordance with instructions received from you.

I have the honor to be,
Very respectfully, your obedient servant,

H. STURM.

Romero to Sturm.

[Translation.]

No. 256.] WASHINGTON, February 25, 1867.

MEXICAN LEGATION
IN THE
U. S. OF AMERICA.

After having heard your explanations, and having maturely considered the affair relative to the cargo of the steamer Everman, I agree to pay for the goods taken by Don Servando Canales and his soldiers, which goods are shown in the documents marked "C" and "F" annexed to the report of Mr. Stocking.

As to the value of the goods sold at Roma, by Mr. Stocking and carried afterward to Tampico, and in general the rest the value of which is due to the original owners, I authorize you to use the price for which said goods have been sold by your agent, provided you agree in taking charge, to pay the creditors so as not to leave any claim pending against my Government, which you will be so kind as to send to me with the receipts which said creditors will give you.

I would be very glad if this arrangement determines you to conclude at once the affair alluded to.

I repeat to you the assurances of my most attentive consideration.

M. ROMERO.

General H. STURM,
New York.

Romero to Sturm.

[Translation.]

No. 257.] WASHINGTON, February 25, 1867.

MEXICAN LEGATION
IN THE
U. S. OF AMERICA.

By the present I authorize you to purchase as many as twelve million percussion caps, or the greatest possible quantity, the former one being the maximum. The price to be paid in bonds of the Mexican Republic, and the contract to be revised by Consul General Navarro in the same way as he had to do heretofore according to my instructions.

I repeat to you the assurances of my attentive consideration,

M. ROMERO.

To General H. STURM,
New York.

Sturm to Romero.

No. 258.]
TAYLOR'S HOTEL,
JERSEY CITY, N. J., March 3, 1867.

Senor M. ROMERO,
    Mexican Minister, etc.,
        Washington, D. C.

I have the honor to herewith enclose the following vouchers for goods shipped per steamer Vixen to Minititlan:

Bill of A. C. Campbell for carbines	$64,804 00
Bill of Mr. Whitfield for surgical instruments	3,000 00
Bill of Geo. M. Ramsay for caps, fuses	539 50

All of which bills are receipted in full; also receipt in full from

Hall & Ruckel for medicines sent per same steamer	460 97
Also a correct copy of bill of goods purchased of Schuyler, Hartley & Graham, for same steamer	87,187 79

The receipt for the bonds delivered to Messrs. Schuyler, Hartley & Graham in payment of the last amount you have in your possession. I send you these duplicate vouchers in place of those which I have heretofore forwarded you, but which you stated to me are not in your possession.

Be kind enough to acknowledge the receipt of these documents at your convenience.

        I am Sir, very respectfully,
            Your obedient servant,
                H. STURM.

Sturm to Romero.

No. 259.]
TAYLOR'S HOTEL,
JERSEY CITY, N. J., March 3, 1867.

SENOR M. ROMERO,
    Mexican Minister, etc.
        Washington, D. C.

Sir: I have the honor to report that I have made to Mr. Walter H. Gilson, agent for Messrs. Merritt, Wolcott & Co., and Messrs. Dewhurst & Emerson, a proposition to settle their account for goods sent to Matamoras per steamer Everman. The terms of this proposition, you will find in my letter bearing date March 1st, 1867, addressed to Mr. W. H. Gilson, agent, etc., accompanying this.

The terms I proposed to them are in accordance with my verbal understanding with you, and the letter of your instructions regarding this matter, contained in your order of the 25th ultimo. I also enclose herewith a copy of their reply to me, dated March 2d, 1867, from which you will see that they claim payment for the goods delivered to Mr. Pierce, to recover the cargo from the hands of Don Servando Canales, as also the payment for cash advances made by them for inspection, insurance, etc., in New York.

This latter claim I consider a just one, but so far as the goods are concerned, I submit the matter for your judgment as to its equity.

Should you accept their proposition the whole matter can be settled at once. In that case, please send me an order for the requisite amount of bonds, and I will obtain from them a receipt in full of all claims against the Government. The amount of money required to pay them according to their proposition is as follows:

For goods delivered to General Canales, and taken by his
troops and delivered to Mr. Laing.................................$21,031 50
For goods delivered to Mr. Pierce..................................... 13,912 00
For cash advanced for insurance, etc............................. 11,341 00

    Total..$46,284 50
Or in Mexican Bonds at 60c...$77,140 83
Or in even money.. 77,150 00

I enclose a statement herewith showing in detail the manner of proposed settlement for goods. Be pleased to communicate to me your views on this matter.

I am, Sir, very respectfully,
Your obedient servant,
H. STURM.

[Statement enclosed in No. 259.]

Statement of Articles to be paid for in Bonds to the credit of Walter H. Gilson, agent for Messrs. Merritt, Wolcott & Co. and Messrs. Dewhurst & Co.

STATEMENT.

A	155 Revolvers, at $18...................................	$2,790 00
"	500 Sabres, at $4.50.....................................	2,250 00
"	250 Cavalry Belts, at $2.10...........................	525 00
O	580 Rifles (Enfield), at $16.50......................	9,570 00
T	111,000 Rifle Cartridges, at $28....................	3,108 00
	29 Enfield Rifles, at $16.50.........................	478 50
	1,000 Pistol Cartridges, at $25.....................	25 00
	29 Paulins, at $40...	1,160 00
	250 Sabres, at $4.50.....................................	1,125 00
		$21,031 50

Statement of Cash received and remaining due for Goods sold.

Draft on New York (deducting sale of powder for account S. & R.),
    currency $4,746 37
Specie due from Tampico, $12,000 at 1.38 premium.......................... 16,560 00
Statement Q—Currency due from Mr. Pierce for sales 300 Rifles....... 3,000 00

                                                                               $24,306 37

Statement of Expenses incurred on account of Goods sold.

	COIN.	CURRENCY.
Aug. 31—Freight on goods from Brownsville to Brazos......	$760 68	
Oct. 18—Drayage and labor on goods to steamer to Brazos,	25 38	
Oct. 19—Freight on goods from Brownsville to Brazos......	206 00	
Sep. 12—Watchman and labor on goods at Brazos............	10 75	$22 00
Proportion of storage on goods from Aug. 19th, ⅓,	215 25	
Freights to Roma, and proportion of storage there, ¼..	526 27	
$1,744.23 coin reduced to currency at 1.38......................		2,393 02
Total..		$2,415 02

Statement of Goods which can not be paid for under this Agreement.

Statement B—	400 Enfield Rifles, at $16.50...............................	$6,600 00
	400 sets Infantry Accoutrements, at $4..................	1,600 00
	204,000 Rifle Cartridges, at $28...........................	5,712 00
Statement M—	120 Enfield Rifles, at $16.50...............................	1,780 00
	1,000 Infantry Belts, at 85c.................................	850 00
	1,000 Cap Pouches, at 80c..................................	800 00
	1,000 Bayonet Sheathes, at 75c...........................	750 00
	1,500 Haversacks, at 85c.....................................	1,275 00
	916 Cartridge Boxes, $1.60..................................	1,465 60
Total..		$21,032 60

Sturm to Romero.

No. 260.] JERSEY CITY, N. J., March 4, 1867.

Senor M. ROMERO,
    Mexican Minister, etc.

Sir: I have the honor to enclose herewith a copy of an account of goods purchased of Mr. Ames and other friends, the purchase of which has this day been approved by Consul-General Navarro, and he states to me that he will so inform you to-day.

The total amount of these purchases, including packing boxes, etc., is $229,461.44, U. S. currency, or in Mexican Bonds at 60c on the dollar, $382,450. These goods, as you are aware, were contracted for, and purchased by me before instructions were received to stop all purchases, and they have been in my possession since December 5th, 1866.

I would now respectfully ask you to send me an order for $382,450, Mexican Bonds, so that I may be enabled to pay for these goods.

Be pleased to state in your order the date of the coupons of said bonds.

As soon as I shall have paid for these goods I will remit to you the proper vouchers. Mr. Ames writes to me to-day that he will be here on Thursday of this week, expecting me to be ready then to close this tranpaction.

I am sir, very respectfully,
Your obd't servant,
H. STURM.

NEW YORK, March 4, 1867.

Bill of Goods bought of J. T. Ames and others.

Two thousand three hundred cavalry sabres at $7.50	$17,250 00	
One thousand two hundred engineer's swords at $6.00	7,200 00	
One officer's sword at $35.00	35 00	
Two cavalry at $7.50	15 00	
Two artillery sabres at $7.50	15 00	
Two engineer's swords at $6.00	12 00	
One hundred and thirty-six boxes at $3.00	408 00	
Freight and drayage	91 54	
		$25,026 54
One thousand five hundred infantry accoutrements at $4.50	6,750 00	
Two hundred and fifty cavalry accoutrements at $7.00	1,750 00	
One thousand cartridge boxes for infantry at $1.65	1,650 00	
Two thousand three hundred sabre belts (complete) at $2.25	5,175 00	
One thousand two hundred engineer's belts (complete) at $2.00	2,400 00	
		17,725 00
Two thousand Maynard's carbines at $30.00	60,000 00	
Two hundred thousand cartridges at $40.00	8,000 00	
Two hundred and forty packing boxes at $1.00	240 00	
Freight and drayage	170 00	
		68,410 00
Twenty-six thousand equipments at $4.50	117,300 00	
Three hundred and three cases and cooperage at $3.30	999 90	
		118,299 90
		$229,461 44

The above goods were contracted for and purchased by me before I received instructions to stop making purchases.

H. STURM,
Agent for the Republic of Mexico.

Sturm to Romero.

No. 261.] JERSEY CITY, March 4, 1867.

Senor M. ROMERO,

Dear Sir: I have tried for some days to obtain from Captain Bradford a copy of the report of the investigation in regard to the loss of the Suwanee, but have not, as yet, been able to get it, as the Captain is just now busily engaged in some investigations, but shall get it as soon as he has the time, when I will at once forward it to you. Col. Mejia saw me on Saturday and is to meet me again to-morrow, when he will give me a list of articles which he desires to obtain. I will then see what I can get and report to you.

Yours truly,
H. STURM.

P. S. Have you heard as yet from Mr. Cushing about the Everman?

H. S.

Sturm to Romero.

No. 262.]   JERSEY CITY, N. J., March 5, 1867.

Senor M. ROMERO,

Dear Sir: Enclosed please find a statement of articles which Col. Mejia desires to obtain, of those which I now have on hand; also a statement of such articles as he desires me to obtain for him, but which I will have to purchase for him.

Be pleased to give me your instructions in regard to this matter, and I will then see what I can obtain.

I am, Sir, very respectfully,
Your obedient servant,
H. STURM.

Statement of articles Required by Col. Mejia of those which I have now on hand.

One hundred and fifty sabres and belts.
One hundred and fifty cavalry accoutrements.
Six hundred engineer's swords and belts.
Six hundred infantry accoutrements.
Six hundred equipments.
Six hundred Maynard's carbines.
Six hundred cartridges for do.
Six hundred uniforms.
Six hundred great coats.
One hundred shelter tents for hospital.

Statement of Articles which Col. Mejia desires me to purchase for him.

Two three-inch rifled cannon complete.
Two mountain howitzers.
Six hundred rounds shot, shell, and cannister for each cannon.
Four hundred rounds shot shell, and cannister for each howitzer.
Eight hundred rifles.
One hundred cartridges for Enfield rifles.
Eight hundred sets equipments (complete.)

One hundred cartridges for Enfield rifles.
One hundred and fifty revolvers.
Six cartridges for revolvers.
One hundred pouches and belts complete for revolvers.
Fifty new commissioned officer's swords.
One hundred and fifty cavalry saddles complete.

Sturm to Romero.

No. 263.] NEW YORK, March 4, 1867.

Senor. M. ROMERO,
  Mexican Minister, etc.

Sir: I have the honor to acknowledge your communication dated Washington, March 6, 1867, in which you ask me to remit to you invoices of the goods purchased by me, together with the original approval of Dr. Navarro, Consul-General of the Republic of Mexico. I herewith transmit to you a correct copy of the four accounts, signed and approved by Dr. Navarro.

I was not aware, heretofore, that you wished to have me send you copies of such accounts, and with the original certificate of the Consul-General attached, but I shall hereafter ask Dr. Navarro to approve and sign all accounts for purchases made on behalf of the Mexican Government in *duplicate*, so that I may be enabled to send one to you and the *other* to the parties from whom the goods may be purchased.

You are aware, of course, that I notify every party with whom I am doing business for and on account of the Mexican Government, that according to instructions I have received from you, every agreement I may make on behalf of the Mexican Government must first be *approved* by and signed by you or the Consul-General of the Republic, before it is valid and binding on the Mexican Government, and therefore, to protect themselves, the parties are justly entitled to a copy of such agreement as I may make with them, with the original signature of the proper authority of the Mexican Government attached thereto.

I think it would be well, and I hereby respectfully ask you to inform Dr. Navarro to sign all contracts in triplicate, then I will have one contract for the parties interested, one for you, and one for myself, as it may save some difficulty in case any of these papers should be lost in transmitting them.

I am, Sir,
  Your very obedient servant,
    H. STURM.

NEW YORK, March 4, 1867.
Bill of Goods bouyht of J. T. Ames and others.

[No. 1.]

Two thousand three hundred cavalry sabres at $7.50.......$ 17,250 00
One thousand two hundred engineer's swords at $6.00..... 7,200 00

One officer's sword at $35.00	$35 00	
Two cavalry sabres at $7.50	15 00	
Two artillery sabres at $7.50	15 00	
Two engineer's swords at $6.00	12 00	
One hundred and thirty-six boxes at $3.00	408 00	
Freight and drayage	91 54	
		$25,026 54

[No. 2.]

One thousand five hundred infantry accoutrements at $4.50	$6,750 00	
Two hundred and fifty cavalry accoutrements at $7.00	1,750 00	
One thousand cartridge boxes for infantry at $1.65	1,650 00	
Two thousand three hundred sabre belts (complete) at $2.25	5,175 00	
One thousand two hundred engineer's belts (complete) at $2.00	2,400 00	
		17,725 00

[No. 3.]

Two thousand Maynard carbines at $30	$60,000 00	
Two hundred thousand cartridges at $40.00	8,000 00	
Two hundred and forty packing boxes at 1.00	240 00	
Freight and drayage	170 00	
		68,410 00

[No. 4.

Twenty-six thousand equipments for cav. and inf. at $4.50.	$117,300 00	
Three hundred and three cases and cooperage at $3.30	999 90	
		118,299 90
		$22,461 44

I hereby agree to exchange the Mexican Bonds paid for this account for others guaranteed by the U. S. Government, in case such guarantee be obtained.

H. STURM,
Agent for the Republic of Mexico.

According to the instructions received from the Mexican Legation, I hereby certify that Gen. Sturm has power to make the above contract, and it is valid and binding on the Mexican Government.

NEW YORK, March 4, 1867.

JUAN N. NAVARRO.

Sturm to Romero.

No. 264.]   JERSEY CITY, March 6, 1867.

Senor M. ROMERO,
    Mexican Minister, etc.

Dear Sir: Your letter of March 6 I have received, but you are a day ahead of me, all your letters being dated March 6, 1867. Of course this is a mistake, but I simply ask your attention to the fact to prevent error. I have been busy for the last few days to see what I could do in regard to paying the interest, and to settle the old accounts; also to obtain what Col. Mejia needs, and what you desired me to purchase. I hope to be able to purchase all these goods on reasonable terms. In regard to the charges for insurance, etc., of Mr. W. H. Gilson, I reply to you officially. By looking over the original file which I sent to you after the sailing of the steamer Everman, you will see that these charges are all specified, and I think they ought to be paid, in justice to the parties. I have no doubt that I shall be able to settle this very disagreeable matter to your satisfaction.

Very respectfully yours,
H. STURM.

Romero to Sturm.

[Translation.]

No. 265.]   WASHINGTON, March 6, 1867.

MEXICAN LEGATION IN THE U. S. OF AMERICA.

I have received your note, dated 4th inst., with the enclosed list of goods, and their prices, that you had bought before you received the order to stop purchasing. You tell me that Consul Navarro was to advise me that he had approved the contracts relating thereto; and said gentleman, under date 2d inst., tells me he has done so, writing the necessary note on the four invoices that relate to said goods; but as he does not state the prices, nor even the total sum approved by him, it is necessary you should send me a copy of each of said invoices, covered by Mr. Navarro's original approbation and signature. When this condition is fulfilled, I will attend to the payment of the bonds due to the sellers.

I reiterate to you the assurances of my attentive consideration,
M. ROMERO.

General H. STURM,
  New York.

Romero to Sturm.

[Translation.]

No. 266.]   WASHINGTON, March 6, 1867.

MEXICAN LEGATION IN THE U. S. OF AMERICA.

Your note of the 3d inst. came to hand, with a copy of a letter which you addressed to Mr. W. H. Gilson and a copy of the answer which this gentleman gives about my proposals to you for the settlement about the cargo of the Everman. I have already told you, and repeat it now, that I am ready to pay for the goods taken by Canales or his soldiers, and as to those which it is said were received by Mr. Laing for Governor Viesca, I shall be ready when I receive about this fact the official information which I have asked for.

As to the goods delivered to Mr. Pierce, as is said to save the cargo, I can not assume the responsibility of paying for them, but will await the resolution of the Government.

In regard to the money advanced by the sellers of the goods ($11,341), for inspection, insurance, etc, since this is the first notice which I have from you in the matter, I can not pay it till I get satisfactory explanations specifying what is the insurance referred to, what the other expenses were, and why timely advice of the same was not given to me.

If the parties interested agree to await the resolution of these points, I am ready to pay them immediately in bonds for the goods taken by Canales and his soldiers, and for those which were sold in Texas and went to Tampico, with the money which you have received and are about to receive as their price; always in case such creditors agree to take that as payment in full for the latter.

I renew to you my attentive consideration.

M. ROMERO.

To General H. STURM,
    New York.

Romero to Sturm.

No. 267.]   WASHINGTON, March 6, 1867.

General H. STURM,
    New York.

My Dear Sir: I have received your letter of the 3d inst., enclosing vouchers relative to the Vixen.

I am also in receipt of yours, dated on the 4th, and speaking of your interview with Colonel Mejia.

Mr. Cushing has not yet given his opinion about the cargo of the Everman, but I think he will do so in two or three days.

I answer you officially concerning other subjects.

Very sincerely yours,

M. ROMERO.

Do not omit sending me a copy, in English, of Gen. Carvajal's powers.

Sturm to Romero.

No. 268.]   TAYLOR'S HOTEL,
JERSEY CITY, March 7, 1867.

Senor M. ROMERO,
    Mexican Minister,
        Washington, D. C.

Sir: I have the honor to acknowledge the receipt of your letter, dated March 6th, in which you say that you are ready to pay for the goods taken by General

Canales and his soldiers, and also for those delivered to Senor Laing, as soon as I forward you the official receipt therefor.

The goods delivered to Mr. Pierce, you say you are not willing to assume the responsibility of paying for, until you have received the resolution of the Government in the matter.

In regard to the amount of $11,341, advanced for inspection, insurance, etc., you say that this is the first notice you have received from me of this matter, and ask of me explanations, and why timely advice was not given to you. In reply, I have the honor to state, that on the 8th day of August last, I remitted to you the contract made with Mr. W. H. Gilson, together with the bill of the goods, for which payment is now claimed by him. By referring to this bill, you will find all the items of expense in cash incurred by him for insurance, inspection, labor, etc. At the time I purchased these goods, I had not sufficient funds in my possession to defray these expenses myself, and I required him to advance this amount of cash, expecting to pay them in the same way as the goods might be paid for, and had the different items charged in the bill with the goods. Having remitted this bill as before stated, I, of course, believed you to be fully cognizant of the particulars. From your letter, however, I infer that you are under the impression that this is a new and separate charge. This, however, is not the case, but it is a part of the original bill, amounting to $176,624, currency.

I have the honor to be,
Very respectfully,
Your obedient servant,
H. STURM.

Romero to Sturm.

[Translation.]

No. 269. WASHINGTON, March 7, 1867.

MEXICAN LEGATION IN THE U. S. OF AMERICA.

I have your communication of yesterday, in which you send me one list of the goods which Col. Mexia wants of those you have on hand, and another, of those which the same Colonel desires you to purchase for him.

In answer, I have to say to you that the orders of the Government are very strict that all purchases for bonds must be stopped, and it is not possible for you to give to Col. Mexia anything, except of those which you now have on hand.

Of the articles which you have on hand, you may deliver to him the following: 200 Maynard carbines, 20,000 cartridges for the same, and 50 tents.

You may also give to him, if he should ask for it, a proportionate amount of the powder which you have in the magazine of Messrs. Dupont de Nemours & Co., advising me of the quantity beforehand, so that I may determine what is to be done.

I repeat to you the assurances of my attentive consideration.

M. ROMERO.

Senor General H. STURM,
New York.

Sturm to Romero.

No. 270.] JERSEY CITY, N. Y., March 8, 1867.

Senor M. ROMERO,
  Mexican Minister, etc.

Sir: I have the honor to herewith transmit copies of General Carvajal's powers, also copy of your certificate, which documents were given to me by General Carvajal in May last, before his departure to Mexico.

I have the honor to be, Sir, very respectfully,
  Your obedient servant,
  H. STURM.

Romero to Sturm.

[Translation.]

No. 271.] WASHINGTON, March 8, 1867.

MEXICAN LEGATION
  IN THE
U. S. OF AMERICA.

I have received your communication of the 6th inst. with the four invoices of goods purchased of Mr. Ames and others, which were approved on the 4th inst. by Consul Navarro.

Enclosed herewith you will find an order (a draft) on Messrs. Corlies & Co., in order they deliver to you three hundred and eighty-two thousand four hundred and fifty ($382,450) dollars in Mexican Bonds, with which you will pay the amount of said goods.

I renew to you the assurances of my consideration.
  M. ROMERO.

General H. STURM,
  New York.

Sturm to Romero.

No. 272.] TAYLOR'S HOTEL,
  JERSEY CITY, N. J., March 18, 1867.

Senor M. ROMERO,
  Mexican Minister, etc.
    Washington, D. C.

Sir: At the request of General Sturm, I write you to inform you that the General left this morning for Boston, having been called there by a telegraphic dispatch. He will probably return to-morrow. He was compelled to leave immediately upon receipt of the dispatch, and could not write you, but desired me to say, that he had strong hopes of accomplishing something toward the payment of the interest on the coupons due in April.

The General has been so occupied trying to pacify the parties interested in the cargo of the Everman, that he had not time to make the statement as you requested regarding the Woodhouse swindle.

Immediately upon his return, he will forward it to you.

I have the honor to be, very respectfully,

Your obedient servant,

WILBUR F. STOCKING.

Romero to Sturm.

No. 273.] WASHINGTON, March 12, 1867.

General H. STURM,
Jersey City.

Dear Sir: I have received Mr. Cushing's opinion on the several points submitted to his examination. As regards Mr. Cattell's claim for the charter of the Suwanee, Mr. Cushing's opinion is that he is not entitled to anything. I sent yesterday to Mr. Cattell a copy of that opinion.

I take up and decide as soon as I can the other cases.

Respectfully,

M. ROMERO.

Romero to Sturm.

No. 274.] WASHINGTON, March 14, 1867.

General H. STURM,
Jersey City, N. J.

Dear General: I have received your favor of yesterday, informing me that you can not obtain for bonds the goods for General Diaz. If you think there is no prospect of getting them, give up your efforts in that direction.

You speak to me of a private enterprise of yours to send some *materiel* of war to Tampico, to sell it there for cash, and you ask me if I can assist you in that undertaking. Please tell me in what way I could do it.

As for the plan of your brother to get a commission in our army, I send you the enclosed letter.

Very sincerely yours,

M. ROMERO.

Sturm to Romero.

No. 275.] JERSEY CITY, March 16, 1867.

Senor M. ROMERO,
Mexican Minister, etc.

Dear Sir: I have received your note, enclosing a letter of recommendation for my brother, for which please accept my hearty thanks. My brother is a good man, and has persistently tried to serve your Government, and I shall be very glad if I hear that he has at last succeeded.

I enclose you herewith a list of the goods which I desire to send to Tampico to sell for private account. I shall send them per steamer a week from to-morrow, I think. The parties who are furnishing me these goods are Mr. Ames and his friends, the Sharp's Arms Co., and some individual friends of mine. I have offered Col. Mejia free passage for himself, and I will also take all such goods as you may wish to send free of charge. All I ask of you in the way of assistance is, that this matter will be properly represented to the authorities there, so that no difficulty may occur, and that I may be allowed to take these goods there free of charge, and also get my money out free, and obtain such assistance from the officers there, as they can grant me consistently with their duty to the Government.

These facilities have heretofore been given to men who are trading in arms, and as my goods are all of the first quality and *new*, and I can sell them either to the Government at very reasonable prices, or else to private parties. I believe the country will be the gainer by my operation. I would also like to hear any suggestions that you might be able to make to me, to further the success of this enterprise, as I of course desire that these arms shall go to such parties as are *beyond doubt* loyal. It may be possible that there is not money enough at Tampico to pay for all these goods; in that case, I should send them to such other place as you might suggest, or might be deemed advisable. The goods I am instructed to consign to the American Consul, and I would like to have your opinion about this.

I also send you to-day the authority of Mr. Laing, and his receipt for the goods at Roma, so that you may send me an order for the bonds requisite to pay for the goods, which you think you will agree to pay for in bonds. I am anxious to close all this matter.

In case you wish to send any goods by my steamer, please specify them, so I may get them ready.

Yours truly,
H. STURM.

Sturm to Romero.

No. 276.]   JERSEY CITY, N. J., March 16, 1867.

Senor M. ROMERO,
  Mexican Minister, etc.

Sir: I have the honor to herewith enclose the original authority of Senor Don Julio Laing, according to which he was empowered to receive on behalf of the Government, the goods which were left at Roma. I also enclose the original receipt which Mr. Laing gave to Mr. Stocking for these goods.

Be pleased to communicate to me at your earliest convenience, what decision you have arrived at, with regard to settling for the cargo of the steamer Everman.

Hoping to hear from you soon,

I remain, very respectfully,
Your obedient servant,
H. STURM.

Romero to Sturm.

No. 277.] WASHINGTON, March 17, 1867.

General H. STURM,
Jersey City.

Dear Sir: I enclose to you a copy of Mr. Cushing's opinion in regard to the charter of the Suwanee which has been communication by me to Mr. Cattell.

Respectfully,
M. ROMERO.

Sturm to Romero.

No. 278.] TAYLOR'S HOTEL,
JERSEY CITY, N. J., March 20, 1867.

Senor M. ROMERO,.

Dear Sir: I returned yesterday from Springfield, Mass., where I tried, in connection with other matters, to obtain some money to pay the interest due on the April coupons. So far, I have not succeeded, for reasons which I will explain to you verbally at some future time.

On my return, I received your note enclosing Mr. Cushing's opinion. Do me the favor to communicate this to me officially, so that I may answer the same.

Such an opinion could not have been formed from a proper knowledge of the facts in the case, and appears to me as a strained attempt upon his part to traduce my character, which the whole tenor and wording of his letter confirms.

This opinion having been communicated by you to Mr. Cattell, it places me in a false position, which my honor demands I shall rectify.

I have not as yet heard from you in regard to shipping my Government goods to Mexico. If you wish to have this done, please inform me at once, so that I may make my arrangements accordingly.

I have had a very severe letter from Mr. Simons, and I hope that this matter, as well as that of the cargo, will be settled very soon in some way.

Very respectfully yours,
H. STURM.

Sturm to Romero.

No. 279.] JERSEY CITY, N. J., March 21, 1867.

Senor M. ROMERO,
    Mexican Minister, etc.

Sir: I have the honor to enclose herewith the original receipt of Messrs. Hall and Ruckel, for two thousand eight hundred and fifty ($2,850) dollars Mexican Bonds, which amount you instructed me, on the 29th of December last, to pay to these gentlemen, for medical stores sent by them to Mexico, as a part of the cargo of the Everman. I have not succeeded in settling this account until to-day, as these gentlemen were dissatisfied with having the coupons dated November 24th, claiming that they are entitled to full interest.

    I am, Sir, very respectfully,
        Your obedient servant,
                H. STURM.

Romero to Sturm.

[Translation.]

No. 280.] WASHINGTON, March 22, 1867.

MEXICAN LEGATION IN THE U. S. OF AMERICA.

In consequence of the opinion given by Hon. Caleb Cushing in regard to the cargo of the steamer Everman, I have resolved, animated by a spirit of justice, to pay at once two-thirds of the amount due for same cargo, deferring to pay for the other third until my Government shall decide whether it is right to pay for the total amount, notwithstanding all the legal considerations presented by Mr. Cushing.

Herewith enclosed you will find a copy of this lawyer's opinion, which I beg you to communicate to Mr. Henry Simons, asking him whether he agrees to receive two-thirds of his claim. If so, I shall send you at once the order, that he may receive the proper amount of bonds.

I renew to you my attentive consideration.

                M. ROMERO.

To General H. STURM, New York.

Romero to Sturm.

[Translation.]

No. 281.] WASHINGTON, March 22, 1867.

MEXICAN LEGATION IN THE U. S. OF AMERICA.

I have received your communication, dated on the 16th inst, with which you accompany General Escobedo's order to Mr. Laing, to receive the arms and other goods that were in Roma, (Texas) and at the same time the receipt which that gentleman gave to Mr. Stocking for said articles.

As these documents are enough to prove officially that Mr. Laing received five hundred and eighty rifles in behalf of the Government, but not the rest, the receipt not specifying what it was, I enclose herein an order on Messrs. J. W. Corlies & Co. to deliver to you fifteen thousand eight hundred and fifty dollars ($15,850) in bonds, which amount is the value of said rifles, deferring to pay for the rest until the necessary vouchers are presented.

I renew to you my attentive consideration.

M. ROMERO.

To General H. Sturm,
New York.

Romero to Sturm.

[Translation.]

No. 282.]   WASHINGTON, March 26, 1867.

MEXICAN LEGATION   Please place at the disposal of Col. Enrique A. Mejia,
IN THE   Commissioner of Desiderio Pavon, Chief Commanding the
U. S. OF AMERICA.   third line of the State of Vera Cruz, besides the goods specified in my note of the 7th inst., two hundred sword bayonets for the carbines he will receive, and two hundred cartridge boxes from the goods you bought for the Mexican Government.

I repeat to you the assurances of my attentive consideration.

M. ROMERO.

To General H. Sturm,
New York.

Romero to Sturm.

No. 283.]   WASHINGTON, March 23, 1867.

General H. Sturm,
Jersey City, N. J.

Dear Sir: I have received your three letters of the 16th, 20th and 22d, the latter having been brought by Mr. Stocking.

I enclose you one letter for General A. Gomez, and another for Mr. Chase, which will enable Mr. Stocking to do his business. I can not specify the facilities they might give you there, but I generally recommend them to extend yo as many as they conveniently can.

If you do not succeed in the disposal of the goods at Tampico, I would suggest to take them to Alvarado or Matamoras.

As I don't know if the steamer will go to either of the latter ports, I can not improve your offer of conveying some goods sent by me on account of my Government, with the exception of those to be given to Colonel Mejia, on which I write to you separately. Were it not so, I could send some goods to Alvarado and some also to Matamoras.

When you decide the voyage of the steamer for any of these ports, I will give you letters for Mr. Stocking alike to that which he will take to Tampico.

In regard to your wish of having an official copy of Mr. Cushing's opinion, which you consider injurious to your character, allow me to tell you that I can not consistently, and that it is sufficient for you that I have a fuller knowledge of the facts than Mr. Cushing could have in what concerns you personally.

I remain, dear Sir,
Sincerely yours,
M. ROMERO.

I sent you yesterday, by mistake, a copy of a letter from Mr. Walker instead of Mr. Cushing's opinion, which is now enclosed. Please return that letter to me.

Romero to General A. Gomez.

No. 284.] WASHINGTON, March 23, 1867.

General ASCENSION GOMEZ,
Tampico.

My Esteemed Sir: Mr. W. F. Stocking goes to that place as agent of some manufacturers of arms and other materials of war of this country, carrying some articles of this kind to sell them on private account, and without myself or any commissioner of our Government having anything to do with this undertaking. Nevertheless, as I know Mr. Stocking and the persons for whom he goes to negotiate the said sale, to be friends of our cause, I recommend him to you, in order that should occasion offer for the purchase of his goods, because of his selling them at advantageous prices and on equitable terms, you will afford him the facilities that may be in your power, and which shall not be in opposition to the national interests, in order that the referred to undertaking may have good results.

I remain, as always,
Your very attentive friend
And obedient servant,
M. ROMERO.

NOTE.—This letter was returned to my brother some time in 1868.   H. STURM.

Sturm to Romero.

No. 285.]
TAYLOR'S HOTEL,
JERSEY CITY, N. J., March 31, 1867.

Senor M. ROMERO,
    Mexican Minister, etc.

Sir: I have the honor to herewith transmit four (4) vouchers, all properly receipted, viz:

Mr. J. T. Ames...	$41,700,	Mexican Bonds.
Mr. Gaylord...	29,550,	" "
Mass. Arms Co..	114,000,	" "
C. W. Mitchell..	197,150,	" "
Total amount...	$382,400	

This amount corresponds to the amount of bonds you placed at my disposal on the 8th of March, for the purpose of paying to these gentlemen the amounts respectively due to them, less fifty dollars of bonds left over and still in my hands. This discrepancy occurs in consequence of the fact, that in settling for these four accounts separately, I was unable, by paying in bonds, to make the exact change, and therefore I have adopted the rule to pay fifty dollar bonds only in case the account of the respective party exceeds the sum of twenty-five dollars; and so it happens that I have now in my hands, of the amount which you placed at my disposal, the sum of fifty dollors, Mexican Bonds, which you will please charge to me.

My account will, therefore, stand thus, viz.

Received March 8th, of Senor M. Romero..$382,450
Paid March 30th, as per vouchers... 382,400

    Balance due the Government in bonds.. $50

I have the honor to be, Sir,
    Very respectfully,
        Your obedient servant,
            H. STURM.

Romero to Sturm.

Gen. H. STURM,
    Jersey City.

No. 286.]   WASHINGTON, April 8, 1867.

Dear Sir: I have not heard from you for several days. Now that your steamer has left I suppose you are less engaged, and therefore will have leisure to finish your report of the Woodhouse affair. I would like to have this at your earliest convenience.

Gen. Berriozabal wishes me to send to Matamoras such part of the goods purchased from Mr. Ames as is intended for him. He would pay the freight at Matamoras on receipt of the goods. Do you think it possible to send them under such terms?

The balance of these goods are intended for Gen. Diaz, and I would prefer to have them sent to Alvarado.

As you know Gen. Garcia and Gen. Benavidez are there now blockading Vera Cruz. They lack heavy artillery, and I doubt very much whether they can take that place unless they are supplied with heavy artillery and the necessary ammunition. As the capture of Vera Cruz is of very great importance I have no doubt that they would be willing to pay well for any artillery that any enterprising party might take to Alvarado. If you should be willing to have any of your friends undertake this, let me know it. I can send all goods for Gen. Diaz. Gen. Baranda will be at headquarters of Gen. Garcia and Benavidez.

The Mexican Government has requested me to return the Sheridan to Mr. Simons, if this can be done. Mr. Mariscal has already written to Mr. S. on this subject, but as yet he has had no answer.

Mr. S. said to me that you had not communicated to him my determination about the charter of the Everman. I wish you would at once attend to the subject and persuade Mr. Simons that my proposition is the best thing he can have, and it would be useless to grumble and denounce everybody. He can have at once his bonds and wait for the answer of the Mexican Government.

I am, Sir, in great haste,

Your respectfully,

M. ROMERO.

Sturm to Romero.

TAYLOR'S HOTEL,
JERSEY CITY, N. J., April 9, 1867.

No. 287.]

Senor M. ROMERO,

Dear Sir: Yours of yesterday came duly to hand this morning, and I will at once see what I can do toward carrying out the suggestions you make.

I also, at the same time, received a communication from Mr. Henry Simons, dated yesterday, in which he says: "You will send me the two-thirds of the amount due for charter of steamer J. W. Everman, as you propose." Mr. Simon also says he wants full interest from October 1st, 1866.

Be pleased to send me an order for such bonds as you may desire me to pay to Mr. Simons, and I will attend to it at once.

I will send you my Woodhouse statement by to-morrow night. I would have sent it before, but was anxious to hear from Gen. Wallace before finishing it, as he was one of the principal parties connected with Gen. Carvajal in transacting the business with Woodhouse.

The General has telegraphed that he would write me fully, but I have not heard from him as yet.

Yours truly,

H. STURM.

Romero to Sturm.

[Translation.]

No. 288.] WASHINGTON, April 10, 1867.

MEXICAN LEGATION
IN THE
U. S. OF AMERICA.

Your favor of yesterday wherein you manifest to me that Mr. Henry Simons agrees on receiving the two-thirds of what he asks for charter of the steamer Everman according to my proposals is at hand.

Under this intelligence, and that Mr. Simons will give you a receipt for the whole amount of the charter, or expressing that the other third will be subject to the decision of the Mexican Government, I send you the enclosed order to Messrs. J. W. Corlies & Co. to deliver you in bonds $89,130, which is the equivalent at the rate of 60 per cent. of what Mr. Simons charges for the charter of the Everman. The coupons to be dated October 1, 1866, to pay Mr. Simons the interest he claims.

I repeat to you the assurances of my attentive consideration.

M. ROMERO.

To Gen. H. STURM,
    Jersey City, N. J.

Sturm to Romero.

No. 289.] TAYLOR'S HOTEL,
JERSEY CITY, N. J., April 12, 1867.

Dear Sir: Be pleased to communicate to me as soon as possible what proportion of the goods on hand you wish me to send to Matamoras. I think I shall be able, if the cargo is sufficiently large, to send these goods forthwith on condition that the freight for the same is paid on their arrival at Brazos where Gen. Berriozabal will have to receive them, and before I can make a definite arrangement for the price of freight, it is necessary that I know the exact quantity to be sent.

I am also trying hard to arrange matters for Gen. Diaz, and hope to be able to write more definitely about this in a few days.

Yours truly,

H. STURM.

Sturm to Romero.

No. 290.] TAYLOR'S HOTEL,
JERSEY CITY, N. J., April 12, 1867.

Senor M. ROMERO,
    Mexican Minister, etc.

Sir: I have the honor to herewith enclose the original receipt of Mr. R. J. Dewhurst for the sum of fifteen thousand nine hundred and fifty dollars, Mexican Bonds, this being the correct amount due Mr. Dewhurst for five hundred and eighty Enfield rifles delivered to Mr. Laing.

The order which you sent to me called only for fifteen thousand eight hundred and fifty dollars, being one hundred dollars less than the amount due to Mr. Dewhurst, an error which I detected, and corrected upon settlement of the account.

I am, Sir, very respectfully,
Your obedient servant,
H. STURM.

Romero to Sturm.

[Translation.]

No. 291.]   WASHINGTON, April 15, 1867.

MEXICAN LEGATION.
IN THE
U. S. OF AMERICA.

In answering your communication dated on the 12th inst., in which you inquire which are the goods I wish to send to Matamoras from those you have on hand, I must say that the articles I should like to remit to Gen. Berriozabal, the freight of which shall be paid for at its arrival at Brazos, as you wish to, are as follows.

Five hundred Maynard's carbines.
Fifty thousand metallic cartridges for the same.
Five hundred uniform overcoats.
Five hundred uniform coats.
Two thousand equipments.
Three hundred cavalry sabres.
Three hundred cavalry belts.
One hundred engineer's swords.
One hundred engineer's belts.
Five hundred infantry accoutrements.
One hundred tents.
Powder and caps as would be sufficient for five thousand men.

I renew to you the assurances of my most distinguished consideration.
M. ROMERO.

Gen. H. STURM.

Romero to Sturm.

[Translation.]

No. 292.]   WASHINGTON, D. C., April 17, 1867.

MEXICAN LEGATION.
IN THE
U. S. OF AMERICA.

When the vessel in which Mr. Fuentes will send some goods to Vera Cruz to General Benavidas will be ready, you will ship by her on account of the Mexican Government the following goods from those which you have on hand, consigned to the Chief commanding the Eastern Line:

One thousand Maynard carbines.
One hundred thousand metallic cartridges for the same.
One thousand uniform overcoats.
Two thousand uniform coats.
One hundred camp tents.
Ten thousand equipments.
One thousand two hundred cavalry sabres.
One thousand two hundred cavalry belts.
One thousand engineer's swords.
One thousand engineers belts.
One thousand infantry accoutrements,
Two hundred and fifty cavalry accoutrements.
One thousand infantry cartridge boxes.
One officer's sword.
Two cavalry swords.
Two artillery swords.
Two engineer's swords.
Powder and percussion caps for ten thousand men.

As I have some passengers for the vessel I beg you to tell me conveniently the day of her departure.

I reiterate to you the assurances of my most distinguished consideration.

M. ROMERO.

Sturm to Romero.

No. 293.]

TAYLOR'S HOTEL,
JERSEY CITY, N. J., April 18, 1867.

SENOR M. ROMERO,

Dear Sir: I send you this day the two copies of the "Woodhouse report," and also the letter of Mr. Henry Simons, which you sent to me.

In regard to the expense and delay on account of the steamer Sheridan, which Mr. Simons claims, I can not give an opinion, as I have no means of ascertaining their correctness; there is, however, no doubt but Mr. Simons has been put to expense in keeping this vessel at Brazos.

Mr. Simons will probably be here on Saturday, for the purpose of getting his bonds. I will then have some conversation with him in regard to the matter, and will then report to you.

It is *my* opinion, however, that it would be of greater advantage to the Government, particularly at the present time, to retain this vessel, as she can certainly be *very* usefully employed on the coast, and would do much toward ending this war, if properly manned and employed.

As soon as I am ready to send the goods that you have ordered me to ship, I will give you due notice of the same.

I am, Sir, very truly yours,

H. STURM.

Sturm to Romero.

No. 294.]
TAYLOR'S HOTEL,
JERSEY CITY, N. J., April 26, 1867.

Senor M. ROMERO,
  Mexican Minister, etc.

Sir: I have the honor to state that I have settled with Mr. R. J. Dewhurst, receiver for Messrs. Merritt, Wolcott & Co., and Dewhurst & Emerson, the account for that portion of the cargo of the steamer Everman, which was taken by Mr. Stocking to Tampico, and there sold by him.

As payment for these goods, I have just given to Mr. Dewhurst a draft for $6,146.36, which Mr. Stocking brought with him. Out of this draft Mr. Dewhurst has paid to Messrs. Smith & Rand the sum of $1,400, which amount was due to them for powder sent out in the Everman. In addition to this draft, I have given Mr. Dewhurst an order on Messrs. D. Holder & Co., of Brownsville, and Mr. Franklin Chase, of Tampico, for a certain draft of $12,000 specie, or thereabouts, this being the balance due on the arms sold at Tampico, and remaining in the hands of Mr. Chase, at the time of Mr. Stocking's return.

Enclosed please find the proper vouchers, according to which the Mexican Government and myself are released from any further responsibility, and from any and all claims which Messrs. Merritt, Wolcott & Co. and Dewhurst & Emerson have on that portion of the steamer Everman, shipped for sale to Tampico, Mexico.

I have the honor, Sir, to be very respectfully,
  Your obedient servant,
      H. STURM.

Romero to Sturm.

No. 295.] WASHINGTON, April 28, 1867.

General H. STURM,
  Jersey City.

Dear Sir: I enclose to you my letter for General Berriozabal stating what I have ordered to be sent to him. Please forward it by the vessel which will take the cargo.

I hear that General Wallace is in New York. I regret that I can not see him. Please ask him to write the report I begged of him long ago to prepare for me on the Woodhouse case.

I received yesterday your letter in regard to the settlement of goods sent to Tampico by Mr. Stocking.

In great hurry,
  Respectfully,
      M. ROMERO.

Sturm to Romero.

No. 296.] JERSEY CITY, N. J., April 30, 1867.

Senor M. ROMERO.

Dear Sir: Your letter of the 28th inst. has been received, enclosing one for General Berriozabal. I shall forward the letter to him by the vessel carrying the goods.

Enclosed please find an invoice of the goods that I sent to General Berriozabal, according to your orders, signed by myself. I also send you the written agreement of Mr. Woodhouse (owner of the vessel) for the freight charges on the above goods to Brazos, Santiago, both of which documents, or copies of them, if you prefer, I desire you would communicate to General Berriozabal for his information.

The charges, I have been informed, are very reasonable, and you will see that I have been very careful to stipulate that the goods are delivered at *Brazos*, either to Messrs. D. Holder & Co., or to any vessel that General Berriozabal may send to Brazos for the goods, free of any other charge except the freight charge mentioned, so that General Berriozabal may not be imposed upon by parties making charges for primage, which is customary.

General Berriozabal will have ample time to make preparations for receiving these goods at Brazos, but in case he should by some accident be prevented from doing so, Messrs. D. Holder & Co.—gentlemen well known to General Berriozabal—will hold these goods subject to his order.

Yours truly,
H. STURM.

Sturm to Romero.

No. 297.] TAYLOR'S HOTEL
JERSEY CITY, N. J., April 30, 1867.

Senor M. ROMERO.

Dear Sir: I have just received several letters from my brothers and Mr. Stocking, dated Tampico the 16th, 17th and 18th inst., and it is with the greatest sorrow I have to inform you that the news from Tampico is very discouraging indeed. The statements are, that when the vessel arrived there, Tampico was in a state of revolt. Gomez, although not yet having pronounced for anybody, had however, refused to obey the orders of President Juarez. He is controlled by a certain Gardet, who, being a bitter enemy of Colonel Mexia and General Pavon, and the friends of Juarez generally, had not allowed Colonel Mexia and party to land, and at the last advices (per letter of 18th inst.), Colonel Mexia was still on board the steamer, and General Pavon was momentarily expected to come on board for protection.

My friends expected to leave Tampico, and go to Alvarado, but Gomez would not allow the steamer to leave, but demanded as the vessel had cleared for Tampico, that the cargo should be discharged there, and has exacted heavy duties. Colonel Mexia, under the circumstances, of course is powerless to aid or protect my friends.

What the result of this trouble will be, I can not of course say at present, but I am apprehensive that it will tend to injure me very materially, as under the circumstances the goods can not be sold there, nor can they be taken away from there, as Gomez refuses to let the vessel proceed.

On the 18th inst., after hearing of the capture of Puebla, Gomez, probably being somewhat frightened, stated that before he would allow the vessel to proceed, or anything to be done with the cargo, he must first ascertain the determination of the Government in regard to the matter. This, of course, will take considerable time, and will cause me a great deal of expense.

Mr. Stocking and my brothers state that Mr. Chase told them that a letter from you, explaining what I have done for the Mexican Government, and that I have sent the Mexican officers and the Government goods aboard the steamer at my own expense, without expecting to charge the Government anything, etc., would influence Gomez in releasing the vessel and cargo, and to do me justice in the premises. Will you do me the favor, if it is not inconsistent with your position, to explain this fully to Gomez, and also to the Government. You will thereby confer a great favor on me; for it would indeed be a heavy blow to me, if this property should be lost.

It is very hard, and it makes me feel sad to see these continuous troubles in Tamaulipas, and I only hope that the Government may soon be in a position to quell these disturbances, and to punish the offenders.

I am, Sir, very truly yours,
H. STURM.

Sturm to Romero.

No. 298.]   JERSEY CITY, May 1, 1867.

Senor M. ROMERO,

Dear Sir: Your telegram of yesterday, asking me to insure with bonds, has been received, and to-day I tried to effect this, but find it impossible. I can, however, insure the cargo here at the regular rates, and have the premium collected at Brazos on delivery of the goods, in the same manner as the freight charges.

If you approve of this, please let me know, and I will effect it at once.

Yours truly,
H. STURM.

Romero to Sturm.

No. 299.]   WASHINGTON, May 1, 1867.

General H. STURM,
New York City.

Dear Sir: Your letter of yesterday has been received. I send to-day a copy of it and the two papers therein enclosed to General Berriozabal. A duplicate of my letter to General B. is herewith enclosed, with a view that you would send it to its address, in the way you think best.

I had yesterday a telegraphic dispatch from you, asking me if you should insure the goods sent to General B. I answered it at once, as follows: If it can be done with bonds at current prices, do so.

You will oblige me very much by asking General Wallace to make his report on the Woodhouse affair before he leaves New York, as I am very anxious to have it.

In great hurry,
Respectfully yours,
M. ROMERO.

Romero to Sturm.

No. 300.] WASHINGTON, May 2, 1867.

General H. STURM,
Jersey City, N. J.

Dear Sir: Yours of the 30th ult. is at hand, and contents noticed.

I am very sorry that such difficulties occur in Tampico; but think all will be settled favorably with the cheering news of the interior. I write with this date to General Gomez, according to your suggestion. Perhaps before my letter arrives the difficulties will have disappeared.

Yours very truly,
M. ROMERO.

Yours of yesterday at hand. I have no objections to your getting insurance to be paid at Matamoras. You may do it so.

Romero to Sturm.

No. 301.] WASHINGTON, May 10, 1867.

General H. STURM,
Jersey City.

Dear General: I remember having signed a promisory note to you for $700 in gold, which you advanced to Mr. F. D. Macin. Please let me know if you still keep it, to have it paid to you, and in case you have transferred it, tell the holder to apply to Mr. J. Fuentes, who will pay it in my behalf.

I am, dear Sir, very truly yours,
M. ROMERO.

Romero to Sturm.

[Translation.]

No. 302.] WASHINGTON, May 23, 1867.

MEXICAN LEGATION IN THE U. S. OF AMERICA.

I ask you to tell me if Mr. Simons received the bonds that I sent you some time ago to pay him the third part of the charter of the steamer Everman that he claimed.

If Mr. Simons has received those bonds, be so kind as to send me the corresponding receipt as you have done at other times; and if he has not, be so good as to explain to me the difficulties still pending for the settlement of that affair.

I repeat to you the assurances of my attentive consideration,

M. ROMERO.

Sturm to Romero.

No. 303.] NEW YORK, May 24, 1867.

Senor. M. ROMERO,
Mexican Minister, etc.

Sir: I have the honor to acknowledge the receipt of your official communication of yesterday, and in reply would state, that Mr. Simons has not as yet called for his bonds; for what reasons I know not. I have repeatedly notified him that the bonds are ready to be delivered to him upon his signing the proper vouchers for them.

I shall remit these vouchers to you, as soon as Mr. Simons signs them and receives his bonds, which I hope will be very soon.

I am, Sir, very respectfully,
Your obedient servant,
H. STURM.

Sturm to Romero.

No. 304.] NEW YORK, May 24, 1867.

SENOR M. ROMERO,

Dear Sir: I reply to your official letter to-day. As soon as I can get Mr. Simons to sign the vouchers for the bonds, according to your instructions, as per enclosed copy of receipt, I will pay over the bonds to him, and send you the vouchers at once; until this is done, or until you order me to do otherwise, I can not hurry this matter any.

I wish all the old matters could be settled definitely in some way, as the parties are calling on me daily, asking me for settlement of their accounts, which of course I have no power to do.

I had a dispatch from Mr. Stocking to-day, according to which, he will be here about Tuesday next. When he arrives, I will tell you all the news.

Yours truly,
H. STURM.

P. S. I have underscored the important part of the receipt.

Romero to Sturm.

[Translation.]

No. 305.]   WASHINGTON, May 25, 1867.

MEXICAN LEGATION IN THE U. S. OF AMERICA.

General Don Desiderio Pavon in his note, dated the 1st inst., tells me he received the goods sent on the steamer McCallum, with the exception of the 20,000 metallic cartridges for the carbines, which cartridges he says did not arrive in time to be shipped by you, but that he knew you were going to send them by the first ship going to Tampico.

Allow me to tell you that certainly you forgot to tell me that those cartridges had been left; and as the carbines, in my opinion, are of little use without them, I feel obliged to ask you to send those cartridges to General Pavon as soon as possible, if they have not been sent already.

I repeat to you the assurances of my most distinguished consideration.

M. ROMERO.

Romero to Sturm.

No. 306.]   WASHINGTON, June 4, 1867.

General H. STURM,
New York City.

Dear Sir: Your remarks on Saturday evening, as appeared in yesterday's "Herald," embarrass me very much, as you will readily understand.

I do not think they were opportune, as far as Mr. Seward was concerned.

I hope you will give a satisfactory answer to the enclosed letter.

In great haste,
Respectfully yours,
M. ROMERO.

Romero to Sturm.

No. 307.]   WASHINGTON, June 4, 1867.

General H. STURM,
New York.

Dear Sir: I have noticed in yesterday's "New York Herald," your remarks.

at a serenade tendered to you on Saturday last, as the Special Agent of the Liberal Government of Mexico, in your city, by several citizens of New York.

I regret very much that the tenor of your remarks is calculated to convey the impression that I share them in any. With a view to avoid misunderstandings, you will oblige me by answering the following questions:

1st. Whether you are an Agent of Mexico for anything but formally to make some purchases of supplies and war material, under certain conditions?

2d. Whether in your remarks on that occasion, you expressed my views in any way, or your own individual ideas, formed not through conversations with me, on public affairs relating to Mexico?

I am Sir, very respectfully,
Your obedient servant,
M. ROMERO.

Sturm to Romero.

No. 308.] NEW YORK, June 6, 1867.

Senor M. ROMERO,

Dear Sir: I have just received your two notes of the 4th inst., in one of which you ask me to reply to two questions propounded by you.

In reply I must say that I was very much surprised on reading the contents of your notes.

You know full well the position that I hold toward you and your Government, and the many sacrifices that I have made, and the arduous labors that I have performed during more than two years in aiding your Government, and the practical results arising therefrom in assisting to overthrow the so-called empire of Mexico, using, in the meantime, my own personal means and those of my family and friends to assist your Government and its officers in every way possible without having as yet received any benefit therefor whatever. It is therefore unnecessary for me to reply to your first question.

In answer to the second question, allow me to say that I can not see how anybody can hold *you* responsible for any remarks that *I* may choose to make.

The prominent officials connected with the Government of the United States in Washington fully understand my position as a citizen and former officer of this Government, and will of course accord to *me* the right to express *my own views whenever and wherever* I may choose to do so.

I regret, however, that *you* have been embarrassed in any way in consequence of the remarks *I* made last Saturday. Had I known beforehand that such a thing was intended by my friends, and particularly that what I did say in a private social circle in my own house, would be published and commented upon, and misinterpreted as it has been by the press, I should have prepared myself a little and spoken much more to the point than I have done.

About half-past 10 o'clock on Saturday night last, a party of merchants and members of several clubs of New York and Jersey City, all tried and staunch friends of your Government, called to congratulate me, *as a friend of your Government,* upon its recent successes. In reply, I stated to them that the success was not due, as has been lately claimed by several prominent papers, to any *active* interference on the part of, or any *material* aid given by the U. S. Government in behalf of Mexico, but was due solely to the determination and patriotism of the Mexican people, and the officers of its Government at home and *in this country*, and also to the efforts made in behalf of your cause by a few *American* citizens. I then said, that so far as the Government was concerned, while the President, Gen. Grant and other members of the Cabinet had always been friends of our sister Republics, Mr. Seward, as Secretary of State, had not shown himself as a friend *either to Mexico or any other* Republic on this continent, and that the fact that his nephew, Clarence Seward, and his intimate friend, Mr. Blatchford, had connected themselves with enterprises inaugurated under grants and franchises obtained from the so-called Emperor, Maximilian, had tended largely to sustain the Empire to the detriment of the Liberal cause, and that I regretted to see that our Secretary of State and a portion of the public press should *now* make strenuous efforts to save the life of Maximilian, while no such efforts had been made by them to save the lives of Cols. Arteaga, Salazar, and other noble Mexican patriots who were executed under Maximilian's bloody decree for the only crime of being true to their country. I then alluded to the fact that it was a disgrace to *us Americans* that we had no representative at the seat of the Mexican Government, and I declared it a great injury to the cause that Mr. Campbell was allowed to remain in New Orleans under the excuse of not being able to find President Juarez, etc., etc.

Now, my dear Sir, I have given you about the substance of what I said in regard to the points mentioned in your notes, and I think, it is high time, and *very opportune just now*, for the people of the U. S. to fully understand the difficulties under which your Government and your people have labored during the last five years, and the miserable policy that has been pursued toward our sister Republics.

In all my remarks, however, I spoke only *my own* sentiments, and without any reference whatever to what might or might not be *your* views on the subject.

Hoping that this reply will be satisfactory,

I am, Sir,

Yours truly,

H. STURM.

Romero to Sturm.

No. 309.] WASHINGTON, June 7, 1867.

General H. STURM,
New York.

Dear Sir: Your letter of yesterday has just been received. I see that you did not exactly understand the object of my letter to you on the 4th inst., and as I can not enter into any explanations in this letter, I will leave this matter for such time as I may have a conversation with you. You, as an American citizen, are of course perfectly free to express any opinion you think best on any subject.

You have not answered my question about whether the goods for Gen. Berriozabal have left or not. I am anxious to know it.

Your remarks have produced quite a sensation here.

In great haste,
Truly yours,
M. ROMERO.

Sturm to Romero.

No. 310.] NEW YORK, June 11, 1867.

Senor M. ROMERO,
Mexican Minister, etc.

Sir: I have the honor to herewith enclose to you the receipt of Mr. Henry Simons for eighty-nine thousand one hundred and fifty ($89,150) dollars, Mexican Bonds, in payment for two-thirds of the amount of the charter of the steamer Everman.

Mr. Simons objected to sign the receipt as drawn, but as it was drawn according to instructions received from you, I refused to pay him unless he so signed it.

I have been ready to pay Mr. Simons the above amount ever since I received your order for the bonds, and the delay in settling this account is to be attributed to Mr. Simons alone.

I am, Sir, very respectfully,
Your obedient servant,
H. STURM.

Romero to Sturm.

[Translation.]

No. 311.] WASHINGTON, June 11, 1867.

MEXICAN LEGATION.
IN THE
U. S. OF AMERICA.

Gen. Berriozabal tells me, under date of the 31st May last, that the steamer Sheridan, bought by you from Mr. Simons, with my approval, was received by the Mexican authorities of the frontier.

As the delivery is made I am under the obligation of paying the price of said steamer which, according to the contract agreed between you and Mr. Simons the 2d of last August, was ($88,000) currency, or in Mexican Bonds at 60 per cent.

You will find enclosed a bill to your order on Messrs. J. W. Corlies & Co., of New York, for $146,650 in Mexican Bonds, which is the equivalent of $88,000 in currency at the stipulated price.

Before delivering this amount to Mr. Simons, you will ask from him the bill of sale of said steamer according to contract.

M. ROMERO.

Romero to Sturm.

No. 312.] WASHINGTON, June 12, 1867.
General H. STURM,
    New York.

Dear Sir: Your letter of yesterday, with a receipt from Mr. Simons, has been receieed.

General Berriozabal informs me that he has received the steamer Sheridan; therefore I will have no difficulty now in paying for it, and you will find enclosed a draft on Messrs. John W. Corlies & Co. for the necessary bonds to make the payment. In accordance with the contract, the payment has to be made only when the receipt of the steamers is given up to you.

I wish you would see my official letter to Mr. Simons, on this subject, before you make the payment. I hold that he is only entitled to the interest of the bonds from the date on which he presents the receipt of the steamer. I will, however, be willing to have them dated on the day of the arrival of the steamer to Brazos, should he renounce all claims for indemnity on account of our delay in receiving it. This seems to me just and fair.

    I am, Sir, very respectfully,
        Your obedient servant,
            M. ROMERO.

Sturm to Romero.

No. 313.] NEW YORK, June 14, 1867.
Senor M. ROMERO,
    Mexican Minister etc.

Sir: I have the honor to acknowledge the receipt of your communication of June 12th, 1867, enclosing an order on Messrs. John W. Corlies & Co. for one hundred and forty-six thousand six hundred and fifty dollars ($146,650), Mexican Bonds, which, in your letter, you instruct me to pay to Mr. Simons as payment *in full* for the steamer General Sheridan, recently delivered to General Berriozabal.

I also received, this day, a letter from Mr. Simons in regard to the same subject. As soon as Mr. Simons delivers me the *bill of sale* of said steamer, in accordance with his contract, I will deliver him said bonds, in accordance with your instructions, and remit to you his receipt for the same.

I have to state, however, that Messrs. John W. Corlies & Co. informs me that they have not sufficient bonds on hand to meet this payment.

Be pleased, therefore, to give them instructions occordingly.

    I am, Sir,
        Very respectfully,
            Your obedient servant,
                H. STURM.

Sturm to Romero.

No. 314.] NEW YORK, June, 17, 1867.

Senor M. ROMERO,

Dear Sir: I have received two communications from Mr. Simons in regard to a settlement for the steamer Sheridan.

Mr. Simons insists on the following points: 1st, That the coupons of the bonds be dated August 25th, 1866, the day that the steamer was ready for delivery at Brazos. 2d, That the expense incurred by him in keeping the vessel there so long a time, be also paid to him. He is willing, however, to take the amount of bonds you offer, provided the coupons are dated as above, on account, leaving the balance open for settlement hereafter.

Be pleased to advise me what to say to Mr. Simons under the circumstances. I would have sent you Mr. Simons' letters, or rather copies of them, but the terms in which he writes, are such that I refrain from doing so.

I enclose herewith some newspaper slips, which may be interesting to you. A party of my friends called to see me yesterday, and I learned from them that one of the gentlemen present at the serenade, took a full short-hand report of what I did say on that occasion, and they have promised to get me a copy of it, which as soon as I get I will forward to you, from which you will see that the newspapers have not stated exactly what I did say on the occasion.

Yours truly,

H. STURM.

Sturm to Romero.

No. 315.] NEW YORK, July 9, 1867.

Senor M. ROMERO,
Mexican Minister, etc.

Sir: I have the honor to state that Mr. Henry Simons called this morning for his bonds, which I delivered to him. I enclose herewith his receipt for one hundred and forty-six thousand six hundred and fifty ($146,650) dollars, given according to instructions from you.

I have the honor to be,

Very respectfully, your obedient servant,

H. STURM.

Romero to Sturm.

[Translation.]

No. 316.] WASHINGTON, July 10, 1867.

MEXICAN LEGATION.
IN THE
U. S. OF AMERICA.

The port of Vera Cruz having come back to the obedience of the Constitutional Government of the Mexican Republic, I ask you to send as soon as possible to said port on a sailing vessel, which shall be as good as possible all the war materials that you have on hand belonging to said Government, consigning them to the General in Chief of the Army of the East.

You will make the contract for the freight at the price current, and it will be paid in Vera Cruz, on the delivery of said goods.

I remain, very respectfully,
Your obedient servant,
M. ROMERO.

Original not found.

Memorandum of an Interview with Mr. Romero.

No. 317.] July 11th, 1867.

Arrived in Washington at 6 A. M. Called on Mr. Romero at 11 A. M.

Requested him, if he had not heard from the Government yet, to take the responsibility to settle the claims of Mr. Cattell, Simons, Dewhurst & Emerson. and all the unsettled accounts.

I also stated that I was endeavoring to the utmost to forward the goods for General Diaz, as he had requested, and would have done so before, but for the difficulty to get a sailing vessel, on account of the various rumors, set afloat since Maximilian's execution, that a foreign fleet has been dispatched to renew the war against Mexico.

I also advised him of a scheme of certain parties in league with Santa Anna and Ortega, to get up a filibustering expedition against his Government; and requested him to communicate this fact at once to Mr. Seward and General Grant.

In reply, Mr. Romero said, he wished I would lose no time in forwarding the goods on hand to Vera Cruz, and said he wrote to me yesterday to that effect. He says there is no truth in the rumors of further war in Mexico; and he wishes me to write him about the filibustering scheme, after I hear from the parties investigating this matter, so he can lay the facts before Mr. Seward.

Mr. Romero says, he is going in a few weeks to Mexico, and is very busy to-day, and will speak with me to-morrow about the settlement of all old accounts, and also particularly about the remuneration for my services, etc., etc., and wants me to call at ten to-morrow morning.

Friday, July 12th, 1867.

Called on Mr. Romero at 10 o'clock A. M.

Mr. Romero said, as he was going home soon, he desired as much as possible to settle all claims before going, and wished to speak to me freely and friendly about this matter, especially in regard to settlement of my own claims and those of friends, who had served his Government. He said his position was an embarrassing one; he had always tried to promptly pay all accounts that citizens of this country had against his Government for aid furnished during the war; had written several times to his Government for instructions to settle the various pending matters, but had no reply and could not take the responsibility upon himself, except as to claims that had originated by his own direct instructions to me.

The various circumstances connected with General Carvajal's contracts are not fully understood at home, and in consequence of the Woodhouse contract and the revolt at Matamoras, many false stories have been circulated in Mexico about General Carvajal. The amount of indebtedness created by him has been magnified and grossly exaggerated, so that everything done by his (General C.) orders, and the parties who had anything to do with him, are looked upon with suspicion by the Mexican Government.

He said I had been a very good friend of his country, and he had always fully advised his Government about my efforts in behalf of the Mexican Republic and the valuable assistance I have furnished politically and in the shape of arms. He desired and believed I would be fully remunerated for all, and would assist me in every way to accomplish this.

As many of the contracts originating under General Carvajal's authority are yet unsettled. and I know all about them, he had concluded it would be best if I should go with him to Mexico, and there give all the information his Government might require; and he thought this would save much delay and trouble.

He said he appreciated the importance of settling all those claims as soon as possible; and nearly all the Mexican friends who were here at the time, and had gone in the Everman, Vixen, etc, are now in Mexico, and hold prominent posi, tions there, they will also do their best to assist me in settling these claims, and in obtaining what is due to me.

He said, I had several times spoken with him about projects to develop the resources of his country, by building railroads, starting steamship lines, etc., and that I would accept as payment for my claims, some charter or privilege from his Government that would remunerate me. He said that I was correct in my idea that the Government could not pay in cash a very large amount at the present time, and he requested me to tell him frankly what I would like to have, and he would communicate it to his Government.

In reply, I said to Mr. Romero, that I was not now prepared to specify anything particular, as he himself could not give me any definite information about it; that at a former interview, I had stated to him my belief that his Government would require all the money it could command to support itself, unless it should succeed in negotiating a loan in this country; and to make that possible, the credit of his Government must first be raised to a higher standard, and one way to accomplish that was; to encourage American capital and enterprise to come to his country, to assist in developing its resources; and, above all, that every American citizen who had aided his country, must be promptly satisfied and settled with.

If his Government would do this, and would pursue a liberal policy toward foreigners, as the United States are doing, and would adopt a wise financial policy and system, all this would be accomplished.

I said, that his own reputation and interest, as well as my own, demanded that our American friends should be liberally dealt with; and if that should be done, I had no doubt that I myself could, with the assistance of those very friends, who had assisted me heretofore, raise a large capital for investment in Mexican enterprises; and I would then not demand cash payment from his Government for all it owes me.

I said, that he had not understood me correctly; that I had not offered to take grants or franchises for all; only as part payment.

I said, that Mr. Romero more than any other man, except perhaps General Carvajal, knew fully what I had accomplished for his Government. That to do this, I had received no assistance from his Government or people at all, but had now advanced something like one hundred and fifty thousand dollars in cash, al of which, I had paid out in the full belief that his Government and Nation were not what her enemies had stated, but would gratefully repay it.

That the expenses incurred by me, directly in connection with the purchase and shipment of arms, such as pay to inspectors, agents, clerks, and their expenses, drayage, etc., would amount to some fifty thousand dollars alone, for the greater part of which I had already furnished him the bills and accounts; and I requested him to consider the large number of contracts made by me since May 1st, 1865, a great part of which had not been carried out, owing to the inability of General C. to raise funds on the Mexican Bonds; and that any person acquainted with the business would tell him, that this amount would be considered very reasonable, and I had no doubt his Government would find I had managed business very economically.

I reminded him that I had taken up the drafts of Dupont & Co., when he could not hear from his Government about them, so as to save the credit of his country, and obtain the powder it needed. I had also paid out a considerable amount on interest coupons of Mexican Bonds, as an advance and an inducement to parties to take bonds in payment, by showing them that I had faith in the stability and honesty of his Government. For this latter outlay, I had the coupons in my possession, and this account was separate from the money otherwise expended.

I then said to Mr. Romero, that he was aware that I had rendered important political services of a secret and delicate nature to his Government, and that as he knew I was obligated to many persons, for the payment to them for their assistance, that I had necessarily expended large sums for myself and for agents employed in this business; but that I wanted;

First. Full and fair settlement with Messrs. Dewhurst & Emerson, Mr. Cattell, and Mr. Simons, and others who had furnished the material of war, and the steamers to transport them to Mexico.

Second. I wanted an arrangement for the payment of the interest on the bonds I had been instrumental in disposing of for arms, etc.

Third. I wanted payment in cash, with interest, for that part of money expended by me for purchases and shipment of arms; also payment for the drafts of Dupont & Co.

And that in regard to payment for secret and political services rendered, for which I was obligated to others, and the cash I had expended in that way; I would arrange with my friends, many of whom had already agreed to it, that we accept from the Mexican Government some franchise or grant that we can make useful and paying to us.

I said I would write out a full report of all my transactions, except the secret service, which I could not do, and deliver it to him before going home, together with the balance of the vouchers not yet furnished; and I would go with him to Mexico, if he thought it necessary or advisable.

In reply, Mr. Romero said: "He knew fully what had been done for his country through me, and would lay all the facts before his Government; and he wished I would go with him to Mexico, as many things had to be explained there, and he felt sure everything would be settled as I wished, when we arrived at the Mexican capital.

"He desired me to make out such a report as I spoke of, in as short a way as possible without going into details, of all transactions connected with the purchase and shipment of arms about which he has officially communicated the reports to his Government, and that the balance can be settled in Mexico, when he and I will both communicate with the Government in person."

I then said to Mr. Romero: "That I was desirous to do something to show the Mexican people the friendly feelings entertained by Americans toward them, and if he had no objection, I desired that he should invite some prominent Americans to go with him to Mexico to see the country and its people. If he would take care of them while in his country, I would buy or charter a steamer to take him and his guests to Mexico and return them to this country, and would pay all expenses connected therewith myself.

Mr. Romero gladly accepted the offer, and requested me to inform him as soon as I could procure a vessel, and he would invite some gentleman to go with him. He also said he expected to leave about the latter part of August or first of September.

Before leaving, I stated to Mr. Romero "that I had arranged with Messrs. Boker & Co. not to present now, to the State Department, their claim for the amount of a certain draft of Placido Vega for arms furnished to him, of which I spoke at our last interview; but they had agreed to wait until the Government had fully re-established itself; and I said if he thought it best, I would propose to Messrs. Boker & Co. to present their claim also to the Mexican Government for settlement, when I should arrive at the Mexican capital. Mr. Romero requested me to do so.

Correct copy of memorandum. H. STURM.

Sturm to Romero.

No. 318.] NEW YORK, July 13, 1867.

Senor M. ROMERO,
    Mexican Minister, etc.

Sir: I have the honor to inform you that the rumors which have been afloat, since the execution of Maximilian, that some parties inimical to the Mexican Government are endeavoring to get up an expedition to commit a raid on Mexico, are but too true. I have endeavored, for several days, to ascertain the truth of these rumors and the names and standing of the parties connected with the movement, and their probable plan of operation; and after careful inquiry, I find that quite a number of persons, and some of them men of very fair standing in society, are connected with the proposed movement; and are doing their utmost, by means of the public press and private meetings, to create an excitement and enlist the sympathies of ambitious and rash young men in favor of their enterprise.

The leading spirits of this movement are mostly persons engaged in, or sympathizing with the rebellion against our own Government, and some of them have been connected heretofore with similar fillibustering expeditions against Cuba and Nicaragua These persons pretend to be in the confidence of our Government, and claim that said Government is not adverse to such an undertaking, provided it can be carried out in such a way as not to openly infringe upon the neutrality laws of this country.

These schemers, therefore, propose to go to Mexico under the disguise of emigrants; to carry with them their arms and necessary stores; to make a descent upon some place on the coast of Mexico (not yet determined), where they expect to be joined by Mexicans disaffected towards the Government.

That the object of these fillibusters is only plunder, and that our Government does not approve of any such act, is of course clear; and it is equally certain that a movement of this kind can only meet with a disastrous defeat. Yet there is no doubt that unless this movement is checked at once, trouble and expense may ensue to the Mexican Government, which, at the present moment, requires quietude to reorganize its own internal affairs I would, therefore, respectfully suggest the propriety of informing our Government of this proposed scheme, so that proper steps may be taken to prevent its consummation. I urge this more especially, as the leaders of this movement *pretend* to be acting under the *auspices, and with the support of our Government* and that of France and Austria, from which latter they claim to have the promise of five million dollars towards defraying the expenses of the expedition. They also expect to raise one million dollars in this city by subscription.

The expedition is to start from different places, particularly New York, Baltimore, Mobile and New Orleans. I do not think it advisable, for prudential reasons, at present to mention the names of the parties connected with this movement, but shall do so whenever you desire it.

I have the honor to be, Sir,
Very respectfully,
Your obedient servant,
H. STURM.

Romero to Sturm.

No. 319.] WASHINGTON, July 15, 1867.

General H. STURM,
New York.

Dear Sir: Your two letters of the 13th inst., and one of the 14th, have been received.

You very likely have seen Mr. Seward's memorandum on the Santa Anna case, which settles entirely that matter.

It is not correct that the order prohibiting the exportation of arms from the United States has never been revoked. It was revoked on the 4th of May, 1865. There will be, therefore, no trouble in shipping from New York any articles for Mexico. Please send to Vera Cruz the Mexican goods just as soon as you can do so. It is of the utmost importance that this matter will not be delayed for a single moment.

In great haste,
Respectfully,
M. ROMERO.

Sturm to Romero.

No. 320.] NEW YORK, July 17, 1867.

Senor M. ROMERO,
Mexican Minister, etc.

Dear Sir: By General Sturm's order I write to you to say, that the General received your note of yesterday. He is very busy endeavoring to get the arms shipped to Mexico, but finds it very difficult to do so, in his (the General's) condition, as the people here are afraid to take munitions of war to Mexico, on account of the rumor of the French and Austrian fleets visiting Vera Cruz.

Another objection is raised, that under the existing circumstances there is no probability of a return freight, and also that all the charges are to be collected at Vera Cruz.

By direction of the General, I herewith enclose you several slips from the newspapers. The article from the "Tribune," the General says, is from the pen of a very particular friend of *ours.*

The General has just come in, and he instructs me to say, that he is using his utmost endeavors to get the goods shipped, and as soon as he can accomplish it, he will notify you at once.

Very respectfully,
Your obedient servant,
S. D. STOCKING,
By order General H. STURM.

Romero to Sturm.

No. 321.] WASHINGTON, July 18, 1867.

General H. STURM,
Jersey City, N. J.

Dear Sir: Your letters of the 15th, 16th and 17th inst., signed by Mr. Stocking, have been received, and its enclosures duly noticed.

I will be glad if you can send soon the articles existing there. There is no danger that any European man-of-war will make any demonstration against any U. S. vessel carrying American goods. I am sure of this.

In great haste,
Yours respectfully,
M. ROMERO.

July 19, 1867.—Your favor of yesterday, with enclosures has just been received.

Original missing.

Sturm to Romero.

No. 322.] NEW YORK, July 23, 1867.

Senor M. ROMERO.

Dear Sir : I received your answer to my telegram of this A. M. Enclosed I send you the proposition made by Mr. Woodhouse, the same party who took the goods to Matamoras. Dr. Navarro does not know the rates, and Mr. Fuentes, to whom he referred, says that $3,200 is the regular rate, but can not say what would be reasonable under the circumstances, in consideration of the money advanced for insurance, etc., which will be considerable.

This has reference to a portion of the cargo (fourth-fifths of the whole now on hand) which I proposed to send per Woodhouse's offer for $4,000. The difference would be, therefore, $800.

The balance of the goods; mostly equipments and ammunition, will go in another vessel for $1,000, as all the goods can not go in one vessel unless it be a large one, as my goods are very bulky.

To-morrow I will see another party, and perhaps I may do better.

Yours truly,
H. STURM.

Romero to Sturm.

No. 323.] WASHINGTON, July 23, 1867.

General H. STURM,
New York.

Dear General: I have received your two letters of the 22d inst., one enclosing Mr. Horton's report. As you suggest, it is not worth spending any money to ferret out what the dreamy filibusters may plan, after the action of the U. S. Government, which will defeat their schemes.

As for the freight of the Government stores which I instructed you to send to Vera Cruz: I have answered to-day your telegram, and will now repeat, that in case the ship takes *only* the Government goods, they are sure not to be demanded any port charges, but not otherwise, viz.: if they take any goods to Vera Cruz.

The price of the freight shall be approved by Consul Navarro, and will be paid at Vera Cruz, as well as the insurance price, all at regular market rates.

Very truly yours,

M. ROMERO.

Sturm to Romero.

No. 324.] NEW YORK, July 25, 1867.

Senor M. ROMERO.

Dear Sir: I enclose you to-day an offer from Messrs. Alexander & Sons (the party to whom Mr. Fuentes had referred me) in regard to freight to Vera Cruz. These gentlemen are doing a regular business with Mexico, and for that reason Mr. Fuentes thought I might obtain better rates, but on comparing their offer with that of Woodhouse's, I find they ask $600 more for the freight, besides commissions and interest for advances on insurance, etc., etc.

I have been negotiating with them all day to-day, hoping to reduce the rate, which I think I can accomplish, and will notify you of it if I succeed.

In the meantime Mr. Woodhouse's offer has been withdrawn, which I regret exceedingly. He seems to be afraid of trouble. I am very much annoyed, indeed, that the American newspapers, instead of strengthening the confidence, of merchants and others in relation to Mexico, are really doing all they can to injure American commerce to Mexico, by publishing every now and then such absurd statements as we constantly see in the papers, thereby driving the whole trade into the hands of a few men who, fully understanding the situation, and having thus no opposition to contend with, have it all their own way and charge their own price.

I am as desirous as you are to get the goods shipped as soon as possible, but the delay is only caused by my efforts to get the freight taken as low as possible.

Enclosed I send you a few more slips from the papers.

Yours truly,

H. STURM.

Sturm to Romero.

No. 325.] NEW YORK, July 27, 1867.

Senor M. ROMERO,

Dear Sir: I have received your letter of yesterday, and have called twice at the Consular office (but learned from Mr. Fuentes that Dr. Navarro had gone to the country) for the purpose of closing the arrangement for freight to Vera Cruz to-day, as I have received a note (a copy of which I enclose) from Messrs. Alexander & Sons, and since then a message from them, which makes it necessary for me to either accept or decline their offer before 3 P. M. to-day. I do not wish to decline their offer, for I can see no other immediate opportunity for sending the goods to Vera Cruz, and then it is a question whether I can get freight on better, or as good terms.

Besides the policy of insurance on the goods expires at the end of this month, and unless I send these goods now I would have to insure again; the cost of this, together with the storage and charges, would be more than could possibly be saved by delay.

I have, therefore, in the absence of Dr. Navarro, taken the responsibility to accept the offer made by Alexander & Sons.

A copy of my letter of acceptance I herewith enclose.

Hoping you will approve my action in the premises I remain,

Very respectfully yours,

H. STURM.

Sturm to Romero.

No. 326.]   NEW YORK, July 27, 1867.

Senor. M. ROMERO,

Dear Sir: Since writing you to-day about the acceptance of Alexandre & Sons' offer of freight, Mr. Fuentes has called, saying that Dr. Navarro has sent him a note approving of Alexandre's terms, so everything is all right now in regard to this matter. The goods will be loaded as fast as possible, and I would be obliged if you would write to the proper officer in Vera Cruz, also to give me his address. I shall send you an exact invoice of the goods as soon as I know the exact amount I can send in the vessel.

Yours truly, in haste,

H. STURM.

I send you more slips to-day. The "Times" has some scurrilous articles again.

H. S.

Romero to Sturm.

No. 327.]   WASHINGTON, July 31, 1867.

General H. STURM,
  New York.

Dear Sir: I suppose Mr. Tifft has informed you that my trip to New York was postponed. I may leave to-morrow or Monday next. I will let Mr. Tifft know by telegraph.

There is a poor Mexican here who wishes to go home and has no means to pay his passage. Could he go on board the vessel taking our goods to Vera Cruz? He is a hardy man, and could be of some use on board.

Respectfully,

M. ROMERO.

Sturm to Romero.

Senor M. ROMERO,

No. 328.]   NEW YORK, August 2, 1867.

Dear Sir: Your two notes have been received, but I could not answer them sooner. I can send your man to Vera Cruz in the Bark, without charge, and have so arranged it to-day.

Be pleased to have him here by Tuesday morning next. I am using every spare moment to write out the statement you desire of me, and hope to have the same ready very soon.

Yours truly, in haste,

H. STURM.

Sturm to Romero.

No. 329.]   NEW YORK, August 10, 1867.

Senor M. ROMERO.

Dear Sir: I have the honor to herewith transmit to you the invoices and duplicate bills of lading of the goods shipped per barque Zingarella to Vera Cruz. The bill of lading is duly approved by the Consul General, Juan N. Navarro, the original of which, approved in the same way, is in the hands of the Captain of the vessel.

The charges to be collected at Vera Cruz, and which are expressed on the bill of lading, are as follows:

For freight, in gold	$3,800 00
For advance charges, storage, insurance, etc., reduced to gold	6,119 87
Total, in gold	$9,919 87

I am, Sir, very respectfully,
Your obedient servant,

H. STURM

Sturm to Romero.

No. 330.]   NEW YORK, August 23, 1867.

Senor M. ROMERO,
    Mexican Minister, etc.

Sir: Enclosed I have the honor to transmit to you the statement of cash received and expended by me since December 24th, 1866 (at which time I transmitted to you an account up to that time), on account of purchases and shipments made for the Mexican Government. Also a statement of the bonds received and expended for purchases, the vouchers for which I have heretofore transmitted to you at such times as I made the payments.

Owing to sickness in my family, I shall not be able to send you my report until Monday night.

I am, Sir, very respectfully,
Your obedient servant,
H. STURM.

Romero to Sturm.

No. 331.] WASHINGTON, August 24, 1867.

General H. STURM,
New York.

Dear Sir: Your two letters of yesterday have been received. I will submit to my Government your account for cash expenses enclosed to one of them.

I can not tell exactly when I will be able to leave New York It can not be before the 20th of September. I will take with me my mother and sister, U. S. Grant, Jr., and Senor Degollado, my private secretary.

I am very glad to hear that Mrs. Sturm is recovered.

I am sir, very respectfully,
Your obd't servant,
M. ROMERO

Romero to Sturm.

No. 332.] WASHINGTON, August 26, 1867.

General H. STURM,
New York City.

Dear General: I notice in your account an item for logs of mahogany. My impression is that General Baranda sent that mahognay to Mr. Fuentes to be sold, and the price to aid the payment of the steamer. Thus I do not understand the reason of the charge you make, and which might be a mistake. But I am not positive of anything in this connection, and I merely ask you a short explanation on this point, not finding at home any letter concerning it.

Very truly yours,
M. ROMERO.

Sturm to Romero.

No. 333.] NEW YORK, August 27, 1867.

Senor M. ROMERO,

My Dear Sir: Your two notes of the 24th and 26th inst I have duly received. I am glad you called my attention to the mahogany, so that I can explain this transaction without complicating my accounts.

At the time the Vixen left for Minititlan, I instructed my brother (who went out as supercargo) if possible to obtain some return freight at that place, or if that could not be done, to purchase some fustic or logwood, provided he could do so at such rates as would enable me, from its sale here, to somewhat reduce the expense of the steamer Vixen. I also explained this to General Baranda, stating to him that whatever profit might arise from this, would inure to the benefit of the Government. I gave my brother five hundred ($500) dollars in gold to enable him to pay the necessary expenses. At Minititlan it was found impossible to obtain freight, except some hides, and some passengers, and by the advice of General Baranda, who aided him, he purchased forty-three (43) logs of mahogany, for which he paid four hundred and eighty ($480) dollars in gold.

On the arrival of the mahogany here, I caused it to be unloaded, inspected, and sold to the highest bidder, as is usual under such circumstances, and by examining voucher No. 5, statement "A," (Merritt, Bridgeford & Co.,) you will see that the sum of one thousand and forty-three dollars and thirteen cents ($1,043.13) was realized therefor. By examining statement "B," of cash received by me, you will also see that I have charged myself with whatever money I have received from freight of hides and on account of passengers. This money I have again expended, as you will see from the statements submitted to you.

I enclose herewith a statement referring only to the mahogany, and the money received for freight and passengers, to show you how much the Government has made by the transaction.

The hope expressed in your letter about the recovery of my wife, I am sorry to say, has not been realized. On the contrary, I fear for the worst; but hope that with proper care and attention she may recover. Hard as it may seem, I have positively determined, that unless I am physically disabled in the meantime, I shall go to Mexico whenever you are ready. The vessel will be ready this week, and you can therefore rely upon it whenever you may determine to go.

In haste, yours truly,

H. STURM.

Statement.

	Currency.	Specie.
1867.		
Jan. 5—Cash paid for mahogany...		$480 00
" " " Charges on mahogany.....................	$129 05	
	$129 05	$480 00

CONTRA.

	Currency.	Specie.
Cash received from sale of mahogany................................$1,043 13		
" " for passages from Minititlan......................		$200 00
" " " freight on hides..		140 00
" " " passages from Key West.......................	80 00	
	$1,123 13	$340 00

Figuring gold at $1.35 there is a saving to the Government of $805.08 on this transaction.

Romero to Sturm.

[Translation.]

No. 334.] NEW YORK, September 4, 1867.

MEXICAN LEGATION
IN THE
U. S. OF AMERICA.

I have to-day received your communication dated 23d last August, in which you deemed it convenient to make me a statement of all the services that you have done to my Government, and in general terms of the sundry bargains and forwarding of amunition made by you, either on account of the said Government or for your own private account; enclosing at the same time a notice of all the contracts, amount of the bonds that you have received and expended on different occasions, and of the advances made by you on buying and embarking said goods, etc.

I have manifested to you in answer, that my opinion in general is favorable on the merit of your services; which I acknowledge now with satisfaction; moreover, on the different special points mentioned by you in your communication, I have also expressed my opinion, both in the letters and notes that I have addressed to you, and in our private conversations. I refrain, therefore, from entering here into details, and I confine myself to transmit to my Government your aforesaid communication, with the annexed accounts, and I do not doubt that, with the information that it has already received and with that I am ready to send upon some facts, if necessary, ample justice will be done you.

I avail myself of this opportunity to reiterate to you the assurances of my attentive consideration.

M. ROMERO.

Senor General HERMAN STURM,
New York.

Extract of a Publication in the Diario Oficial of Mexico.

[Translation.]

No. 335.] AT HOME (MEXICO,) November 21st, 1867.

Senor M. ROMERO.

My Esteemed Friend: A few days before your arrival at this capital, some newspapers had spoken about the various contracts which were made in the U. S. by the commissioners of the Mexican Government. As the newspapers referred to affirmed that all those contracts were ruinous, and that they would originate numerous claims on the part of the North American contractors, which are altogether inexact, I hasten as the editor of the *Diario Oficial* to deny these reports which, vague as they are, notwithstanding, might claim the attention of the public.

The *Ferro-carril* of this Capital has announced that it will make certain disclosures concerning the contracts which it pretends to be acquainted with; and, whereas, it has not made them, nor is it possible to anticipate what they will be, I will refrain from saying anything more on this subject from want of data which I do not possess.

As you are now among us, I think it proper that you, as an authorized person, should state all that has transpired in reference to these matters, for no one else better than yourself, who so much deserves the esteem and trust of your fellow-citizens, could represent this matter in its true light.

I have taken the liberty to make this request of you, hoping you will be kind enough to note and answer it at your earliest convenience.

I am, Sir, &c.,
JOSE DIAZ COVARRUBIAS.

No. 5, SECOND VANEGAS STREET,
MEXICO, November 21, 1867.

Senor Don JOSE DIAZ COVARRUBIAS,
Present.

My Esteemed Sir, and Friend: I have just received your favor of this date, in which referring to the rumors published by some city newspapers about the contracts made by the agents of our Government in New York, you ask me to state, for the benefit of our fellow-citizens, what has passed relative to these subjects. It is but natural that they should wish to be acquainted with whatever the Government has done abroad to provide itself with arms and munitions of war during the late struggle with France, and in order to satisfy this desire, I anticipated it while in Washington by making two publications, circulars No. 14 and 15, which I believed would contain the information required, to form a correct idea of what had been done. On my arrival in this city I learned that only circular No. 14 had been received, and accordingly I gave you the copies immediately of circular No 15, which I understand will soon be published in the "Djario Oficial."

It would not be necessary for me to reply further to your communication were it not that among the remarks made by the city press there are expressions which require my notice, for the honor of the nation and of its Government.

Although I have not immediately at hand all of the data concerning these negotiations, I will make a brief but complete statement of all that occurred, which will satisfy all persons who carefully examine it, that with small charges or expenses, comparatively speaking, much more was obtained than could have been reasonably expected. I shall not here undertake the defence of the acts of the Government in this matter, not so much for the reason that it is not my place to do it, as because I do not wish to associate that question with the direct object of this letter. Therefore I will limit myself to refer to the facts, from which every one, according to his own judgment, will arrive at his own conclusion.

There were four persons appointed by the Government of Mexico to obtain resources from the United States: Dr. Juan A. Zambrano, General Gaspar Sanchez Ochoa, General Jose Maria de Jesus Carvajal and myself. The authorization granted to Sr. Zambrano was issued by the Treasury Department and was limited to giving him authority to dispose of the proceeds from confiscated property of traitors. Mr. Zambrano was convinced that it was not possible to realize anything in virtue of said authorization, and while he was always ready to do all he could in behalf of our cause, he had the good judgment to make no use of his authority.

General Sanchez Ochoa was authorized to negotiate a loan of ten millions of dollars by pledging the receipts of our custom houses on the Pacific. In San

Francisco he printed bonds for that amount which he mortgaged for the payment of thirty thousand dollars in gold, advanced to him for the printing and for the private expenses of himself and those who accompanied him. Besides, he made in that city other contracts, the greater part of which came accidentally to my knowledge and that of the Government, and not because he communicated them to us. I did not interfere in these transactions, nor did I know even, the powers the General possessed till after his arrival in New York. All of them have nevertheless been declared null by the Government.

Being not able to sell the bonds he had printed at San Francisco, he came to New York, thinking he could realize them here. When the Government knew that the General was in New York it ordered him to act in accordance with me, needing my approval for his acts. On the 2d of February, 1866, he signed a contract with General Fremont, by virtue of which he gave him six of the ten million dollars he had in bonds and the grant for a railway, in exchange for the various obligations which the General contracted.

Thinking this contract onerous for the nation I denied my approval. The Government pronounced it null as soon as it come to its knowledge.

General Sanchez Ochoa, not being satisfied with this, disavowed the authority of the Government, and solicited and succeeded in having his contract expressly or tacitly approved by Don Jesus Gonzalez Ortega, who had assumed the position of President of the Republic in New York. With a view of explaining all this to the Government of the United States, taking as ground for my explanations data and irrefutable documents, I addressed a note to Mr. Seward on the 4th of June last which will render impossible claims on this subject on the part of that Government. My note to Mr. Seward, and four of the one hundred and sixty-eight documents enclosed therewith, were published in the circular No. 14 above referred to.

When I saw that General Sanchez Ochoa disobeyd the Government, I notified the firm that kept the bonds deposited, that these should be at the disposition of the Government, whose property they were, and not at the disposition of the one who had printed them, who had ceased to be its agent. Thanks to this notification we procured that Fremont did not obtain those which General Sanchez Ochoa pretended to give him in his contract.

However, he delivered to him some of them that he kept as samples, and the amount of which is not known; but these can not be considered as legal obligations to bind the nation, as much on account of the manner in which they were disposed of, as that,—as it appears, they were imperfect bonds and unnumbered.

The ten millions of dollars printed by General Sanchez Ochoa in San Francisco being subjected to the payment of the amount of thirty thousand dollars in gold, which were advanced to him with one and a half per cent. interest per month, it will not be possible to redeem until the payment of this amount be made. The Legation of the Republic in Washington received instructions to redeem these bonds as soon as possible, and I redeemed a million and a half dollars of them, and they were canceled without delay. The remaining eight millions and a half are deposited in a safe place, and there is no fear that they will be improperly disposed of.

General Carvajal arrived at Washington in April, 1865. His powers were independent of mine, and they were communicated to me neither officially nor privately. At the end of July, the same year, he made in New York a leonine and ruinous contract with Daniel Woodhouse, purporting to have been signed some days before in San Carlos, State of Tamaulipas. Although in his powers he was not advised that he needed my approval for the validity of his acts, he tried to obtain it, but I would not give it. The Government declared this contract to be null, when it came to his knowledge. Notwithstanding, Woodhouse printed the whole or a part of the fifty millions of dollars in bonds that should be issued according to contract. Before I left Washington I got together all the proofs, and I took the necessary steps to prove that Woodhouse had proceeded by fraud; that for that reason the contract was null and void; that all bonds he might print accordingly would be fraudulent, and that the Government of the Republic would never consider them as legitimate obligations against the nation. I published official notices, which I thought proper, in order to prevent fraud upon persons who, in good faith, not knowing the circumstances of the case, might purchase these bonds; and addressed to the Government of the United States a note dated the 20th of April last, in which I so plainly and evidently stated all this, that I am sure that this unfortunate affair will not bring any claims on the part of the Government at Washington. Besides, I succeeded in having all these documents officially printed by the Government of the United States and sent to Congress, and in this manner they are within the reach of all the citizens of the American Union.

On the 11th of September, 1865, General Carvajal concluded another contract with the house of Messrs. John W. Corlies & Co., of New York. In this contract, all the ruinous clauses for Mexico, which existed in the former one, were omitted, and it was agreed with said house to sell thirty millions of dollars in bonds of the Republic, giving it a good commission for those that might be sold at a fair price, and giving besides an indemnity for the expenses incurred in bringing about a sale, in case the sale should not be effected. Several clauses of this contract were altered in a manner favorable to us, in an additional contract which I made with the same house the 16th of May, 1866, and in which the commission for the sale of the bonds were reduced to very favorable terms.

When General Carvajal made this contract, he had already received instructions from the Government ordering that he should obtain my approbation in all his acts. It would be very tedious to mention, in this connection, the many and serious motives which induced me to approve this contract, in which some of the reforms proposed by me had been introduced. I communicated the whole business to the Ministry of Relations at length, and I think that, as well in the archives of that Ministry as in former acts, my conduct is fully vindicated.

In the aforesaid contract it was agreed, that of the thirty millions of dollars in bonds, only ten millions should be put in the market. And, indeed, that amount was not struck off. Of the printed bonds, only nine thousand dollars were sold for cash, as appears from the aforesaid accounts.

General Herman Sturm, Chief of Ordnance of the State of Indiana, had been appointed, by General Carvajal, agent for the purchase of munitions of war for Mexico.

Notwithstanding I regarded with natural distrust all the persons whom General Carvajal had brought around him, because, as a general thing, they inspired me with no confidence, I received such good recommendations of General Sturm, and he manifested such good sense when he addressed me about the purchase of arms, that I thought I ought to retain him in the character given to him by General Carvajal, giving him instructions that would prevent any abuse of his position. Thanks to the untiring energy and activity of this General, arms and munitions of war were purchased with bonds; and even their transportation in steamers, to the Republic, was paid with them.

The first remission was made under the auspices of General Carvajal. General Sturm contracted, in his own name, for a whole cargo, which was to have been paid in gold, at reasonable prices, on arriving at Matamoras. Considering the danger of the operation, and in case the payment should not be thus verified, it was to be paid in bonds at sixty per cent., which was the market price. The cargo left New York, greatly to my surprise, (for I did not believe the operation could be made,) on board the steamer Everman, which arrived safe at Matamoras. Unfortunately, when General Carvajal received the effects, the revolution of Servando Canales broke out, which prevented the effects from being used immediately. The agent sent by General Sturm with them, succeeded in saving the greatest part of them, which were at length handed over to Generals Escobedo and Viezca, and which well served both gentlemen in giving a death-blow to the traitors. Said effects not having been paid in gold in Matamoras, I paid in bonds that part of them which fell into the hands of the national forces.

Satisfied that General Sturm could purchase munitions of war with bonds at fair prices, I commissioned him to procure those needed by General Pedro de Baranda, an agent from General Alejandro Garcia, second in command of the Eastern line. He bought what he could, and they were sent on the steamer Vixen to Minatitlan. Fortunately they arrived safe, and did good service. General Diaz used them in taking Puebla.

Mr. Juan Jose Baz had been commissioned by General Regules to procure arms and munitions of war. The cargo of the Vixen having been sent, I recommended to General Sturm the purchase of effects asked for by Mr. Baz, for General Regules. Another cargo was purchased; but in procuring a vessel to take it to the Pacific, great difficulties were experienced on account of the great distance and the long time employed in arriving at the point of destination. For this reason I determined to send said arms to Tampico or Tuxpan, and that Mr. Baz, whom I commissioned to take them, should deliver a part of them to the patriots of the Huasteca and State of Mexico, and the other part to General Diaz.

Mr. Jose Ferrer, who had bought arms for the troops of General Alatorre, put them aboard the Suwanee, which was the same steamer in which Mr. Baz was bringing those arms. Unfortunately this steamer foundered on the coast of South Carolina, and all was lost. This disaster and the favorable aspect the affairs of the Republic were assuming, made me determine to forward no more armament. A short time after I received instructions from the Government to suspend all purchases. General Sturm, nevertheless, to supply the demands made by Messrs. Benitez, Baz and General Baranda, had made contracts which placed at our disposition other effects. Of these, some were sent to General Berriozobal at Matamoras, at the time he was in a difficult situation in that city, and when they were of great utility in keeping that city subservient to the authority of the Government. Another portion was sent to General Pavon at Tampico, on board the steamer General McCallum, when he was besieging the insurrectionists headed by Ascencion Gomez, and the receipt of these arms contributed to their capitulation. The remainder of said effects was sent to Vera Cruz, to the order of General Diaz, who, having command of only a division, placed them at the disposition of the Supreme Government.

When General Carvajal was ready to start to go to take charge of the Government of the State of Tamaulipas, he recommended me to send him a steamer to blockade Matamoras. When this city should be occupied, she would be of service to take Tampico, which was yet in power of the traitors. I was told by General Sturm that they had proposed to sell him one, which answered our purposes, at a very reasonable price. After mature deliberation, I determined to buy it for eighty-eight thousand dollars. Unfortunately she arrived at Matamoras when General Carvajal had been displaced by the rebellion of Canales. No legitimate authority was found to whom to deliver her, and she remained at Brazos de Santiago. When General Escobedo occupied Matamoras, he was told that the steamer was at his disposal, but not having any instructions on this matter, he declined to receive it. General Berriozobal received her at last, after having layed idle about a year at Brazos de Santiago, and armed her in order to blockade Vera Cruz after the French left, and going to that port, she sunk on the coast of Tamaulipas.

Among the instructions I gave General Sturm, to purchase arms, there was one by which it was expressly agreed that each contract he would make should require my approval for its validity, with the view of satisfying myself that he purchased only those articles which were wanted, and that their prices were reasonable. Having manifested to me that in these proceedings he often lost the opportunity of making purchases, because persons that one day were ready to sell their goods for bonds, changed their minds on the next, I determined to authorize the Citizen Juan N. Navarro, Consul of the Republic in New York, in whose integrity and patriotism I had the purest confidence, to approve of the purchases whenever he thought their prices reasonable. This was so much more convenient, for, as he lived in New York, it would be easier for him than me to know the market prices of the goods purchased. With the exception of two or three cases in which I approved of the contracts of General Sturm, all the rest were ratified by Mr. Navarro, and once approved, I had nothing to do but to draw on the firm of Messrs. Corlies and Co., for the amount of bonds wanted by General Sturm to pay for them.

As for the prices of the goods bought, I must say here, that considering the want we had of them and the circumstances and manner in which the purchase was made, they were very fair. Could we have had money to have bought them for cash, undoubtedly we could have gotten them at lower prices; but we must recollect that we paid in bonds issued by a Government that was not established and much less consolidated, and whose success was so doubtful; that, therefore, the holders of such bonds did run the risk, in case that our enemies would triumph, that they would not be recognized by them; or, at least, if we should triumph, of not being paid the interest, as it has happened. If we take into consideration all these matters, and, yet, that the Government of the United States, with an excellent credit, had to sell its dollars at thirty cents, and that the Confederates gave a bale of cotton for each gun, we will come to the conclusion that the price of sixteen dollars in bonds we paid for Enfield and Springfield rifles was not so high.

When we consider all that we bought at a time, when each gun was of inestimable value to us, and when our credit neither was, nor could be very high, and we reflect that the arms were sent under circumstances that were necessarily very urgent, to Generals Carvajal, Escobedo, Viezca, Diaz, Garcia, Berriozabal, Pavon, and others, the good service which they have rendered, the moral effect which the issuing of the bonds and the purchase of arms, produced in the Republic, discouraged our enemies, including Napoleon, and encouraging our friends, which I had an opportunity to know, by the number of commissions sent to me from all parts at Washington; and when we consider that all this was accomplished with less than two millions of dollars in bonds, which at their market price, can now be bought up for two hundred thousand dollars, I think that nobody will believe that there was any bad management, or that the Republic was unjustly brought in debt.

In many other nations, it will be believed on the contrary, that prodigies have been effected, with an amount relatively insignificant.

The power the Government gave me to procure means was very ample. Not expecting to obtain those means, I made use of my authority to approve or disapprove of the arrangements of other commissioners, and to authorize the purchase of articles of war.

The labors I underwent at Washington were very serious, and occupied all my time. Among my official obligations neither the purchase of arms nor the management and direction of the sale of our bonds was included. I accepted both obligations, although the first had never been entrusted to me by the Government, because I thought I was doing my country a service, and to carry out which I made supreme efforts, which at any other period of my life would have cost a sacrifice of my existence.

Well did I know that an intervention in affairs where money is concerned exposes one to the accusation of bad faith, and even of lack of honesty; and in deciding to do so, I had to make another sacrifice, the greatest of all, in the supposition that having no other patrimony than that of integrity with which my acquaintances honor me, I desired not to see it exposed, not even to suspicion or unfounded attacks. If any one has charges to make against me, I am ready to answer them, and to demonstrate that if I have acted wrong it has always been in good faith, and always with good intentions in my conduct.

The accounts presented by the house of Messrs John W. Corlies & Co., and by General Sturm, which I published in my circular No. 15, have not yet been settled. Not wishing to take upon myself the responsibility of settling them, I submitted them to the Government. As some explanations were necessary, the interested parties have thought fit to come to this city, to have a settlement here. They availed themselves of my coming, believing that, as I had intervened in those affairs, I could contribute to do away with the difficulties presented, and to make the necessary explanations. They do not come, then, to present reclamations of any kind, but to have a liquidation. Nor is it true that the Government of the United States has made, or is about to make, any reclamation against our country, on account of the debts contracted by the nation in the United States. General Banks and Senator Morton were coming with me, not representing any reclamations against our Government, but invited by me to study and learn something of the Republic, believing that in the future the relations between the two countries will be more intimate and useful.

The rumor that these pretended reclamations have caused my return to the Republic, is also unfounded and inexact. The documents which you published in the "Diario Oficial" yesterday, express the true and only motives I have had in returning to the Republic. It is useless for me to say to you that the rumor of our Government having received $30,000,000 from the United States in 1861, is unfounded. We do not owe to the Government of the United States one cent for money lent us during our war with France, nor for any other matter.

General Carvajal nominated Mr. Jesus Fuentes y Muniz as his agent for the signing of bonds; and in his absence he commissioned Mr. Francisco Zarco; and he being absent, Mr. Pantaleon Tovar.

It was never necessary that either of these two gentlemen should sign any bonds; but Mr. Zarco, who remained in New York while all these things were taking place, is well informed as regards everything that transpired. I should not do him the justice he deserves, if I should fail to mention here, that he did all he could to serve his country, intervening unofficially and in a friendly manner, in those affairs.

Desirous that in the United States the most dispassionate and exact data concerning the Republic, and of what takes place within its limits, might be known, I requested the editor of the New York "Tribune" to send one of its editors as a correspondent to said paper to Mexico, and I offered to facilitate the person sent, in any way it might be in my power for the best success of the mission.

Mr. Kane O'Donnell, a distinguished writer, was appointed for that object. I gave him a passage in the steamer Wilderness, which brought me to Vera Cruz; and I took him to Tehuacan, to see the second division of our army; and I brought him with me to this city. I was very far from thinking that any one should see in this a net, set to entrap our country, or that any one should think that I had acted wrong, believing as I did, that it suited the interest of the nation.

I see that I have extended this letter beyond what I desired; but I believe the importance of the subject referred to will justify me in so doing.

I am your very attentive and affectionate friend and humble servant,

M. ROMERO.

Sturm to Romero.

No. 336.] CITY OF MEXICO, December 5, 1867.

Senor M. ROMERO.

Dear Sir: You are aware, in March last I sent the steamer General McCallum to Tampico with a cargo of arms to aid your Government in annihilating the Empire, then in its last stages. The undertaking was a private one entirely, but being informed that the Liberals, who were then besieged at Queretaro and other places needed urgently, supplies of this kind, and they could and would pay for them, I arranged with certain parties in Boston and New York to send out this cargo, and I agreed to bear all the cost of transportation to this country, and in case of their not being sold, I am compelled to return them to New York, free of cost, to the parties interested, and in the same good order as I received them.

These arms are now in Tampico, and Vera Cruz, and as I sent them there to your Government, and, unfortunately, the revolt at Tampico prevented me from delivering them at the time, when they were so much needed by the Government, I desire very much the Government buy these arms, and thus save me a great loss, that must inevitably follow, if I am compelled to return these arms to the United States.

Enclosed, I send you a complete list of the arms, also of a battery of rifled cannon, also some new Springfield rifles that I bought recently.

Will you do me the favor to report this matter to your Government.

Yours truly,

H. STURM.

Mejia to Sturm.

[Translation.]

:::::::::::::::::::::::::::::::
: Stamp of the :
: War and Navy Dep't. :
:::::::::::::::::::::::::::::::

No. 337.]

DEPARTMENT OF ARTILLERY,
BUREAU No. 2,
MEXICO, December, 18 1867.

H. STURM, Esq.

In reply to your letter of the 5th inst., relative to the arms which you offer for sale, I have to state that the Supreme Government does not wish to purchase them, on account of the difference of their calibres, and the high prices asked for them.

MEJIA.

Sturm to Romero.

No. 338.]

MEXICO, December 24, 1867.

Senor. M. ROMERO,

Dear Sir: I have come to the conclusion not to have a personal interview with Mr. Lerdo this evening, but instead to submit to him in writing, in as concise a manner as possible, what I have to say. All I ask of the Government is some decision in regard to my affairs, and by adopting this plan much time will be saved, and annoyance and misunderstanding avoided.

Be kind enough to hand the enclosed letter to Mr. Lerdo, and accompanying the same with such verbal explanations as you, understanding all the particulars, may deem it advisable to make.

I am, dear Sir,

Yours truly,

H. STURM.

Sturm to Lerdo de Tejada.

No. 339.]
Mexico, December 24, 1867.

Senor D. S. LERDO DE TEJADA,
  Minister of Foreign Relations.

Sir: Being desirous of trespassing as little as possible upon your time or your official engagements, and of inconveniencing you as little as may be, with my affairs, I have determined to address you in *writing* in regard to the settlement of the different accounts that I have against your Government, begging you at the same time to remit to me its decision in regard to this mattter at your earliest convenience.

To enable you to fully understand the extent of the services that I have rendered to your Government, and the sacrifices that I have made on its account, both of which I have good reason to believe are not understood nor appreciated by the Government; I will here state, that at the time when I became connected with your Government, its prospects were very gloomy indeed, and its success was considered very doubtful. I found the commissioner, sent by your Government to obtain aid from the United States, in a very embarrassing and difficult position, without money to defray even *the most urgent* and necessary expenses, and surrounded by swindlers who, taking advantage of the unfortunate position of your country, and *his* patriotism and anxiety to serve his Government, deceived him, and by false pretences succeeded in inducing him to enter into negotiations with them that threatened, at one time, to involve your country in serious difficulties, and cause it the loss of millions of dollars without receiving therefrom the least benefit.

Relying upon the promise made to me by your commissioner, that the Mexican Government would do prompt and full justice to me for whatever services I should render to it, or whatever expenses I might incur on its account, I undertook the then almost hopeless task of obtaining for your Government material aid upon its credit, for its bonds, which at that time were considered of no value.

For over two years and a half, faithfully assisted by my brother and other true personal friends, I have been constantly engaged in rendering effective service to your country, and by energy and perseverance I have succeeded in overcoming the intrigues of your enemies, and to the astonishment of even your friends, have been enabled to send to your assistance a large amount of war material at very low prices. I have also rendered to your country important political services, and I am bold enough to say, have done much toward re-establishing your credit in the United States, which, as you are well aware, was at a very low ebb; and have, besides, saved your country many millions of dollars, and from many entanglements that would certainly have embarrassed it in the future. During all this time I have not received from your Government any pecuniary assistance whatever, (except the sum of two hundred and fifty dollars in silver, a few days since) or even any acknowledgment of my services; on the contrary, to accomplish the results attained, I have expended over a hundred and fifty thousand dollars of my own means and those of my friends. In addition, I have sent to this country, some months before the fall of the so-called empire, and at a time when they were urgently needed, a large amount of arms and ammunition, to enable the Government to have them within its reach. These arms, as you are aware, were not bought by the Government, or sent under any orders of the same, but it was expected that they would be sold on their arrival in this country. Unfortunately, however, a revolt at Tampico, to which place they were shipped, has prevented their sale, and as yet I have not been relieved of this burden, and have consequently suffered a heavy loss on this account.

On my arrival here, it was my intention to make the most liberal arrangement with your Government in regard to the payment of the debt it owes me, and to this end I have made to it various propositions for settlement of my accounts, for cash advanced by me, services rendered, and the sale of the arms which I now have in this country. Had either of these propositions been accepted, they would have protected me against loss, (*which was all that I desired,*) without causing the Government any great outlay of cash, or embarrassing it in the least; on the contrary, *your Government would have reaped a large advantage therefrom.* But my propositions have been declined, and I have also this morning been informed by the Secretary of War, that the Government does not wish to purchase the arms mentioned above.

As the expense incurred on account of these arms exceeds already the sum of forty thousand dollars, and I necessarily have to incur another large sum in returning them to New York, I am now compelled to ask the Government to pay me at once, both for the cash advanced by me, with interest added, as also to arrange with me the remuneration for the services that I have rendered.

To enable the Government to do this with the least inconvenience, I propose, for instance, to accept as payment an order for the exportation of a certain amount of silver coin, free of all duties, *proportionate to the amount due me*, similar to orders given by the Government on previous occasions.

Having already spent over a month in this city, vainly endeavoring to settle my affairs with the Government, and as every day's delay adds to my expenses, I respectfully ask that the Government now come to some determination in regard to my affairs, so that I may be enabled to return home without further delay and expense.

I have the honor to be, very respectfully,
Your obedient servant,
H. STURM.

To Senor LERDO DE TEJADA,
Minister of Foreign Relations.

Sturm to Romero.

No. 340.] MEXICO, January 16, 1868.
Senor M. ROMERO.

Dear Sir: Since you kindly wrote to the Governors of several States in regard to the arms which I have in this country, I have received replies from some of them, informing me that it is not possible for them to purchase arms at the present moment, on account of the present depleted state of the treasury.

As I have, however, good reason to believe that these arms will be bought as soon as the treasury of the different States is in funds, I think it beneficial for the parties who are interested in these arms, that they are left in this country for the present at least, in the hands of my agents.

To avoid any possible misunderstanding between them and the Government, I desire very much to make a definite arrangement with the Government in regard to any privilege it has or may grant to me; and as you, who are fully conversant with these matters, are now Minister of the Hacienda, I take the liberty of asking you to give me a permit to the following effect, viz.:

1st. The Government grants me, free from all charge and expenses, safe storage in the custom houses of Vera Cruz and Tampico, for all the munitions of war which I now have in these two ports, for a definite time, allowing me or my agents the liberty to overhaul or examine them, when it may be necessary or desired.

2d. The Government grants me the privilege to sell these munitions to itself, any State, or officers of the Government or of any State, without demanding of me the payment of any duties whatever, on any arms thus sold.

3d. The Government allows my agents the privilege to take samples of these arms out of the custom house free of charges.

4th. The Government shall fix certain definite duties on the articles I now have in this country, which duties, I only pay when the arms are sold to private parties. This will save much trouble, and I am thus enabled to make correct calculations.

As you know the kind intentions toward your Government of the parties interested in those arms, and as they have incurred a heavy expense and loss, in consequence of the failure to sell said arms, I ask you for the privilege to sell these arms, or any part of them, to any private party or parties, free of all duties.

Enclosed, I send you correct lists of these arms, and if you can grant these requests, be kind enough to give the privilege separately, for those in Tampico and for those in Vera Cruz.

I am, Sir, very respectfully,
Your obedient servant,
H. STURM.

Romero to Sturm.

[Translation.]

No. 341.]   MEXICO, January 20, 1868.

To Gen. H. STURM, Esq.

The subscriber has received your letter dated 16th inst., in which you request an exemption from duties for the arms which you hold, deposited in the custom houses of Tampico and Vera Cruz.

I have to state to you in reply, that on informing the President of the matter, he has ordered me to say to you, in reference to said petition, that, in consequence of the important services which you have rendered to the Government, should you wish to export the arms for the United States, you can do so without paying any duties; likewise, if you should sell said arms to the Government of the Union; but should you dispose of them to any one or more of the Federal States, you will be obliged to make an arrangement with them, in each case, and if you should, with the approbation of this Government, dispose of them to any private individuals, you shall pay the duties imposed on warlike arms.

M. ROMERO.

Sturm to Romero.

[Private.]

No. 842.] MEXICO, February 7th, 1868.

Senor M. ROMERO,

Dear Sir: I received this morning several letters from the States, which together with the last mail I received, instruct me to return home at once.

As Mr. Tifft had already gone to the Palace when I received these letters, I came to see you in person, but found you so much engaged, that I finally concluded not to wait any longer, but express in this note what I desire very much you will do for me, viz: To explain to Mr. Lerdo the necessity of answering as soon as possible a letter, which I intend to write to-day to him, and remit through you, if agreeable, and in which I ask him to return to me the draft of Placido Vega, in favor of Louis Schumacher, which draft, as you will remember, Mr. Lerdo stated can not be paid by the Government, for certain reasons, which reasons (as I am so instructed) I desire Mr. Lerdo to give to me in writing, if convenient.

I also request Mr. Lerdo for an answer in regard to the Suwanee, Everman and Sheridan matters, and the balance due on the cargo of the Everman.

Will you do me the favor to see Mr. Lerdo about these different matters. It is very important indeed for the Government as you fully understand, that I should not return home without having its decision in regard to these affairs.

Mr. Tifft informed me yesterday that you assured him that my matters should all be arranged, so that I might start for Vera Cruz on Tuesday next; and had I not received additional pressing letters this morning, I would not trouble you with this matter now; but I have engaged a stage for Tuesday morning, and on account of my past experience here, I am afraid that Mr. Lerdo, on account of more important matters, may still further delay, and I trust therefore that you will pardon me for trespassing upon your time with these requests, as you know full well that you are the only one who can aid me in this matter. Be kind enough also to state to me whether you have any objections, under the present circumstances, to hand my letter to Mr. Lerdo. If you have not, I will send it to you as soon as finished.

In haste,

Yours truly,

H. STURM.

Sturm to Lerdo de Tejada.

No. 343.]   MEXICO, February 7, 1868.

Senor Don SEBASTIAN LERDO DE TEJADA,
       Minister of Foreign Relations.

Sir: I would respectfully state to you, that in letters which I received this morning from the United States, I am requested to return home at once, and I have therefore engaged stage on Tuesday morning for Vera Cruz. Under these circumstances, and especially as the letters which I received this morning urge me to do so, I take the liberty of asking you to inform me of the decision of the Mexican Government in regard to the settlement of the different accounts which I submitted to you, and about which we had the interview on December 20th and 30th, 1867, viz:

1st. The payment of the draft of Placido Vega in favor of Louis Schumacher for $63,699.60, which draft, as you stated to me verbally, can not be paid. In case the Government should still entertain this same opinion, will you be kind enough to return to me said draft, stating to me at the same time, in writing, the reasons, on account of which the Government declines accepting and paying this draft, so that I may be enabled to make the proper explanations, in a satisfactory manner, to the parties concerned.

2d. The settlement of the charter of the steamer Suwanee.

3d. The settlement of the charter of the steamer J. W. Everman.

4th. The settlement of the claim for detention of the gunboat Sheridan.

5th. The settlement of balance due on the cargo of steamer J. W. Everman.

I deem it of the utmost importance to your Government, that I am enabled on my return home, to give to my friends in the United States who are interested in these different accounts, and who so cheerfully aided your Government during its time of adversity, its determination in regard to their accounts.

As regards the settlement of my own accounts, we have already come to a verbal understanding, which you determined to put in the shape of a written proposition, and promised to send to me, and as soon as I receive the same, I will reply to it, when this matter also will be determined.

Hoping to receive an early reply,

     I remain, very respectfully,
         Your obedient servant,
                 H. STURM.

Lerdo de Tejada to Sturm.

[Translation.]

No. 344.]   MEXICO, February 9, 1868.

Mr. Lerdo de Tejada's compliments to General Herman Sturm, and would be pleased if the General could find it convenient to come to his house, No. 16 Calle de Santa Clara, to receive some papers.

Lerdo de Tejada to Sturm.

[Translation.]

No. 345.] Mexico, February 8, 1868.

General H. Sturm.

Sir: In your letter of yesterday you have manifested to me your desire that the Government should express its judgment on the following points:

1st. The payment of a draft drawn by Placido Vega in favor of Mr. Lewis Schumacher, in San Francisco, California.

2d. The arrangements of the charter of the steamer Suwanee.

3d. The arrangement of the charter of the steamer J. W. Everman.

4th. The arrangement of the balance due on the cargo of the steamer J. W. Everman.

With regard to the first point, as I have already stated to you verbally, the Government of the Republic has decided, some time since, that it could not accept any responsibility on account of the obligations contracted by Placido Vega, without power, authority, or instructions from the Government to such effect. The commission taken by him to California was solely to purchase arms and warlike effects with the money placed in his hands for that purpose, but no power or authority was conferred upon him to contract any obligations; and the persons wishing to contract with him, should have previously assured themselves that he had power or authority to do so, in the name of his Government, if those persons pretended to reserve any right of action against the latter, as requested. I return to you the drafts referred to.

In respect to the other points mentioned in your letter, I have also stated to you verbally, that from information in the possession of the Government, it has some remarks to make in reference to the sums of which payment is asked; but at the same time it is well disposed to make a just and equitable arrangement.

As you inform me that you are only charged to inform yourself, without having any authorization and power from the parties interested, and also that you are unable to treat on any arrangement in relation to these points, I can, therefore, only repeat to you, that whenever any person sufficiently authorized presents himself, the Government will be glad to make proper arrangements.

S. LERDO DE TEJADA.

Lerdo de Tejada to Sturm.

[Translation.]

No. 346] Mexico, February 8, 1868.

General Herman Sturm.

Sir: When you arrived in this city in November last, for the purpose of settling the account of what is owing to you by the Government of the Republic for the commission in which you was employed in the United States, Senor Matias Romero, the last Minister of Mexico at Washington, accompanied you to speak to me on the subject, and we agreed that you should come to an arrangement with him as the commissioner of the Government in the case, on account of knowledge of all the antecedents, and in order that he might inform the Government what definitive understanding was proper.

Mr. Romero having made his report in reference to the accounts which you presented to him, we all three then had several conferences, in which the different points of those accounts were considered.

The Government being animated by the wish to provide for the services rendered by you, and to bring the matter to an equitable termination, we fixed the basis of an understanding in our last conference, agreeing that I should communicate the same to you in writing, and you, in like manner, would express your conformity, so that at once the proper order of payment might be issued.

The bases agreed upon were as follows:

1st. The payment of the account of the expenses incurred by you, amounting to.. $47,978 57

2d. The payment of two drafts—one for $1,622.53, and the other for $4,773.09, both drawn on the 12th of October, 1860, by Mr. Chas. Butterfield, in favor of Messrs. Kemble & Warner, in payment of powder forwarded to the Government at Vera Cruz, which drafts are held by you; and also the payment of interest, at 7 per cent., up to December 1st, 1860, say... 9,642 91

$57,621 48

3d. That those payments, estimated in currency of the United States at 132 per cent, amount in hard Mexican dollars..................... 43,652 63

4th. That to this amount there are to be added the expenses paid by you in the United States, in gold—the net balance in your favor being.. 856 00

$44,508 63

5th. That deducting from the sum total the amount paid to you by the General Treasury in this city.. 2,550 00

The net balance in your favor being..$41,958 63

6th. That the total payment shall be made to you in three installments, namely: one-half at once, and the other half in two installments of equal amounts at three and six months.

7th. And that the three amounts be paid to you, by the Custom House at Vera Cruz, in silver dollars of Mexican coinage, allowing you to export those amounts free of duties. This exemption from duties having been agreed upon, together with the exchange fixed at 132 per cent., instead of remitting the money to make payment at New York with whatever exchange might be current at the time of so doing.

In fixing the preceding points of agreement in our last conference, there remained open that relating to the promise made to you by General Jose M. de J.

Carvajal, of ($20,000) twenty thousand dollars in bonds, as compensation for the services you might render to the Republic. Inasmuch as no decision was reached in reference to the approval of the promise of General Carvajal, I have stated to you that instead of approving it, it would seem preferable to the Government, as well as yourself, to pay you a yearly salary of $4,000, which, counting from May 1st, 1865, to January 31st of the present year, amounts to $11,000. You said in our last conference, that you would reserve the right to decide whether you would accept that sum as compensation for your services; and in case you decide to do so, it will be added to the sum total above mentioned, so as to be distributed proportionately in the three installments of payment.

I trust you will be pleased to inform me, in reply, of your conformity with the bases referred to, with the understanding that by this arrangement the Government of the Republic will be relieved of all responsibility towards you for the performance of your commission.

I am, Sir, very respectfully,
Your obedient servant,
S. LERDO DE TEJADA.

Sturm to Lerdo de Tejada.

No. 347.]   MEXICO, February 10, 1868.

Senor Don S. LERDO DE TEJADA,
Minister of Foreign Relations.

Sir: I have the honor to acknowledge the receipt on this morning, of your communication of the 8th inst., in which you make two distinct propositions for the settlement of my accounts; and in reply I would respectfully state that I accept with pleasure the first proposition which you make me in regard to the payment of certain cash advances that I have made on account of your Government, with the understanding that I shall meet with no delay at the custom house in Vera Cruz in the payment of the amounts which you specify.

The amount which is due me on this account, as you correctly state in your letter, is, after deducting the sum of $2,550, which I have already received from the general treasury in this city, $41,958.63 specie. In liquidation of this account you will, therefore, be kind enough to give me one order for $20,972.32, payable at sight; and one order for $10,489.65, payable at sight on or after the 10th day of May, 1868; and one order for $10,489,66, payable at sight on or after the 10th day of August, 1868. I will also mention that in order to avoid future trouble, I think it would be well to mention on the face of each order, that the corresponding amount shall be exempt from all duties whatsoever for the purpose of exportation. By doing this you will enable me, in case of necessity, to sell my orders without having any further trouble with them.

The other proposition contained in your letter, in regard to the payment to me of $11,000, as payment in full for all claims that I have against your Government, both for myself and brother, for services rendered and expenses incurred up to the present time, I must respectfully decline.

When you take into consideration the fact that you do not pay even interest on that portion of my cash expenses which I had to advance directly on account of the purchase and shipment of arms, to enable you to get them to your country; and that in coming to Mexico, with my clerks, for the purpose, as I expected, of fully settling all pending matters, I have already expended the sum of $3,600, brought with me, and $2,550 which I have drawn from the national treasury here, and that this amount will necessarily be increased before reaching the United States; you will perceive that the sum of $11,000 will be barely sufficient to defray my traveling expenses and repay me for my time and trouble that I have had in coming here. I therefore prefer to leave this matter open for the present, with the other affairs yet pending, hoping that I may be able to make an arrangement with your Government, whereby, as I have suggested, I may be fully repaid for all my expenses, time, and trouble, without requiring any more cash from the national treasury.

I am, Sir, very respectfully,
Your obedient servant,
H. STURM.

Romero to Sturm.

No. 348.]   MEXICO, February 11, 1868.

My Dear General: Mr. Lerdo handed me your letter to him, and requested me to see you about it. I asked Mr. Tifft to tell you to see me at six. I had to leave my office a few moments, and was sorry to hear, when I returned, that you did not wait for me.

Please come to me to-morrow at ten o'clock.

Yours truly,
M. ROMERO.

Memorandum of an Interview with Mr. Romero in the City of Mexico.

No. 349.]   *February 12, 1868.*

Called on Mr. Romero at 10 o'clock, as requested. He was very much embarrassed at first, and begged me to listen to the advice he was about to give me as a sincere friend.

He said Mr. Lerdo had requested him to return me the letter I had addressed him on the 10th inst. After a long conversation, during which we both repeated old stories, Mr. Romero requested me to change the phraseology of the letter so as to make it acceptable to Mr. Lerdo, and he handed me a memorandum in his own handwriting, of a clause he wished me to insert in my letter, instead of the latter part of the letter I had submitted to Mr. Lerdo.

In reply I said to Mr. Romero that "this clause meant a virtual abandonment of all my claims without any further consideration."

Mr. Romero said: "Oh, no; I will see to it that the President does justice to you and your friends. Just pacify Mr. Lerdo, and all shall be right."

I said: "I have offered to relinquish my own individual claims for services and expenses if necessary, provided your Government will shortly, and before I return home, make a fair and honorable proposition for the settlement of all claims of those who have sent arms and ships to your country at my request and through my agency; or will make any arrangement with the parties themselves that shall be satisfactory to them, so that I may be relieved from blame and trouble; but I do not intend to be forced into relinquishing everything in this way. My friends will demand an account of me on my return, and will justly blame me if I do not guard their interests." I said that "Mr. Lerdo's conduct was simply outrageous, and looked like an attempt to take advantage of the fact that I had already engaged and paid for stage and railroad for Vera Cruz, and to force me to accept his terms, just or unjust."

Mr. Romero took hold of both my hands and begged me to favor him by modifying my letter. He said he would do his best with the President, and Cabinet, and Congress to have full justice done me and my friends. He feared that I would not get a cent now, unless I humored Mr. Lerdo; but if I did, all should be right, and perhaps before arriving home something will have been done for all of us.

After a long conversation, the details of which I can not now put down, as I am too excited, I told Mr. Romero that, out of consideration for the interests of my friends, and his own promises to see us fairly dealt by, I would change the form of the latter portion of my letter, but that would be the last change I would make in it, and if Mr. Lerdo did not accept, I should be able to obtain money enough to see me and my clerks home. I then instructed Mr. S. D. Stocking to insert the following clause, which being done, I returned the letter to Mr. Romero:

"Knowing, however, the condition of your treasury, I will not demand any cash from your Government for my services, trusting that when the whole circumstances of the case shall become fully understood by the members of the Government, it may of its own free will, see that I am remunerated in some other manner.

It may, therefore, be distinctly understood, that the question of compensation for my services is left entirely to the generosity of yourself and associates."

True copy of Memorandum made at 11 o'clock at night.

H. STURM.

Memorandum handed by Mr. Romero to General Sturm.

No. 850.]

I therefore can not accept your offer, and I prefer to render the services I have to the Mexican Government free from all compensation, expecting that this will be considered by the present administration, or any other, when I may be able to make an arrangement with your Government.

Sturm to Lerdo de Tejada.

No. 351.]   MEXICO, February 10, 1868.

Senor Don S. LERDO DE TEJADA,
    Minister of Foreign Relations.

Sir: I have the honor to acknowledge the receipt on this morning, of your communication of the 8th inst., in which you make two distinct propositions for the settlement of my accounts; and in reply I would respectfully state that I accept with pleasure the first proposition which you make me in regard to the payment of certain cash advances that I have made on account of your Government, with the understanding that I shall meet with no delay at the custom house in Vera Cruz in the payment of the amounts which you specify.

The amount which is due me on this account, as you correctly state in your letter, is, after deducting the sum of $2,550, which I have already received from the general treasury in this city, $41,958.63 specie. In liquidation of this account you will, therefore, be kind enough to give me one order for $20,972.32, payable at sight; and one order for $10,489.65, payable at sight on or after the 10th day of May, 1868, and one order for $10,489.66, payable at sight on or after the 10th day of August, 1868. I will also mention that in order to avoid future trouble, I think it would be well to mention on the face of each order, that the corresponding amount shall be exempt from all duties whatsoever for the purpose of exportation. By doing this you will enable me, in case of necessity, to sell my orders without having any further trouble with them.

The other proposition contained in your letter, in regard to the payment to me of $11,000, as payment in full for all claims that I have against your Government, both for myself and brother, for services rendered and expenses incurred up to the present time, I must respectfully decline.

Knowing, however, the condition of your treasury, will not demand any cash from your Government for my services, trusting that when the whole circumstances of the case shall have become fully understood by the members of the Government, it may, of its own free will, see that I am remunerated in some other manner.

It may, therefore, be distinctly understood that the question of compensation for my services is left entirely to the generosity of yourself and associates.

    I am, Sir, very respectfully,
        Your obedient servant,
                H. STURM.

Lerdo de Tejarda to Sturm.

[Translation.]

No. 352.]   MEXICO, February 12, 1868.

General HERMAN STURM.

Sir: In reply to your communication of day before yesterday, I send you a copy of the communication addressed by me this day to the Secretary of the

Treasury, requesting him to issue the corresponding orders of payment, according to the arrangement accepted by you for the payment of your account.

The Government of the Republic will take pleasure, should occasion hereafter arise in other matters, to give you such attention as is due to the services you have rendered.

I am Sir, very respectfully,
Your obedient servant,
LERDO DE TEJADA.

Romero to Sturm.

No. 353.] MEXICO, March 8, 1868.

General HERMAN STURM,
New York.

My Dear General: I hope that now, that you have seen how everything promised you was complied with, your mind will be a little more at ease, and you will judge more calmly about Mexico and Mexican affairs.

You have gained a great deal by coming here, and if you know how to behave, you will be able to accomplish almost all you want.

The two Republics has been assailing you, as you will see in the enclosed slip. I will defend you in our official paper.

Mr. Tifft left soon after you did, and if he did not go pleased, it certainly was not our fault.

My principal object in writing you now is to request of you to do me the favor of buying the following articles for me:

One good pair of revolvers, each in its case, with all its utensils, and besides, a leather case to carry them on horseback.

One good repeating rifle, of Henry's, Spencer, or any other author you think best, with a leather case, to carry it on horseback.

One pair of pocket pistols of Elliott's patent, both in one case, with its utensils.

Ammunition for all these weapons.

I would not like to spend, in all these, more than one hundred and fifty dollars, which Mr. Tifft will give you in case your engagements will not permit you to advance that money to me.

I would be obliged to you, if you fix all these arms in a box and send it to me, to the care of the collector at Vera Cruz, as a piece of my baggage.

The collector told me that he could not possibly get any eagle dollars for you, and that he had to pay you in small change. I regretted this very much, but he says that he could not help it. I instructed him, besides, to pay you the difference between eagle dollars and change, which he informs me he has already done so.

Matters go on here quite satisfactory. All we want is the confidence of the money men in the United States, so that they will invest their money in Mexican enterprises. Could you form a mining company with a capital of two or three hundred thousand dollars? I can have the control of some very good mines.

In great haste,
Most truly yours,
M. ROMERO.

Romero to Sturm.

No. 354.]   CITY OF MEXICO, August 10, 1868.

Gen. H. STURM,

Dear Sir: Yours of the 16th of July was duly received. I also regret to have left without seeing you at the time of my departure. With reference to the conversation you remind me of, be sure I will not forget it. I hope to hear from you again, as you say.

Accept my sincere thanks for your congratulations, and believe me as ever,
Yours truly,
M. ROMERO.

Sturm to Romero.

No. 355.]   *New York,* August, 28, 1868.

Senor M. ROMERO,

Dear Sir: At our last interview, just before your return to Mexico, I promised to write you more fully in relation to the subject of our conversation, as neither time nor opportunity would permit as full an interchange of views at that time as was mutually desired. Having been absent from this city for some time I have delayed until the present. In the meantime I have been pained by the attacks of the Mexican press upon me, and am convinced that they have their foundation in an entire misunderstanding of my position, and the character and value of the services I have rendered your Government at critical periods of its existence. From the nature and source of these attacks I feel that I can be excused for laying aside somewhat of modesty, and that my own self respect demands that I should place myself where impartial persons may know the truth and judge, with a full knowledge of the facts, as to the justice or injustice of these attacks.

The nature and value of my services, as well as the motive influencing my acts, is, I believe, well-known to you, and yet, as you desired at our last conversation, I shall take this means and opportunity of explaining, somewhat in detail, what may be misunderstood by some, or forgotten by others. For this purpose I must be pardoned for referring to the position held by me before I became actively interested in the success of your cause. For four years previous to that time I had held the honorable and remunerative position of Chief of Ordnance of the State of Indiana, and should have held that position until 1869. Unfortunately, as it seems, for myself, I became very much interested in the success of your cause in Mexico, and at the solicitation of your commissioner, and relying upon the good faith of the promises and pledges made by him as inducements to enter actively into the support of your cause, I resigned the position I then held, against the protestations of my friends, and entered with zeal into my new labors, which, from the almost hopeless condition of affairs in Mexico at that time, I believed to be, as I have since learned from experience, very arduous.

Advised by my friends that even should the Republic succeed, there was small chance of my receiving a recognition of my services, or even of obtaining the money which might be due me for salary, or even a return of the monies I must necessarily advance, I still determined to do what I considered my duty, relying upon the good faith of yourself, your Government and its commissioner, in whose patriotism and good intent I had confidence. What inducements were offered me, in view of the risk to be incurred, you are informed of.

From the unfortunate position of affairs in Mexico, and the complications which had arisen in the United States through the fraudulent acts of bad men who pretended to be acting under authority given them by agents of your Government, my duties, almost from the outset, were of a varied and difficult nature, and necessitated much more labor and expense than was at first contemplated, being not only military, but secret and confidential in their character.

A contract having been privately made, and intended to be executed between the Mexican Government and one Daniel Woodhouse, who claimed to represent a very wealthy and influential mercantile organization, was *not* executed, and all proceedings previously taken were annulled, in consequence of information obtained and communicated by me, that there was no foundation, stability or reliability to the pretended company, and that the representations made by Woodhouse were untrue in every respect.

This company had commenced negotiations with your accredited commissioner, for the placing of a loan of $50,000,000 in behalf of your Government, covenanting to make certain advances, and to give certain considerations, which agreements, on their part, were not executed. This rendered it necessary that other and reliable parties should be found who would undertake what had so disastrously failed in the first instance. Your commissioner (General Carvajal) desired me to do this, as money must first be obtained before my plans could be carried out. Having first had full conversation with the members of the house of John W. Corlies & Co., a mercantile house which I believed to be upright and capable of executing their pecuniary obligations, and finding them disposed to aid the financial part of the plan proposed by General Carvajal, I introduced them to General Carvajal, with whom they proceeded to make a contract covering the objects in view. With the full details of this contract I was not at that time fully conversant, a fact which I consider it but just I should state here, as much has been done through this connection for which I may have been blamed, and our different positions and duties to the Mexican Government, seemingly, has been misunderstood, since much that I have accomplished has been erroneously accredited to them.

At this time the financial credit of Mexico was at such a low standard, and so little confidence was felt in either her ability or good faith, that I found my own credit was being seriously affected by my active connection with her interests. Having for over three years, however, endured the mistrust of my business friends and the abuse of the American press, either inimical to your Government or subsidized by your active enemies on account of my so-called fanaticism in behalf of Republican Mexico, I feel confident of my ability to withstand and outlive the ungrateful and unjust attacks recently made upon me through the Mexican press, and rely solely upon time and the facts of my record to disabuse the minds of those wrongly informed, or maliciously and jealously unjust.

The true way to ascertain the value of your friends, is to judge of the motive which actuates, and the results accomplished for your good by them; and from this standpoint, I desire to be judged. You are fully aware of the motive, nature and extent of my services, but will excuse my referring briefly to them here, as with the pressing cares of your present position, something of the past may not be at once recalled.

In addition to much time and money spent by me in secret service, necessitated by the complications constantly arising, in procuring the influence of our most prominent men in behalf of Republican Mexico, and aiding the attempted passage of a bill through the American Congress looking to the guaranteeing of the payment of your bonds; to which expensive service, I was ordered by your commissioner, I have, individually, succeeded in obtaining credit for, as well as procuring on your bonds, at fair rates, large amounts of munitions of war, in value nearly 3,000,000 of dollars; and have shipped them to your country at different times during the war for independence, which you were then waging against a foreign invader. The Mexican Government, during the entire period, not having furnished me with *one dollar* to meet the necessary expenses attendant upon the transportation of these goods to and from different places in the United States, and from here to Mexico, such as drayage, lighterage, and the charter of vessels necessary to transport them to the ports most available for ready service. I was compelled to either deprive the Government of the use of these arms and munitions, and thereby endanger the success of the cause, or advance the required money myself, which I did promptly, and whenever there were goods enough on hand to warrant a shipment, taking therein what was considered by business men, to whom I unsuccessfully applied, to join me in advancing money, an unwarrantable risk of ever being repaid.

It was a fact, that though I procured from my personal friends, and by reason of the high character I had previously borne, such a large amount of material of war for Mexican Bonds, it was found impossible for your financial agents to sell, during the whole time, more than $9,000 worth of bonds for cash. An officer of your Government, who in exile was much distressed for food, was refused even a loaf of bread for $1,000 dollars of Mexican Bonds.

I simply desire to call these facts to your mind, since my motive has been so ungratefully assailed, and I think you, at least, in remembering these and other services rendered by me, can not endorse these misstatements, or impugn my motive.

The statement made, that my accounts were paid without even the presentation of vouchers, is untrue as you know, I having transmitted them to you with a full and tabular statement of all my operations, made in the form required in the United States service, and for which, I hold your receipt. On the contrary, it *is* true that *not all* for which I presented vouchers was paid; and equally true that I left Mexico dissatisfied with the course pursued toward myself and my friends, who had risked and accomplished so much, from which Mexico derived great benefit.

Without wishing to detract from the value of services attempted by others, though unsuccessful, so far as any practical results were attained, I can not fail to remark here, that if for the placing of $9,000 of bonds, your financial agents (Messrs. John W. Corlies & Co.) have received from your Government a return of the small advance made by them, and $1,000,000 in bonds, together with other and special and valuable advantages through their connection; I can not see how you can be surprised at my dissatisfaction, in being offered a partial return of money advanced by me (and that only upon vouchers presented) and the salary of a Brigadier-General in the Mexican service. This matter, however, being merely personal, and perhaps no more than was to have been expected in view of the warnings I had received from those less earnestly devoted to the success of your Government, could have been borne with less mortification, had the pledges been kept, which I had been authorized to make to my friends, and, relying upon which, they had so nobly aided me, and, through me, your cause.

I have been censured even by those who ought to be my firmest friends for my connection with the meeting of Mexican creditors, held at the Fifth Avenue Hotel, in May, 1868, and have been charged with being an enemy to Mexico, and the "mouthpiece and tool of American speculators." How much I deserve this, you will readily understand, when you consider the relations I held toward a large number of the creditors present at this meeting.

All the military goods purchased for the Mexican Government with bonds, were obtained by me, upon the representation that the contracts made with your Government would be faithfully executed, and the goods paid for as agreed. As the seat of your Government was however being constantly changed from place to place, until the fall of the so-called Empire, you were unable to obtain the desired instructions, and consequently you did not wish to take upon yourself the responsibility of settling the claims which had arisen through my negotiations, until you could obtain from your Government such instructions as would authorize you to do so. All this I explained, from time to time, as you communicated it to me, to the parties interested; and although it was difficult, and exceedingly unpleasant to me not to have these accounts settled at that time, I succeeded in pacifying the claimants; and I believe, with one exception, they patiently waited until such time as you, in full communication with your Government, might be enabled to adjust them.

One of my principal objects in going to Mexico last October was, as you are aware, to bring about a full settlement of all the accounts which had been contracted through my negotiation. You know how earnestly I urged you, during my stay in Mexico, and Mr. Lerdo, through you, not to compel me to return without having accomplished this result. Mr. Lerdo, however, for reasons unknown and inexplicable to me, declined then to adjust the accounts. I was thus compelled to return and meet your creditors, without being able to give them any good reason for this neglect. To their manifold questions, I gave such answers as were in accordance with truth, and after explaining your position, I urged them to correspond with you directly, as I had no doubt you would endeavor to bring about a settlement as soon as possible. Just at this time, your financial agent, Mr. Tifft, returned from Mexico, and almost immediately thereafter, I was besieged by a number of these creditors, who represented to me that they had seen Mr. Tifft, and from his conversation, they had formed the idea that the whole thing was a "big swindle;" that no interest upon the bonds would be paid for a long time, if then, etc., etc.; and they also stated to me that he (Mr. Tifft) had advised them to sell their bonds at whatever price they could get. Following this, came the news from Mexico, that a large sum of money had been sent here to buy up bonds at a discount, and that your Government did not pay the interest then past due and falling due, in order to depreciate the bonds, and enable your agents to buy them in at a low price, etc., etc.

Is it not natural that, under these circumstances, men who had given their goods for your bonds in good faith, during the most critical period of your late war for independence, relying upon the representations I had made to them, the good name I had borne, and *your* integrity; should have become incensed, and that some of them even began to doubt my honesty, and to intimate that I was in league with Mr. Tifft in this scheme, and was making money for myself at their expense?

You surely can not be surprised at their taking this view of the case, and must accord me the credit of having anticipated what I knew must inevitably follow the course pursued, and marked out by the Government in connection with these matters, for you will remember, that before leaving Mexico, I stated to you my belief that the creditors, who had waited long and patiently, would begin to suspect of bad faith, all who were connected with their claims, directly or indirectly, unless something was done looking to their settlement at least, before I should return.

You will remember that so fully did I appreciate the importance, both to myself and the Government, of these creditors being satisfied that I proposed to defer the settlement of my own personal accounts, should it interfere or intrude upon the time required to investigate and adjudicate the claims spoken of above.

Had you settled these claims, or placed me in a position to do so, I would have been enabled, on my return, to take a bold stand in favor of your Government, and referring to these very creditors, could have openly stated that the Republic of Mexico would settle all its just debts; that it had done so in this case and would continue to do so with all, when satisfied of their justice. But this pleasure was denied me, and on the contrary, I was compelled to be silent, that my motives might not be misjudged, and I not considered a party to a wrong act, or to a speculation, that under the circumstances, could reflect nothing but discredit.

When in May last, it was determined by some of your creditors to take some steps to obtain redress and to compel a settlement of their accounts, I was invited to be present, and at the meeting held, I urged a policy which was conciliatory and honorable, certainly not unjust, and could not but be advantageous to both, but more especially to your Government, viz.: The appointment of a Joint Commission, exactly as has just been arranged between the United States and Mexico.

Let us consider this matter, and then judge as to the justice of the charge, that I have acted unwisely or unfriendly toward Mexico. During the terms of various administrations in Mexico, that Government has conceded various grants and privileges to American citizens, the validity of which grants the present Government ignores, for various reasons. Numerous persons have presented claims also for personal damages, outrages to person and property, etc., etc.

During the recent struggle in Mexico, a variety of new claims have sprung up. These claims all remain *unsettled*, because the Mexican Government claims, that some of them are unjust, and in regard to the others, that it is not in a position to *pay* them at the present time.

It is quite supposable that a large number of these claims are fraudulent, illegitimate, extravagant, etc., and ought not to be paid by Mexico.

There is and has been a party here in the United States favoring the annexation or conquest of Mexico by the United States to satisfy these claims. This is backed up by Europeans. The American public have no means of judging of the justice of the claims presented, as no effort is made by the Mexican Government to settle them or determine their equity; and of course the public take it for granted that all these claims are valid and just, and believe that the administration of to-day, like some preceding ones, simply contracts but does not settle its accounts. This course causes bad feeling, and gives the interested parties the best opportunity to gain sympathy and to secure favor to their schemes.

The honest creditors are not the ones that have *created* bad feeling; they hope for a better state of affairs, relying on the justice of their claims. The *other* creditors will keep up the excitement; for the longer the trouble can be continued in Mexico, the more likely they regard it that eventually their claims will be acknowledged.

Of all the pretended claims against Mexico, the most infamous is that of Woodhouse, with his contract for bonds, etc. To-day all the witnesses to this attempted swindle are alive: yourself, General Carvajal, myself, Mr. Stocking, Fuentes, Navarro, etc., as well as different members of your own Government. Defer the settlement of this pretended claim for a few years, and Woodhouse will succeed in interesting a large number of persons (by selling or giving them bonds), to such an extent that this Woodhouse matter, easily settled now, will then assume perhaps the proportions and character of the Jecker fraud, and this simply from the fact that the Mexican Government has as yet taken no steps to set this matter in its true light before the public, and may one day be charged with complicity, in not having acted promptly to avoid seeming acquiescence in the pretensions of Woodhouse & Co. If it should eventually cost Mexico much money to settle with the innocent holders of these bonds, the fault will rest with Mexico and its Government solely. Have you thought of this?

The Commission can adjust and determine the validity of all claims, and although Mexico may not be able to pay all just dues at once, it can *arrange* for their payment, and thus vindicate itself from the stigma sought to be cast upon it, by these fictitious and fraudulent claimants; and can stand before the world as a nation that *is just*, and will not be regarded otherwise; jealous of its honor, and, from the independence which an innate sense of justice creates, not willing to be imposed upon. The Government of the United States will not allow our neighboring Republic to be swindled by citizens of the United States, but it must protect its own citizens as against injustice from Mexico.

When the labors of this Commission are concluded, and the just claims against Mexico have been ascertained and separated from the unjust ones, there will be left a comparatively small sum for Mexico to pay; and should it not be able to pay this amount at once, can there possibly be a difficulty in arranging a mode of payment which will be equitable and acceptable? I believe not; for the commercial advantages mutually enjoyed by both adjoining Republics can be so utilized by each as to make it to the interest of each to aid the other; and an easy method will be devised to settle amicably and advantageously all claims held by one against the other.

Mexico, being rid of all pretended claims, and having promptly settled its just indebtedness, will, if continuing this policy, command credit and confidence abroad, and secure peace and prosperity, such as it has never been her fortune heretofore to enjoy. For this I have labored earnestly and faithfully; and believing that in no *other* course is there true policy or hope of stable prosperity, in *this* course I shall continue, even though at present I may be misunderstood and my labor unappreciated.

I hope you may find it consistent with your sense of justice and propriety to make my views and consequent acts fully known to your Government.

Very respectfully,
Your obedient servant,
H. STURM.

Sturm to Romero.

No. 356.] September 28, 1868.

Senor M. ROMERO.

My Dear Sir: I received your letter of August 10th, and I send you to day the letter that I promised you. I commenced this letter in August last, but was delayed in forwarding it, on account of the cares I have had on my hands lately, principally on account of the insurance on the cargo of the schooner lost last fall, previous to our arrival in Mexico.

In my letter I say to you, as nearly as possible, what I intended to say when you were here; although much that I desired to say to you in person has, for the present, been withheld, as there are some things which I do not yet desire to commit to paper.

I may be in Mexico next winter, and in that case shall have an opportunity of conversing with you personally.

Neither your people or Government have understood me; but time will develop all this, and I believe that before long, they will see that the course pursued by me toward Mexico has been such as to serve her best interests; and if your Government would see its true interest, by assisting me in the course I have laid for myself in this matter, I believe that much good would result therefrom.

In great haste,
Yours truly,
H. STURM.

Sturm to Romero.

[Confidential.]

No. 357.] October 1, 1868.

Senor M. ROMERO,

Ever since our conversation here, I have thought of what you told me in relation to the bonds. I have also had repeated interviews with your bondholders, at which the matter of redemption of your bonds was discussed.

While I consider it a very unfortunate circumstance that the rumor was set afloat here that bonds were being bought up, and especially at the time and in the manner in which this report gained circulation, yet, as I told you at the time you were here, I consider it eminently right and proper, as well as beneficial, that you and the parties who have received these bonds should come to a direct and amicable arrangement, if it is desired to retire the bonds; and I have spoken freely but confidentially with several parties who received their bonds from me, and I believe that an arrangement can be effected with a large number which will be satisfactory both to you and to them.

I am now authorized to say, that bonds, probably to the amount of $250,000, can be arranged for at once; and I communicate this to you, and send you enclosed a copy of a note received in relation to this matter. *I desire it distinctly understood*, however, that in this matter my object is simply to render a service to these gentlemen, and also to the Government, if it desires to call in the bonds; and I do not desire, nor will I accept of any brokerage or commission, *in any way*, in connection with the matter. I am willing to aid both parties interested, in effecting any just arrangement, which shall be mutually satisfactory; and I believe that by an open, straightforward course, such as I suggest, (although confidentially and privately pursued to avoid speculation,) you may be able to obtain the larger part of your bonds. Although the greater portion of those having them, prefer to hold them now, yet if the matter treated of above is of any interest to you or your government, and you write me or them what you can pay for the bonds, I will give my services in trying to effect an arrangement.

I desire to say here, that this matter is confidential, and whether you write me or the parties holding the bonds, you will have to arrange the matter so that it shall not pass through the hands of third parties, (excepting, perhaps, Dr. Navarro or Government officials); for if any real good is to be secured, this is the only direct way of dealing; otherwise, doubt and suspicion will attach to the transaction, and the object would be defeated, and I could not have anything to do with it.

Hoping to hear from you again, and wishing you best success,

I am, Sir,

Yours truly,

H. STURM.

Sturm to Romero.

No. 358.] October 15, 1868.

[Private.]

Senor M. ROMERO,

My Dear Sir: When I last wrote you I intended to enclose a few documents which would show you exactly what ground I had taken in connection with Mexican creditors, and thus refute some statements made about me which are not in accordance with facts, but arose from a want of knowledge of myself and my doings. I send them to-day (having accidentally forgotten to mail them the last time) to you for your own private information and use there.

Had the Government, or yourself, only fully comprehended the disagreeable position in which I have been placed in consequence of my connection with purchases here, I am sure that not for a moment the thought would have been entertained, that I was assuming an inimical position toward Mexico from mercenary motives.

I think now that I shall be in Vera Cruz some time during November (in consequence of the lawsuit I have about the insurance of the schooner S. T. Keese, lost at sea just before my arrival in Mexico last year) and may then have an opportunity of writing you more from there. Until then I remain,

Yours truly,

H. STURM.

Sturm to Romero.

[Private.]

No. 359.] New York, October 28, 1868.

Senor M. ROMERO,

Dear Sir: I have now positively determined to sail for Vera Cruz per steamer Grenada on the 10th of November, for the purpose of collecting evidence in regard to the insurance on the Keese. The insurance companies have refused to pay, and are endeavoring to prove by Mr. Gamboa, Mr. Ritter, Mr. Carrau, a Mr. Tomayo, and a Mr. Oliver, (all of Vera Cruz) that there was no market for arms in Mexico, and that it was unusual for arms to be sent there, etc.: thus trying to make out that the only object I had in sending arms and munitions to Mexico was to defraud the insurance companies, as I could not possibly sell them in Mexico.

I find it, of course, very difficult to explain before the Court all my relations with Mexico, and how I came to send arms to your country, and the companies argue that no business man would take such a risk as I have taken unless he had some ulterior object in view, viz.: to make a dishonest profit out of the insurance companies.

When you see the complaint and allegations set up by the insurance companies in defense, you will observe how my good intentions and acts in behalf of your country are now being used to the detriment of myself and those of my friends whom I induced to send these arms to Mexico.

As you fully understand the whole history of my shipment of arms, and as I fear Mr. Gamboa may not so fully understand all the particulars, I take the liberty of asking you to inform Mr. Gamboa (who I know is a friend of yours) of the true facts in the case, and ask him to assist me in every way possible while in Vera Cruz on this business.

Should I lose the amount which I have in this shipment in addition to what I have already lost during the last three years, it will be a very severe blow.

By extending to me your kind offices in this matter you will confer a great favor, as you know I am a stranger in Vera Cruz and do not understand the language as well, perhaps, as the parties representing the insurance companies.

I shall remain but a very short time in Vera Cruz, and do not think it possible (owing to my engagements here) to go to the City of Mexico.

Trusting this may find you and your family in good health,

I am yours, etc.,

H. STURM.

Romero to Sturm.

No. 360.] MEXICO, October 24, 1868.

General H. STURM,
New York.

My Dear Sir: Last mail from the United States brought me your two letters of August 28th and September 28th, and your confidential letter of the 1st instant.

Although I do not have much time at my command, yet I will try to give you my views on the several points you mentioned in your letters. I am, indeed, very sorry that you was displeased with your trip to Mexico. My opinion is, that nothing was done while you was here which would give you a real offense. Some things were not done that might have been done to advantage; but if you had been a little more famillar with Mexican society and Mexican politics, you would not have taken any real exception at what was done. Both the President and Mr. Lerdo desired to please you; and you may not know it, but it is a fact, that but few others obtained what you was promised. Had you accepted all, and gone back to the United States to explain to your friends how you found matters, and what chances they had of making a settlement; to return to Mexico six or eight months later, affairs would have gone very differently. You could then have served better your friends and done more yourself. I remember I tried to persuade you to adopt this course. I was sincerely as anxious as you was yourself, that there should not be any misunderstanding between yourself and our friends and the Mexican Government.

I was a witness of your efforts to serve Mexico in her hour of need. I always did you full justice about this, as about everything else. Even when I thought you was trying to injure Mexico, I never said nor wrote, or much less published anything against you. I did not stop the payment of the money which was due to you, as I might have done.

Unfortunately, you misunderstood some things while here, and left somewhat offended. You took then a course which everybody here supposed was inimical to Mexico; and as there was no sufficient reason for it, the feeling was, of course, somewhat that of disappointment. While I was here the press did not say any thing against you, nor has it said anything since my return.

My desire is to settle, in good faith, the claims of all Americans who helped us in any way during our war with the French. One of my principal objects in going to Washington last summer was to come to an understanding with the Government of the United States about this. Fortunately we succeeded in this, and you know the treaty which was signed, and which is almost the same as you proposed at the meeting at the Fifth Avenue Hotel.

Our means do not allow us to make immediate settlement with all our creditors; but it is, and has been our policy to be always willing to make partial settlements with all those who are satisfied with little and offer some inducements. Mr. Tifft, Mr. Henry, and some others, have been settled with in this way; and if you have seen my last report on the finances, you may have noticed what a large amount we have employed in paying our debts.

As regards the subject of your confidential letter, I have to say, that should it be convenient for you to visit again Mexico, we might then come to an understanding about that and many other important matters, and that I would be very glad to again see you here.

In great hurry, I am, my dear General,
Very respectfully,
Your obedient servant,
M. ROMERO.

Romero to Sturm.

No. 361.] MEXICO, November 10, 1868.

General HERMAN STURM,
New York City.

Dear Sir: I received a few days ago a letter from you enclosing some printed documents about your position toward Mexico and the Mexican Government. I am very much obliged to you for your kindness in sending me these papers, which are interesting.

Mr. Tifft advised me of the lawsuit you are engaged in, and about the probable proceedings which may take place at Vera Cruz. I write to-day to Senor Gamboa about this.

Affairs continue to improve here. Congress has just passed a law authorizing the free exportation of silver and gold ore.

In great haste, I am,
My dear General,
Very respectfully,
Your obedient servant,
M. ROMERO.

Romero to Sturm.

No. 362.] MEXICO, December 12, 1868.

General H. STURM,

Dear Sir: You are aware how anxious I have been to make equitable settlements with the citizens of the United States holding reasonable claims against Mexico. We have just signed a treaty for this purpose, and have made, besides, partial settlements with several creditors.

As you are about returning to New York, I should be very much obliged to you, if you conveniently can inform me, after conversing with the interested parties, whether it is possible to make settlements with such of the claimants as are not willing to avail themselves of the stipulations of the treaty.

This information I desire for my own guidance and further action on the subject.

I am, General,
Very respectfully,
Your obedient servant,
M. ROMERO.

Garcia to Romero.

[Translation.]

[No. 363.] PUEBLA, December 12, 1868.

To Mr. MATTIAS ROMERO,
Minister, Mexico.

My Dear Sir and Friend: I have received both of your letters dated the 10th, and respond to them at once. I render to you my thanks for what I am informed in the one, which assures me that my recommendation of Don Ignacio Reynoso, of Chalchicomula, as been attended with good results; and in the other, by which you are pleased to interest me in favor of the credit of General Sturm against the State, which will be duly complied with in the shortest possible time, first for its justness, and lastly in compliance with your desires.

At this time I should make known to you that the payment of this credit has been delayed against my will, and which results from the immense difficulties which exist in the treasury of the mountain campaign, affecting nearly $200,000.

As an indication of my desire to comply in this case I have at once drawn in favor of said credit, on a small sum which I had in Vera Cruz.

I remain, as ever,
Truly your friend and
Obedient servant,
R. J. GARCIA.

Romero to Sturm.

[Translation.]

[No. 364.] MEXICO, December 15, 1868.

General STURM,
Hotel Yturbide,
Present.

Dear Friend: I enclose to you a copy of a letter sent to me by R. J. Garcia,

Governor of Puebla, in which he advises me of having attended to what I advised him to do, in reference to the payment of your credit.

I remain, as ever,
Your friend and truly,
M. ROMERO.

Sturm to Romero.

No. 365.]   MEXICO, December 16, 1868.

Senor M. ROMERO.

My dear Sir: Your kind note enclosing one from Governor Garcia of Puebla has come to hand, and I thank you heartily for your efforts in this matter.

In regard to the answer of the Governor, I can only say that I am much disappointed in not receiving the money due; were it my own only, I would not care so much, but as it is not, I shall have to make the most strenuous efforts to recover payment. The Governor has made so many promises, and violated all of them, even from one day to the other, that I can not place any more faith in him. As soon as the time arrives when I can see you with propriety, I will explain all this to you.

I have now determined to remain here for some days longer, as letters of importance from the United States, as also certain statements made here, and other disagreeable facts which have come to my knowledge, render it prudent that we should converse together fully before I depart.

Respectfully,
Yours truly,
H. STURM.

Ritter to Holder, Boker & Co.

[Translation.]

Vera Cruz Telegraph Line.

All despatches shall have the seal of [SEAL.] *this office.*

Sent from Vera Cruz.

No. 366.]   Received in MEXICO, December 17, 1868, at 3:25 P. M.

Messrs. HOLDER, BOKER & Co.:

This custom house has only nine hundred and odd dollars belonging to the Governor, but we have no order for its delivery to us.

RITTER.

Sturm to Lerdo de Tejada.

No. 367.]   MEXICO, December, 24, 1868.

Senor D. SEBASTIAN LERDO DE TEJADA,
    Minister, etc.

Sir: I take the liberty of writing to you, that owing to my protracted stay here, my funds are nearly exhausted, and I would respectfully ask you, in case the state of the Treasury permits it, to direct the payment to me of a small sum, say twenty-five hundred ($2,500) dollars, on account of the difference still existing in my favor.

Should you be able to grant this request, 1 should like to have this money by to-morrow, as I intend to return to Vera Cruz early on Monday next.

            I am, Sir, very respectfully,
                      Your obedient servant,
                                    H. STURM.

Sturm to Lerdo de Tejada.

No. 368.]   MEXICO, December 26, 1868.

Senor D. S. LERDO DE TEJADA,
    Minister, etc.

Sir: About one year ago you made to me an offer of a certain sum in payment for services rendered and expenses incurred by me while aiding your Government in the United States.

In my reply I think I stated, that as the sum was too small I respectfully declined your offer, hoping that at some future time your Government would remunerate me. I now take the liberty to again respectfully call your attention to the services rendered by me, and as I have left the specific amount to the generosity of your Government, I now simply ask you to favor me with a small sum of twenty-five hundred dollars on account.

Hoping to hear from you soon in reply,
        I remain,
                Respectfully yours,
                                    H. STURM.

Lerdo de Tejada to Sturm.

[Translation.]

No. 369.]   MEXICO, December 26, 1868.

General H. STURM,
    Present.

Sir: I have received your letter of this date in relation to the payment to you of the sum of $2,500 on account of the remuneration of the services rendered by you to Mexico, during the war against the foreign intervention.

For the various reasons explained to you in some of our conferences, I said to you in my letter of February 8th of the present year, tha. the Government was disposed to remunerate the services rendered by you during the period of two years and nine months, allowing you a salary of $4,000 per year, which would amount, for that time, to $11,000.

Although you did not accept this amount in your reply of February 10th, nevertheless, for the reasons pointed out by you in the conferences, the sum of $3,000 was ordered to be paid you, which sum was comprised in my communication of February 12th to the Treasury Department, a copy of which I sent you with my letter of the same day, and which also refers to other sums which have been paid to you in full.

As you do not inform me in your letter of to-day, whether you have decided to accept the whole or a part of the $8,000 remaining unpaid of the amount offered by the Government, I respectfully beg of you to take into consideration the difficulty necessarily in way, as a public functionary, in ordering the payment, out of the public funds, of an amount which has not been agreed upon and accepted.

I have no objection to ordering the payment to you of the $2,500, of which you speak in your letter of this date; but I would invite yorr attention to the necessity of your stating whether you accept wholly or in part the balance mentioned of the offer of the Government, so that payment may be made on account.

I am, Sir, very respectfully,
Your obedient servant,
S. LERDO DE TEJADA.

Sturm to Lerdo de Tejada.

No. 370.]   Mexico, December 26, 1868.

Senor LERDO DE TEJADA,
Minister, etc.

Sir: I have the honor to acknowledge the receipt of your letter of to-day, in which you inform me that you will dispose to pay me the sum of twenty-five hundred dollars, on account of services rendered by me (in addition to what you have previously given me) and you ask me again to fix definitely the sum I demand. In reply I can only refer to my previous letters, in which I have already said that I shall accept whatever the generosity of your Government may see fit to pay me in addition as a settlement in full.

I am sir, respectfully,
Your obedient servant,
H. STURM.

Romero to Sturm.

No 371.] MEXICO, December 27, 1868.

General H. STURM,
National Hotel.

My Dear General: I enclose to you Mr. Lerdo's answer to you, with a copy of his order to the Treasury. I send to-morrow this order by telegraph to Vera Cruz.

Respectfully,
Your obedient servant,
M. ROMERO.

Lerdo de Tejada to Sturm.

[Translation.]

No. 372] MEXICO, December 27, 1868.

General H. STURM,
Present.

Sir: I have to-day received your letter, dated on yesterday, in answer to mine in reply to the other letter you wrote to me on that date.

In view of what you state, I forward to the Minister of the Treasury on this day, a letter (the copy of which I herewith accompany) so that he may order the payment to you of two thousand five hundred ($2,500) dollars, which amount you requested to be paid to you on account of remuneration for the services you rendered to Mexico during the foreign invasion war.

As you persist in saying that you will leave it to the Government to fix the amount for the remuneration of your services, I must inform you that its consideration of this matter has not been pending, but was determined upon from the date of the letter I wrote to you on the 8th of February last.

I must reiterate what I said in my former letter to you, that there exists a difficulty in my repeatedly requesting the payment to you of sums on account of an amount which you have not expressed yourself as willing to accept, and should you desire to reserve the right to dispose of the balance of the sum determined upon on the 8th of February last, I deem it necessary that you at once decide whether you accept and conform to the said sum as remuneration for your services.

I am, your most obedient servant,
S. LERDO DE TEJADA.

Sturm to Romero.

No. 373.] PUEBLA, December 28, 1868.

Senor M. ROMERO.

My Dear Friend: I arrived here this day safe and sound. Not being able to obtain pen and ink, I write in pencil.

I received your note enclosing Mr. Lerdo's letter late last night. From the tenor of his letter, I believe he has not truly comprehended my motives and views. This does not matter, however, for the present.

I wish now to say a few words to you privately, as a sincere friend to your country and myself, viz: I wish you, if you can, to arrange with the Government to take the arms I have in this country at the prices I have stated, and I will give eighteen months' time to pay the same in, in regular installments; and I wish them to pay me individually $2,500, besides what I have already received from the Government, and I will give the Government a receipt in full of all demands. I am so anxious to go home and satisfy those friends that sent those arms.

You know that I can be of great assistance to your country, and of my willingness to do this, you certainly can have no doubt; for I have sacrificed much, and will now sacrifice all I have paid out, just to be able to do justice to those who helped you when I begged for aid for your country. All the expenses I have had in shipping these arms, and subsequent expenses, I will cheerfully lose, if I can only succeed in maintaining their good feeling towards Mexico and its affairs. *Do me the favor, therefore,* to explain this at once to the President and Mr. Lerdo, and telegraph me the result at Vera Cruz; and if you are certain that it can be done, I may return to settle everything in Mexico myself.

You may rest assured that I may be able to save Mexico ten times the cost of these arms, and immensely benefit her in many respects, if I succeed in settling all these pending affairs here.

I write this in a great hurry, as it is already very late; but I have thought of this all day, and am so anxious to let you know my ideas at once, that I send this by special messenger, so it may not miscarry.

Yours respectfully,

H. STURM.

Romero to Sturm.

No. 374.]   MEXICO, December 29, 1868.

General H. STURM,
   Vera Cruz.

My Dear General: I have just received your esteemed letter of yesterday, dated at Puebla. I am glad to hear that you had arrived well and safely to that city, and hope you will have a happy and pleasant trip.

I received last evening a telegraphic dispatch from Mr. Gamboa, stating that he had not been summoned to give his testimony in his case, so that I suppose you will arrive there in time.

Mr. Cripps sent me this morning a copy of a letter from Mr. Fitch to you, which I enclosed to Mr. Tifft by the extraordinary the English steamer.

Do not give yourself much concern about your services to Mexico. I know what they are, and will do what I can to compensate them.

I will mention to the President and Mr. Lerdo what you say about the arms, and will send you their answer.

By the English steamer I instructed Dr. Navarro of the President's disposition about the redemption of bonds. When you arrive in New York, see him, and you will find him fully instructed about it.

We have examined, too, the case of Messrs. Dewhurst & Emerson, and have concluded to make you the following proposition:

If they give up their bonds to Dr. Navarro, and all their claims against the Mexican Government for past transactions, we will pay them $25,000 in installments of $3,000 a month.

In great haste,
I am, my dear General,
Most truly your obedient servant,
M. ROMERO.

Sturm to Romero.

No. 375.] VERA CRUZ, January 5, 1869.

Senor M. ROMERO.

My Dear Friend: I have received your letter and also your telegram about the $2,500. General Foster informed me yesterday that this money is ready at the Commissioners, and I will obtain it to-day.

As regards my own salary and remuneration, it matters but little; but I am so anxious, as my letter will have shown you, that others should be satisfied. This is of more importance to me and your country than the settlement of my own affairs; and, as I stated to you, I will give up everything myself to have this done.

I notice what you say about settling the claim of Dewhurst & Emerson, but I don't think that they will accept the offer you have made. Be pleased to return to me, to New York, the letters from them which I left with you to show you my authority. I forgot to get them at the last moment.

I hope to hear from you in detail in regard to all those matters, at New York, and you may rest assured that I will do all I can to harmonize these different affairs.

Hoping that yourself and family are enjoying prosperity and happiness,
I am, dear Sir,
Truly yours,
H. STURM.

Romero to Sturm.

No. 376.] MEXICO, January 21, 1869.

General H. STURM,
 New-York City.

My Dear Friend: I duly received your letter of the 5th inst., dated at Vera Cruz, the day before you sailed for New York. I hope you had a pleasant trip, and are already at home.

I am glad to hear that the order for $2,500 on the Vera Cruz Custom House was received by you before you left Vera Cruz, and therefore in good time.

I am sorry you do not think it acceptable, the proposition I made to you to settle Messrs. Dewhurst & Emerson's claims against the Government of Mexico. We have considered again this matter, and being anxious as we are to make any sacrifice to settle all pending questions with American creditors, I am authorized to make you a new and more liberal proposition, to wit: That we will pay Messrs. D. & E. $35,000, instead of $25,000, I offered you in my last letter on this subject. This payment to be made in installments not to exceed of $3,000 or $4,000 a month; Messrs. D. & E. will give up all their claims against Mexico, and besides, surrender their bonds.

When you arrived in New York, I suppose you found Dr. Navarro authorized to treat with you on the other subject.

There is nothing new here. Congress is going to adjourn to-day. The law authorizing the free exportation of ore has already passed, so have the grants for the Tehuantepec and Guaymas railroads.

In great haste, I am, dear Sir,
 Very truly yours,
  M. ROMERO.

Sturm to Romero.

 WILLARD'S HOTEL,
No. 377.] WASHINGTON, D. C., February 3, 1869.

Senor M. ROMERO,

My Dear Sir: I arrived here safely a week ago, after having spent a week in Cuba; and although I have not time to write you much in detail, there are some matters concerning which I wish to speak to you at once. I have made the proposition to Messrs. Dewhurst & Emerson, as you requested me to, to settle their claim by paying them $25,000, but they have refused to accept this. I ascertain that they have sold their bonds to Mr. Tifft or Corlies & Co., for 17 per cent. currency. Of course, for the future, the idea of their returning the bonds paid to them is out of the question. They, like a number of others, are determined to place their claims before the Commission, and it is on this subject that I wish now to write you.

While in Mexico, I stated to you the advisability of settling *privately* all the contracts made during the late war, for material, etc. But as this has not been done, another difficulty presents itself, namely:

According to the strict interpretation of the wording of the Treaty, claims of this nature can not be placed before the Commission, as has already been ascertained by several parties here who are anxious either to be commissioners or attorneys for the claimants, and you may rest assured that as soon as this becomes publicly known, there will be disappointment and a renewal of the bitter feeling by those holding such claims against your country; and I, therefore, urge you, as a friend and as one who has the interests of both countries at heart, and who intends to deal justly throughout, to take this matter into immediate consideration, and endeavor if possible, by a voluntary act on the part of your Government, to avert this, and take into the provisions of the Treaty. all existing claims between the citizens of each country against the Government of the other.

I have explained to you fully in regard to this matter, and you understand the object I have at heart. This, however, can not be accomplished, unless all existing difficulties can be satisfactorily arranged; and to do this, it seems to me no better way can be devised than this plan of the settlement of *all* claims by a Commission.

I write this letter hurriedly, as the mail closes soon, and I must send it to-night in order to get it into the mail for the steamer to-morrow, and have not time to go into detail, nor is it necessary, as you fully appreciate the importance of this matter to your country, and also to yourself.

I shall await with anxiety a letter from you concerning this matter.

You may rest assured that I shall try to aid you in every way that shall tend to bring about a harmonious feeling between the citizens of the two countries, and tend to the development of the immense resources of Mexico.

Yours truly,

H. STURM.

My address is,
Postoffice box 1701,
New York City.

Sturm to Romero.

No. 378.] WASHINGTON, February 3, 1869.

Senor M. ROMERO,

Dear Sir: Since closing my letter of this date to you, it occurs to me to inform you that I saw Dr. Navarro in New York, but he had not received instructions from you as yet. If he has since that time, I have not been informed of it, nor have I had an opportunity of seeing the parties authorizing me to make the proposition I did to you.

Dr. Navarro is in Washington, but I have not been able as yet to see him, unfortunately calling always at the wrong time. I hope, however, to see him soon, and will try to arrange that affair, if he has received your instructions. I would also mention that Mr. Priest (the agent of the Insurance companies) left New York last Friday for Mexico, and I have no doubt that he will continue his nefarious proceedings in your country, and may take advantage of the letters of recommendation that you and others gave him, at my request, at the time. I then believed that he was engaged in *honorable* business. I now consider it my duty, therefore, to inform you of his departure hence for Vera Cruz I myself do not propose to follow him to frustrate his schemes in Mexico, whatever they may be, having neither time nor money to spare further, in counteracting his villainous acts, being fully satisfied that if the case requires that fraud should be resorted to by the companies, their case rests on a very insecure foundation.

Please give my kind regards to your family and my other friends in your city, and believe me,

Yours truly,

H. STURM.

P. S. Please do me the favor to tell Governor Baz, Fuentes, Macin, and others, that I neglected to leave my photograph with them as promised, but will send it shortly.

H. S.

Romero to Sturm.

No. 379.]   MEXICO, February 9, 1869.

My Dear Sir;

I have been deprived, of late, of the pleasure of hearing from you. Knowing the interest you take in Mexican affairs, it gives me pleasure to inform you that the condition of things at large continues to improve in this country, although slowly and with some difficulties.

Unfortunately we have now and then some military mutinies which, although easily subdued, cause us trouble and contribute to give us a bad character abroad. One of these mutinies took place at Puebla on the 3d instant under Don Miguel Negrete. He succeeded in causing a squadron of troops, which was on duty there, to rebel against the Government, in exacting some money, using of the most violent means, and he left the city as soon as he heard that the Government troops were about the town. A sufficient number of troops have been detached in pursuit of the rebels, and it is believed that they will not be able to keep their ground but a few days. This result shows that the military mutinies which, in former occasions, have caused so much harm in Mexico, are of little consequence now. It is likely this will discourage other parties from embarking in such undertakings in the future.

I am, my dear Sir, in haste,

Most truly your obedient servant,

M. ROMERO.

I will write you more fully by next mail. Negrete took your guns at Puebla.

General HERMAN STURM,
  New York City,
    New York.

Romero to Sturm.

No. 380.] MEXICO, February 27, 1869.

General HERMAN STURM,
  New York City.

My Dear General: The political condition of affairs has improved of late. Negrete's revolt ended very easily as soon as the Government troops were able to reach him. His men disbanded almost without fighting on the 20th instant. All the material of war he had with him was captured. Lewis Malo, the officer commanding the squadron which rebelled at Puebla, was killed in the engagement. Esteves, second in command, and several others were captured, and the affair is altogether ended.

The parties who started another rebellion at Apam were also routed and dispersed. So was Servando Canales, in the State of Tamaulipas, by General Escobedo's forces.

All these events will necessarily contribute to consolidate public peace in Mexico. The malcontents see now that they can not succeed any more in their machinations against the peace of the country, and it is not likely they will rise again.

The people are really tired of war, and quite anxious to consolidate peace. The opposition to the Government, formed of a very few persons who sympathized with the rebellion, have been clamoring for a change of Cabinet. As their motives for asking this are not patriotic and noble, and they can not in any way represent the country, their desires have not been complied with.

The commercial prostration unfortunately prevails as the natural consequence of the long war we have suffered.

In great hurry,
  I am, my dear General,
    Most truly yours,
      M. ROMERO.

Romero to Sturm.

No. 381.] MEXICO, February 27, 1869.

General H. STURM,
  New York City.

My Dear General: I enclose you, for your information, copy of a letter I addressed on the 23d instant to Messrs. Dewhurst & Emerson.

In great haste,
  I am, my dear General,
    Most truly yours,
      M. ROMERO.

Romero to Sturm.

No. 382.]   MEXICO, March 5, 1869.

General H. STURM,
New York City.

My Dear Sir: Yesterday I was favored with your two letters dated at Willard's Hotel, Washington, on the 4th ultimo. I am very glad to hear of your safe arrival in the United States.

I entirely agree with you about the convenience of extending the treaty for the settlement of claims between Mexico and the United States to all pending claims between both countries.

You very likely will hear before this of the proposition we had made to Messrs. Dewhurst and Emerson for the settlement of their claim. I am sorry they have disposed of their bonds, as this circumstance will make it a little more difficult to come to a settlement.

I sent you, a few days ago, a copy of a letter written by me to Messrs. D. & E. on this subject, under the basis that they still held these bonds.

Dr. Navarro has certainly received, long ago, my instructions about the bonds. Please see him about it again.

I notice what you say about Mr. Priest, and will act with caution.

It will give me pleasure to give your message to Governor Baz, Messrs. Fuentes, Macin, and others.

A gentleman by the name of H. R. Ludlow has come to this city as agent for Messrs. Schuyler, Hartley & Graham, of New York, for the settlement of some claims, connected with Captain McGaffey, about a cargo of arms sent to Tampico.

By next mail I will write you more fully, as I am now very much pressed for time.

In great hurry,
Most truly yours,

M. ROMERO.

Romero to Sturm.

No. 383]   MEXICO, March 2, 1869.

General HERMAN STURM,
New York City.

Dear Sir: Last mail from the United States brought me your favor of the 15th ultimo. I have written you fully in my previous letters about Messrs. Dewhurst & Emerson's claim. I really hope the terms of settlement I have offered them, will be acceptable to them.

Dr. Navarro has received instructions for the purpose you suggested while here, and they are repeated again by this mail for fear that the former ones sent to him might have been misled. I hope, with the aid of this instruction, your wishes will be realized.

We are very anxious to know here what will be the policy, as regards Mexico, of the new administration at Washington.

The condition of things continues to improve here, although slowly.

I am engaged now in preparing a system of reform of our financial laws, to lay it before Congress on their next session. If approved it may contribute, in a great measure, to the development of this country.

I was very anxious that we should have been represented at General Grant's inauguration, and have advised President Juarez to send General Porfirio Diaz as representative of Mexico in Washington. I hope the President will lose no time in making a fit appointment.

In great hurry,
  I am, dear Sir,
    Most truly,
      Your obedient servant,
        M. ROMERO.

I will speak to the President and Mr. Lerdo about your suggestions regarding the treaty of claims.

Romero to Sturm.

No. 384.]   MEXICO, April 28, 1869.

My Dear Sir:

I had none of your favors by last mail. As I know you would like to hear from Mexico, I give you the following news:

Political affairs here continue to improve, although slowly. We are now on the eve of our elections to Congress and the canvass is nearly as lively as it is in the United States on similar occasions. There is, however, small founded fear of any public disturbance, whatever may be the result of the elections.

There is not sufficient confidence felt yet on the part of the business class of the community in the consolidation of our institutions and the maintenance of public peace to encourage them to invest their money in enterprizes of public good. The result is, of course, that business is paralyzed, and that the national development of the country does not go on as rapidly as we desired. Otherwise the condition of things is satisfactory.

It has been rumored here that a revolution took place near Acapulco under General Alvarez. This, I am glad to hear, is not true.

        Most truly yours,
             M. ROMERO.

General HERMAN STURM,
  New York City,
    New York.

Romero to Sturm.

No. 385.]   MEXICO, June 21, 1869.

General H STURM,
  New York City.

My Dear General: I enclose to you, for your information, a slip from the "Two Republics," of this city, purporting to be in regard to an insurance affair concerning you.

    I am, General,
      Yours very truly,
         M. ROMERO.

Sturm to Romero.

[Private.]

No. 386.] INDIANAPOLIS, July 22d, 1869.

My Dear Mr. Romero:

I was very much pleased to receive this A. M. your letter of June 21st, and hasten to reply to it, so it may be sent by the next steamer, which leaves I think on Saturday or Monday next, from New York.

I have carefully and repeatedly read the extracts from the "Two Republics," which you enclosed, and I am of the opinion that the article never was written in Washington, but concocted in Mexico, or else sent there for publication, to be used here, whenever the trial should come off, or at such other time as it might be useful to influence somebody.

The article itself is incorrect in every particular; besides this, it appears very strange, that a correspondent in Washington should write thus, when, to my knowledge, not a single paper in this country has ever alluded to the subject; when, as you know from experience, correspondents of newspapers are very apt to publish everything they can get hold of, even if not true.

As I have not much time to day to write fully, for fear that my letter may not reach the steamer in time, I beg of you to take the paper containing the article, and compare it, while you are reading this letter, and you will come to the same conclusion as myself.

The vessel (Keese) was lost in October, 1867, while I was on my way to Mexico.

While I was in Mexico, Mr. Priest came to Vera Cruz and quietly prepared the way for a second *official* visit.

The crew of the Keese was not obtained from Chili; but was, on their arrival at New York, (from Vera Cruz,) at once taken hold of by the agents of the Insurance Company, who paid and maintained them till their examination, *August*, 1868, at which examination, the mate and steward testified positively against the companies, and the other three men in such a way, that while the testimony did me no harm, it yet showed clearly that they had been manipulated, and only testified thus because we would not pay them as the company did.

Mr. Priest, who had just returned from Chili, at the time of his first visit to Vera Cruz, was then sent to Vera Cruz to take *officially* the testimony of the men he had seen a year before. Apprised of this, I went also to Mexico, and we arrived in Vera Cruz (with General Rosecranz) the latter part of November, 1868. On our arrival, Mr. Priest, who found I was looking into matters, objected to taking testimony then, as he wished to go with General Rosecranz to Mexico; and arranged that nothing should be done till we both returned.

On our arrival in Mexico, he at once proceeded to betray me, by interesting or trying to interest various parties against me, and paying special attention to that class of persons, who were known or supposed to be *inimical* to the Government. Mr. Priest freely used his acquaintance with General Rosecranz, and also a certain letter of introduction given him by the *State Department* of the *United States*, to give himself weight, with such persons as he desired to manipulate.

You will recollect how singularly we found this out. Colonel Gagern, *a prisoner* at the time, had already written out a long article against you, Mariscal Baz, and others, containing almost the same statements contained in the article of the "Two Republics."

Mr. Priest, after obtaining from you and Mr. Mariscal, upon my recommendation, strong letters of recommendation, suddenly left, and the first we heard, was that he and Consul Saulnier, at Vera Cruz, (who at the same time was the agent of some of the New York insurance companies, in Vera Cruz,) had proceeded to take the testimony of the witnesses, without my being present as agreed. The testimony, however, was decidedly against the companies; and upon my return to Vera Cruz, the examination was suddenly closed, as Mr. Priest, *the official person* whom Saulnier recognized, refused to go on further, (the testimony being all in my favor.) You will also recollect the efforts made by Priest to obtain false testimony from Fitch, Green, Enking and others. The object simply was to bemuddle the case, so that if the companies should not be able to beat me on other grounds, the jury might at least be very doubtful about my whole connection with Mexico, and thus award me as little as possible.

Now let us look at the counter claim, or plea of the insurance companies. They claim,

1st. That the goods were not sent.

2d. If sent, the goods are valued too high, as they were bought with Mexican Bonds, of "little or no validity and doubtful legality, on which no interest has or will be paid, and which can to-day be bought in this market for five cents."

3d. That they are not bound to pay, because the whole transaction is illegal, as the arms were intended against a Government with which the Government of the United States was then at peace, and the shipment was therefore a violation of the neutrality of the United States, of which fact *your orators* (the companies) were at the time ignorant.

You will see on how weak grounds the companies stand, and they must, therefore, use intrigue and bribery to beat me, or else to delay me as much as possible to wear out my patience. But in this, they have reckoned without their host, and judgment day will come before my patience gives out entirely; and I will rather lose all I have, than to be defrauded out of what is justly due me, or those I represent.

In regard to the attempt to mix up the Suwanee, it is clear that Mr. Priest's object is to create some ill-feeling in *Mexico*, so that he may succeed to have plenty of false rumors, etc., in the newspapers.

Messrs. Schuyler, Hartley & Graham, Mr. Cattell and the American Arms Co., are amply able to show that the arms were delivered on board, and the whole affair of the loss was *bona fide*. I can not have anything to do with it as I have paid them, and have their receipt, they delivering the goods on board themselves; and besides this, three of my men, Captain McComb, Mr. Partridge and Mr. Southard. checked the goods as they went aboard. So we need not fear *scrutiny* at all; but the attempts to create false reports and manufacture evidence, etc., ought to be stopped if possible; but I can not know here what is said in your city. In this country, the companies will not be likely to attempt anything of the kind, but at a distance, where I cannot be, except at great expense, this is much safer for them.

I shall be much obliged to you, if you inform me of what is going on, and to do what you can to defeat these combinations.

I remain, in haste,
Yours truly,
H. STURM.
Postoffice Box 1701,
New York.

Romero to Sturm.

No. 387.]   MEXICO, August 11, 1869.

General HERMAN STURM.
  Postoffice Box 1,701,
    New York City, N. Y.

My Dear General: I have just received a press copy of your letter of the 22d ultimo, dated at Indianapolis, in answer to mine of the 21st June last

I agree with you that the correspondence published here by the "Two Republics" was written here, and not in Washington. Similar cases have occurred of late, in which I know the editor of that paper has made up letters from several places.

I have not had any of your letters for several months, and now only received a press copy of your favor.

Matters continue to improve here, although slowly. General Rosecranz is very earnest about forming a company to build a railroad here. I wish you would help him in that, as it will be a great and profitable undertaking. We need now more than ever the investment of foreign capital and skill, and especially American capital, in the development of the resources of Mexico.

In great haste,
  I am, my dear General,
    Most truly yours,
      M. ROMERO.

Sturm to Romero.

No. 388.]   INDIANAPOLIS, September 25, 1869.

Senor M. ROMERO.

My Dear Sir: I received yours of August 11th by to-day's mail. My original letter of July 22d has, doubtless, by this time arrived I can not understand how it happened I sent you a press copy, unless owing to the great hurry in which I wrote, two letters of the same kind were written, as I was writing a number of other letters at the same time, some of them in the city and some at home. I notice what you say about General Rosecranz and the railroad project. I write about that another letter.

You know about my suits against the twelve marine insurance companies of New York and Baltimore, arising out of the loss of the schooner S. T. Keese, on board of which were fifty-four thousand dollars worth (or more, I believe) of goods belonging to your Government, but insured in my name, and for which I have assumed the responsibility. The attempt of the companies, and their manner of defending themselves by bribed and perjured testimony, and of injuring my character is simply infamous.

You also know of the infamous and miserable attempt which J. Sampson Priest, the agent of the New York Board of Underwriters, made in your city to bribe men, who were supposed to be inimical to you and President Juarez, to make false affidavits about you and me, as well as other prominent gentlemen, and to suborn the press to publish certain articles against us; all of which he intended to use here in favor of the insurance companies and to defeat my claims. I wrote you in my last about this also. Since then, however, I have become fully convinced that other agents of these companies have bribed some of the sailors and are attempting to bribe several of my witnesses. Various rumors detrimental to my character and that of some of my friends, have been industriously circulated here, by means of the public press, for the purpose of injuring me and them in the estimation of the public, and no doubt with a view to influence the minds of persons who may be called on a jury to try and decide my cases.

In all these articles my connection with the "Mexican Swindle" is especially mentioned, and the fact commented upon, that I made large sums out of your Government and have trumped up claims against it.

I now wish to say to you, that my position is becoming almost unbearable; and if it is in your power at all to persuade your colleagues, composing the Cabinet of President Juarez, to come to some conclusion in regard to the claims contracted by me as the Agent of your Government, or even to officially and publicly state the exact status of my connection with your Government and the various matters that have been existing between us, you will confer a benefit on me and mine, for which I shall be ever grateful.

It is a hard thing for a man to bear, to be treated with coldness and ingratitude by those to whom he has been a true friend in their hour of adversity, and for whose salvation he has sacrificed himself and his all. But still harder is it when, in consequence of this, those from whom he has begged for and obtained the wherewith to support the life of a nation, begin to mistrust and accuse him of bad faith; and this nation looks calmly on, and does not think it worth while to pay any attention to the wants and sufferings of her former friend.

This, Mr. Romero, is actually the position in which I find myself placed. The parties who sold me the arms, and furnished me the ships to transport them to Mexico to assist your country in her hour of need, see no movement made looking to a fair settlement of their claims. The parties who accepted your bonds in payment for goods or services rendered, see no sign that looks like an attempt, even, of providing for the payment of the interest. Mr. Ames, Mr. Palmer, and several other gentlemen who forwarded at my request, (induced by the promises made of fair and honorable dealing towards them,) per steamer McCallum, and subsequently the arms, etc., to Tampico and Vera Cruz, are beginning to mistrust, and can not conceive that the Mexican authorities should be so callous to all feeling of honor as to treat me and them in the way we have been. And *all of them,* I fear, suspect that the many rumors afloat are true, and that an arrangement exists between me and the Mexican authorities by which we both profit at their expense; and they begin to fear that the whole thing is a "swindle."

Besides, there are not wanting those who chuckle over this state of affairs and regale my (and many of them your) friends with "*I told you so,*" and pointing to the past history of your country, they remark that "treachery" is one of the natural attributes of a Mexican.

I speak freely and frankly to you to-night, the same as I have often done before. I know you can not be held responsible for the shortcomings of your Government, nor can you individually and alone take ground against, and act contrary to the direct wishes and instructions of your Government, and I will do you the justice to say, that I believe, if you were alone, and could act as your heart dictates, all would be well, and Mexico would be a "nation" in the eyes of the world; but you now hold the responsible position of Secretary of the Treasury, and as such are a member of the Cabinet of President Juarez, and also know how generously my friends have assisted you and your Government, and how unselfish I have been in my endeavors to aid your country. You will remember that before leaving Mexico the last time, and several times previous, I offered to relinquish all my claims against your Government provided it would honorably settle with, and satisfactorily arrange the accounts due to those whom I induced to trust to "Mexican honor," and I now, for the last time, repeat this offer, and beg of you to induce your Government to clear up the cloud that is hanging over me in consequence of my connection with your Government. As you are aware, I do not fear labor, and can suffer all sorts of privations to assist a cause I believe to be right and just. I *can not,* and *will not,* allow my fair name and honor, and that of my family and friends to suffer in consequence of rumors which, *as you fully know, and your Government knows,* are false in every respect, and undeserved by me.

For one single individual to be opposed by a Government, and by all the creditors of that Government, made so by and in consequence of his zeal to assist it in a struggle against a European usurpation, and at the same time to fight against the intrigues of twelve corporations, with millions at their back, may seem difficult, and it may be thought by some that I will soon be crushed out of existence, but I assure you it shall not be done if I can help it. If I cannot gain any thing further, I will, at least, that the public and my children shall fully understand my whole connection with the Mexican Government, and they may judge whether I acted dishonestly, and have ever deserved such treatment as I have received at the hands of your Government.

Be pleased to let me hear something definite immediately, and remember,

Yours truly,

H. STURM.

Sturm to Mariscal.

No. 389.] WILLARD'S HOTEL,
WASHINGTON, D. C., November 23, 1869.

To his Excellency,
  IGNATIO MARISCAL,
    Minister, etc.

Sir: At your request I have furnished you with a copy of the pamphlet which I was about to publish, and, since you proposed that I should withhold the further circulation of the pamphlet until you could communicate with your Government, I submitted your proposition to my attorneys, Messrs. Johnston and Stanton, who have this morning had an interview with you on the subject.

They inform me that you express a desire that there should be an amicable, just, and honorable settlement between your Government and myself, and with this understanding they advise me to accept your proposition to withhold the further circulation of the pamphlet for fifty days, upon your assurance that you will use your good offices with your Government to procure a settlement. I have adopted their views, and am willing to accept your proposition, and after the acknowledgment of the receipt of this note, I will transmit to you, for the information of your Government, a statement of my demands, which are all based upon valid contracts, and actual services performed under them.

I am, Sir, very respectfully,
  Your obedient servant,
    H. STURM

Mariscal to Sturm.

No. 390.] WASHINGTON, November 23, 1869.

General HERMAN STURM,
  Washington, D. C.

MEXICAN LEGATION Sir: I am in ~~receipt of~~ your communication of to-day
  IN THE informing me that you have adopted the views of your
U. S. OF AMERICA. counsel, Messrs. Johnston and Stanton, to the effect that
  you should withhold the circulation of your pamphlet entitled: "The Republic of Mexico and its American Creditors," for the term of fifty days, as I have proposed, with a view to communicate with my Government in order to procure an amicable and just arrangement. You further inform me that, after my acknowledgment of the receipt of your note, you will transmit to me, for the information of my Government, a statement of your demands, based upon contracts and services rendered under them.

While confirming my proposition to Messrs. Johnston and Stanton, I have only to explain that the fifty days should be counted since the 4th of next month, or any other day when the steamer direct to Vera Cruz leaves the port of New-

York, as there is no other earlier opportunity to send my dispatches to Mexico. I shall wait for the statement you promise me, as well as four or five copies of your pamphlet, for the proper information of the Mexican Government.

Very respectfully,
Your obedient servant,
IGNATIO MARISCAL.

Sturm to Mariscal.

No. 391.]
TAYLOR'S HOTEL,
JERSEY CITY, N. J., November 25, 1869.

To His Excellency,
   IGNATIO MARISCAL,
      Minister, etc.

Sir: I have the honor to acknowledge the receipt of your communication of November 23d, and herewith send you five copies of the pamphlet as you requested:

Messrs. Johnston and Stanton have assured me of the kind feeling you entertain toward me, and of your expressed desire to bring about a friendly settlement of my claims against your Government, and in accordance with the wish expressed in your letter, to prevent the circulation of my pamphlet, I have, yesterday and to-day, requested those friends to whom I had already furnished some copies, to withhold them from the public for the present.

I need not assure you that the kind feelings you have expressed for me are fully reciprocated. and I sincerely hope you will be able to convince your Government that a prompt and amicable settlement will conduce largely to its benefit, and will simply accord me tardy justice. The statements, etc., of my demands, though known to your Government, I will transmit you to-morrow.

Very respectfully,
Your obedient servant,
H. STURM.

No. 392]
TAYLOR'S HOTEL,
JERSEY CITY, N. J., November 26, 1869.

To His Excellency,
   IGNATIO MARISCAL,
      Minister, etc., etc.

Sir: I herewith give you the statement of my demands against your Government, as I promised in my letter of November 23d, viz:

1. For cash expended by me while aiding your Government in various ways, during the years 1865, 1866, 1867...................... $157,500.00
2. For personal services during that time....................................... 100,000.00
3. For secret service, performed by numerous friends, to whom I am obligated for the amount, as per agreement with General Carvajal, dated August 25th, 1865 .... 500,000.00

Total in United States currency.. $757,500.00
Interest at 7 per cent. per annum from January 1st, 1868 .... 106,050.00

Total.. $863,550.00

4. For gold advanced to anticipate payment of interest on bonds, coupons of which are in my possession, the sum of $13,300.00
Interest at 7 per cent. for three years.. 2,793 00

Total, in gold.. $16,093.00

Grand total in United States currency.......... $863,550.00
Grand total in gold....................................... 16,093.00

The above amount is subject to a credit for the moneys I have received from the Mexican Government. This amount I have not the means of ascertaining correctly now, as my papers are at Indianapolis, but can readily be obtained hereafter, and is fully known to your Government.

When in 1867 I went to Mexico with Senor Romero, for the purpose of settling my accounts with your Government, I was lead to believe that your Government would fairly remunerate me, and confident that it would gladly accept my generous offers, I proposed to accept cash for those expenses only, incurred directly in connection with the purchase and shipment of arms, and in paying old drafts against your Government, which stood in the way of obtaining goods for bonds, for which expenses I have rendered Senor Romero detailed accounts and vouchers; and for payment for my own services and the services of others, I offered to accept, in lieu of money, either some franchises, grants, lands, or other privileges; and I left it to the generosity of your Government to determine the amount due for my own personal services; and, during my last visit to Mexico, I again offered in writing, to make a *present* of my claim for personal services to your Government, if it would promptly settle for the amounts due those whom I had induced to trust your Government; but as your Government has not seen fit to accept my proposition, and as the amount offered me ($11,000) is entirely inadequate, as it will not even pay my traveling expenses, I am reluctantly forced to state my own figures, which I think every fair minded man will consider very reasonable.

Hoping to hear from you as soon as you receive a reply from your Government.

I remain, very respectfully,

H. STURM.

Mariscal to Sturm.

No. 393.]   WASHINGTON, November 30, 1869.

General HERMAN STURM,
    Jersey City, N. J.

MEXICAN LEGATION IN THE U. S. OF AMERICA.

Sir: I have received your communication, dated on the 26th inst., containing a statement of the sums which you claim from the Mexican Government, and at the same time five copies of your pamphlet, "The Republic of Mexico and its American Creditors." As agreed with your attorneys, I will send your statement and some copies of the pamphlet to my Government, with such explanations as may be conducive to have the subject of your claims reconsidered; and as soon as I may receive an answer, I will communicate it to you. In the meantime, I rely on your promise that the circulation of said pamphlet will be stopped.

I have also to acknowledge the receipt of your letter, dated the 23d inst., and assure you that you are not mistaken in considering my determination to consult my Government before your pamphlet is further circulated, as prompted by a friendly feeling to yourself, no less than by the wish to serve the interests of my country.

                I remain, General, respectfully,
                          Your obedient servant,
                                    IGNATIO MARISCAL.

DEPOSITIONS.

Deposition of William H. H. Terrell.

No. 894.]

Deponent deposes and says, that his name is William H. H. Terrell; his age is forty-four years; he was born in Henry county, Kentucky; is a citizen of the State of Indiana, and resides at present in the city of Washington; his occupation is Third Assistant Post Master General of the United States; that at the time of the happening of the events concerning which he testifies, he resided in the city of Indianapolis, in the State of Indiana, and his occupation that of Adjutant General of said State, with the rank, pay, and allowances of a Brigadier General in the Army of the United States; and that he has no interest, direct or indirect, and is not the agent or attorney of any one having any interest, direct or indirect, in the claim concerning which he now testifies.

Deponent, upon his oath, further says, that he is acquainted with the claimant in this case, General Herman Sturm; that he has known him intimately since June, 1861, at which time said Sturm was Superintendent of the Indiana State Arsenal, at Indianapolis, Indiana; and that he was subsequently Chief of Ordnance of the State of Indiana, with the rank of Colonel; and that afterwards, in consideration of his faithful services, he was commissioned by the Governor of said State a Brigadier General. That as such Superintendent of the Indiana State Arsenal, and as Chief of Ordnance of said State, as aforesaid, said Sturm had official and personal charge and control of said Arsenal and of the general ordnance affairs of the State as relates to the fabrication of ammunition and the care and custody of large quantities of ordnance stores, including small arms, field and heavy ordnance, equipments, etc., issued by the State during the war of the Rebellion for and on behalf of the State and United States governments to over two hundred and fifty thousand (250,000) troops, who were enrolled in said State as volunteers, militia, etc., during said war. That as such Superintendent of the Arsenal and Chief of Ordnance of said State, said Sturm served continuously, under his several appointments and commissions, until some time about the first of May, 1865, when he retired from active service; though, for the purpose of making settlement with the Government of the United States of the State Ordnance accounts, he rendered considerable and valuable service to the State after that date.

Further testifying, deponent says, that during all the time, from June, 1861, to May, 1865, said Sturm was compelled to assume, and did assume, under the orders of the Governor of the State and other superior officers, great responsibility and labor, as well in superintending and managing the Arsenal, purchasing supplies, and conducting its business—amounting, altogether, to the sum of $788,838.45—as in receiving, storing, repairing, and issuing arms, equipments, and other property of immense value belonging to the United States and placed under the control of the Governor for the use of volunteers, including also arms, equipments, etc., belonging to the State for the use of the militia thereof. That in conducting, managing, and superintending the great and important business entrusted to and performed by him, as aforesaid, General Sturm displayed the highest order of ability, the most inflexible integrity and indefatigable energy and industry. That his accounts, books, and vouchers were audited and allowed by reliable and sworn officers of the State government, after the most thorough and rigid examination and scrutiny; and that deponent, though officially and personally familiar with all his transactions with the State and United States governments, can not now recall a single instance in which the official or personal conduct of General Sturm was found to be improper; on the contrary, deponent expressly states, that throughout the entire term of General Sturm's long and honorable, as well as responsible service, as hereinbefore set forth, he was repeatedly endorsed and commended by the Governor and military authorities of the State and by the State Legislative Committees, by whom his transactions were examined.

Deponent further says, that about the month of June, 1865, he learned from gentlemen of high official position in the United States, and subsequently from General Sturm himself, that he (General Sturm) had been engaged by the Republican Government of Mexico to act as Agent for said Government in the purchase and shipment of arms, ammunition, quartermasters' and commissary supplies, and to do and perform all necessary and proper acts appertaining to said agency; that said Sturm made his plans known to deponent, from time to time, and exhibited to deponent the written authority and orders under which he proposed to act for said Republican Government of Mexico; that he invited and urged me to take an interest with him in the Mexican cause, earnestly maintaining that it was the duty of every citizen of the United States to sustain and aid the legitimate Republican Government of Mexico, and secure the overthrow of the usurper, Maximilian. Being on terms of confidential intimacy with General Sturm, he frankly made known to me the promises, agreements, and powers that had been made and granted to him by the authorities of the Mexican Government, and exhibited to me all the documents appertaining thereto, except such as related to secret service, and expressed his entire faith and confidence in the integrity of said government, and in its ability to overthrow the so-called Empire of Maximilian and restore the Republic. General Sturm was very earnest, industrious and enthusiastic in his efforts to aid the Republican Government of Mexico, and by his personal influence and the influence of prominent men in the State of Indiana and elsewhere, succeeded in creating a very favorable public opinion in behalf of the Mexican cause; he enlisted the press and leading banks in his endeavors to raise the credit of the Republic, with the view of securing the sale of its bonds, and, on all occasions, wherever opportunity offered, displayed the utmost zeal and energy in building up public sentiment in favor of the Republican Government of Mexico.

Deponent knows that through the efforts and influence of General Sturm, a resolution highly favorable to that government was passed by the Legislature of the State of Indiana, which was subsequently transmitted by the Governor of said State to the Congress of the United States and to the Executives of the several States.

From deponent's long and intimate acquaintance with General Sturm, personally and officially, he now states that he believes said Sturm, during his whole service under the Mexican Government, acted in the most perfect good faith and exerted himself in the most faithful and zealous manner to advance its interests in this country, spending his own private means to that end and contributing in every possible way to the success of the cause he had espoused.

And deponent further saith not.

W. H. H. TERRELL.

Deposition of John J. Hayden.

No. 395.]

The said John J. Hayden being first duly cautioned and sworn to tell the truth, the whole truth, and nothing but the truth, deposes and says, that his name is John J. Hayden; his age is fifty-one years; he was born in Indiana; his residence is in Indianapolis, and his occupation is that of insurance agent, and that at the time of the happening of the events concerning which he testifies, his residence was in Indianapolis, and his occupation that of insurance agent, and that he has no interest direct or indirect, and is not the attorney or agent of any one having any interest direct or indirect in the claim concerning which he now testifies.

Deponent further says that he is now, and has been for several years last past intimately acquainted with the above named claimant, General Herman Sturm; that in or about the month of May, A. D. 1865, said Sturm held the position of Chief of Ordnance for the State of Indiana, and also held a very high and honorable position, both as an officer and a citizen in this community; and was always esteemed a man of the strictest integrity and high sense of honor, and was possessed of valuable real estate in this city, and that when said Sturm proposed to resign his position as Chief of Ordnance of said State to enter into the employment of the Mexican government, many of his warm political and personal friends doubted the propriety of his undertaking, both in regard to its financial as well as social views, as but little confidence was felt as to the stability of the Republic of Mexico.

Some time in the fall of 1865, General Sturm made an arrangement with deponent to endeavor to make sale of bonds of the said Republic of Mexico at and for the price of sixty cents in United States currency, for each dollar of Mexican bonds. Deponent during a visit to the city of New York and Washington made some inquiry concerning said bonds, and believing they were duly authorized by said government of Mexico, and that there was no objection on the part of the United States government to the sale of said bonds, made considerable effort to negotiate and make sale of the bonds of said Republic of Mexico, by the distribution of printed circulars in relation thereto, through the mails and otherwise, but was never able to effect the sale of a single bond, for the reason that he could find no one who had sufficient confidence in them to make such investment of their funds, and therefore voluntarily abandoned all further effort to dispose of the same.

Deponent however believes, from frequent conversations with General Sturm, that he still had faith in the success of the Mexican cause, and that he still continued his efforts in her behalf, expending money freely and liberally, and personally advocating the cause of the Republic of Mexico, and in fact appeared to be devoting his whole time and energies in her behalf—but has recently been informed by said General Sturm that in consequence of the non-fulfillment of the agreement or contract on the part of the Mexican government with him (the said Sturm) that he has been seriously injured—financially and in business credit, and that he now seeks indemnity of said government for his outlay of time and money for the last several years past—and to which deponent believes he is justly entitled, as he has been zealous, active, and energetic in his labors in behalf of said Republic of Mexico—enduring the privation of home for long periods of time, and evidently to the great neglect of other interests which would have yielded him handsome profit by proper care and attention.

Deponent further states that during his long acquaintance with General Sturm, his personal characteristics, in addition to those of a perfect gentleman, an honorable citizen and an upright man, are untiring energy in his every undertaking, faithfulness to every trust, and splendid executive ability to accomplish whatever he has undertaken; to which and for which he can doubtless submit abundant and more valuable proof.

JOHN J. HAYDEN.

Deposition of Thomas B. McCarty.

No. 396.]

The said Thomas B. McCarty being first duly cautioned and sworn to tell the truth, the whole truth, and nothing but the truth, deposes and says that his name is Thomas B. McCarty; his age is fifty-one years; his residence is in the city of Indianapolis, in said county and State, and his occupation is that of a general manufacturer, and at the time of the happening of the events concerning which he testifies, he was Auditor of the State of Indiana, and his residence was in said city of Indianapolis; that he was born in Meade county, State of Kentucky; that he has no interest, direct or indirect, and is not the attorney or agent of any one having any interest direct or indirect, in the claim concerning which he now testifies.

Deponent further says that he has been intimately acquainted with the above-named claimant, General Herman Sturm, for several years last past; that in the year 1865, said Sturm was Chief of Ordnance for the State of Indiana, which said position he resigned for the purpose and object in view of engaging in the cause of the Republic of Mexico; that upon different occasions deponent met said Sturm, both in the cities of New York and Washington, where said Sturm gave large parties and entertainments at which many prominent men were present, with whom he labored energetically to enlist their sympathies and aid for the cause of the Republic of Mexico; that said Sturm used money freely and liberally by employing many agents throughout the United States, and by enlisting the sympathy of his many warm personal friends, and by advocating through the public press of the country, and in the Legislatures of several States, and in the Congress of the United States, the cause of the Republic of Mexico; that said Sturm was untiring in his efforts for said cause, and deponent says that the success said Sturm met with, is due mainly to his high social and political standing, and the liberality with which he furnished means for the advancement of the interests of the Republic of Mexico; deponent further says, that in consequence of the non-fulfillment on the part of the Mexican Government of its pledges and promises to said Sturm, the latter has been seriously injured in his credit and business standing, and in many cases suffered in his reputation with such persons as were not intimately acquainted with him, the condition of Mexican affairs, the true relations said Sturm held toward the government, and the many difficulties and obstacles he had to meet in his endeavors to aid the Mexican Government; deponent knows that some of the parties who furnished material through the agency of General Sturm upon Mexican credit, under the misapprehension of facts, sued said Sturm, and held him personally responsible for debts due them from the Mexican Government, for interest on Mexican bonds that they had purchased, for material of war, or other aid or services furnished or rendered by them to the Mexican Government, and in this way said Sturm has for more than two years been annoyed and harrassed, and unable to attend to his manufacturing interests and other business in this city, which he had to leave in the hands of agents, and deponent being intimately acquainted with General Sturm, his family and his interests in this city, verily believes that said Sturm has lost largely in a pecuniary sense, and also in reputation, except with his intimate friends, in consequence of his connection with the Government of Mexico, and of his zeal to aid the cause of that country; and deponent believes that said Sturm is entitled to the most liberal allowance from, and the grateful acknowledgments of the Republic of Mexico for the many, and under the circumstances, invaluable services he has rendered to the Republican cause of Mexico, and the material aid he has succeeded in obtaining for the government of that country, when but few men were willing to believe in its perpetuity, and further deponent saith not.

THOS. B. McCARTY.

Deposition of Charles A. Ray.

[No. 397.]

The said Charles A. Ray being first duly cautioned and sworn to tell the whole truth, and nothing but the truth, deposes and says that his name is Charles A. Ray; his age is forty-two years; his residence is in said city of Indianapolis, and his occupation at present is that of an attorney at law, and that at the time of the happening of the events concerning which he testifies, his residence was said city of Indianapolis, and his occupation that of a Judge of the Supreme Court for the State of Indiana, and that he has no interest, direct or indirect, and is not the attorney or agent of any one having any interest, direct or indirect, in the claim concerning which he now testifies; deponent further says that he is well acquainted with the above-named claimant, General Herman Sturm, and he has known him intimately for about ten years last past; that in the year 1865 said Sturm was Chief of Ordnance for the State of Indiana, and held a very high and honorable position in this community, both as an officer and citizen; that some time in the year 1865 said Sturm resigned his position as said Chief of Ordnance for said State, and entered into the employment or service of the Government of the Republic of Mexico for the purpose of aiding that Government in its struggle with its foreign invaders; deponent further says that while in the city of New York he met said Sturm upon different occasions, who was always advocating the cause of the Republic of Mexico; that said Sturm seemed untiring in his efforts in behalf of that Government; deponent further says that said Sturm continued these efforts by using money freely and liberally, by employing many agents throughout the United States, and also by enlisting the sympathies of his many warm personal friends, and by advocating through the public press of this country, and in the legislatures of several States, and in the Congress of the United States the cause of the Republic of Mexico, he succeeded in obtaining for the Mexican Government a large amount of sympathy and material aid in the shape of arms and other necessary supplies. Deponent further says that he met General Sturm repeatedly in Washington City, and that claimant labored industriously with the prominent men of this country in behalf of the Mexican cause. Deponent further says that in consequence of the non-fulfillment of the pledges and promises of the Mexican Government made to said General Sturm, the latter has been, as deponent verily believes, seriously injured in his credit and business standing, and has also in many instances suffered heavily in reputation, as many persons who did credit the Mexican Government and failed to receive from it the promised payment, attributed this failure to a plan or scheme of that Government to defraud them, to which they finally—but deponent did not, and does not—believed said Sturm to be a party. Deponent further says that General Sturm has been almost constantly, from the early part of the year 1865 until some time in the summer of the present year, separated from his home here and his family, and been compelled to have his manufacturing and other business interests here, as also his real estate property, in the hands of agents; and that, as deponent believes, in consequence of his absence, he has lost heavily, so much so that he has been compelled to mortgage his property, and otherwise borrow money to enable him to prosecute his claims against the Government of the Republic of Mexico; that, considering the many cares and responsibilities attached to the employment of said claimant for the Mexican Government, as well as the many services and material aid rendered that Government by said Sturm; considering the many difficulties and obstacles with which he must necessarily be overcome while advocating the cause and obtaining assistance for said Government; considering the time he was absent from his home, family, and business interests here, and also the losses he might, and as deponent believes, did sustain by reason of such absence, deponent does not hesitate to say that General Sturm is entitled to the most liberal treatment and pay from the Government of the Republic of Mexico.

CHARLES A. RAY.

Deposition of William R. Holloway.

No. 398.]

The said William R. Holloway, being first duly cautioned and sworn to tell the truth, the whole truth, and nothing but the truth, deposes and says, that his name is William R. Holloway; that his age is thirty-four years; that he was born in the county of Wayne and State of Indiana; and that his residence is now in said city of Indianapolis; and that his occupation is that of Postmaster of said city, and is one of the proprietors of the "Indianapolis Daily Journal;" and that at the time of the happening of the events concerning which he testifies, his residence was in said city of Indianapolis and his occupation that of one of the proprietors of said "Indianapolis Daily Journal;" and that he has no interest, direct or indirect, and is not the agent or attorney of any one having an interest, direct or indirect, in the claim concerning which he now testifies.

Deponent further says, that he is personally and intimately acquainted with the claimant, Gen. Herman Sturm, a citizen of Indianapolis in the said State of Indiana, and has known him for ten years last past; that some time during the spring of 1865, said claimant approached this deponent, in the city of Washington, D. C., and repeatedly thereafter in said city of Indianapolis, in reference to engaging and securing the support and influence of said "Indianapolis Daily Journal" in behalf of the cause of the Republic of Mexico, and against the usurper, Maximilian and his French allies; that said claimant represented to this deponent that he was the Agent of the Republic of Mexico, duly authorized and empowered to act as such; that this deponent, through influential friends and persons in official positions at the city of Washington, D. C., ascertained from Senor Romero, then the Minister of the Republic of Mexico, at said city of Washington, that said General Herman Sturm was the duly authorized Agent of the Republic of Mexico, and was duly empowered to act as such in the United States, and would be so respected by the government of Mexico; that in accordance with the information so received, this deponent further says, that he agreed with said Sturm to render, and that he did render, to the cause of Mexico the influence and support of the Indianapolis Daily Journal against the then existing foreign invasions and usurpations, and that said support and influence of said Daily Journal was continued until all foreign enemies were ejected from the soil of Mexico; that the above mentioned services were rendered to the Republic of Mexico upon the personal request and solicitations of said Sturm. This deponent further says, that he knows from his own personal knowledge, during the years 1865 and 1866, said Sturm did employ many agents in different parts of the United States, in the interests of the cause of the Republic of Mexico, and expended large sums of money in the furtherance of the objects he was endeavoring to accomplish in behalf of said Mexico; that said Sturm at all times manifested great zeal in behalf of the cause of Mexico, and was indefatigable and untiring in his efforts and labors therein; that at various times this deponent accompanied said Sturm to different cities in the United States, where said Sturm was laboring in the interests of Mexico, and that at many times capitalists and business men warned said Sturm and advised him against expending his time and means in behalf of a government so notorious for its bad faith as Mexico, but that, upon the other hand, such seemed to be his implicit confidence in the good faith of the government of Mexico, that such warnings and repre—

sentations had the effect only to confirm him in his judgment, and to call forth from him renewed energies in the accomplishment of his purpose; that in the winter of 1865, said Sturm labored earnestly and for a long time with the Legislature of the State of Indiana to obtain from them the adoption of a resolution in favor of aid to the Republic of Mexico, and against the intervention of foreign powers in that country, which said resolution was finally passed; that this deponent was also present several times in the city of Washington, D. C., in the early part of 1866, and was a witness to the exertions of said Sturm to obtain from the United States a guaranty of a Mexican loan; this deponent also states, from his own personal knowledge, that the rooms of said Sturm, in said city of Washington, were visited hourly and daily by prominent and influential citizens and officials of the United States, with whom said Sturm was laboring for the good of Mexico, and that he spent his money freely, and must have incurred, as this deponent believes, expenses to the amount of many thousand dollars; that the efforts and exertions of said Sturm, for the purposes hereinbefore stated in behalf of the Republic of Mexico, were continued and did not end until after the cessation of all foreign invasions therein, and until the establishment of President Juarez and the Republican form of government; and from his own knowledge knows, that in consequence of the violation of the pledges and promises made to said Sturm by the government of Mexico, he has been entangled in vexatious lawsuits and annoying disputes, and has borne, pecuniarily, serious embarrassments, and has been unable to attend to any other business until the month of July, 1871, and has been compelled to place his business and property at this place in the hands of an agent, and has consequently and thereby suffered a loss of many thousand dollars; and finally this deponent states that in May, 1865, said General Sturm was Chief of Ordnance of the State of Indiana, and, against the advice of his friends and the wishes of Senator Oliver P. Morton, then the Governor of the State of Indiana, he resigned said position for the purpose of aiding the Mexican Government. And further deponent saith not.

W. R. HOLLOWAY.

Deposition of Isaac L. Gibbs.

No. 399.]

Isaac L. Gibbs deposes and says, that he is forty-seven years of age; that he was born in the State of Ohio; that his occupation is that of a lawyer, and that his residence is in the city of Washington; that during the winter of 1866, while Congress was in session—the deponent then residing in Washington—the said Sturm called on him for the purpose of employing him to aid the said Sturm in advancing the interests of the Republic of Mexico, which was then engaged in a war with the Maximilian Empire of Mexico and its French allies; and that the said Sturm represented to the deponent that he was the Agent of the Republic of Mexico, and fully empowered to employ others, and to make such agreements as to their compensation as the circumstances required.

Deponent further states, that the services in which the said Sturm wished to engage him were of a secret and confidential character, and that before commencing the performance of them, he wished to have every assurance possible as to the authority and powers of the said Sturm; that the said Sturm showed him documents from the Mexican Republic to General Carvajal, and from the said Carvajal to the said Sturm, as evidence of authority; that the deponent also called on Mr. Romero, who was at the time the Minister of the Republic of Mexico at Washington, for more complete information; that in his interview with Mr. Romero, the said Romero stated that the said Sturm was fully empowered to act for the Republic of Mexico, and that any contract or engagement made by the said Sturm would be scrupulously and religiously observed by the Mexican Republic.

Deponent further states, that being thus fully assured, he made an agreement with the said Sturm, and devoted his entire time, for the period of a year, in co-operation with him in maintaining the cause of the Mexican Republic and forming and advancing plans and movements for its benefit, at Washington and other places, and that the said Sturm had in his employment a number of others, besides himself, engaged in aiding him in the performance of his duties as Agent of the Republic of Mexico.

The deponent further states, that the said Sturm devoted himself with extraordinary diligence to the affairs of Mexico, expending his money freely and whenever the interests of the Mexican Republic demanded it, and also induced the deponent and others to expend their money in the cause, in addition to his own advances; and that the services and expenditures required in the large number of transactions incident to the proper management of the interests of the Republic of Mexico in this country were necessarily of a secret and confidential character.

Deponent further states, that the engagements made by the said Sturm to him for compensation for services rendered in the cause of the Republic of Mexico, have been satisfactorily settled by the said Sturm; that the deponent has no interest in the claim of the said Sturm against the Republic of Mexico, and that he (deponent) is not an agent or attorney of the claimant or of any person having an interest in the said claim

ISAAC L. GIBBS.

Deposition of William H. Sanders.

No. 400.]

William H. Sanders, being first duly cautioned and sworn, to tell the truth, the whole truth, and nothing but the truth, deposes and says that his name is William H. Sanders; his age is forty-one years; his residence is in the city of St. Louis, Mo.; that he was born in the city of New York, and State of New York, and his occupation is that of a note and stock broker, and that at the time of the happening of the events concerning which he testifies, his residence was in the city of New York, and his occupation that of a stock and note broker, and that he has no interest, direct or indirect, and is not the attorney or agent of any one having any interest, direct or indirect, in the claim concerning which he now testifies.

Deponent further says that he has come to Indianapolis at the urgent request of General Herman Sturm, to give this his testimony: that he has known said Sturm since the summer of 1864; that during the latter part of 1865, in New York City, deponent was repeatedly requested and urged by said Sturm to purchase the bonds of the Republic of Mexico, at the rate of sixty cents on the dollar, and to endeavor to sell the same to others, for which a liberal commission was promised; deponent did use his best endeavors for a long time, and until the Spring of 1866, to dispose of these bonds, but although the financial agents of Mexico, in New York City, had guaranteed the payment of the first year's interest on said bonds, that is up to October 1st, 1866, such was the want of faith of the moneyed men in the ability or disposition of the Mexican Government to pay its indebtedness, and so low was the credit of that Government in financial circles, that this deponent was unable to dispose of or sell a single bond; that, sometime in the month of September, 1866, General Sturm stated to deponent that the financial agents of Mexico had declined to further guarantee the payment of the interest on the Mexican bonds; and the Mexican credit was so low and unless something was done to bolster it up it would be impossible to obtain any further aid for that government in this country; that said Sturm then requested deponent to buy up the coupons for October, 1866, to 1867, being for one year of such Mexican bonds as said Sturm might refer to him, and it was distinctly understood between deponent and said Sturm that not more than five per cent at the utmost should be charged by deponent as a discount; deponent further says that, in accordance with this understanding, he did, from September, 1866, to some time in the spring of 1867, purchase different lots of the coupons of the Mexican bonds issued by Corlies & Co., the Mexican financial agents in New York city, for which deponent paid in full the gold, and in some cases its equivalent in United States currency, to the amount, as nearly as deponent now recollects, of over ten thousand dollars in gold, all of which was however, from time to time duly repaid to said deponent by said Sturm; deponent must state, however, that he deducted from the amount paid by him for the said coupons his commission or discount previously mentioned which deponent kept for his labor and trouble in this transaction, and in no case has this commission or discount exceeded five per cent. called for on the face of the coupons; deponent knows that said Sturm also employed other brokers for a similar purpose, but he can not state how many nor the amount purchased by them; deponent also states that said Sturm was both energetic and persevering in relation to these financial transactions in behalf of the Republic of Mexico, and deponent was often surprised at the indefatigable energy and labors displayed by said Sturm in overcoming all difficulties and obstacles, they being so many and great as would have discouraged most men; deponent further says that said Sturm, during the latter part of the summer of 1865, and from that time until the fall of 1866, gave many entertainments, parties and excursions, at many of which deponent was present, and that prominent persons, merchants and bankers, as well as many Mexican officers and refugees were present on these occasions, and that as deponent knows, said Sturm's object and endeavor was to manufacture public opinion and create sympathy for the Mexican cause, and obtain from the persons present, or through them or their friends, some aid, either in money or material of war for the Mexican government, and that said Sturm has paid large sums of money in this way, the amount of which deponent can not state, but he knows that on one of these occasions said Sturm paid at the Maison Doree, on Fourteenth Street and Broadway, in the city of New York, over two hundred dollars, and on another occasion, a trial trip of steamers that said Sturm was endeavoring to obtain for the Mexican government, he paid over five hundred dollars for expenses, and deponent firmly believes that the great success said Sturm finally met with in obtaining aid for Mexico is mainly due to the frank and gentlemanly behavior and the great liberality which he displayed on all these occasions, and the earnestness with which he pleaded with those present for the almost forlorn cause of the Republic of Mèxico; deponent also says that it is his firm conviction that the government of the United States, though the first and greatest in the world, had during the late war in this country no such energetic and patriotic friend in Europe or other foreign country, as General Sturm showed himself to be in the cause of the Republic of Mexico, and that he is entitled to, and ought to receive and have the most liberal treatment and compensation at the hands of that government.

W. H. SANDERS.

Deposition of Alexander H. Conner.

No. 401.]

The said Alexander H. Conner being first duly cautioned and sworn to tell the truth, the whole truth, and nothing but the truth deposes and says that his name is Alexander H. Conner; his age is thirty-nine years; that his residence is in said city of Indianapolis, and that he is by profession an attorney at law, and that at the time of the happening of the events concerning which he testifies he was engaged in the newspaper business, being a co-proprietor of the Indianapolis "Daily Journal," and that he has no interest direct or indirect, and is not the agent or attorney of any one having any interest direct or indirect, in the claim concerning which he now testifies.

Deponent further says that he is well acquainted with the claimant, General Herman Sturm, and has known him for more than ten years last past; that said Sturm was Chief of Ordnance for the State of Indiana, and that some time in the year of 1865, he resigned his position as said Chief of Ordnance and entered into the service or employment of the Republic of Mexico; that during the time said Sturm was so engaged in the service of the Republic of Mexico; deponent met him at the city of Washington, and also in the city of New York, and frequently visited his rooms; that his rooms were visited by many influential men, with whom General Sturm labored for the cause of the Republic of Mexico; that said claimant at all times whilst in said service, so far as deponent was able to observe, manifested the greatest activity and the warmest enthusiasm and earnestness for said Republic, and seemed untiring while making efforts for the good of that country; that said claimant spent large sums of money from time to time in influencing public opinion and sympathy in behalf of Mexico; that said General Sturm has been absent from his home in said city of Indianapolis, most of the time during the past six years, and has been in no other business, to deponent's knowledge, since then until the summer of this year, and consequently his private interests here, by reason of vexatious law suits and disputes, must have, and did suffer severely, which has placed the claimant pecuniarily in an embarrassed condition, so much so that deponent has aided said Sturm pecuniarily to assert his rights and prosecute his claim against the said Republic of Mexico; that the said embarrassed condition of said Sturm, as deponent believes, grew out of the fact of the violation of the agreements and promises of the Republic of Mexico with him made. Deponent further says that considering all the circumstances of the case, the many invaluable services rendered by said Sturm, the many and costly sacrifices made by him to the Republic of Mexico; considering that she had no credit at all in this country, and considering the reasonable fees ordinarily paid to attorneys of railroad and other corporations, as well as to government attorneys and agents, the said Sturm is fairly entitled to a remuneration and fee of at least fifty thousand dollars per annum, not considering or including his expenses and the many obligations he has entered into with others, for which, as deponent knows, he is in some cases held personally responsible.

A. H. CONNER.

Deposition of Samuel M. Douglass.

No. 402.]

The said Samuel M. Douglass being first duly cautioned and sworn to tell the truth, the whole truth, and nothing but the truth, deposes and says that his name is Samuel M. Douglass; his age is forty years; that his residence is in said city of Indianapolis, and that at the time of the happening of the events concerning which he testifies, his residence was in said city of Indianapolis, and that his occupation was that of co-proprietor of the Indianapolis "Daily Journal," a newspaper then, and now, published in said city, and that he has no interest direct or indirect, and is not the agent or attorney of any one having any interest direct or indirect, in the claim concerning which he now testifies.

Deponent further says that he is personally well acquainted with the claimant, General Herman Sturm, and has known him intimately since the year 1856; that in the spring of the year 1865, said General Sturm was Chief of Ordnance of the State of Indiana, which position he resigned against the protestations of his personal and political friends who were were well acquainted with the past history of Mexico, for the purpose of aiding the Republic government of that country against foreign invaders. Deponent further says he has followed the course of said Sturm during the years 1865, 1866, and 1867, having met him repeatedly in the cities of New York, Washington, and Indianapolis, and can testify of his own knowledge to the untiring zeal and energy with which he labored for the cause of Mexico, and in spite of the many difficulties and discouragements with which he was surrounded in consequence of the bad repute which the Mexican government then had in regard to her ability and disposition to pay and meet her obligations. This deponent knows that especially in the years 1865 and 1866 said Sturm spent large sums of money to agents and others for the purpose of manufacturing public opinion in favor of the Mexican government, and obtaining materials of war and other supplies for said government in the United States; that this deponent further knows of his own personal knowledge that said Sturm has embarrassed himself by borrowing large sums of money, and obtaining material of war and other aid for said government of Mexico, for which he is now held personally responsible; that he has been entangled in law suits and has been compelled to make many sacrifices for the purpose of settling claims and pacifying claimants to whom he had personally obligated himself in the belief that the Republic of Mexico would fulfill and keep in good faith her contracts with him. And deponent further says that said Sturm has had, and still has, a large amount of real estate in the city of Indianapolis, county of Marion, and State of Indiana, and is also a part owner of a brass manufacturing establishment in said city of Indianapolis, all of which he has been compelled to leave in the hands of agents, in consequence of the many difficulties and law suits arising out of his connection with the government of Mexico, and has been compelled to absent himself from home, since the early part of the year 1865, until about the month of July of this year; that said Sturm has lost largely in a pecuniary sense, not taking into consideration the many cares, mental anxieties and other troubles to which he and his family, from whom he has been separated a great part of the time, have been subjected; to many law suits, annoyances, and troubles, and many cares, growing out of his connection with the Mexican government; and deponent has within the last two years individually aided the said Sturm financially to assist him in asserting his rights and prosecuting his just claim against the Mexican government.

S. M. DOUGLASS.

Deposition of William Francis Elston.

No. 403.]

The said William Francis Elston being first duly cautioned and sworn to tell the truth, the whole truth, and nothing but the truth, deposes and says that his name is William Francis Elston; his age is twenty-eight years; his residence is in Crawfordsville, State of Indiana, and his occupation is that of the Mayor of the city of Crawfordsville, Indiana, and that at the time of the happening of the events concerning which he testifies he was a law student at Harvard University, Cambridge, State of Massachusetts, and that he has no interest direct or indirect, and is not the attorney or agent of any one having any interest direct or indirect, in the claim concerning which he now testifies.

Deponent further says that he is intimately acquainted with the claimant, General Herman Sturm, and has known him personally for eight or ten years last past, and by reputation for more than that time; that during the years 1865 and 1866, deponent knows that from the spring of 1865 and for two or three years thereafter said Sturm was energetically and industriously engaged aiding and assisting the Republic of Mexico, and repeatedly urged deponent, whose relations were in high position in Indiana, politically as well as socially and pecuniarily, to become connected with a scheme he and General Lewis Wallace had formed of liberating the Republic of Mexico from its foreign invaders; this deponent and many other acquaintances of this deponent did so aid the government of the Republic of Mexico in this country, and did assist General Sturm and General Wallace to help Mexico, until in the winter of 1865, deponent was informed by General Sturm that the effort to obtain money on the credit of the Mexican government had failed, and he would therefore not be responsible for any further arrangements; deponent thereupon paid no further attention to the matter, having been fully reimbursed by General Sturm for his troubles and expenses by promises and otherwise. Deponent further says that he has subsequently followed the career of said General Sturm, and that said Sturm, in his opinion, has done all he could do, and much more than any government would have the right to expect of him, considering all the circumstances; this deponent would not consider that an award of fifty thousand dollars per annum would be at all unreasonable as a remuneration for the time, trouble, and services rendered by the said Sturm to the Republic of Mexico, as a matter of course without considering any expenses he might have entered into with others.

And deponent further says that he has come to the city of Indianapolis, Indiana, to-day, at the urgent request of General Sturm, and after hearing the statements of General Sturm in connection with the reasons that compelled him to call deponent here, this deponent is free to say, and does say that all the foregoing statements are true, and that he cheerfully and voluntarily deposes to the same.

WILLIAM FRANCIS ELSTON,
Mayor of the City of Crawfordsville,
State of Indiana.

Deposition of Herman Funke.

[No. 404.]

The said Herman Funke being first duly cautioned and sworn to tell the truth, the whole truth, and nothing but the truth, deposes and says that his name is Herman Funke; his age is forty-six years; he was born in Germany, and that his residence is now at College Point, Queens county, New York, and his occupation that of a merchant in the city of New York, and that at the time of the happening of the events concerning which he testifies, his residence was in the same place where he now resides, and his occupation that of a merchant, and that he has no interest, direct or indirect, and is not the agent or attorney of any one having any interest, direct or indirect, in the claim concerning which he now testifies.

Deponent further says that he has been engaged in the general hardware business in the city of New York since the year 1842, as a member, first of the firm of Herman Boker, and subsequently of the firm of Herman Boker & Co., of which latter firm he is now the senior partner, and has been such since the year 1861.

Deponent further says as follows: I have known General Herman Sturm, the claimant herein, for a number of years, both by reputation and personally. Said Sturm, during the years 1866 and 1867, repeatedly urged and importuned me in person, and through other parties, to sell to the Mexican Government arms and munitions of war, and receive in payment therefor, Mexican bonds issued by John W. Corlies & Co., No. 57, Broadway, New York, the financial agents of the Republic of Mexico. I made investigation, both personally and through prominent friends in Washington, and ascertained that said bonds were acknowledged as legitimate by Senor Don Matias Romero, the then Minister of Mexico in Washington, and that General Sturm's authority as agent of said Government was also duly acknowledged, and that the Mexican Government had promised to faithfully pay the interest on said bonds as it should accrue and become due.

I soon found, however, that the merchants and financial men of the city of New York and elsewhere, had little or no confidence in the ability or disposition of the said Mexican Government to fulfill its obligations, and declined to trust said Government. I, seeing that through the energy and perseverance of said Sturm, many merchants and others in the United States did invest in said bonds, and furnished large quantities of war material to the Mexican Government, and believing that the statements made by said Sturm, Senor Romero, and others, regarding the good faith of the Mexican Government, would be verified—I finally did sell to General Sturm, for the Mexican Government, a large lot of arms and munitions of war, and received for the same from the said General Herman Sturm, the bonds of the Mexican Government, at the rate of sixty (60) cents on the dollar.

I further depose and say, that the Mexican Government has not carried out its promise, and has not paid interest on said bonds as it became due, and I still hold the said bonds, and more than four years interest has accrued, and is now due and still unpaid on said bonds.

I further say that I know that General Sturm has faithfully and energetically labored for the good of the cause of the Mexican Republic until some time in the year 1868; that in his endeavors to manufacture credit for the Republican Government of Mexico, and obtain material aid for the same in the United States, said Sturm has expended his money freely, and has personally obligated himself to others to a large amount; and in consequence of the non-fulfillment on the part of the Mexican Government of its promises and obligations to said Sturm and others, said Sturm has been seriously damaged financially, and has been harassed and annoyed by vexatious lawsuits, which, as I verily believe, never would have taken place if the Mexican Government had kept its promises faithfully.

During this year, 1871, I have repeatedly advanced said Sturm large sums of money to enable him to prosecute his just claims against the Mexican Government, for which advances I now hold, among other collaterals, a large amount of interest coupons of Mexican bonds, for which said Sturm had advanced the money to enhance the credit of the Mexican Government, and to facilitate efforts of that Government to obtain in the United States the very material, by the aid of which it was finally successful in driving the invaders from its soil, and re-establishing its own power.

The total amount so advanced by me to said Sturm is over twelve thousand dollars.

In consequence of said Sturm's connection with the Mexican Government, and of his efforts to aid the same, and in consequence of the lawsuits and other troubles growing out of the same, the said Sturm has been compelled to neglect his own private business, and separate himself from his family for a number of years, and the treatment said Sturm has received from said Mexican Government in requital for his untiring labors and zeal in behalf of the same, has been anything but fair and honorable, and he is deserving of, and ought to receive the most liberal compensation.

The value of the arms and munitions of war sold by me to General Sturm, as agent of the Government of Mexico, was about one hundred and fifty thousand dollars in the currency of the United States.

HERMAN FUNKE.

Deposition of John C. New.

No. 405.]

The said John C. New, being by me first duly cautioned and sworn to tell the truth, the whole truth, and nothing but the truth, deposes and says that his name is John C. New; his age is forty years; that his residence is in said city of Indianapolis, and that he is a stockholder in, and cashier of the First National Bank of Indianapolis; and that at the time of the happening of the events concerning which he testifies, his residence was in said city of Indianapolis, and his occupation was that of cashier of, and stockholder in, the said First National Bank; and that he has no interest, direct or indirect, and is not the attorney or agent of any one having any interest, direct or indirect, in the claim concerning which he now testifies.

Deponent further says, that he has known the claimant, General Herman Sturm, for several years last past; that during the month of October, 1865, said claimant, General Herman Sturm, urged deponent to aid the Government of the Republic of Mexico, by endeavoring to dispose of the bonds of said Government, and by giving to the sale of said bonds the benefit of the financial standing and reputation of said bank; that said claimant did place in the hands of deponent, as an officer of said bank, a large amount of said bonds, and offered him a liberal commission on all bonds he should succeed in selling, at the rate of sixty cents on the dollar, either himself, or through other banks or bankers; that deponent labored industriously for several months to accomplish said object, and by advertising it gave all possible publication to the matter, but the credit of the Mexican Government, which at that time was almost out of existence, was so bad, and its character and reputation for not fulfilling its obligations so notorious, that deponent failed in the enterprise, and could not succeed in selling and disposing of a single Mexican bond. During this time, and from the summer of 1865 to the present time, October, 1871, this deponent has watched with much interest the acts of said Sturm, and his many and various efforts to aid the Liberal Government of Mexico, and although, during this time, and especially during the years 1865 and 1866, said Sturm met with discouragements and disappointments from almost every quarter, and although many of his personal friends and acquaintances, this deponent being one of them, fearing, as has since proved true, that the Mexican Government, after availing itself of said

Sturm's aid and support, and the aid, support, and money of his friends, would not fulfill its contracts and obligations to and with him, endeavored to dissuade him from further prosecuting his efforts in behalf of the Mexican cause; yet such was his patriotism and confidence in the good faith of the Mexican Government that he continued, if not redoubled his efforts, neglected all his private business, property and interests here in Indiana, separated himself from his family almost continuously, and spent his means freely in his endeavors to aid the almost forlorn Government of the Republic of Mexico, in its endeavor to overthrow its foreign invader; although this deponent is well-acquainted and intimate with General Sturm, he can not state what amounts of money he has spent to aid the Mexican Government, but deponent knows, and says, from his own knowledge, that he has met said General Sturm during the years 1865, 1866, 1867, and 1868, in the city of New York, Washington, Indianapolis, and other places, and that during this time the said Sturm was industriously endeavoring to aid the Mexican Government financially and otherwise, and in his efforts to manufacture public opinion in favor of the Mexican cause, and to obtain material aid for the Mexican Government, he exhausted his own means, and drew largely on the means of his friends, and generally spent his money liberally for the good of the Republic of Mexico, and deponent knows that in consequence of the non-fulfillment of the pledges of the Mexican Government to said Sturm, he has been placed in a very embarrassing position in consequence of lawsuits, etc., commenced against said Sturm by persons to whom he had personally obligated himself in his efforts to raise credit, money, and material of war for Mexico; and deponent knows that said Sturm has been very largely injured, pecuniarily and otherwise, in consequence of his connection with the Government of Mexico; and deponent further says that during the last two years he has repeatedly assisted said Sturm pecuniarily, both as an officer of the bank and individually, for the purpose of enabling him to prosecute his claims before said Commission, and obtaining from the Mexican Government what is justly due him; deponent further states that, taking into consideration the social, political, as well as the financial standing of General Sturm during the years 1865, 1866, and down to the present time, and the many and extraordinary efforts he made to aid the Republic of Mexico, when scarcely anybody could be found willing to trust that Government, and considering the fact that whatever said Sturm accomplished for the good of Mexico, was accomplished by means of him, his friends, his social standing and reputation alone, coupled with the means that he and his friends brought to bear upon the subject, and considering the fact that the Mexican Government did not furnish him with any means whatever, it is the honest conviction and belief of this deponent that the very lowest amount that ought to be awarded to said Sturm for his services in and during this time, not considering what he might have advanced cash, or what he might have obligated himself to others, should be fifty thousand dollars for each year the said Sturm was engaged as the agent of Mexico, or was prevented from engaging in other business in consequence of lawsuits and other entanglements to which he was subjected; and deponent finally states that he returned to said Sturm, all and every bond of the Government of the Republic of Mexico that had been placed in his hands as hereinbefore stated. And further deponent saith not.

JOHN C. NEW.

Deposition of Adolphus Ahromet.

No. 406.]

The said Adolphus Abromet, being first duly cautioned and sworn to tell the truth, the whole truth, and nothing but the truth, deposes and says, that his name is Adolphus Abromet; his age is forty-one years; his residence is in said city of Indianapolis; his occupation is that of an insurance agent for the Ætna Insurance Company; and that at the time of the happening of the events concerning which he testifies, his residence was in said city of Indianapolis, and his occupation that of agent of the Ætna Insurance Company, of Hartford, Connecticut; and that he has no interest, direct or indirect, and is not the attorney or agent of any one having any interest, direct or indirect, in the claim concerning which he now testifies. Deponent further says that he has been personally acquainted with the above named claimant, General Herman Sturm, since the year 1861; that during the year 1865 and 1866 said claimant was then, and for some time subsequently, energetically endeavoring and laboring to obtain money, means and credit for the Government of the Republic of Mexico, to assist it in its struggle with its foreign invaders; among other things said Sturm urged deponent to invest some money in the bonds of that Republic, and although deponent found, upon inquiring, that said Government was not considered reliable in financial circles, and had no credit with the mercantile community of this country, yet knowing General Sturm to be an honorable man, and relying in good faith upon the statements and representations of said Sturm, deponent did purchase of the financial agents of said Government, Messrs. Corlies & Co., of New York City, five hundred dollars of Mexican bonds, for which he paid three hundred dollars in United States currency. Deponent further says that since October, 1866, no interest has been paid on said bonds, and he has been informed, by said Corlies & Co., that the Mexican Government has made no provision whatever for the payment of said interest. Deponent also knows many other cases where the Mexican Government has failed to comply with her agreements and contracts, and in consequence of these violations of good faith, the said General Sturm has been placed in an embarrassed condition, and has been sued in the courts, because of the shortcomings of that Government, by parties who, not fully understanding the full status of affairs, held said Sturm personally responsible for the aforementioned violations of good faith on the part of the Mexican Government, and many of them were led to believe by the enemies of said Sturm, and did believe, that said Sturm willfully made false representations to them, and obtained said material aid under false pretences, and that said Sturm was in reality a party in conjuction with the Mexican Government and others, to a grand scheme to defraud citizens of this country. And further deponent saith not.

A. ABROMET.

Deposition of John A. Bridgland.

No. 407.]

The said John A. Bridgland being by me first duly cautioned and sworn to tell the truth, the whole truth, and nothing but the truth, deposes and says that his name is John A. Bridgland; his age is forty-four years; he was born in Lynchburg, State of Virginia, and that his residence is now in the city of New York, and his occupation that of a merchant, and that at the time of the happening of the events concerning which he testifies, his residence was in the State of Indiana, and his occupation that of a merchant and an officer of the army, and that he has no interest, direct or indirect, and is not the agent or attorney of any one having an interest, direct or indirect, in the claim concerning which he now testifies.

Deponent further says that the attorneys for General Herman Sturm have requested an affidavit from me concerning his fidelity to the United States as Chief of Ordnance of the State of Indiana, during the late rebellion, and his subsequent efficiency and fidelity to the present government of Mexico as its special agent in the United States.

From my knowledge of General Sturm, his great efficiency in the former position has only been excelled, as a result of his experience in that position, in the remarkable tact and ability shown in the latter; for in both positions I knew him well, and do say in sincerity that in my opinion there were but few men, if any, that would or could have produced such results, with the same class of people, financially and otherwise, in favor of the Mexican government at that time.

Without being interested, directly or indirectly, to the amount of one dollar in General Sturm's faithful performance of his work for either government, I unhesitatingly say, that in my opinion he would not present a claim for disbursements or services rendered, that was not in full accordance with the efforts of a faithful agent.

I had the pleasure, several times during his efforts for the Mexican government, of introducing him to gentlemen of large wealth and influence, in New York and other places, that I thought as bankers and business men would be of service to his Mexican enterprise, with the belief that such introductions would sustain the Republican movement in Mexico, and thereby break down an attempt to establish a monarchy on our continent. Not having General Sturm's pecuniary interest in view for one moment, but that his success would reflect credit upon my own country, I watched his movements from month to month and from year to year with great interest, and I can say of my own personal knowledge, that he made large disbursements in handsome dinner parties, opera boxes, and other elegant entertainments to this class of gentlemen, with the hope that these disbursements would result in the accomplishment of the work that had been assigned to him by the Mexican government.

JOHN A. BRIDGLAND.

American and Mexican Commission—No. 676.

Deposition of Major General Lewis Wallace.

No. 408.]

Before me, the undersigned, a Notary Public in and for the county of Marion and State of Indiana, on this 9th day of May, 1870, personally appeared Lewis Wallace, of Crawfordsville, Montgomery county, Indiana, who, being by me first duly sworn according to law, on his oath deposes and says:

That in the spring of 1865, one General Jose M. J. Carvajal, Governor of the State of Tamaulipas, came to the United States, as agent, specially authorized of the Republican government of Mexico.

That, generally speaking, the authority of the said General Carvajal was to buy arms and material of war, engage foreigners for military service, and raise funds by loan for his government. That, as he might rightfully do under his said authority, the said General Carvajal engaged deponent to aid and assist him in the performance of his said agency in the United States; that the said General Carvajal being further desirous of obtaining the services of a reliable officer, familiar with ordnance and ordnance stores, and their purchase and procurement in the United States, was by deponent introduced to General Herman Sturm, some time in April, 1865; that the said General Carvajal thereupon appointed General Sturm a general contracting agent for him and his government; that the said appointment was in writing, which, on its face, appears to have been executed by the said General Carvajal at Sota La Marina, March 1, 1865, while in fact it was executed in the United States, the object being, as suggested by deponent, to avoid all possible complication under the neutrality laws of the United States; that the said General Carvajal, at the time he so appointed General Sturm, was of opinion that he could accomplish his mission in the United States and return to his State in the period of three or four months; that his promise to pay General Sturm ten or twenty thousand dollars as remuneration for his services while in the United States was based upon that idea; that it was also agreed by General Carvajal, that the said General Sturm, after concluding his labor in the United States, should go to Mexico, in the capacity of Chief of Ordnance for the Republic and with the rank of Brigadier General in the regular army; that later, in September, as deponent now believes, General Carvajal also agreed that General Sturm should have and receive a grant of mineral and agricultural lands; that General Sturm's authority extended to the purchase of ordnance and ordnance stores, quartermaster, commissary and medical supplies, and everything ordinarily required by an army for active operations in the field; including the appointment of Assistants and the chartering and purchase of vessels for transportation and other purposes; that, in the said authorization to General Sturm, General Carvajal reserved to himself, or in his absence to this deponent, the right to approve the contracts which the said General Sturm might make; that the said General Sturm entered at once and zealously upon the discharge of the duties entrusted to him, and continued to discharge the same for a long period, to-wit: until some time in 1868; that he made large purchases of arms and *materiel* of war generally, employed assistants and chartered steamers for transportation; that his contracts, purchases and actions in the premises, down to August, 1866, were fully approved and sanctioned by General Carvajal, or in his absence by this deponent; that the said appointment of General Sturm was duly reported by General Carvajal to Senor Don M. Romero,

Mexican Minister, resident in Washington, and also, as deponent believes, to his government in Mexico; that deponent, though often in communication with the said Romero touching the said General Sturm and his purchases and conduct generally, never heard from that official a word of denial of his authority; but, on the contrary, in many instances, both in New York and in Washington, he heard admissions from the said Minister of the validity of the said authority, and approval of the zeal, energy and competency of the said General Sturm; that deponent was resident for several months in Chihuahua, the Mexican seat of government, and in frequent communication while there with President Juarez and his cabinet ministers, Mejia, Iglesias and Lerdo de Tejada, and never heard from them, or any of them, a word of disapproval, either of Carvajal's appointment of said Sturm or of said Sturm's actions in and about the management of his said agency.

That when General Carvajal returned to his State and command in Mexico, he instructed said Sturm to continue his agency in concert with Senor Don M. Romero and this deponent; that so well satisfied was the said Romero with the conduct of the said Sturm, that he did not hesitate to continue the agency conferred, as aforesaid, by General Carvajal, abating nothing, but on the contrary, by his own instructions, enlarging the said Sturm's authority; that, in the course of his said Agency the said General Sturm was necessarily put to great labor, care, responsibility and expense, without compensation or means furnished him by the said Mexican government or any of its officials; that he always cheerfully obeyed the orders and directions of General Carvajal and Senor Romero, some of which were outside of the scope of the written authority aforesaid; amongst other duties of that kind was the execution of a secret agency in Washington, in connection with an effort to obtain material aid for Mexico from the United States government, and also a labored endeavor to sell the bonds of the Mexican Republic, and create credit and sympathy for that Republic; that the entire operations of said Sturm were at his own expense, as deponent verily believes, and upon no other basis than that of a Mexican credit, which he himself was largely instrumental in creating in the United States; that he did not hesitate to pledge his own credit and incur individual liability to accomplish his objects; that he advanced moneys to General Carvajal for the personal support of that official and to relieve the necessities of Mexicans captured in battle and returning home through New York, from the French prisons, and for other purposes, and this when high Mexican authorities in the United States, from inability or disinclination, refused to help the unfortunate patriots; that at the time of his appointment by General Carvajal as aforesaid, the said General Sturm was Chief of Ordnance in the State of Indiana; that to accept the said appointment the said Sturm was compelled to resign his said position in Indiana; that ever since accepting the said appointment, the said Sturm has been compelled to give his time and attention almost exclusively to the complications incidental to the contracts made by him in the course of his said agency and growing out of the repudiations, refusals to pay, and the general bad faith of the Mexican officials; that he has been, and is now, harassed by vexatious law suits and other troubles founded upon his undertakings in aid of the Mexican government; that he is now liable in large amounts to parties with whom he formed engagements in the course of his secret agencies; that failing to obtain settlements for himself and his contracting parties in the United States, he has been compelled to go repeatedly to the Mexican capital for the same purpose, but as deponent believes with no better success; that said Sturm has long since rendered a full account of his services, labors and management as agent aforesaid and demanded compensation and repayment, and fulfillment of engagements solemnly made to and with him by the said Mexican government, through its officials aforesaid, and while his labors and services have been received and his accounts approved by the said government, his demands have been constantly refused by it; that, to deponent's knowledge, the services of the said General Sturm have been of very great importance to the Mexican government, and by no person has their value and difficulties been more broadly stated than by Senor M. Romero, Secretary of the Mexican treasury, in his report of his own conduct and management while resident Minister at Washington; that deponent is not interested directly or indirectly in the claims preferred by the said Sturm for said services; and further deponent saith not.

LEWIS WALLACE.

{Notarial Seal.} Sworn to and subscribed before me, at Indianapolis, in witness whereof, I have have hereunto set my hand and official seal, the day and year above written.

WILLIAM WALLACE,
Notary Public.

In the Joint Commission of the United States and Mexico, under the Convention of July 4th, 1868,

IN THE MATTER OF THE CLAIM OF

HERMAN STURM vs. THE REPUBLIC OF MEXICO.

Deposition of Norman L. Latson.

No. 409.]

The deposition of Norman L. Latson, taken before me, the undersigned, a United States Commissioner, duly authorized to administer oaths and take depositions, in the city, State, and county of New York, on the 30th day of December, 1871, between the hours of three and five o'clock P. M., at the United States Commissioner's Office, 41 Chambers street, in the city of New York, and intended to be used and read in evidence in behalf of the claimant in the above entitled cause.

The said Norman L. Latson, being by me first duly cautioned and sworn to tell the truth, the whole truth, and nothing but the truth, deposes and says, that his name is Norman L. Latson; his age is thirty years; he was born in Rhinebeck, Dutchess county, State of New York, and his occupation is that of a merchant in said city of New York, which was his residence at the time of the happening of the events concerning which he testifies.

Deponent further says, that he is well acquainted with the claimant, General Herman Sturm. Some time in the month of February, 1867, General Sturm applied to me for the purpose of chartering a steamer to convey a cargo of munitions of war to Mexico. On the 27th day of March, 1867, I chartered to said General Herman Sturm the steamer General McCallum for the aforesaid purpose, for the term of forty (40) days; said charter-party being hereto annexed—marked "Exhibit A" by the Commission. According to the terms of said charter-party, General Sturm was obliged to furnish all the coal, provisions, engineer's and other stores, as well as to pay the wages of the officers and crew, and further pays all port and other charges of said steamer (while in ports of the Gulf of Mexico or the United States) during the time of employment by him. ·

On the 31st day of May, 1867, said steamer sailed from the port of New York, being filled with a large cargo of munitions of war, and having on board a number of passengers, and arrived at the port of Tampico on or about the 14th day of April, 1867, and returned to the port of New York on the 2d day of June (1867) of the same year, in a disabled condition. On the arrival of said steamer at the said port of New York, I was informed by the Captain and other officers of the said steamer, whose statements were fully corroborated before court by them and the crew, that on their arrival at Tampico, the commandant of that place, General A. Gomez, took possession of the steamer and would not allow her cargo to be discharged unless the duties and other charges on said cargo and vessel had first been paid to him by General Sturm's super-cargo.

After several days detention, they were compelled to proceed with the steamer to a place some (60) sixty miles or (70) seventy miles up the Panuco River, for the purpose of discharging there a portion of the cargo which, as they said, belonged to the Mexican Government.

On her return voyage to Tampico, the said steamer was driven ashore in consequence of the swiftness of the current in the aforesaid river, which was at that place very tortuous; and said steamer was seriously damaged in her machinery, wheels, and hull.

They further stated, that on their return to Tampico, the aforesaid General Gomez still continued to hold said steamer, and refused to allow the discharge of said cargo unless all the duties and charges aforesaid were first paid; neither would he allow the said steamer to proceed to sea, for the purpose of going to the port of Alvarado, but forced the super-cargo, Mr. Stocking, to discharge the whole of the cargo on board of said steamer in Tampico. In consequence of this action on part of said General Gomez, said steamer was detained until the —— day of May, 1867, when she was allowed to proceed to sea; but as in the meantime the coal, provisions, and other stores provided by General Sturm, had become exhausted, the said steamer was compelled to proceed to Galveston, Texas, for the purpose of replenishing her stores, but being unable to obtain sufficient coal at that port, the steamer went to Key West, Florida, and there took in sufficient coal to take her to New York. where, as before stated, she arrived on the second (2d) day of June, 1867, and was discharged from further service on the 3d day of (June) the same month.

Deponent further says, that as soon as possible I had the said same steamer repaired, for which repairs I had to pay. Thereupon I presented to the said Gen. Sturm my bill of expenses incurred for the aforesaid coal and other stores purchased at Galveston, Texas, and Key West, Florida, and for repairing said steamer, as aforesaid; and also for the demurrage on account of the detention of said steamer beyond the original term of charter, and loss occasioned to me in consequence of the damage to said steamer, as I could not use her until she was repaired. In fact I lost more than six thousand ($6,000) dollars by detention in putting the vessel in seaworthy condition on her return to New York. A copy of this account is herewith annexed and marked Exhibit "C," J. A. O.

General Sturm refused to pay me for this account, on the ground, as he said at the time, that the detention and damage of said steamer was not occasioned by any fault of his, but through the unlawful acts of the Mexican authorities and by superior military force.

After some weeks had passed, General Sturm had become convinced that according to the laws of the State of New York, he was bound to pay me the expenses and loss incurred in consequence of the damages incurred by said steamer, and he fully settled with me for that part of my claim, amounting, after deducting previous payments, as the annexed account will fully show, to about ten thousand ($10,000) dollars, and which he paid to me; but he declined to pay the balance of my aforesaid account for detention. For this balance, amounting to nine thousand seven hundred and thirty-one dollars and fifty-seven cents ($9,731.57), I have since sued him before the United States Court of Brooklyn, New York, which court has decreed to me a verdict against said General H. Sturm for the full amount claimed by me, amounting, with costs and interest, to twelve thousand one hundred and one dollars and thirty-seven cents, for the payment of which General Sturm has given me security. Certified copy of said judgment is hereto annexed, Exhibit "B," J A. O.

Deponent further says, that the said steamer, General McCallum, ought not to have been detained at Tampico longer than three days, at the utmost, to unload her cargo, as stated by the captain and engineer; in fact I believe all the cargo could have been discharged in twenty-four hours.

NORMAN L. LATSON.

I, John A. Osborn, a United States Commissioner, do hereby certify that, at the request of Norman L. Latson, I caused the above-mentioned Norman L. Latson, deponent in the foregoing deposition, to come before me at the time and place in the caption mentioned; that said deponent was by me carefully examined, cautioned and sworn, according to the laws of the United States, then and there to testify the whole truth.

That said deposition was wholly reduced to writing by him in my presence, and was carefully read by deponent before being signed by him; and deponent then and there, in my presence, subscribed the same; and I further certify that I have no interest, direct or indirect, in the claim to which the above deposition relates, and am not the agent or attorney of any person having any interest therein, and that all interlineations and erasures were made known to deponent before signing his deposition.

Witness my hand and official seal at the city of New York, this 30th day of December, 1871.

JOHN A. OSBORN,
U. S. Commissioner,
Southern District of New York.

Commissioner's Seal.

UNITED STATES OF AMERICA, } ss.
SOUTHERN DISTRICT OF NEW YORK.

I, Kenneth G. White, Clerk of the Circuit Court of the United States of America for the Southern District of New York, Second Circuit, do hereby certify, that I am well acquainted with the handwriting of John A. Osborn, whose name is subscribed to the annexed deposition and certificate, and that the signature to the same is in his proper handwriting. And I do further certify, that he was, at the time of signing the same, a United States Commissioner, duly appointed by the Circuit Court of the United States of America for the Southern District of New York, Second Circuit.

[Seal of the Court.] In testimony whereof, I have hereunto subscribed my name, and affixed the seal of the said Circuit Court, this 3d day of January, in the year of our Lord one thousand eight hundred and seventy-two, and of the Independence of these United States the ninety-sixth.

KENNETH G. WHITE, Clerk.

[U. S. Rev. 5c. Stamp.]

Memorandum of Agreement.

MEMORANDUM OF AGREEMENT made and entered into this twenty-second day of March, eighteen hundred and sixty-seven, between Norman L. Latson, of the city of New York, owner of the steamship called the "General McCallum," of five hundred and twenty tons, or thereabouts, measurement, party of the first part, and General Herman Sturn, of the city of Indianapolis, party of the second part, showeth, that the party of the first part agrees to charter the above named steamer, for a term of not less than forty days, for a voyage from New York to Tampico, or other Mexican ports, with the privilege of Brazos Santiago, or Galveston, or New Orleans, at the rate of one hundred dollars per day, United States currency, payable in advance, with the additional privilege of ninety days further service at the same rate of per diem, payment to be made in New York every ten days; and with the further privilege, on the part of the party of the second part, to close the purchase of the steamer at the price of thirty-five thousand dollars, payable in United States legal currency, whenever or wherever the steamer may be during the time limited by the charter.

It is further agreed, that the steamer shall be fully covered by insurance at the expense of the charterers, which shall be done at the best obtainable rates; and that the party of the first part shall appoint the commander and chief engineer to serve during the term of the charter—the wages of the captain to be two hundred dollars per month, and the wages of the engineer to be one hundred and fifty dollars per month.

The charterer (party of the second part) hereby agrees to provide the steamer with a full complement of officers and men in every department at his own cost, together with coals, and all other necessary provisions and stores; to pay all port charges, pilotage, and other expenses attending the proposed voyage. In the event of loss by seizure, the charterers are to be held fully responsible to the party of the first part in the sum of thirty-five thousand dollars.

It is further agreed, that this vessel shall be in readiness for sea March 27th, 1868, and the charter party shall commence at that date, with the ship in good and seaworthy condition.

The party of the second part shall have the privilege of loading while ship is repairing.

Copy.

N. L. LATSON.

Charter Party of the Steamer General McCallum.

This Charter Party made and concluded upon in the city of New York, this twenty-sixth day of March, 1867, between Norman L. Latson, owner of the steamer General McCallum of New York, of the burthen of five hundred and twenty tons or thereabouts, now lying in the harbor of New York, of the first part; and Herman Sturm, of the city of Indianapolis, of the second part:

Witnesseth, that the party of the first part, for and in consideration of the covenants and agreements hereinafter mentioned, to be kept and performed by the party of the second part, does covenant and agree on the freighting and chartering of the said vessel unto the said party of the second part for a voyage from the port of New York to Tampico or other Mexican ports on the Gulf of Mexico, agreeable to the insurance, with the privilege of the ports of New Orleans, Galveston, and Brazos Santiago, as the party of the second part may select, and for a term not less than forty days, with the privilege of additional ninety days after the expiration of the first forty days, on the terms following, that is to say:

First. The said party of the first part does engage that the said vessel in and during the said time shall be kept tight, staunch, well fitted, tackled, and provided with every requisite necessary for such a voyage.

Second. The said party of the first part does further engage that the whole of said vessel shall be at the sole use and disposal of the said party of the second part during the time aforesaid, and no goods or merchandise shall be laden on board or otherwise than from the said party of the second part or his agents without his consent on pain of forfeiture of the amount of freight agreed upon for the same.

Third. The said party of the first part does further agree to take and receive on board the said vessel during the aforesaid time and voyage all such lawful goods and merchandise as the said party of the second part or his agent may think proper to ship.

And the said party of the second part, for and in consideration of the covenants and agreements to be kept and performed by the said party of the first part does covenant and agree with the said party of the first part, to hire the said vessel as aforesaid on the terms following, that is to say:

First. The said party of the second part does engage to provide and furnish the said vessel with provisions, coal, and stores and to pay the expenses of manning, port charges, pilotage, and other expenses of said steamer, during the voyage or time she may be employed.

Second. The said party of the second part does further engage to pay to the said party of the first part or his agent for the said charter or freight of said vessel during the voyage aforesaid in the manner following, that is to say:

One hundred dollars U. S. currency for each and every day the said vessel may be employed. Four thousand dollars to be paid in advance at the time of sailing of said vessel, and if said vessel should be detained by said party of the second part beyond the term of forty days, then the sum of one thousand dollars at the end of every ten days immediately after the expiration of the first forty days.

Third. The said party of the second part does further engage to pay to the said party of the first part for the insurance of said vessel during the time she is employed the sum of

Fourth. The said party of the second part further engages to deliver said vessel to the said party of the first part at the port of New York at the end of the expiration of this charter.

It is further agreed by and between the said parties that the said party of the second part may at any time during the time of the charter become the owner of said vessel by paying or causing to be paid to said party of the first part or his agent the sum of thirty-five thousand dollars legal currency of the United States; and

It is also further agreed that the said party of the first part shall appoint the Captain and Chief Engineer of the said vessel at a monthly salary not exceeding the sum of two hundred dollars for the former and the sum of one hundred and fifty dollars for the latter, currency of the U. S. But the party of the second part shall have the privilege of appointing all other officers and crew.

The party of the second part also hereby agrees to pay to the said party of the first part the aforesaid sum of thirty-five thousand dollars in full payment for said vessel in case said vessel should be seized in any way and confiscated.

This charter to commence at 12 M., on the 27th day of March, 1867.

To the true and faithful performance of all the foregoing convenants and agreements, the said parties, each to the other, do hereby bind themselves, their heirs, executors, administrators, and assigns.

In witness whereof, the said parties have hereunto interchangeably set their hands this twenty-seventh day of March, 1867.

NORMAN L. LATSON.
H. STURM.

Signed, sealed, and delivered in the presence of }
    WALTER H. GILSON.
    D. B. BRIDGFORD.

U. S. Rev.
5c. Stamp

Decree of the Court.

[Exhibit B. J. A. O., U. S. C.]

At a stated term of the District Court, of the United States of America, for the Eastern District of New York, held at the United States Court Rooms in the city of Brooklyn, on the 19th day of December in the year of our Lord one thousand eight hundred and seventy-one.

Present:

The Honorable Charles L. Benedict, District Judge.

NORMAN L. LATSON
v.
HERMAN STURM.

The report of Edward L. Owen. Esq., U. S. Commissioner, to whom it was referred, to ascertain the amount due the libelant, herein, from the respondent, for breach of charter of the steamer General McCullum, being presented to the Court, from which it appears that there is due the libelant, by reason of the breach of such charter, of the steamer General McCullum, the sum of eleven thousand eight hundred and eighty-eight and 67-100 dollars, and no exception to said report having been filed—

Now on motion of Benedict, Tracy & Benedict, libelant's proctors, it is ordered, adjudged, and decreed, that said report be and the same is hereby in all things confirmed, and that the libelant, Norman L. Latson recover, herein, for the breach of the charter of the said steamer Gen. McCallum, the amount so reported due, together with his costs, taxed at two hundred and twelve and 68-100 dollars, making in all the sum of twelve thousand one hundred and one and 35-100 dollars.

And on like motion, It is further ordered that unless an appeal be taken from this decree within the time limited, and prescribed, by the rules, and practice of this Court, the libelant have execution, to satisfy this decree.

(Signed)   CHARLES S. BENEDICT.

:Seal of the: A true copy from the original on file.
: Court. :   SAMUEL T. JONES,
                                                Clerk.

General H. Sturm in account current with the Steamer General McCallum and Owner.

[Exhibit C. J. A. O., U. S. C.]

1867.

M'ch 27–To charter of str. Gen. McCallum from 27 M'ch to 3 June, 1867, 69 days, at $100............	369 "	493 73 100 17	6,900
" Insurance on $35,000 for 3 mo., at 4 per ct.	"	9 46	1,400
" extra labor on str. pr. your order............	"	6 37	132 50
" shipping crew.......................................	"	2 22	90
" cash paid Osborn Custom H. Fees...........	335	61	31 15
" two telegrams from Galveston.................	297	254 56	13 40
" cash pd. pay roll of crew.........................	"	63 64	4,408 35
" Capt. Barton's st. dft. from Key West......	"	34 10	1,102 08
" " " " " Galveston......	"	9 13	595 90
" " " " " "	"	95 63	158 63
" " " " " "			1,656 34
" repairing wheel damaged going up the Panuca River, Mexico.............................	286	556 11	10,000
To balance interest...................................		$1,625 73	1,625 73
			$28,114 08
To balance..			$20,324 43

CREDIT.

1867.

M'ch 27–By cash on acct. charter money....................	369	286 22	4,000
Apr. 1 " " " " pay roll.............................	365	196 27	2,773 33
17 " " " " insurance........................	348	33 83	500
" interest in red...		$516 32	516 32
Balance...............................			20,324 43
			$28,114 08

E. O. E.

NEW YORK, April 1, 1868.

NOTE.—In the manuscript from which the above table was set the first and second columns of figures were written in red ink.—PRINTER.

Deposition of Jonathan N. Tifft.

No. 410]

The said Jonathan N. Tifft being by me first duly cautioned and sworn to tell the truth, the whole truth, and nothing but the truth, deposes and says that his name is Jonathan N. Tifft; his age is forty-three years; he was born in the town of Nassau, Rensselaer county, State of New York, and that his residence is now in the city of New York, and his occupation that of merchant, and that at the time of the happening of the events concerning which he testifies his residence was in said city of New York, and his occupation that of merchant, and that he has no interest, direct or indirect, and is not the agent or attorney of any one having any interest, direct or indirect, in the claim concerning which he now testifies. Deponent further says that he is well acquainted with the claimant, General Herman Sturm. Sometime in the month of May, 1865, he, said Tifft, was in the city of Washington on business, and while there he called upon General Sturm, who was then stopping at Rullman's Hotel, corner of Thirteenth street and E street in said city, and he found him, said Sturm, in company with several officers of our army, and during the several days he, said Tifft, remained in that city he, said Sturm, seemed actively engaged in entertaining them. Upon one occasion he, said Tifft, was introduced by him, said Sturm, to General Lew. Wallace who, on that evening, made a speech to a considerable assemblage particularly on the subject of the necessity and desirability of United States aid to Mexico.

In the month of August following General Sturm spent an evening at the said Tifft's house, and informed him confidentially that he, said Sturm, desired to purchase a large quantity of picks, shovels, mess plates, forks, etc., suitable for army use, and on said Tifft's inquiring whether the articles were intended for the State of Indiana—of which said Sturm was then, or had been, Chief of Ordnance—he informed said Tifft they were for the government of Mexico and to aid President Juarez in maintaining the stability of that government. Said Sturm also told deponent that his orders came from General Jose M. J. Carvajal, of Mexico, who was then staying incognito in this city and was, he said. duly authorized by the Mexican government to contract for such supplies as might be needed.

As deponent was in the hardware business he proposed to supply the needed articles provided the pay was made satisfactory; whereupon General Sturm informed him that the The United States and West Virginia Land and Mining Company would furnish the money, and desired deponent to investigate as to the responsibility of said company, at the same time expressing some doubts as to their solvency. In making such investigation he, said Tifft, discovered that the company was utterly incompetent to pay moneys as promised, and therefore deponent, on behalf of his firm (John W. Corlies & Co.), declined to furnish the articles desired. Immediately on notifying General Sturm of this decision said Sturm desired to introduce deponent to General Carvajal, and upon such introduction deponent found General Carvajal in very distressed circumstances—without money, and annoyed beyond measure in consequence of his arrangement with the irresponsible company—but on his urgent request deponent furnished him with a lawyer and promised him to personally aid by all reasonable means in extricating him from his difficulties. Subsequently, as the result of various interviews with General Carvajal, a contract was made between him, acting for the Mexican government, and deponent's firm of John W. Corlies & Co., by which said firm were made the financial agents of of that government and directed to issue and if possible dispose of thirty millions of dollars of the bonds of that country, the proceeds to be used in such manner as the authorities should direct. This contract having been approved by His Excellency M. Romero,

Minister, etc., at Washington, deponent's firm caused the bonds to be engraved and printed so far as needed, and commenced their sale. Unfortunately but little demand was found for the bonds, and deponent was directed by General Carvajal to apply to the United States government for its guaranty to the payment of fifty million dollars of Mexican bonds; and by said Carvajal's written directions, General Sturm, who had been by him appointed his agent, remained with deponent at Washington working indefatigably for that object during the greater part of two sessions of our Congress. In the meantime General Sturm presented to deponent's firm an order from General Carvajal for fifteen hundred thousand dollars United States currency or its equivalent in Mexican bonds at sixty per cent., but as said firm had been obliged, in order to dispose of the bonds at all, to guarantee personally the payment of the first year's interest (viz 1866), they declined to deliver them unless the interest was first deposited with deponent's firm or the coupons cut off from the bonds; and even then deponent informed General Sturm that the bonds were not in his possession ready for delivery, because of the lack of the personal signature of Jesus Fuentes y Munis, the agent appointed by the Mexican government to sign all bonds, and who only signed upon direction of His Excellency, M. Romero, who himself only authorized the signing of such bonds as were required for immediate use. Subsequently General Sturm again presented the order, but in the meantime deponent's firm had received official notice from the Mexican government that General Carvajal's orders were not to be honored unless approved by His Excellency, M. Romero, which approval the order presented did not bear; hence it was utterly out of said firm's power, for this additional reason, to comply with said Sturm's demand.

Deponent further states that to the indefatigable and persistent efforts of General Sturm, pursued without intermission for more than two years at great expense to him, is largely due the purchase and shipment to the Mexican government of large quantities of arms and other munitions of war, which happily aided that government in the capture of Maximilian and the expulsion of the French from that country.

J. N. TIFFT.

Deposition of William C. Peckham.

No. 411.]

The said William C. Peckham, being first duly cautioned and sworn to tell the truth, the whole truth and nothing but the truth, deposes and says, that his name is William C. Peckam; his age is forty years; he was born in Rhode Island; and that his residence is now in the city of New York, and his occupation that of a stenographer; and that at the time of the happening of the events concerning which he testifies his residence was in Seventeenth Street, in the city of New York, and his occupation that of a clerk, and that he has no interest, direct or indirect, in the claim concerning which he now testifies.

Deponent further says, that sometime during the summer of 1865, he was engaged as book keeper and clerk by General Jose M. J. Carvajal, Commissioner of the Mexican Republic, then temporarily residing in New York city. On or about the 16th day of May, 1866, said General Carvajal sailed for Mexico, and before his departure he ordered deponent and several officers of said General to report to General Herman Sturm, the agent of the Mexican government in the United States, who, as he said, had full instructions in the premises. On or about the 26th of July, of the same year, deponent sailed for Brazo, Santiago, Texas, in the steamer J. W. Everman, and on the 11th of August he arrived at Matamoras, Mexico, where he reported to General Carvajal. On the 12th of August said General was deposed and driven from the city by his officers and men, and as there was no immediate prospect of a settlement of the difficulties caused by the deposition of General Carvajal, deponent returned in the same steamer to New York.

Deponent further says, that General Herman Sturm has faithfully kept and performed the promises of payment made to deponent by General Carvajal, who had, amongst other things, given to him a draft on Messrs. J. W. Corlies & Co., the financial agents of the Republic of Mexico, at No. 57 Broadway, New York city, but as said agents had no funds to the credit of that government from which to pay said draft, General Herman Sturm settled with deponent and paid him the amount due, which, as deponent now recollects, was fifteen hundred dollars in gold.

WILLIAM C. PECKHAM.

Deposition of Marcellus Hartley.

No. 412.]

The said Marcellus Hartley being first duly cautioned and sworn to tell the truth, the whole truth, and nothing but the truth, deposes and says that his name is Marcellus Hartley; his age is forty-two years; he was born in New York city, and that his residence is now in the city and State of New York, and is at present a partner of the firm of Schuyler, Hartley & Graham, importers and wholesale dealers in military goods and fancy goods, at No. 19 Maiden Lane; and at the time of happening of the events concerning which he testifies, his residence was also in the said city of New York, and his business the same as before stated. Deponent further says:

I am well acquainted with the claimant, General Herman Sturm, and have known him since about the breaking out of the late rebellion, and have had business transactions with him as an officer of Ordnance for the State of Indiana. Some time in the year (1865) eighteen hundred and sixty five, and subsequently, I was repeatedly urged by the said General Sturm, and the Hon. Robert Dale Owen, to sell to said Sturm, as agent for the Republic of Mexico, arms and other munitions of war, and take in payment therefor the bonds of that government, at the authorized rate of sixty cents on the dollar. I was assured by said Sturm that the Mexican government would, without fail, make due and full arrangements for the prompt payment of the interest on said bonds, as it should accrue and become due, as soon as said government should be fully re-established and in possession of its sources of revenue.

Having satisfied myself that General Sturm was acting under proper authority from, and that the bonds he offered in payment were issued by, the legitimate government of Mexico, recognized by the government of the United States and Senor M. Romero, the Minister of said Mexican government at Washington, D. C., I did sell, some time in the months of October and November, 1866, to said Sturm, as agent aforesaid, a large amount of arms and other munitions of war, amounting, at the rate aforesaid, in all to about six hundred thousand dollars in Mexican bonds, which bonds were duly paid to me by said General Sturm.

I further say, that the said General Sturm, by his persistency, induced me to sell the goods to the Mexican government; and, so far as I know, labored faithfully and earnestly for the best interests of Mexico, and endeavored, to his utmost, to raise the credit of that government, and obtain for its bonds the military and other supplies it stood so much in need of. And I believe the said Sturm to be an honorable and faithful man, and during all transactions our house or I have had with him, both as an officer of the United States and of the State of Indiana, and as Agent for the Republic of Mexico, his business with us has been promptly settled; and at no time has he received from our house, as the agent of either government, either directly or indirectly, any commission, or present, or any other gratification; and I further say, that I have no interest, directly or indirectly, in the claim of the said General Herman Sturm against the said government of Mexico.

MARCELLUS HARTLEY.

Letter from Carvajal.

No. 413.] La Joya, Texas, July 28, 1869.

The undersigned certifies: That General Herman Sturm, late of the Ordnance Department of the State of Indiana, served faithfully under my orders as Agent of the Republic of Mexico, in the years of 1865 and 1866, raising a credit for my country, buying arms and munitions of war, and enlisting many influential and able men of the first order in the United States to use their efforts at their own expense, to obtain means and valuable assistance in favor of my country's cause: That in the discharge of his duties, General Sturm has expended large sums of money out of his own private funds, without receiving any moneys from my Government, to my knowledge; and generally, that the services rendered by General Sturm and his friends to the cause of Mexico, cannot be adequately repaid with money, as they were rendered at a time when we were passing our darkest hour.

And, in justice to General Sturm, who also acted as *secret* Agent with ample powers, I give the present, as above.

JOSE M. J. CARVAJAL,
Late Agent of the Republic of Mexico, and
Governor of Tamaulipas and San Louis Potosi.

Deposition of Charles E. Capehart.

No. 414]

The said Charles E. Capehart, being first duly sworn and cautioned, deposes and says, that during the war of the rebellion he was an officer of the United States army; that his rank, at the time of the closing of said war, was that of Colonel of cavalry; that he became acquainted with the claimant, General Herman Sturm, during the month of May or June, 1865, and learned that said General Sturm was then actively engaged in making friends and obtaining assistance for the Government of the Republic ot Mexico, then engaged in a war with the usurper, Maximilian and his French allies; that General Sturm had at that time a great many active and enterprising young men, chiefly those who had been officers in the army of the United States, whose reputation and merits would inspire confidence, all of whom were actively and effectively employed in promoting the cause of the Liberal Government of Mexico, in this country.

Sometime in the month of January, 1866, General Sturm informed deponent that the Mexican Government was in the greatest need of pecuniary assistance, and that an effort would be made to obtain such aid from the Government of the United States, by an act of Congress, and that he, the said Sturm, had been instructed, as the agent of the Government of the Republic of Mexico, to secure, if possible, the enactment of a law guaranteeing a Mexican loan of fifty million of dollars.

General Sturm exhibited to the deponent several documents authorizing him, the said Sturm, to act in the United States as the *military* as well as the *confidential* agent of the Mexican Government, and he proposed to engage the deponent to assist him in aiding the Mexican Government; that said Sturm informed deponent that he had an obligation for a secret service fund of half a million of dollars, given him by General J. M. J. Carvajal, to be used in promoting the interests of the Republic of Mexico in the United States, and said Sturm proposed to pay deponent for the services he desired deponent to render, and to reimburse him for the expenses he might incur in such service, a specific sum of said fund, which said Sturm agreed to pay deponent when said secret service fund should be received from the Government of Mexico; and General Sturm referred deponent to Senor M. Romero, Mexican Minister in the United States, for a confirmation as to General Sturm's authority to make such engagements and his power to dispose of said secret service fund as stated.

Deponent thereupon went immediately to Senor M. Romero (with whom the deponent was acquainted) and stated to him the representations and proposals that had been made to deponent by said Sturm, and asked Senor M. Romero if General Sturm was fully empowered to make such contracts in behalf of his Government. In reply M. Romero stated to deponent that General Sturm had derived his authority from General Carvajal, the duly authorized Commissioner of the Mexican Government, and that he was acting in perfect concert with him, Mr. Romero, and in accordance with the wishes of his Government, and Mr. Romero assured deponent, in the most positive manner, that any contract or engagement which General Sturm would make by virtue of his authority from General Carvajal, would be binding on and be faithfully observed by his Government, and that any promises the said General Sturm should make, for payment for services out of the secret service fund before mentioned, would be kept, and he, Mr. Romero, would guarantee the payment thereof.

Upon these assurances on the part of the Mexican Minister, the deponent made an agreement with General Sturm, and for the period of over a year co-operated in advancing and maintaining the cause of the Mexican Republic, and rendered whatever services were required of him by said Sturm, many of which were of a secret and confidential character.

During this time General Sturm had in his employment many other agents, and the said Sturm devoted himself with extraordinary diligence to the affairs of the Republic of Mexico, endeavoring to his utmost to manufacture public opinion in favor of and create sympathy for that distressed Government, and to counteract, by means of secret agents and in various other ways, the plans and machinations of the agents of the Maximilian, French and Austrian Governments in this country, many of whom were in this city of Washington, well supplied with money and industriously engaged in preventing, by all possible means, the Liberal Government of Mexico from obtaining in this country any aid it so much needed and sought, and in defeating any measure of relief, or any other public act or expression of assistance or sympathy in favor of the Mexican Republic.

Deponent further says that in consequence of his connection with General Sturm and many of his agents, he is fully aware of the fact that General Sturm has expended large sums of money, and has induced others (including deponent) to spend their money freely in the interest of the Mexican Republic, and that many agents employed by said Sturm, although willing to render their services for promises to pay, required *cash money* for incidental daily expenses, and that said Sturm, as well as deponent, have advanced of their own means the money thus required.

Deponent further says that the money he thus expended, and the services which he rendered were cheerfully given upon the confident anticipation that the Mexican Government would faithfully keep its promises, as Mr. Romero had assured deponent it would; but at no time has he received payment for services rendered and expenses advanced either for himself or for the other agents employed by deponent, and he still holds General Sturm responsible for the amounts thus due him. And further deponent saith not.

CHARLES E. CAPEHART.

Deposition of Richard M. Hall.

No. 415.]

Deponent being duly sworn, deposes and says that he has known General Sturm ever since the spring of 1855; that his reputation then was, and has ever since been of the highest character for honor and integrity. His profession in Indianapolis was that of a Civil Engineer.

During the winter of 1865 and 1866 I was in daily intercourse with General Sturm concerning affairs in Mexico, and was taken into a somewhat confidential relation with him as to his purposes and aims in aiding the Government of Mexico, then in conflict with Maximilian. He showed me certain papers purporting to give him full authority from the Mexican Government to make contracts, and to secure for that Government from the United States, a guarantee of a fifty million loan.

There being at the time so many conflicting rumors about the affairs of Mexico, in order to assure myself and friends to the utmost extent as to the regularity of General Sturm's authority, I put myself in communication with gentlemen of the highest standing, and through them ascertained that Mr. Romero, then the Mexican Minister at Washington, recognized the authority of General Sturm to make contracts and promises in behalf of his (Romero's) Government, and that he (Romero) was acting in concord with General Sturm in the interest of Mexico, and that he stood pledged to carry out General Sturm's agreements.

Subsequent to this I entered into an engagement with General Sturm to aid him in all proper ways to secure the endorsement and support of the United States in the then proposed Mexican loan; that, pending legislative action thereon, during said winters of 1865 and 1866, I was active in aiding General Sturm as far as possible, spending both time and money; that, under and by General Sturm's direction I made certain engagements and promises for him with other influential persons to aid him, and I know that they did assist in promoting the interest of said loan, and generally the affairs and interests of the Mexican Republic.

General Sturm promised me, and others through me, a liberal fee for services in this direction, but up to this time have had no compensation whatever, and yet hold him responsible for his promises and engagements.

And further, that being so constantly with General Sturm during said winter and spring, I had occasion to notice the unremitting labors of said General Sturm in behalf of Mexico, and to remark upon the enormous outlays of money he incurred to accomplish his mission or purpose in her behalf. He (General Sturm) had constantly around him the very best and most representative men of the country, whom he had interested for the imperiled Republic of Mexico.

R. M. HALL.

Deposition of Godlove S. Orth.

No. 416.]

The said Godlove S. Orth, being by me first duly cautioned and sworn to tell the truth, the whole truth, and nothing but the truth, deposes and says, that his name is Godlove S. Orth; that he is fifty-four years of age; that he was born in the State of Pennsylvania, and his residence is now in the city of Lafayette, Indiana. That he was a member of Congress from 1863 to 1871, and during the sessions of Congress between the years aforesaid he was in the city of Washington. That during his entire service he was a member of the Committee on Foreign Affairs.

Deponent further says: I am well acquainted with the above complainant, Herman Sturm, and understood he was, during the recent rebellion, on the staff of Governor Morton, and Chief of Ordnance of the State of Indiana, and I have always understood that he discharged his duties to the entire satisfaction of the public authorities.

During my service in Congress I became well acquainted with Hon. M. Romero, the Mexican Minister accredited to our Government.

In the year 1866 some propositions were introduced into Congress with reference to extending material aid and sympathy from our Government to the Republic of Mexico, among which I recollect one, to guarantee the bonds of said Republic to the amount of fifty millions of dollars, or to issue on behalf of said Republic the bonds of this Government for a similar amount.

Pending these propositions, General Sturm was frequently in Washington, and called several times at my rooms in Washington, alleging that he was a confidential agent of Mexico, and advocated and persistently urged the passage of some measures of relief, and especially the issuing of the bonds.

The Mexican Minister (M. Romero) manifested great interest in the result of these measures, calling to see me quite often, and once at least, if not oftener, he called in company with General Sturm for the same purpose.

I also met General Sturm occasionally at the rooms of other members of Congress, urging and advocating the cause of the Republic of Mexico in that behalf, and am well satisfied that the want of action on the part of Congress was not owing to any neglect or fault on the part of General Sturm, for my present recollection is, that he was constantly, in season and out of season, pleading for relief to Mexico.

I have no interest whatever, directly or indirectly, in the claim of Herman Sturm against the Republic of Mexico. And further this deponent sayeth not.

GODLOVE S. ORTH.

Deposition of Fred. P. Stanton.

No. 417.]

I was born in Alexandria, D. C.; I am fifty-six years of age; I now reside in Washington City, and my occupation is that of a lawyer. In 1866 I was residing in the neighborhood of this city, and was then doing business here as a lawyer. In February or March of that year, 1866, General Sturm, the claimant, called on me and stated that he was the agent of the Mexican Government, deriving his power from General Jose M.J. Carvajal. He exhibited to me all the documents purporting to give General Carvajal authority to act in the name of the Mexican Government, and to employ all necessary agents in the United States to raise money and to purchase arms and material of war, and generally to promote the interests of Mexico by all lawful means within the United States.

I can not now state the full purport of the documents exhibited to me by General Sturm, but they purported to be the original documents, conferring authority by the Mexican Government on General Carvajal, and then by General Carvajal upon General Sturm.

Not feeling myself competent to judge of the validity and authenticity of these documents, I called upon M. Romero, the Mexican Minister in Washington, and inquired of him as to the validity of the powers claimed by General

Sturm. In reply to my inquiries, M. Romero informed me that General Carvajal had full authority from the Government of Mexico, and that General Sturm was duly authorized to act as the agent of that Government in the secret and confidential service in which he was then engaged.

Acting upon the information thus received from the Minister of the Mexican Government in Washington, I made an engagement with General Sturm to assist him by legal advice and counsel in the affairs of the Mexican Government. General Sturm agreed to pay me for my services, and has since satisfactorily settled with me, and I therefore have no interest in his claim against the Mexican Government. I am not his attorney in the prosecution of said claim.

I know that General Sturm was exceedingly active and energetic in serving the Government of Mexico. He devoted his whole time and attention to that business, and spent his money freely. He employed other persons besides myself, who gave their time and exertions in promoting the interests of Mexico and the success of General Sturm's negotiations. I, myself, devoted a great deal of time and labor to the business aforesaid.

I saw Mr. Romero on several occasions and conversed with him on the subject of General Sturm's agency. I remember very distinctly that on one of these occasions, in the spring of 1866, General John A. Logan, now a Senator of the United States, was present, and participated in the conversation with Mr. Romero.

In all these conversations, Mr. Romero admitted the authority of General Sturm as above stated.

FRED. P. STANION.

Deposition of Walter Hawkes.

No. 418.]

The said Walter Hawkes, being by me first duly cautioned and sworn to tell the truth, the whole truth, and nothing but the truth, deposes and says that his name is Walter Hawkes; his age is forty-two years; he was born in Massachusetts; and that his residence is now in the City of New York, and his occupation that of a merchant, and that at the time of the happening of the events concerning which he testifies, his residence was in New York City, and his occupation that of merchant, and that he has no interest, direct or indirect, and is not the agent or attorney of any one having any interest, direct or indirect, in the claim concerning which he now testifies.

Deponent further says that during the years 1865 and 1866, he was repeatedly applied to and urged by the claimant in this case, General H. Sturm, the agent of the Government of Mexico, to sell to the Mexican Government arms and other munitions of war, and receive in payment therefor the bonds of that Government at the rate of sixty (60) cents on the dollar. Deponent, however, ascertained from bankers and merchants, and financial men generally, in New York City, that they had no confidence whatever either in the ability or disposition of the Mexican Government to comply with its contracts or promises, and that the credit of the Mexican Government was so low that it would be injurious to deponent and other business men to deal with the Mexican Government except for cash, and your deponent consequently informed General Sturm that for the reasons before stated he must decline to accept the propositions made by the said Sturm. General Sturm, however, persisted in his efforts, and labored earnestly and for a long time with your deponent, and as he knows, with many other merchants in New York City, to convince them that the Government of Mexico would faithfully carry out its agreements and fulfill its promises to such persons as would aid her in her distress, and deponent, in the fall of 1866, seeing that through the efforts of General Sturm several cargoes of munitions of war, obtained from New York merchants for Mexican bonds, had been shipped to Mexico, proposed to said Sturm to sell him materials of war for bonds, provided the Mexican Government would secure the payment of the interest on said bonds as it accrued and became due. To which said Sturm replied that he had such faith in the honor and integrity of said Government that he would cheerfully advance to deponent money sufficient to meet the payment of one year's interest on all Mexican bonds deponent (in payment) would receive for arms, &c., sold to the Mexican Government. Thereupon, deponent agreed with said Sturm some time in October or November, 1866, to furnish said Sturm a large amount of arms, equipments, knapsacks, haversacks, percussion caps, &c., at the then ruling prices, for which he agreed to take in payment the bonds of the Mexican Government, at the rate of sixty (60) cents on the dollar, provided said Sturm would advance one year's interest on said bonds. Deponent having been out of the arms' business for the last three (3) years, has not, at the present moment, access to his books, and can not state the exact amount of arms he sold to said Sturm, nor the exact amount of bonds he received in payment therefor; but deponent states that the total amount of money advanced to him by said Sturm, as interest on said bonds, amounts to seven thousand nine hundred and twenty-four ($7,924.70) dollars and seventy cents in currency of the United States, which sum was paid to deponent at three (3) different times by checks on the Banking House of Winslow, Lanier & Co., of New York City, which said checks are hereto attached. Deponent further says that since that time he has not received a single cent of interest on said bonds, and has transferred said bonds to other parties interested with deponent in arms transactions. Finally, deponent says that it is his honest conviction and belief that the success of the Mexican Government to obtain munitions of war in this country on its promises to pay, is mainly due to the enterprise and energy of its agent, General Sturm, and to the liberal and practical use he made of money in furthering, and the earnestness with which he plead the cause of that Government, and further deponent saith not.

W. HAWKES.

Deposition of O. H. Burbridge.

No. 419.]

Oscar H. Burbridge, being duly sworn, deposes and says that some time in the early part of (1866) eighteen hundred and sixty-six, General Herman Sturm was introduced to me by my brother, General S. G. Burbridge. General Sturm represented himself to be the agent of the Mexican Government in this country, for the purpose of obtaining aid and assistance for that Government to sustain it in its efforts against the European intervention. He was very highly recommended by many influential persons with whom I was acquainted, and I watched with much interest his effort with the members of the Congress of the United States Government, to obtain through them a guarantee from the Government of the United States to the Mexican loan of fifty millions ($50,000,000) of dollars. While so engaged, General Sturm urged me and other friends to advance our money to the Mexican Government by investing in its bonds, stating to me that it was the duty of every American citizen to support the Liberal Government of Mexico, and its President, Juarez, and that said Government would surely prove itself grateful to its friends in this country.

The Congress of the United States adjourned, however, without guaranteeing said loan, and some time during the month of July, (1866,) eighteen hundred and sixty-six, General Sturm begged me (supposing that I had capital at my command) to induce my friends to form an association and collect a sufficient amount of money for the purpose of purchasing a sufficient quantity of arms to form a cargo to be sent to the Liberal force of Mexico. General Sturm showed me various documents, purporting to be authorization from the Mexican Government, and he requested me to go myself, and also to introduce my friends to Senor Romero, the Minister of the Mexican Government to our Government at Washington. Being myself strongly opposed to the foreign intervention in Mexico, and being strongly impressed, by the statement made to me by General Sturm, that a fair and liberal offer of remuneration would be made to me, I called on Senor Romero, Minister as aforesaid, at his house, corner of Thirteenth and K streets, in Washington City, for the purpose of satisfying myself, as well as my friends, that General Sturm was acting under proper authority from that Mexican Government, which was at the time recognized by the Government of the United States; during this interview, and subsequent ones that I had with said Romero, he assured me that General Sturm had received his power and authorization from General Carvajal, the regularly appointed Commissioner of the Mexican Government, and that any contract or arrangement he might make under that authority would be duly recognized by the Mexican Government. Mr. Romero said to me, however, that as Minister, he himself would have nothing to do with transactions in arms, etc., etc., and referred me to said Sturm in such a manner, however, that I was forcibly impressed with the idea that it was the urgent wish and desire of said Minister to obtain speedy assistance in the shape of arms for his Government, and have them sent to that Government, in fact, although I do not now recollect the exact language used. He assured me that his Government was in the utmost need of assistance, and would be very grateful to me and other friends if we would comply with the wishes of General Sturm, and furnish aid to his Government. After several interviews with said Sturm, having made arrangements with a few friends and bankers for the money necessary to purchase the arms General Sturm desired for the Mexican Government, I agreed with him to furnish at fixed prices, which Mr. Romero himself had assured me were equitable and fair—arms and other munitions amounting, as near as I can recollect now, to the sum of over seven hundred thousand ($700,000) dollars. This contract was made between General Sturm and myself and partners, in the city of New York, in the early part of (1866) eighteen hundred and sixty-six; and General Sturm said to me that according to his instructions, before this contract would be binding on the Mexican Government, it would be necessary to submit it to Mr. Romero for approval, which would, however, be speedily obtained; and he urged me not to lose any time on account of that formality, but proceed at once to purchase and furnish him the arms, so that his inspectors might be able to go on with the inspection and packing of said arms, and no time be lost.

Thereupon I made arrangements with the firm of Schuyler, Hartley & Graham, dealers in arms, New York City, for the purchasing of said arms as were required by General Sturm, depositing with them the sum of one thousand ($1,000) dollars, as collateral security for the fulfilling of the purchase of them on my part, which amount, they stated to me, would barely cover their expense in handling the arms, in case I should not fulfill my contract with them.

While thus endeavoring to aid and facilitate General Sturm as much as possible, I also submitted my contract with the Mexican Government to the Mexican Consul in New York City, who, as I was informed by letters from Mr. Romero, shown me by General Sturm, was authorized to approve the contract in the absence of Mr. Romero, who, in the meantime, had gone with the President of the United States, General Grant, and other prominent men, on a trip through the United States. The Mexican Consul at New York assured me that he approved my contract with General Sturm in every respect, but when I requested him to put this approval in writing, he stated to me that it was not necessary, as General Sturm's authority was in writing, and that it was a formality simply, and that he had not been instructed to approve in writing. As this was my understanding of the word approval, and as I could not see any reason why said Consul should hesitate to sign his name to a document he verbally fully approved, I sent my partner to Cleveland, Ohio, for the purpose of seeing Mr. Romero, who, as I was informed by General Sturm, would be there with the Presidential party, with a view of obtaining his written approval to the contract. Mr. Romero, as I was informed by my partner, assured him that the contract was all right, and that he had instructed the Mexican Consul at New York to approve the contract in writing. On the return of my partner, some time in the commencement of September, we again went to the Mexican Consul together with General Sturm, who exhibited to him certain letters and telegrams from Mr. Romero, instructing him to approve the contract. The said Consul still declined to give his approval in writing, although he did so to the full extent verbally. While thus endeavoring to obtain the approval of the Mexican officials to the contract in writing, news was received and published in the newspapers, that on the arrival of the steamer J. W. Everman, at Matamoras, with the cargo of arms and munitions that had been previously obtained by General Sturm from other parties in New York City and Philadelphia, had been seized by the Mexican officer then in command there, and that the American citizens who came with said cargo and vessel to aid the Mexican Government in various capacities, had on their arrival been imprisoned and otherwise outrageously treated by the Mexican authorities. At the same time, General Ortega, then in the United States, through newspapers and otherwise, proclaimed that he, and not President Juarez, was the legitimate President of Mexico, and the bonds issued by President Juarez and Mr. Romero would not be recognized by him as soon as he would obtain the reins of government. Another party by the name of Woodhouse claimed to have a contract with the Mexican Government, according to which he was the only person entitled to issue bonds for said Government in this country, and that all bonds not so issued by him were illegitimate, and to substantiate this, he exhibited a contract made with the Mexican Government purporting to be approved by Mr. Romero. Under these circumstances, all the friends whom I had induced to participate with me in the enterprise of furnishing aid to Mexico for its bonds, and on whom I relied for contributing a large portion of money necessary to carry out my contract with the Mexican Government, became dissatisfied with the whole Mexican business, fearing that the Mexican Government did not intend to act in good faith towards us; and although the aforesaid contract was finally, about the middle of September, approved in writing by the proper Mexican officials, yet I was, in consequence of this trouble and delay and the refusal of my friends to carry out their parts, compelled to decline to have anything further to do with the furnishing of aid to Mexico, as desired by General Sturm; and yet, to do justice to General Sturm, I must state that he endeavored to the utmost of his ability to persuade us, and even force us to carry out the contract on various grounds. But seeing the injustice of thus forcing me to carry out to the letter an agreement which the Mexican authorities in this country had refused to comply with, he finally released me from further responsibility; and I state further, that at the time of the breaking up of our arrangements as aforesaid, several thousand stands of arms, equipments, etc., etc., had already been inspected by General Sturm's inspectors, and were boxed up ready for shipment, and to satisfy the claim of the firm in New York, of whom I had purchased the arms, for their trouble and expense in the matter, I was compelled to pay them the sum of one thousand ($1,000) dollars, and that I have further suffered a pecuniary loss in the way of traveling and other expenses incidental to the affair, in my endeavors to obtain through the Mexican officials a written approval to the contract, and to furnish the arms called for by the same, of at least one thousand ($1,000) dollars; and further state that I am only interested to the amount of two thousand dollars in said claim, as above described. And further the deponent saith not.

O. H. BURBRIDGE.

Deposition of B. Sellick Osbon.

No. 420.]

The said B. Sellick Osbon being duly sworn, deposes and says, that he followed the sea, professionally, for more than twenty years, serving in the navy of Buenos Ayres, and during the late rebellion as volunteer aide to the late Admiral D. G. Farragut, U. S. N., and signal officer of the U. S. Flagship, Hartford, and aide to Captain J. L. Worden, U. S. N., and signal officer of the U. S. S. Montauk, and having seen much naval service, and being highly recommended to General Jose M. J. Carvajal for ability, zeal, &c., was in the month of September, 1865, induced to enter into an agreement with the said General Jose M. J Carvajal to proceed to Mexico and there take service in the navy of that country; and as the said General Carvajal desired to purchase some vessels in the United States suitable for gunboat service, he instructed me to assist him in obtaining such vessels. General Herman Sturm was the agent of the Mexican Government, authorized to purchase ships, munitions of war, &c In the month of October, 1865, the steam yacht, "Clara Clarita" was offered for sale to General Sturm for the use of the Mexican Government, and I was instructed to examine her thoroughly, and have her put in complete order for Government service. We had one or more trial trips, the expenses of which I have no doubt amounted to several hundred dollars, and were paid by General Sturm. The vessel was suitable, and arrangements were made to purchase her, but as the financial agents of the Mexican Government could not dispose of Mexican bonds for current money, and as the parties owning said vessel were not willing to sell her for bonds, the arrangement to purchase fell through. I remained with General Carvajal until his departure for Mexico, some time in the month of May, 1866, and during this time I assisted him in every way possible to obtain a suitable vessel for his purpose, but in consequence of the many factions among the Mexican Republicans themselves, and the general discredit of that Government in this country, it was impossible to obtain a vessel on credit.

One or two evenings before the departure of General Carvajal, who resided in the same house as I did, he sent for me and W. C. Peckham, his book-keeper, and in the presence of General Lew. Wallace, and W. F. Stocking, his private Secretary, he stated to me that General Sturm expected to succeed in obtaining a steamer such as he (General Carvajal) desired, and he instructed me, as well as Mr. Stocking and Mr. Peckham, to report to General Sturm, and obey his instructions; and he further said that General Sturm had received from him full instructions as to our future movements, and that he (General Sturm) would be fully provided with funds necessary to pay all our expenses, &c., and that we were to look to General Sturm for payment.

In accordance with instructions received from General Sturm, I proceeded to Philadelphia some time in the month of July, 1866, to superintend the fitting out of the steamer "General Sheridan," and on the 6th of August of that year I took passage in her with my officers, who had served during the war in the navy of the United States, and sailed for Brazos Santiago, Texas, with the intention of proceeding to Mexico, and there take service under the Mexican Government. It was agreed between General Carvajal and myself that I should command the "General Sheridan," which was to be delivered to me at the port of Soto la Marina, Mexico, or in that neighborhood. On my arrival at Brazos Santiago, I received telegraphic orders from General Carvajal to report in person to him at Brownsville, Texas. I also heard that he had been deposed by a revolt of his officers and troops, and that the cargo of munitions of war, &c., landed by the steamer "J. W. Everman," had been taken to Matamoras by order of General Carvajal, and that after the landing of the said cargo, it had been taken possession of by the Mexican authorities, but a few hours afterwards the Mexican officers inimical to General Carvajal had caused the aforesaid revolt and had plundered the cargo. I further state that Colonel W. F. Stocking, private Secretary to General Carvajal, endeavored by all means in his power to prevent the arms from being used against the Government of which Benito Juarez was President. General Carvajal was in a very distressed condition, and had no funds whatever to pay me and others who had come out with, or at his instigation, to Mexico. But relying on General Sturm, who, as he said and as I knew, had furnished General Carvajal with nearly all the funds while he was in New York City, and expecting that General Sturm would still assist and help him out of his distressing position, he, General Carvajal, gave me an order on said General Herman Sturm for fifteen hundred and seventy-three ($1,573.83) dollars and eighty-three cents, which was the amount due me for services rendered up to September 29, 1866. I remained in Matamoras, Mexico, until January, 1867, and then returned to the United States, and from the city of New Orleans I transmitted to General Sturm the order of General Carvajal to pay me the aforesaid fifteen hundred and seventy-three ($1,573.83) dollars and eighty-three cents. After some time I received a reply from General Sturm acknowledging receipt of the order, but stating that he had expended such a large amount of money for the Mexican Government, and had not received in return one dollar of money, nor had he bonds at his command at the time to pay me as requested by General Carvajal. He promised, however, to pay me as soon as he should receive the funds which the Mexican Government had promised him.

I communicated with him at various times subsequently, both personally and otherwise, but he always stated that he had not even received yet the return of the money he had advanced for that Government, and to this day I hold him responsible to me for the payment of the aforesaid draft of fifteen hundred and seventy-three ($1,573.83) dollars and eighty-three cents.

B. SELLICK OSBON.

Deposition of W. P. Dole.

No. 421.]

The said W. P. Dole, having been duly sworn, deposes and says, that I am well acquainted with General Herman Sturm, the claimant in this case.

In the fall or winter of the year 1865, General Sturm engaged me as his attorney to assist him in his efforts to obtain material aid from the Government and people of the United States, for the cause of the Mexican Republic in its then desperate struggle against the invasion and usurpation of Maximilian.

General Sturm exhibited to me certain documents, purporting to be a contract, power of authority, and orders signed by General J. M. J. Carvajal as Commissioner of the Mexican Republic in the United States, whereby General Sturm was duly authorized and empowered to act as agent of the Mexican Government, to obtain *materiel* of war, &c., and to perform other services of a secret and confidential nature. General Sturm further stated that he had been promised by General Carvajal ample funds to carry into effect the objects and purposes stated. General Sturm further explained to me that the immediate object then contemplated was to obtain from the Government of the United

States, a guarantee of a loan of fifty million dollars, or to obtain other material aid from the Government and people of the United States.

It was at the time a well-known fact that the Mexican cause was in a desperate and almost hopeless condition; that its Government had been driven to a remote part of its territory, the greater part thereof being, at the time, under the military domination of Maximilian; that its army scarcely existed except in name, being few in numbers, destitute almost entirely of arms, clothing, equipments and supplies, and that its credit was so low that its securities possessed no marketable value, and that unless powerful and speedy assistance could be obtained in the United States, the Mexican cause was utterly hopeless.

It was equally well-known that the emissaries of Maximilian in this country were numerous, able and vigilant, and were supplied with money to enable them to counteract the efforts of the friends of the Republic of Mexico.

General Sturm referred me to the Mexican Minister, Senor M. Romero, for a confirmation of his statements to me, as to the extent and validity of the powers that had been conferred on him as the agent of the Republican Government of Mexico, and I accordingly called upon M. Romero and stated to him the representations that General Sturm had made to me, and I asked Mr. Romero to state explicitly if the powers of General Sturm were valid, and if the contracts and engagements made by General Sturm would be recognized and carried out by the Mexican Government.

In reply, Mr. Romero assured me that the powers and authority derived by General Sturm from General Carvajal were legitimate and valid, and that any and all contracts and agreements made by General Sturm, in accordance with the said powers and authority, would be binding upon the Mexican Government and would be faithfully carried out by it; and Mr. Romero further assured me that General Sturm would be supplied with funds for the purposes indicated, and that the payment of such funds to General Sturm had been guaranteed, both by General Carvajal and himself (Mr. Romero.)

Fully satisfied of the authority of General Sturm to act as the agent of the Mexican Republic, I at once commenced devoting my best exertions to promote the interests of the Mexican Government, for the purpose of obtaining material aid, and from some time in the month of November, 1865, to the latter part of the year 1866, I was actively engaged in co-operating with General Sturm in his efforts to assist the Mexican Government, and during that time I expended a considerable sum of money, but up to the present time I have not been compensated by General Sturm or the Mexican Government, either in whole or in part for my services or expenditures.

General Sturm agreed to pay me out of a *secret service fund* that had been guaranteed to him by, and which he expected to receive from, the Mexican Government, but which, as he informs me, and as I believe, he has not received, and I look to him *only* for payment.

I further declare that I was fully cognizant of the manner in which General Sturm performed his duties as the agent of the Mexican Government; that his energy, activity and zeal were untiring; that his fertility of resource and ingenuity were apparently inexhaustible; that no obstacle, however great, seemed to daunt his inflexible purpose and courage, and the complete success attained by him finally in his efforts to aid Mexico, abundantly attests the possession and exercise on his part of these high qualities, and entitle him to a most liberal compensation from the Mexican Government.

I further declare that General Sturm spent money liberally and judiciously in his efforts to aid Mexico, and that he obligated himself in a similar manner as he did to me, to many other persons, agents and attorneys, who acted with him in aiding the cause of Mexican liberty. And further deponent sayeth not

W. P. DOLE.

Deposition of William J. Taylor.

No. 422.]

The said William J. Taylor, being duly sworn, deposes and says that in April, 1866, I resided in the city of Philadelphia, Pa., and was the senior partner of the firm of Wm. J. Taylor & Co., doing business at No. 208 North Delaware Avenue, in said city. Our firm was extensively engaged in the running of steamers to domestic and foreign ports. During our late war we chartered our steamers to the Government of the United States. Sometime during the aforesaid month of April, 1866, General Herman Sturm requested me to assist him in his efforts to obtain munitions of war for the Republic of Mexico, and steamers to transport them to that country.

I satisfied myself about General Sturm's authority to act as agent for the Mexican Government, and being assured by Mr. Romero that good faith would be kept by his Government, and relying upon the integrity of General Sturm, who was well recommended to me, I entered into negotiations with him, intending to charter to him one of the steamers, the "Agnes," then lying at Jersey City, belonging to my house (Wm. J. Taylor & Co., of Philadelphia.)

General Carvajal, General Wallace, and others with them, called on board of the vessel and examined her, and General Carvajal declared himself fully satisfied with the steamer, and proposed to take her; but before the agreement was perfected I made other disposition of her.

I then agreed with General Sturm to act as his agent and to procure, as secretly as possible, two steamers to convey General Carvajal and his party and cargoes of munitions to Mexico.

According to this arrangement I procured the steamers "Suwanee" and "J. W. Everman," both of which were transports and were well suited for the purpose, having been used as such by the Government of the United States, and they were chartered by General Sturm, as the agent of the Mexican Government.

The "J. W. Everman" was owned in Philadelphia by Henry Simons, who was well and favorably known as a large manufacturer, ship owner, and contractor with the Government of the United States during the war; and he chartered that vessel to General Sturm for a voyage to Brazos de Santiago, Texas, at the rate of $950 per day, and $3 per day for each passenger while on board. This charter included coal, provisions, and everything requisite for the running of a steamer, and I believe that that price was about that paid by the Government of the United States for the same vessel for similar services, as can be readily ascertained by reference to the records of the Transportation Division of the Quarter-master General's Office, United States Army. This charter provided that payment should be made in money, or in Mexican bonds at the rate of sixty cents on the dollar of their par value.

Subsequent to the charter of this vessel, in accordance with instructions from General Sturm and Mr. Romero, I purchased from Henry Simons, aforesaid, a small steamer, called the "General Sheridan," which was constructed and fully equipped as a gunboat, for the sum of $88,000, U. S. currency, payment to be made in Mexican bonds at the rate of sixty cents on the dollar of their par value.

In the contract for the sale of this vessel, it was provided, that Henry Simons should deliver her to General Carvajal, or other officer duly authorized by the Mexican Government to receive her, at or near Bazos de Santiago, Texas.

I know that the "J W. Everman" was in the employ of the Mexican Government until some time in the month of October of the same year, and that the "General Sheridan" arrived out on or about the 12th day of August of that year, and was then ready to be delivered to the Mexican Government.

About the middle of August, 1866, I was informed, through telegraphic dispatches from Galveston, Texas, that a revolt had occurred at Matamoras, and that General Carvajal had been deposed; and on the return of the steamer "Everman" in the commencement of October, 1866, I also learned from her Captain, and others, that owing to the aforesaid revolt, this steamer had been detained a considerable time, there being no Mexican officer there willing or empowered to order her return to New York, and that the "Sheridan" was still waiting to be received by the Mexican Government. I was subsequently informed that this vessel was not formally received by the Mexican Government until the latter part of the month of May, 1867.

Having been instrumental in bringing about the contracts for the "Everman" and "Sheridan," and having pledged myself to Henry Simons, aforesaid, that the Mexican Government would faithfully carry out their contracts with him, I was constantly importuned by him, to obtain for him the bonds that were due him for the two vessels, but the Mexican Minister, Mr. Romero, refused, from time to time, to deliver the bonds. Some time in the month of June, 1867, partial payments were made on those two contracts; and I know that Mr. Simons, aforesaid, has since failed, which failure was largely owing to the long deferred even partial payments, and the great depreciation of Mexican bonds, brought about by the violation of that Government of nearly all its contracts made through General Sturm, and the practical repudiation of its *legally issued bonds*. I further declare, that it is my judgment, as a practical steamboat man, that in consequence of the delay of the Mexican Government to receive the steamer "Sheridan," as agreed, Mr. Henry Simons, aforesaid, was put to great inconvenience and expense, as he was compelled to feed and pay the crew, and to bear the risk of her lying there during the stormy season of the year, for the period of nearly ten months, that the sum of ten thousand dollars would not be more than enough for a fair remuneration for the expenses thus incurred.

At the time of the making of the contracts for the aforesaid steamers, in the forepart of May, 1866, General Sturm stated to me that he would be provided with funds, or with Mexican bonds to make payment when it should become due, and in confirmation of that statement, he exhibited to me, Mr. Simons, aforesaid, and other merchants of Philadelphia, a draft to his order for one million five hundred thousand dollars, U. S. currency, or its equivalent in Mexican bonds, drawn on the financial agents of the Republic of Mexico, Messrs. J. W. Corlies & Co., and J. N. Tifft, and duly signed by General Carvajal.

On the 11th day of July, 1866, I called with General Sturm and others at the financial agency of the Mexican Government, at No. 57 Broadway, New York City, and in reply to several questions from General Sturm and myself, Mr. J. N. Tifft, the financial agent of that Government, acknowledged the validity of the aforesaid draft, and further stated that the Mexican Government would keep him supplied with one million of dollars of Mexican bonds on hand at all times, until the whole loan was placed, and to that extent he would guarantee the delivery of bonds to General Sturm upon his order, and he repeated the same statement, at subsequent interviews; but some time in the month of October, 1866, after the return of the "Everman" to New York City, when I demanded, on behalf of Mr. Simons, aforesaid, the delivery of the bonds due for the charter of that vessel, Mr. Tifft declined to do so except upon the order of Mr. Romero, the Mexican Minister.

I assisted General Sturm, as his agent, from April, 1866, until some time in the early part of the year 1867, during which time I devoted a great deal of time, and expended a considerable amount of money in rendering assistance to the Republican cause of Mexico. Having entire confidence in General Sturm's integrity and honesty of purpose, and firmly believing that the Mexican Government would faithfully carry out its agreements, and fairly and honorably settle all just claims against it as soon as it should be fully reinstated in power, I went so far as to urge numerous friends to aid and assist that Government by all means in their power, but to this day I have not been reimbursed by either the Mexican Government, or by General Sturm, and as it was especially upon the strength of the personal character and credit of General Sturm that I rendered the services and expended the money for the benefit of the Mexican Government, and as General Sturm has always assured me that he would pay me as soon as he should be paid by the Mexican Government, I have always held him, and do now hold him, responsible for the payment for said services and expenditures.

At the time when General Sturm opened negotiations with me it was almost impossible to obtain anything for Mexican bonds, and I was the first one who was willing to furnish General Sturm with the needed steamers for the use of the Mexican Government.

About the time of the purchase of the "Sheridan," I advanced, at the urgent request of General Sturm, for the purchase of two large guns, ammunition, etc., for the use of the Mexican Government, the sum of four thousand three hundred ($4,300) dollars, which advance General Sturm agreed to repay me out of a secret service fund which had been promised him; but to this day, neither said sum has been repaid me, nor any part thereof, and I hold said Sturm responsible therefor, with interest at the rate of seven per cent. from the 12th day of July, 1866. In addition, I also, in the month of August, at the instance of General Sturm, furnished him two more guns, etc., for Mexican bonds.

In justice to General Sturm I must say, that in all his transactions with me, and so far as I know, with others, he has acted in the utmost good faith, and I know that he has suffered heavily in consequence of his connection with the Mexican Government, and to this day I have the utmost confidence in him, and although the Mexican Government has violated its good faith with me and others who have assisted her during her hour of need, I do not regret that I have been connected with General Sturm in his efforts to relieve the wants of a sister Republic. His efforts, although he had no other material to work with than Mexico's promises to pay, were eminently successful, and he deserves great credit, and certainly the thanks of the Mexican nation.

I further state, that in consequence of the depreciation of Mexican bonds, which owed their value mainly to the exertions of General Sturm, and which depreciation was caused solely by the bad faith of that Government, and in consequence of other acts of bad faith by the Mexican Government, General Sturm has been entangled in lawsuits, and has also been unable to collect his claims against certain Marine Insurance companies in New York City and elsewhere, for munitions of war lost at sea while being transported to Mexico, and insured by him, for which goods General Sturm was responsible to the Mexican Government for the full amount until their delivery in Mexico. And further deponent sayeth not.

WM. J. TAYLOR.

Deposition of Wilbur F. Stocking.

No. 423.]

Deponent being duly sworn, deposes and says, that about the first of May, 1865, he was engaged by General Jose M. J. Carvajal, the Commissioner of the Republic of Mexico, then recently arrived in this country, to act for him as private and confidential secretary; that he continued in this position with the said Carvajal until, on the 12th August, 1866, in consequence of a revolt at Matamoras, Mexico, said Carvajal was deprived of his authority as Governor of Tamaulipas; that during the time deponent was thus engaged, covering a period of about fifteen months, he became fully conversant with all General Carvajal's plans and movements, as nearly all of the correspondence of said Carvajal was either written by deponent at the direction of said Carvajal, or written by said Carvajal himself in the presence of deponent, with but very few exceptions. Deponent further says that he has carefully examined certain documents and letters on file before the Mexican Commission, Washington, D. C., as evidence to support a claim of General Herman Sturm, and he says that the documents and letters marked respectively No.'s "9," "10," "11," "13," "14," "15," "17," "19," "22," "23," "24," and "25," are in the handwriting of deponent, and were written by deponent by order of, and at the direction of General Carvajal, and that the signature at the bottom is the signature of said Carvajal, and was attached thereto in the presence of deponent; and deponent further says that the letters and documents on file in this case marked respectively No.'s "1," "6," and "12," are in the handwriting of said General J. M, J. Carvajal, and that the signatures attached thereto are the signatures of him, the said General Carvajal.

Deponent further says that he knows that said General Herman Sturm was engaged by said General Carvajal on or about the 1st day of May, 1865, to act for and on behalf of the Republican Government of Mexico, as its secret and confidential agent in the United States, for the purpose of purchasing a large amount of *materiel* of war, and to transport the same, as well as certain emigrants who had been, and were being engaged, by General Lewis Wallace, and friends co-operating with him, to Mexico. At that time it was fully understood and distinctly stated to deponent, General Wallace, General Sturm, and all those in the confidence of said General Carvajal, that the utmost limit of time to be given to said Sturm for the performance of this duty in the United States would be not exceeding three months, and said Carvajal stated, and it was so believed by deponent, and as he verily believes, by General Sturm, that the money necessary to pay for the purchases made, and for the transportation of such persons as should emigrate, and their pay, would be promptly furnished to said Sturm when called for. Deponent knows that General Sturm reported by letter bearing date, "Indianapolis, July 28, 1865," to General Carvajal that he had completed the necessary arrangements to carry out the plans of General Carvajal, as far as they depended upon him, the said Sturm; and that upon the receipt thereof, by General Carvajal's order, General Sturm was directed by telegraph to come to New York at once, and in obedience thereto, General Sturm arrived in New York on the 5th of August, 1865, and reported to General Carvajal at the "Union Place Hotel."

During that day, Generals Carvajal, Wallace, and Sturm had several conferences in my presence, in which the details of General Sturm's arrangements were discussed and fully approved, and upon that occasion General Sturm handed to General Carvajal a detailed statement of the articles he had contracted for, and of the cash expenditures and bills paid by General Sturm to that date.

On the following day, at the request of General Carvajal, General Sturm handed him a written statement, setting forth the amounts of money required by General Sturm to meet said contracts, expenditures, &c., and deponent filed all of said statements with the papers of General Carvajal connected with the business then in hand; said statement embracing an estimate of the amount of funds required to pay for the materials of war contracted for, and to reimburse General Sturm for expenditures made to that date, was fully approved by General Carvajal. Deponent further says that he has examined *Exhibit No.* 8, on file in this case, and he believes it to be a true copy of said statement.

On the following day, August 7th, 1865, General Carvajal directed deponent to draw two drafts on the "United States, West Virginia Land and Mining Company" in favor of General Sturm, and having signed said drafts he handed them to General Sturm. The *Exhibits No.'s 9 and* 10, on file in this case, shown to me this day, are the original drafts above referred to.

The draft for one million five hundred thousand ($1,500,000) dollars, U. S. currency, General Sturm was instructed to use to reimburse himself for expenditures made, and to pay him for his services to that date rendered to the Republic of Mexico, and to pay various bills, &c., contracted by General Carvajal in New York, for himself and other Mexicans, and also to meet in part the engagements that General Sturm had made for materials of war, and General Carvajal further promised to supply General Sturm with a large sum in addition to complete the payments on said contracts for material of war.

The draft for twenty thousand ($20,000) dollars of Mexican bonds was given by General Carvajal to General Sturm to reimburse him for certain outlays made by him in connection with a newspaper General Sturm had purchased in the city of Indianapolis, Indiana, and which paper warmly advocated the Republican cause of Mexico; deponent further says that neither of those two drafts was paid, and that in consequence of the failure of the aforesaid Company to keep its engagement with General Carvajal to supply him with the necessary funds, the immediate execution of the project contemplated by General Carvajal had to be abandoned, and that at the urgent request of General Carvajal, who promised on behalf of his Government to fairly and liberally reward said Sturm and his friends for their services, General Sturm settled and arranged the difficulties that had arisen in consequence of the failure of the aforesaid Company, to the satisfaction of General Carvajal, and in such a manner that no publicity was given the matter, and but very few persons, not intimately associated with General Carvajal, ever knew of the embarrassed condition of Mexican affairs in New York at that time. The settlement of these difficulties in New York by General Sturm involved the expenditure of a large amount of money, and I know that, being unprepared for such an unexpected demand, General Sturm did borrow for that purpose between twenty-five hundred ($2,500) and three thousand ($3,000) dollars.

Deponent further says, of his own knowledge, that General Sturm endeavored to the utmost of his ability to raise the credit of the Mexican Government; that for some six months in the years 1865 and 1866, he resided in the City of Washington, D. C., and endeavored, as the confidential agent of the Mexican Government, and in compliance with the instructions received from General Carvajal and Senor M. Romero, Mexican Minister in Washington, to obtain through Congress direct aid from the Government of the United States for the Liberal Government of Mexico, Maximilian being all that time in armed occupancy of that country.

Deponent, during the same period, repeatedly visited said Sturm in Washington as the bearer of instructions from General Carvajal, and he knows that General Sturm provided and expended money freely and, as deponent thought, judiciously, and with the aid of many agents and the influence of a very considerable portion of the public press, he endeavored to the utmost of his ability to obtain for the Mexican Government the aid so urgently requested for her through her representatives in the United States; and although the United States Congress did not take final action upon the matters so presented by General Sturm and his assistants, yet such was his success in raising the credit of the Mexican Government in the estimation of American capitalists and merchants, that he was enabled to send to Mexico several ship loads of arms and other munitions of war, amounting in value to several millions of dollars, for which the vendors agreed to receive in payment the bonds of the Mexican Government at the authorized rate of sixty cents on the dollar.

Deponent further says that in consequence of the intimate relations he held with General Carvajal, he knows that neither General Carvajal, nor any other Mexican official known to deponent, furnished General Sturm with a single dollar; that on the contrary said General Sturm provided, not only the means necessary to purchase, inspect, and to get ready for transportation to Mexico, the aforesaid material of war, as well as the means required to agitate, through the public press and otherwise, the Mexican question, and to obtain credit for that Government in this country, but he also furnished, whenever necessary, the means to even clothe said Carvajal, and other Mexican officers with him, as well as to provide food for many of them, and in various other ways to relieve the wants and sufferings of the Mexican refugees in this country, to which facts all those who were with General Carvajal at that time can testify; and deponent further says, that from the knowledge he has, he verily believes that the Mexican Government has never reimbursed General Sturm for these outlays, and that General Sturm has consequently suffered a material loss, not only because of the non payment to him of this money, but in consequence of the non-fulfillment of the pledges of the Mexican Government toward others whom General Sturm had induced to trust said Government, and in consequence of the non-payment of even the bonds to parties who had agreed to receive the same in payment for arms furnished, and the non-payment of the interest on such bonds as had been passed to different parties in payment for materials of war supplied, General Sturm has been harrassed and annoyed by actual and threatened lawsuits; and deponent further says that the fact that the Mexican Government has not paid the interest due on her bonds, and otherwise has not kept her promises and pledges to American citizens, has reduced the value of Mexican securities to less than the interest already due on them, and this fact has been seized upon by certain large corporations, to-wit: several Marine Insurance companies of the city of New York, and Baltimore, against whom General Sturm has claims to a large amount, as an evidence of contemplated fraud, and as a ground of defense against the payment of certain demands in the course of legal prosecution now pending in the proper courts, and deponent knows of many instances where parties, not fully conversant with all of the facts, actually believed, and so charged, that said Sturm, with a full understanding with the Mexican Government, had been acting as its agent for the purpose of defrauding American creditors of that Government, all of which has tended largely to injure the business and financial standing of said Sturm.

WILBUR F. STOCKING.

Deposition of D. Willard Bliss.

No. 424]

The said D. Willard Bliss, being duly sworn, deposes and says: I entered the volunteer army of the United States in May, 1861, and was, during that year and until June, 1862, on duty in the field, a portion of the time Chief Medical Officer on the staff of Major General J B. Richardson and General Berry, and during the Peninsular campaign, Medical Director on the staff of Major General Phil. Kearney. In June, 1862, I was detailed for duty in Washington, D. C., *d remained here until the close of the war as Surgeon in charge of the U. S. General Hospital, Armory Square. I know General Herman Sturm, the claimant in this case, having formed his acquaintance during the war of the rebellion. He was at the time Chief of Ordnance of the State of Indiana.

Some time in the month of May, 1865, General Sturm called on me and informed me that he was the confidential agent of the Republic of Mexico, appointed by General Carvajal, who was in this country as the Commissioner of the Republic of Mexico, with full power from his Government to obtain *materiel* of war and means to enable the people of Mexico to resist the invasion and usurpation of Maximilian.

General Sturm explained to me the precarious condition of the Republican Government of Mexico, which at the time had been forced into one of the most remote States of that Republic, as I now recollect, to a place called Paso del Norte, the greater part of the country being then in the possession of Maximilian and his allies.

General Sturm also informed me of the miserable state of the Mexican army, which was then composed of only a few thousand men, without clothing, poorly armed, and really without any proper organization. He further stated to me, that having been entrusted by the Mexican Government with the duty of purchasing all military supplies required for an army of forty thousand (40,000) men, and with organizing Quartermaster, Commissary, Ordnance, and Medical Departments for that Government, he was especially anxious about the latter Department, it being one of the most important, and he solicited my active assistance and co-operation in organizing that Department, and in providing all military and hospital supplies required for its equipment and organization.

Knowing General Sturm's high reputation for integrity, and confiding in his ability and energy, I was disposed to co-operate with him in the enterprise that he proposed to me in obtaining the *materiel*, Ordnance, Medical, and other supplies for an army in Mexico, and I agreed with him to take upon myself that part of his duty relating to the Medical Department.

General Sturm introduced me to Major General Lewis Wallace, of the U. S. army, and the latter introduced me to General Carvajal. Both of these gentlemen fully approved of General Sturm's agreement with me, and General Wallace, who was acquainted with my record as a Medical officer of the U. S. army, expressed himself as exceedingly gratified with General Sturm's success in having perfected an arrangement with me, and both of these gentlemen took occasion to explain to me, that in a very short time a large amount of funds would be ready to carry into effect their plans for saving the Republic of Mexico.

After several conferences with Generals Carvajal and Wallace, I also agreed to General Sturm's urgent request, that in addition to supplying all the medical stores required for an army of forty thousand (40,000) men, I would proceed to Mexico to personally superintend the organization of the Medical Department there, and to engage, as far as possible, medical officers who had served in the army of the United States, to go with me to Mexico, with a view of assisting the Republican Government of that country, and connecting themselves with her army after arriving in that country, and General Carvajal faithfully promised to furnish me in a short time with the funds necessary to pay for the medical stores I should purchase on account of the Mexican Government, and such other expenses as I should incur in securing Medical officers, &c.; and he referred me to General Sturm as the person who was fully empowered by him to make and approve all contracts, and who would, as disbursing officer, be fully provided with the funds to pay me and those whom I might engage.

As my position and acquaintance enabled me to do so, I conferred with the Secretary of War, the Hon. Edwin M. Stanton, to whom I communicated the nature of my arrangements with Generals Carvajal and Sturm. He fully approved of them and offered to assist in every lawful way, and referred me to the Surgeon General of the U. S. army, with whom I communicated, and upon my application he deferred, twice or more, public sales of medical and hospital supplies which had been advertised to take place in the city of Baltimore, Maryland.

As it was distinctly understood on my part in my conversations with General Carvajal, that the *money* would be ready in a short time to pay for the goods I should purchase, and that all the *materiel* must be shipped to Mexico by the 1st of August, 1865, I at once set about to make the necessary arrangements to that end, and a sale of medical stores was ordered to take place in Baltimore about that time, by the Secretary of War. My estimate of the cost of the medical stores required, based upon the probable cost as bought from the United States at public auction, was forty-five thousand ($45,000) dollars, and so I reported to General Sturm some time in the month of July, 1865. I had also enlisted the sympathies of several medical officers who had agreed to go with me to Mexico and accept there positions in the army of that Republic, and assist me in organizing a Medical Department there. About the latter part of July, 1865, I was ready to carry out, on my part, my agreements made with General Sturm.

Sometime in the month of August, 1865, I was informed both by General Sturm and General Wallace, that the arrangements made by General Carvajal in New York with some company for funds had failed, and it would be necessary for him to make some new arrangements. Learning this, I induced the Surgeon General to postpone the sale of medical stores to enable General Carvajal to obtain the means to purchase them; and I believe that the sale of those stores was postponed on two or more occasions for the same purpose. During a visit made by me to New York in the month of September, 1865, General Carvajal informed me that he had made a new arrangement with the house of Corlies & Co., from which he expected very soon to obtain funds, but at a subsequent visit to New York, I think in the month of November, 1865, General Carvajal informed me, confidentially, that on account of the distressed position of his Government, and the condition of its credit in this country, he feared it would be impossible to obtain funds for some time to come. I then stated to General Carvajal that in view of the existing circumstances I could not continue the arrangement made, the time for its execution being too indefinite.

I stated the same to General Sturm, as well as that I had expended a large amount of money and time, for which I saw no prospect of being compensated, and I asked to be released from my engagement. He, however, urgently requested me to continue with him and render whatever assistance I could to the Mexican Government; and he stated to me that if I would do so, he would be personally responsible to me for whatever time, labor or money I might expend for the Republican cause of Mexico. It was at this time that General Sturm proposed to appeal to the public and endeavor to obtain aid for Mexico through legislative means, a plan which General Carvajal and General Wallace fully endorsed.

During the months of August, September, October, November, and December, I repeatedly visited General Carvajal in New York, and during these visits, he expressed himself, (as did, indeed, every one who was with him,) as in the highest degree satisfied with the energy and perseverance, as well as the generous and unselfish devotion of General Sturm; and I remember distinctly, that during one interview, at a time when the Mexican prospects looked very gloomy indeed, General Carvajal, pointing to General Sturm, said to me in the presence of several other gentlemen, "That man is my only hope, and the only hope of my country, and I believe he will yet succeed."

Some time in the month of January, 1866, General Sturm came to Washington with a view of endeavoring to obtain, through the Congress of the United States, a guarantee to a Mexican loan, or other material aid, and he requested me to assist him, by all lawful means, in his project.

I saw Mr. Romero, the Mexican Minister, in this city, on one or more occasions, and he stated to me that General Sturm's authority as agent of the Mexican Government in the United States was ample, and that any contract made by him, according to his authority, would be binding upon the Government, and that General Sturm had been, or would be provided with funds from which to pay the obligations he might enter into. To do full justice to General Sturm, I must say that, during the early part of the summer of 1865, for a period of nearly three months, while the armies of the United States were passing through Washington on their way to be mustered out of the service, General Sturm had rented one-half of the hotel called "Rullman's hotel," situated at the corner of Thirteenth and E streets, Washington City, and used it as headquarters for the friends of the Mexican Republic. The house was constantly crowded with officers of the army, and every exertion was made by General Sturm and his agents, by means of social entertainments, speeches, and otherwise, to enlist the sympathy of those present in behalf of the Mexican cause.

I have also been a witness to his large expenditures made during the whole time, from May, 1865, to the fall of 1867, and I know that he had in his employ many agents of high standing and character, both in the military and civil circles, who were constantly endeavoring to raise the credit of the Mexican Government, and obtain aid and assistance for it in the United States.

It is my opinion and conviction that the expenses incurred by General Sturm were not only absolutely necessary under the circumstances, but were most judiciously incurred, and I further state, that the duty imposed upon General Sturm by General Carvajal as well as Mr. Romero, was of a very delicate character, and of a secret and confidential nature, and required a man possessed of talent and prudence to carry it out successfully; and it has been repeatedly acknowledged by persons in high positions, with whom I am well acquainted, that General Sturm performed that duty most successfully, to the admiration of those who were cognizant of his labors, and who came in contact with him.

During the time I was engaged with General Sturm and co-operated with him, which extended from May, 1865, to the fall of 1867, I devoted much time and labor to the Mexican cause, and in my efforts to assist General Sturm and the Mexican cause, it very often became necessary for me to expend money, and I have expended a considerable amount of money in this way; and I have also obligated myself to others for services rendered and expenses incurred while serving the Mexican cause by my direction, but up to this date I have not been reimbursed for the same. From the information that I have from reliable sources, I believe, however, that General Sturm has never received the money promised him by the Mexican Government, and has, therefore, been unable to comply with the promises made.

I know, however, that various statements have been made at different times, to the effect that General Sturm had received everything that was due him from the Mexican Government, which have caused General Sturm much annoyance and trouble, and his connection with the Mexican Government has caused General Sturm great injury; and to refute the false rumors afloat, and to maintain his character and honor, he has been compelled, ever since the spring of 1868, to devote, as I believe, his entire time to the business of collecting his claims from the Mexican Government, all of which would have been avoided if that Government had faithfully performed its promises. I also know that General Sturm has obligated himself to a large number of persons for the payment to them for services rendered in the interest of the Republican cause of Mexico.

D. WILLARD BLISS.

Deposition of W. H. Farrar.

[No. 425.]

In the Joint Commission of the U. S. and Mexico under Convention of July 4, 1868. In the matter of the claim of

HERMAN STURM
vs. } No. 676.
MEXICO.

I, Wm. H. Farrar, now of the City of Washington, D. C., first being duly sworn according to law, do depose and say: That I am not interested, directly or indirectly, in the claim of General Herman Sturm vs. the Republic of Mexico, pending before the Joint Commission of the United States and Mexico, in session in the said City of Washington; nor is the affiant the attorney, agent, solicitor, or of counsel for said Sturm in said case or claim, or in any matter or manner whatsoever. Affiant further says that during a portion of the period of time that the Emperor Maximilian was in Mexico, he sought in certain ways, to further his interests, and to contribute to his complete success in the firm establishment of his Imperial rule and ascendency in Mexico; that several persons were associated therein with affiant; that we were in communication with Don Luis Arroyo, and others who were well-known to have been the confidential representatives in the United States of the said Maximilian, and affiant further says that he found that strong efforts were made in this country for the defeat of Maximilian by the upholding of the Juarez party in Mexico; that such efforts were made and prosecuted from some time in 1865 to the death of Maximilian; that affiant ascertained in 1865, that said General Herman Sturm was the principal director of said efforts; that he was unceasingly engaged in manufacturing public opinion and sympathy for Juarez through the press of this country, and by divers other means; that he, in 1866, shipped from the port of New York munitions of war to be used against Maximilian, to the great discouragement of his said friends and cause in the United States; and that it was evident to affiant that said Sturm commanded and expended large sums of money in behalf of the so-called Republic of Mexico. Affiant further says that he visited New York in 1865 and 1866, for the purpose of ascertaining whether the funds or money disbursed by said Sturm came from the sale of the bonds of the so-called Republic of Mexico in the hands of its financial agent or agents, and became thoroughly convinced that no sales thereof were made of any important amount by said financial agents, and we became satisfied that said Sturm derived his funds from some other source, but from whence we did not and could not ascertain.

Affiant further says that he called the attention of Count Montholon, the representative of the Emperor Napoleon of France to the fact that said Sturm was the most formidable opponent in the United States to the success of Maximilian, and that said Sturm and those whom he had employed and directed, kept alive the bitter hostility exhibited in the United States against the establishment of the Government of Maximilian. Affiant says that he now verily believes that the overthrow of the Empire of Mexico was largely due to the skill, ability, and moral and material aid furnished and expended by said Sturm in the United States in behalf of the Juarez party.

W. H. FARRAR.

COUNTY OF WASHINGTON,
DISTRICT OF COLUMBIA.

Sworn and subscribed to before me, the undersigned, U. S. Commissioner for the District of Columbia, by W. H. Farrar, to me well-known; and I certify that I have no interest, direct or indirect, in the claim to which the said affidavit relates.

Witness my hand and official seal this 22d day of February, 1872, [SEAL.] at the City of Washington, D. C.

RANDOLPH COYLE,
U. S. Commissioner.

Sturm to Romero.

Report on the Woodhouse Contract.

No. 426.]   NEW YORK, April 10, 1867.

SEÑOR M. ROMERO,
    Mexican Minister, &c.,

SIR—In compliance with your request of March 13th, I herewith state to you all the facts connected with the transactions between General Carvajal and the

United States, European and West Virginia Land and Mining Company, so far as I am cognizant of them, or recollect them at the present time. On the 5th day of August, 1865, I arrived in the city of New York, from Indianapolis, Indiana, in obedience to a telegraphic order received from General Carvajal.

On my arrival, I at once reported to said General at his hotel in this city, and I was informed by him that he had concluded an arrangement with the United States, European and West Virginia Land and Mining Co., of this city, by which said Company had agreed to negotiate a loan of thirty millions of dollars for the Republic of Mexico, and that they had further agreed, in consideration of certain grants and privileges given to said Company by the Mexican Government, to at once advance to him, General Carvajal, in cash, the sum of three million dollars, U. S. currency, to enable him to procure certain munitions of war for his Government, and for other purposes, and he directed me at once to make all the necessary arrangements to carry out certain instructions he had given me under dates of March 1st and March 11th, 1865, namely: to purchase certain specified amounts of munitions of war, and provide the necessary transportation for them to Mexico, stating that he would provide me with the necessary means on the following Monday, as the Company had promised to furnish him one million dollars on that day. On this same day I visited several prominent merchants and manufacturers, and made partial arrangements for powder, rifles, and some other articles which I was instructed to purchase. On my return to the hotel on the evening of this day, I found in General Carvajal's room two men, whom General Carvajal introduced to me, the one as Mr. Daniel Woodhouse, Secretary of the United States, European, West Virginia Land and Mining Co., the other as Mr. E. B. Sackett, Treasurer of the same Company. These two persons remained with General Carvajal, Major General Lew. Wallace, who was also present, and myself, until after eleven o'clock at night, during which time we discussed the manner of carrying out certain arrangements that General Carvajal had then in view. Mr. Woodhouse and Mr. Sackett stated to me, during the conversation, that their Company had a cash capital of twenty millions of dollars, and had five millions of dollars in U. S. seven-thirty bonds, then on deposit to their credit at the Bank of Commerce in the City of New York, and that they would, on the following Monday, (this being Saturday) furnish General Carvajal with one million dollars, but it would probably be three or four days before they would be able to furnish the General with the whole three million of dollars, as they had agreed, stating as a reason, that the Board of Directors of their Company would meet on Monday, August 7th, and it would necessarily require two or three days after to get all the papers, &c., in proper shape. They urged me, however, to lose no time in making my purchases and completing all my arrangements; that I might rely upon it that payments would be promptly made, and that the General would be able, so far as they or their Company were concerned, to leave for Mexico in a week from that time. They also stated that the meeting of the Board of Directors was a mere formality, and that everything was fully arranged.

The appearance of Woodhouse and Sackett, and the manner of their conversation, and the statements which they made were such, that I formed a very poor opinion of them, and grave doubts arose in my mind as to the ability of their Company to fulfill the promises they had that evening made.

The more I thought of this during the night the more firmly I became convinced that a Company possessing so much wealth as these persons had stated, would not confide the management of its business, and intrust the two most responsible offices of the Company to such individuals as I had met on the previous evening, and I concluded to make my apprehensions known to General Carvajal.

I did so on the following day, Sunday, August 6, but was assured by him that everything was all right, and that he knew it, and he showed me a printed prospectus of said Company, which mentioned as trustees of the Company the names of several gentlemen known to me as among the most respectable and wealthy merchants and bankers in New York city, viz.:

Mr. Paul N. Spofford, of the firm of Spofford, Tileson & Co.; Mr. Ezra Bliss; Mr. Bennett, and several others not known to me. This, together with the confidence expressed by General Carvajal, staggered me somewhat, but I made up my mind not to conclude any contracts until I had fully investigated this matter, and satisfied myself of the stability of the Company. I so stated to General Carvajal, and gave as my reasons that I feared he was being imposed upon, he being a stranger, in a strange land, and as his business necessarily required secrecy at this time, these men had taken advantage of this; and I further explained to him how injurious it would be to the interests of the Mexican Government, if I should make contracts on its account, and it should afterward be ascertained that the Government was not in a position to promptly pay its obligations and fulfill its contracts. This matter was discussed between the General and myself until late at night, and I became fully satisfied that the General's whole soul was wrapped up in the idea of saving his country, and that his anxiety, and his impatience to leave for Mexico with aid to his countrymen, had permitted him to be imposed upon by a set of *designing sharpers*. I therefore, with a view to the credit and best interests of the Mexican Government, concluded it prudent to pursue a course which, without interfering with the General's plans, would, in a very few days, solve all the doubts in the case. Consequently, on the following day, I asked of General Carvajal an order on the said Company for a sufficient amount of money to pay for certain articles that I had partially agreed to purchase on the previous Saturday. Accordingly, the General first gave me two orders on said Company for $50,000, U. S. currency each. He requested me, however, not to present these orders on this day, as according to Woodhouse's statement, the Board of Directors of this Company were to meet then, and said I had better wait until next day before I presented them. This I complied with, but being desirous of losing no time, I did go on this day to the house of J. W. Corlies & Co., with whom I was negotiating for the purchase of a quantity of shovels, axes, and other articles, and explained to them how the money would be paid, etc., and requested Mr. J. N. Tifft, of this firm, to present these two drafts at the office of the aforesaid Company on the *following day* for payment, at the same time requesting him to ascertain the standing of the Company. This he cheerfully complied with, but could give me no satisfactory answer by evening, as no bank, bankers, or merchants seemed to know of the existence of the United States, European and West Virginia Land and Mining Company. Mr. Tifft, however, stated that the Company might be a newly formed one, and therefore unknown, and he further said, after

I had given him the names of the principal trustees, that if Mr. Spofford and others I mentioned were connected with said Company, it certainly was responsible. I therefore, on the following day, presented the two aforesaid drafts myself at the office of the Company, number 71, Broadway, where they were both accepted by Daniel Woodhouse, as Secretary of the Company, but in such a manner that they were not negotiable, Woodhouse not stating in his acceptance the place where they should be payable. Upon asking him at what bank, or where they would be paid, he said, "*Here, of course; we do our own banking; we have more money than all the banks of New York, together*," &c.

To my request, in that case, to pay me the money at once, he replied that the Mexican Government had not as yet complied with all its agreements, and that the Board of Directors had decided at their meeting not to pay out such an amount of money until the contracts were fully concluded; and, further, that he had a telegram from Mr. Seward, (Secretary of State,) a former fellow-student and law-partner of his (as he claimed) who desired him (Woodhouse) to come on to Washington for the purpose of consulting with him in regard to this matter. He stated, however, at the same time, that it would be all right in a few days, as he had assurances from Washington that, in case the Company should be hindered in any way, in furnishing the money as rapidly as it might be required by the Mexican Government, the Government of the United States would advance to their Company any amount to the extent of thirty millions, to aid it in this Mexican enterprise, &c., &c. Mr. E. B. Sackett made similar statements, although not quite as bold as those of Mr. Woodhouse.

All this, however, only served to strengthen me in my opinion that the United States, European and West Virginia Land and Mining Company was a humbug, and that General Carvajal had been imposed upon by men who designed to obtain into their possession the bonds of the Republic of Mexico, and who did not intend to advance to that Government one cent, until money had been received from the sale of the bonds, *if then*.

I again urged Mr. Tifft to seek an interview on the following day with Mr. Spofford and other gentlemen I had named, which he promised he would do. I repeated all this to General Carvajal, who, of course, felt very much dissatisfied, but still hoped on, believing it impossible that any American could be capable of making such misrepresentations, and of committing so gross a fraud.

In the evening Woodhouse and Sackett called on General Carvajal, and then they both repeated to General Carvajal and General Wallace, what they had said to me before about Mr Seward, &c., giving as an additional reason for their delay in paying the money, (which, however, as they stated, they had not felt at liberty to communicate to me) that the Government of the United States had communicated to the President of their Company a desire that nothing should be done by the Company until it could be done all at once, and in perfect concert with the United States Government, as otherwise it might, in case of some unforseen defect or accident, be fatal to the whole project in view.

The hollowness of all these statements and promises General Carvajal either did not see, or was unwilling to acknowledge at the time, for, on this very evening, after the interview with Woodhouse and Sackett, he expressed himself as still confident and hopeful, and assured Messrs. Fuentes & Zarco (who also called upon him and expressed their doubts) that everything would be right yet.

On the following day Mr. Tifft stated to me that, according to my request, he called on Mr. Spofford and others, and that each one of these gentlemen had declared to him that they were not connected with this Company in any way whatever, and that the use of their names was unauthorized by, and the existence of the Company unknown to them. In addition to this, some facts had come to light, which connected Woodhouse with some former not very creditable transactions, and which did not help to raise his credit any. All of which I reported to General Carvajal in the evening, when, of course, he became satisfied that he had been made the victim of a swindle. I then urged upon the General the necessity of prompt measures, and to at once have the contract cancelled, and the parties brought to justice if possible; but this he was not inclined to do, as he feared that the publication of this affair at that time would be injurious to his Government, although I explained to him that instead of injuring the Government then, it could, in my opinion, be benefitted by it, and that it certainly would be much more injurious, at some future time, to pass this over in silence now, and that it would leave it in the power of Woodhouse & Co. to impose upon American citizens, who, not understanding this affair, might invest money in any bonds he might sell under his contract, and that it would be a repetition of the Jeaker fraud. On this occasion I requested permission of General Carvajal, who, up to this time had remained secluded, to introduce to him Mr. J. N. Tifft and Mr. J. W. Corlies, the gentlemen who had aided me in exposing this fraudulent concern, and who had offered me freely their assistance, if any was needed; and upon his consenting, I first introduced Mr. J. N. Tifft, with whom he had a full conference, and who in turn introduced to the General Mr. Louis Henry, a lawyer of great respectability.

After full consultation, it was deemed advisable by all parties, that no time ought to be lost in at once revoking the power of attorney given to Mr. Woodhouse, and in cancelling and annulling the contract.

Subsequently General Carvajal made a new contract with Messrs. J. W. Corlies & Co., and since that time I have had no further connection of any kind with Woodhouse and his Company.

I have the honor to be, Sir,
Very respectfully,
Your obedient servant,

H. STURM.

Sturm to Romero.

Report Rendered Senor M. Romero, August 23d, 1867.

8. 427.]   NEW YORK, August 23d, 1867.

SENOR M. ROMERO,
  Mexican Minister, &c.,
    Washington, D. C.

SIR—The war in Mexico having so happily closed, and the last of the military goods purchased by me having been sent to Mexico, I deem this to be the proper time to render you a statement, or rather a brief recapitulation of what I have done in behalf of your Government, and the purchases I have made for it, and I think this will be more especially desirable just now, as you are about returning to your country, and such a statement will enable you the more readily to explain to the Mexican Government all my transactions, and the services that I have been so fortunate as to be able to render to your Government in its struggle to drive the foreign invader from its soil. In a former communication I have remitted to you copies of the powers conferred on me, and the orders given to me at different times by General Carvajal; and I do not, therefore, deem it necessary to encumber this document with a recapitulation of them. My first efforts on behalf of your Government, under these orders, commenced in the beginning of May, 1865. At that time I believed, from statements made to me by General Carvajal, that the pecuniary means necessary to carry out the instructions given to me, were ready and at hand whenever needed; and as the projects contemplated by General Carvajal were of vast magnitude, it was considered of the first importance to systematize and organize the different branches of the duties imposed upon me.

These duties were of a manifold character. It was intended by General Carvajal to organize an auxilliary army corps of ten thousand American veterans, representing the different branches of the military service, viz.: Infantry, artillery, cavalry, and engineers, and it was intended that these troops should congregate somewhere on the Rio Grande, and there join the Mexican forces. As such an enterprise, to be successful, must necessarily be conducted with the greatest secrecy, it was deemed advisable by General Carvajal, and other gentlemen in whom he confided, that owing to my experience in such matters, and my large acquaintance among army officers in this country, I should take charge of providing all the material of war necessary for said army corps, and for such Mexican troops as were intended to be added to this force on Mexican soil, the whole force contemplated to be thus provided for being forty thousand infantry, three thousand cavalry, fifteen batteries of artillery, and an engineer corps of two thousand men.

In addition to providing the material of war, I was also instructed to provide the Quartermaster, Commissary, Medical, and other necessary stores, as well as the needed transportation, and some vessels to be used at the mouth of the Rio Grande and vicinity. I was further instructed to select for the purpose, from such officers as I knew to be capable and trustworthy, such assistance as I might require for the different departments whose charge had been intrusted to me, and I was empowered to offer to such officers as might be willing to enter the Mexican service, the same position and emoluments as they then held, or had last held, while in the service of the United States. As a guide for the performance of my duties, I was particularly instructed to be governed by the rules and regulations of the army of the United States. Although I knew that the duties thus imposed upon me would, under the most favorable circumstances, be both difficult and onerous, yet conscious of the justice, and confident of the ultimate success of the cause I had espoused, I at once entered upon the performance of my duties.

I first perfected complete and systematic lists of the different articles required to equip the above mentioned forces, and to provide for contingencies for one year. The lists of these articles, and an estimate of the cost, at the then ruling market prices, I submitted on the first day of May, 1865, to General Carvajal for his approval, and after having received the instructions necessary, I left Washington for New York and the West, for the purpose of procuring such officers and aid as I required, and to make the necessary arrangements to obtain the requisite supplies at the times needed. I was busily engaged in this duty until the month of August following, during which time I visited the principal cities of the West, and having received from General Carvajal his written approval and endorsement of the lists I had submitted to him, had made all arrangements to carry out my orders in conformity therewith, waiting only for the necessary funds to be placed at my disposal.

On the 3d day of August, while at Indianapolis, I received a telegram from General Carvajal ordering me at once to New York. I departed for this place the same evening, and on my arrival on the 5th day of the month, I at once reported to the General at his headquarters at the Union Place Hotel. Here I was informed by General Carvajal and Major General Lew. Wallace, who was with him, and who, as I was informed by General Carvajal, had command of the auxiliary American forces, that it was their intention to depart very soon for Mexico; that the required number of men would be ready in time, and it was therefore of the utmost importance that I should have everything in readiness. I was further told by General Carvajal that the requisite funds would be placed at my disposal in a few days; that, however, the whole force would not leave at one time, and I would therefore be required to remain in this country until all the troops and material had arrived in Mexico, and until I had received further orders in regard to my departure, and that I should make all my arrangements accordingly. I soon found, however, to my great disappointment, that the parties from whom General Carvajal expected to obtain several millions of dollars, (viz.: The United States, European, and West Virginia Land and Mining Co.) to enable him to carry out his project, had most shamefully deceived him, and that their only object was to take advantage of the unfortunate position of the Mexican Government, and to use the confidence reposed in them, and the powers conferred on them by General Carvajal, to defraud the Mexican Government.

The particulars of this affair, so far as I am cognizant of them, I have already communicated to you in a former report, under date of April 10th, 1867. Being thus unexpectedly disappointed, after becoming familiar with the details of the General's transactions, and seeing no reasonable prospect of soon obtaining the necessary means, I considered it my first duty to cancel, as far as lay in my power, as many of the contracts and negotiations entered into by me on behalf of the Government, as could not be fulfilled under the existing circumstances. I was happily successful in accomplishing this, without creating any ill-feeling or damage to the credit and good faith of the Mexican Government, and I also advised General Carvajal to state to the different officers who had been waiting, and were dependent upon him, that he was then unable to carry out the proposed programme immediately, (although advised by some not to do this, because they believed that money would soon be easily obtained from other sources.) I was prompted to persevere in my intention by a desire to save the Mexican Government much trouble, annoyance, and expense, and to prevent injury to its credit, which, I regret to say, was at this time, (owing to the unfortunate position of the Government) ascertained to be in a very low state, and I feared that should the true position of affairs become publicly known, and particularly should the numerous officers and men, who had so freely offered their lives, if need be, to aid your cause, be kept in suspense and finally disappointed, after incurring, probably, heavy expense, which it would be impossible for the Government at that time to refund to them, it would tend more to aid your enemies than any other event possibly could.

I also at this time assisted General Carvajal with my own private funds, to relieve him from his embarrassing position, and to take the necessary steps to enable him to get rid of the sharpers who had so deceived him; I also endeavored at once to enlist prominent bankers and capitalists known to me personally or through friends, in behalf of aid to your Government; but in this I was unsuccessful, until Messrs. Corlies & Co., whom I had introduced to General Carvajal, and with whom he entered into a contract for that purpose, undertook the negotiation of a Mexican loan.

With the details of this transaction you are much more conversant than I could possibly be, as I have never known until recently all the conditions of this contract. I deem it necessary to state here, that I have never asked or received a commission for my services in this matter from Messrs. Corlies & Co., nor am I in any way interested in any benefit which these gentlemen may receive from the Mexican Government in payment for their services, or by reason of this contract. I repeat this here in order that the Mexican Government may not labor under the same misapprehension that you were led to entertain, until I informed you that by reason of my understanding with General Carvajal, and my consequent official position, I could not receive payment for any services rendered by me on account of your Government, except from that Government.

After this contract was made, I invoked the aid of several of the most prominent men in this country, among others, the Hon. Robert Dale Owen, in behalf of the Republican cause in Mexico, and introduced Mr. Owen to General Carvajal, and to Messrs. J. W. Corlies & Co., which latter party at once made arrangements to secure his active services to that end.

It is unnecessary for me to dwell here on the particulars of how this loan was offered in the market, as you are fully conversant with them; suffice it to say, that seeing the impracticability of carrying out any military movements until pecuniary means had first been obtained, I threw my whole energy into this new work, and I have made several journeys to the Western States, particularly Kentucky, Ohio, and Missouri, endeavoring to obtain means upon the bonds of the Republic, and to arouse the sympathy of the American people in behalf of the patriots of your country.

In the first, I am sorry to say, I was not at that time successful, but as regards the second, I am happy to say, I felt more encouraged every day, especially, when after several months of arduous effort, I succeeded, on the 21st day of December, 1865, in procuring the passage through the Indiana State Legislature, of a resolution, a copy of which is hereby annexed, in favor of supporting your Republic, to which resolution there was but one dissenting voice.

This action of the Legislature was much commented upon throughout the United States, and did much toward calling the attention of its citizens to the heroic struggle made by your countrymen to free themselves from the thralldom of a foreign intervention and despotism.

Similar resolutions were afterward passed by the Legislatures of other States, and their effect was shown especially by the constantly increasing applications made to me by men who, although but just returned to their families after a four years' struggle for liberty in this country, urgently appealed to me to forward them to Mexico, that they might there take service in the same great cause under the banner of the Republic, side by side with its native heroes and defenders, but I had neither the money nor means to aid them in this. While from every quarter, American patriots offered to leave family and home, and to sacrifice, if need be, their lives to maintain Mexican independence, the moneyed men of this country were unwilling to part with their dollars, deeming the security which Mexico offered them a precarious one, and consequently declined to accept its bonds even at a nominal rate. This was the position of affairs, when on my return to New York on the first day of January, 1866, it was deemed advisable by the friends of your cause, to appeal to the Congress of the United States, then in session, for aid to your Government, and I was ordered by General Carvajal, to proceed to Washington with your financial agent, Mr. J. N. Tifft, of the firm of J. W. Corlies & Co., to assist him in accomplishing this so much desired result.

To this work I at once repaired, and although I had already expended large sums of money in my endeavors to aid your country previous to that time, I made such arrangements as enabled me to proceed at once to Washington, and to meet the additional expenses incident thereto. I arrived in Washington on the 6th day of January, 1866, where I remained almost constantly until the 10th of July the same year, aiding in the endeavors to obtain from Congress a guaranty to a Mexican loan. But new complications and difficulties arose from the fact that General Ortega, who claimed to be the Constitutional President of Mexico, disputed and disavowed the authority and legitimacy of any act of President Juarez. In addition to this, General Ochoa, another Commissioner from your Government to the United States, for purposes similar to those of General Carvajal, had also fallen into the hands of speculators, who, under the garb of friendship to Mexico, took advantage of its unfortunate position, and after obtaining all manner of concessions from him, endeavored only to fill their own pockets, and interposed all manner of obstacles to the success of the proposed measure of relief to your Government; but you are also familiar with these details, and I will therefore not repeat them.

They will forever reflect shame upon those who endeavored to use their prominent political positions, formerly accorded them by the liberty loving people of this country, to rob and extort from a sister Republic, then struggling for its very existence, the exorbitant and unjust terms they demanded for the withdrawal of their opposition. These complications and circumstances rendered it impossible for us to obtain from the Government of the United States, at that time, the aid sought, but the advantages derived from the agitation of this question, and of the affairs of Mexico generally, were great, as the discussion of this subject brought to the knowledge of the American people a great many facts of which heretofore they had only meagre and incorrect information.

Quite a number of pamphlets and articles from the pens of the Hon. Robert Dale Owen and others, relative to the true status of Mexico, financially and politically, were distributed among the members of both branches of the national Congress, and to the prominent men and people generally throughout the entire country.

While engaged in assisting in this duty, knowing full well your wants in regard to munitions of war, I did not lose sight of this, and although I found it impossible to obtain ready money for your bonds, I endeavored constantly to obtain for them, such munitions of war as were most urgently needed at that time, on such terms as I was best enabled to, in conformity with my authorization, and it was with a great deal of pleasure that I was able to inform you, early in July, 1866, that certain parties with whom I had been negotiating for a considerable time, had, after personal consultation with General Carvajal, agreed with me to send to Matamoras some vessels laden with munitions of war, on certain conditions specified in the contracts, copies of which I remitted to you, and after obtaining from the Government of the United States permission to sh'p these goods through the State of Texas, I succeeded in sending, on the 16th day of July, the steamer "J. W. Everman," laden with arms consigned to General Carvajal, via Brazos de Santiago, Texas.

The departure of this vessel naturally caused much excitement, and its moral effect was such as to strengthen materially the confidence of the people generally in the success of the Republican cause, to weaken that of the enemies of your Government, and to contradict the statements so widely and insidiously circulated by them (and made more plausible still, by the fact that there were connected with their enterprises, prominent men in this country), to the effect that the so-called Empire would very soon be without any opposition, and that the Government of the Republic had ceased to exist.

Almost simultaneously with the departure of the "Everman," another steamer (the Suwanee) was contracted for by me, intended to convey, as quickly as possible, to the same place, another cargo of the goods, purchased of the same parties under the same contract.

Believing it to be very important to have a small gunboat in the vicinity of the Rio Grande, on that coast, and being able to obtain one for bonds, I suggested to you the propriety of purchasing her for the use of the Government, and obtained from you the necessary authority for this purchase.

This gunboat (the steamer Sheridan) was also sent to Brazos de Santiago, there to be delivered to the proper officer of the Mexican Government. As it would have been impolitic, and almost impossible at that time, to send this vessel from here with her armament aboard, I loaded the guns, ammunition, and other stores of this vessel, together with other army stores which I had purchased in Philadelphia, on board the steamer "Suwanee," intending that before her departure for Brazos she should come to New York to take on the other stores which I had purchased here. Knowing well that the "Sheridan" would be of no use to your Government without coal, and that provisions also were required, I made, during your absence (although I had no special instructions to do so) contracts for the delivery of a sufficient quantity of both these articles to supply the "Sheridan" in active service for twelve months.

On your return you, however, informed me that these articles could be obtained on as good terms in Mexico, and you could not, for this reason, approve of the contracts for their purchase. Consequently, having made these contracts on my own responsibility, and without the limits of my authority, I at once individually settled these contracts to the satisfaction of the parties concerned, and without prejudice to the Mexican Government. This, although at heavy expense to me personally, I was in honor bound to do.

You requested me at this time to send some military stores to General Porfirio Diaz and others, in care of General Baranda, Senor Benitez, and Governor Baz, Commissioners sent here from your Government for that purpose, and as soon as these gentlemen had furnished me with a list of the articles required by them, I set to work to purchase them, and also made the necessary arrangements for another steamer (the Vixen) to transport the goods for General Diaz to Minititlan, and everything seemed to be in a fair way of being soon accomplished, when unfortunately news was received here from Matamoras that on the 12th day of August, immediately upon the arrival of the first cargo of arms, a revolt at that place had displaced General Carvajal, and elevated to power Don Servando Canales, who had taken possession of all the arms sent out by the steamer "Everman," and which had been taken to Matamoras by order of General Carvajal.

All manner of rumors prejudicial to the credit of Mexico were at once set afloat by our enemies; even private advices were sent by parties in Brownsville to the gentlemen in this city from whom I had purchased these arms, to the effect that the whole affair of the revolt was a preconcerted arrangement for the purpose of enabling the Mexican Government to retain those arms without complying with the terms of the respective contracts for their purchase, and although I used every endeavor to convince the interested parties of the unreasonableness and injustice of these statements, these gentlemen declined to deliver me any more goods under their contract until the first shipment had been satisfactorily settled for, and I was thus compelled to delay further intended shipments until a more opportune time; for this reason also I was unable at once to dispatch the steamer "Suwanee," then lying partially loaded at Philadelphia, as I had intended. The report of my agent relative to the unfortunate and deplorable occurrences at Matamoras, bearing on the shipment by the steamer "Everman," and which also delayed the reception by the Mexican authorities of the steamer "Sheridan," has been submitted to you on a former occasion, together with such other facts as I have been able to gather, and I need not therefore go into detail here. Although this unfortunate occurrence was seriously detrimental to the early accomplishment of all the intended operations, I persevered, however, and after numerous fruitless endeavors to purchase goods with bonds, I succeeded, after an unavoidable delay, in sending, on the 11th day of November, 1866, the steamer "Vixen," in care of General Baranda and Senor Benitez, to Minititlan with another cargo of munitions of war, and subsequently, on the 27th day of November, 1866, the steamer "Suwanee," whose destination under the circumstances was changed, was also dispatched for Mexico, to the State of Vera Cruz, under the care of Governor Baz, with a very large assorted cargo of material of war. Unfortunately, however, this vessel foundered at sea in a gale on the 4th day of December, 1866, and the goods on board of her became a total loss, as they were not insured.

The reason why this was not done lies in the fact that I had never received any instructions to insure anything belonging to the Government, and as the Regulations of the United States Army, which I was instructed to follow, positively prohibit officers from insuring Government goods, I, of course, did not do so.

All the facts relating to this disaster which I have been able to collect, I have heretofore transmitted to you. Nothing daunted, however, by this sad occurrence, which was a heavy blow, both to the Government and to myself, and the consequent unpleasant results, I redoubled my efforts, if possible, to replace the articles lost by this shipwreck, with others, and as you are aware, I have succeeded in obtaining for the bonds of Mexico, from some of the most prominent merchants in this country, a large amount of goods, which, according to your instructions, I have just sent by sailing vessel to Vera Cruz. On the 11th day of September, 1866, you transmitted to me the order of your Government relieving General Carvajal from his command, and that in the future I should not obey any further orders from him, and that to this end whatever I did would have to be submitted to you for your approval, and since the reception of this order I have strictly conformed to its instructions, and all contracts and purchases made by me on behalf of your Government since that time, have received either your sanction or the official approval of the Consul General, Juan N. Navarro, who was deputed by you for that purpose.

Under date of the sixth (6) day of January, 1867, I was informed by you that you had received instructions from your Government ordering the discontinuance of further purchases for bonds, and you instructed me to act accordingly, which has been done.

As it was very desirable, however, at that time, to have more arms, as the army was then besieging the cities of Queretaro, Vera Cruz, and Mexico, and Colonel E. A. Mexia having been sent to this city from the State of Vera Cruz for the purpose of obtaining such needed supplies, I urged several gentlemen of means, friends of mine, to send to that State a cargo of munitions of war for the purpose of selling them for cash to the representatives of the Government. In this I also succeeded, and on the 30th day of March, 1867, I dispatched the steamer "General McCallum," with a full assorted cargo for Tampico. Besides the goods belonging to private parties, as before stated, I took out a quantity of goods belonging to the Government, as instructed by you, the invoices of which I have duly transmitted to you. These goods, as well as Colonel Mexia and some other Mexican officers, have thus been forwarded to Mexico without any expense to the Government.

On the 18th day of May, 1867, I also sent a small cargo of military goods per schooner "Veto" to Matamoras, consigned to General Berriozabel, commanding that city, the invoices of which I also transmitted to you at the time.

These goods were fully insured, and the freight made payable on delivery, in accordance with special instructions received from you to that effect. The balance of the goods which I had purchased, and which, as I have above stated, I have just sent to Vera Cruz, I have also insured to the amount of one hundred and fifty thousand, five hundred ($150,500) dollars, and this amount, as well as the charges that were due on them here for storage, fire insurance, &c., and freight, is also to be collected upon the delivery of the goods at Vera Cruz. This arrangement has also, under your instructions, been approved by the Consul General, Juan N. Navarro. At different proper times I have transmitted to you copies of the contracts entered into by me for purchases on behalf of the Government, as also invoices of goods sent to Mexico, and full reports of all my operations since the time of the first shipment of goods to that country; and on the 27th day of last December, I also submitted to you in person a detailed statement of the cash expenses incurred by me on account of these purchases and their shipment, together with the necessary vouchers therefor, and to-day transmit to you separately similar accounts, with their vouchers, for expenses since that time to the present date.

To enable you, however, the more readily to lay before your Government a complete account of all my transactions, I also transmit you, with this report, and attached thereto, a condensed statement of all purchases made by me on behalf of your Government, the amounts of bonds that I have at different times received and expended, as also a statement of the cash expenses incurred by me on account of the purchases and shipments of goods, as well as a statement of the cash expended by me for other purposes necessarily connected with my endeavors to serve your Government as I have done.

You, of course, being fully conversant with the manner in which I became connected with your Government, and the peculiar services I have rendered, in addition to the making of purchases and shipments, will readily see, that taking into consideration the difficult circumstances under which these services have been performed, at a time when but few men could be found willing to render assistance to your Government, especially, as during all the time that your Commissioner, General Carvajal, was here, he was laboring under the most harrassing difficulties, that it almost constantly became necessary for me to assist him pecuniarily, in relieving him from embarrassments, which otherwise would have reflected discredit upon his Government.

Adding to this the number of journeys that I have made for the benefit of your cause, and in order to secure influence and assistance from various sources, all of which necessarily required considerable outlay, I am confident that you will accord to me the credit of having managed all my affairs as economically as was possible under the circumstances.

In regard to the remuneration for my services, I would respectfully state, that at the time when I became connected with your Government, I agreed with General Carvajal upon certain terms and conditions with which you are familiar, firmly believing that the statements made by General Carvajal about the readiness of the necessary funds would be perfectly correct, I resigned the very honorable and remunerative position which I then held as Brigadier General and Chief of Ordnance of the State of Indiana, and left my home and property in the West in a condition, which in consequence of the non-fulfillment of General Carvajal's expectations, and the fact that up to the present time I have received no money whatever from the Government, has embarrassed me considerably, but as I stated to you verbally some time since, I had no desire to ask a special sum as remuneration for my services at a time, when from the information that I had upon this subject, I fully knew that the Mexican Government was unable to pay me, it being then cut off from all sources of revenue, and in a most embarrassing position, of which I could not conscientiously take advantage, but preferred rather to wait until such time as the Mexican Government might be free from foreign plunderers, and have full control of the sources of income of the country, being confident, even in the darkest hours of the Republic, that its Government would do full justice to me, and accord me such remuneration for my services as, under all the circumstances, would be equitable and just.

In closing this report, I consider it my duty to present to the notice of your Government, the officers, who during the time that I have served your Republic, as before mentioned, have either constantly or for some part of the time been employed by me, and who have, during all the time of their service, faithfully assisted me, and to whose efficient aid I am much indebted for the accomplishment of the results above stated.

Mr. Wilbur F. Stocking and Mr. Robert C. Sturm were actively employed in my service from May 1st, 1865, to March 30th, 1867. Mr. William C. Peckham was employed by General Carvajal, and remained in service from May 15th, 1866, to September 22d, 1866, when on account of family matters, he was compelled to resign. Mr. J. F. Vogel, who has been employed by me from July 15th, 1866, to August 15th, 1867; Captain John R. McComb, from July 15th, to August 15th, 1867. Mr. Geo. A. Partridge, employed by General Carvajal, remained in service from May 5th, 1866, to October 15th, 1866, when he was compelled to resign in consequence of his ill health, contracted while at Matamoras, and Mr Sidney D. Stocking, who was employed by me from October 15th, 1866, to August 15th, 1867. The above named gentlemen faithfully performed the duties incumbent upon them under all, and the most adverse circumstances, and though often inconvenienced by not receiving their salaries at the stipulated times, have continued their assistance, and have cheerfully and with enthusiasm remained steadfast in their valuable assistance to your Government.

As you are fully acquainted with all my transactions, and the difficulties encountered, I would respectfully request you to lay all the facts relating to my connection with your Government, before it, and, in the hope that the manner in which I have discharged my duties, and my conduct of the affairs entrusted to me heretofore may meet the approval of the Government,

I have the honor to be, Sir,
Very respectfully,
Your obedient servant,
H. STURM.

The following statements accompany this report:

Statement A. 1 to A. 6. Articles purchased and sent out at different times.
Statement B. Purchases.
Statement B. 1 to B. 6. Balance sheets for purchase accounts.
Statement C. with one voucher. Incidental expenses.
Statement D. with one voucher. Secret service.
Statement E. with six vouchers. Salaries paid.
Statement F. Various expenses.
Statement G. Cash balance sheets.
Statement H. and H. 1. Bonds received and expended.

LIST OF EXHIBITS

RELATING TO

THE CLAIM OF HERMAN STURM

VERSUS

THE REPUBLIC OF MEXICO.

No. 676.

NO.	FROM WHOM AND TO WHOM.	DATE.	SUBJECT.	PAGE.
1	....	1865 May 1...	Agreement between Gen. Carvajal and Gen. Sturm, respecting the latter's duties as Agent of the Mexican Government, his compensation, secret service fund, etc., etc.	1
2	Gen. Carvajal to Gen. Sturm.	March 1	Power of Authority................................	2
3	....	June 7...	Gen. Carvajal's authority certified by Minister Romero...............................	3
4	Gen. Carvajal to Gen. Sturm.	Mar. 11..	Order to proceed to execute the authority, dated March 1..................................	4
5	Same to same...	July 4...	Authority to buy certain articles for the Government..	4
6	Same to same...	July 4...	Authority to buy articles named for the Government..	5
7	Gen. Sturm to Gen. Carvajal.	July 28..	Reports preparations for movement of fifteen hundred laborers from Memphis complete...	5
8	Gen. Sturm to Gen. Carvajal.	Aug. 6...	Statement of moneys required by his various contracts, purchases, etc. Also, moneys required on account for cash advanced, personal services, payment of salaries and various bills, including $20,000 for "Free Press"....................	5
9	Gen. Carvajal to U. S., E., and W. V. L. and Mining Co.	Aug. 7...	Draft for $20,000....................................	6
10	Ditto...............	Aug. 7...	Draft for $1,500,000.	7

NO.	FROM WHOM AND TO WHOM.	DATE.	SUBJECT.	PAGE.
		1865.		
11	Gen. Carvajal to Gen. Sturm.	Aug. 25...	Concerning the United States, European and West Virginia Land and Mining Co. Satisfied it is a fraud. The good name of his government must not be brought into contempt by exposures in the courts and press. Certain preliminaries to be attended to. Sends agreement, intended to be incidental to agreement of May 1..................	7
12	Same to same...	Aug. 25...	Agreement for a Secret Service Fund....	8
13	Same to same...	Aug. 25...	Schedule of Ordnance, Quartermaster and Commissary Stores, submitted May 1, approved. Order to proceed to contract for them. Instructions as to payment	9
14	Gen. Carvajal to	Sept. 12...	Draft for $20,000.........................	10
15	Corlies & Co...	Sept. 12...	Draft of $1,500,000. Receipts rendered on same..................................	10
16	....	Nov. 8.....	Memorandum of interview with Mr. Romero, November 8, at No. 35 West Thirty-third St., New York..................	13
		1866.		
17	Gen. Carvajal to Gen. Sturm.	Jan. 5.....	Necessity of invoking aid of American government, in the way of money or loan of credit. General Sturm directed to proceed to Washington as confidential agent, to aid Mr. Tifft, &c............	15
18	....	April 29...	Memorandum of interview between Mr. Romero and General Sturm............	15
19	Gen. Carvajal to Gen. Sturm.	May 15...	Is about to return to his military department. Directs execution of proceedings, contracts, etc. New contracts to be made in concert with General Lew. Wallace and Senor M. Romero............	17
20	....	May 15...	Memorandum of interview between Generals Carvajal and Wallace. Colonel Stocking and General Sturm............	17
21	....	May 15...	Memorandum of interview with Carvajal, Wallace, Stocking and Mr. J. N. Tifft..	18
22	Gen. Carvajal to Gen. Sturm.	May 16...	Transmits copies of his authority from his government, with modification in favor of Mr. Romero.....................	19
		1864.		
23	....	Nov. 8.....	General Carvajal's appointment and powers as Governor of Tamaulipas...........	19
24	....	Nov. 12...	General Carvajal's authority as Commissioner of Mexico to obtain aid and raise funds in the United States.............	20
		1865.		
25	....	July 13...	Authority of Mr. Romero in the execution of General Carvajal's commission.	22
		1866.		
26	....	May 16...	Memorandum of interview between General Sturm and Mr. Romero in Washington City............................	23
27	....	July 9.....	Memorandum of interview between Mr. Romero, General Grant and General Sturm in Washington City...............	24
28	Sec. McCulloch to Gen. Sturm.	July 10...	Permission given by the Secretary of the Treasury of the United States to ship certain ordnance, etc. to Br'sville, Tex.	24

NO.	FROM WHOM AND TO WHOM.	DATE.	SUBJECT.	PAGE.
		1866.		
29	....	July 11...	Memorandum of interview with Mr. Tifft, relative to draft for $1,500,000............	25
30	Gen. Wallace to Gen. Sturm.	July 11...	Contract for arms, etc., and arrangements for shipment to Mexico approved.	25
31	Gen. Sturm to Mr. Romero.	July 14...	Contract for steamers completed. Progress of affairs satisfactory................	26
32	Mr. Romero to Gen. Sturm.	July 15...	Officers to report for transportation......	26
33	Gen. Sturm to Mr. Romero.	July 27...	Sailing of steamer J. W. Everman reported. List of her stores reported enclosed............................	27
34	Mr. Romero to Gen. Sturm.	July 28...	Receipt of notice of the sailing of the Everman.........................	27
35	Same to same...	July 31...	Request to embark Col. Licastro for Rio Grande............................	28
36	Same to same...	Aug. 1.....	Touching publication in the *World*. Encloses letters.....................	28
37	Gen. Sturm to Mr. Romero.	Aug. 2.....	Concerning the Sheridan and its purchase............................	28
38	Same to same...	Aug. 7.....	Encloses copies of contract with W. H. Gilson, charter party of steamer Everman, etc. Complains of hindrances by agents to buy for General Escobedo.	29
39	Mr. Romero to Gen. Sturm.	Aug. 8.....	Knows no agent sent to buy arms for Escobedo.........................	30
40	Same to same...	Aug. 12...	Mr Campbell offers to sell 1,600 carbines.	30
41	Gen. Sturm to Mr. Romero.	Aug. 14...	Answer relative to Mr. Campbell's offer.	31
42	Same to same...	Aug. 15...	Mr Jenk's offer of two batteries of field artillery, etc.	31
43	Mr. Romero to Gen. Sturm.	Aug. 17...	Answer relative to Mr. Campbell's offer..	32
44	Same to same...	Aug. 17...	Telegram.—"Will be in Washington tomorrow."..........................	32
45	....	Aug. 18...	Memorandum of interview between General Sturm and Mr. Romero. Corlies & Co.'s refusal to honor General Carvajal's draft for $1,500,000. Sturm asks instructions of Romero...............	32
46	Mr. Romero to Gen. Sturm.	Aug. 19...	Don Benitez, Commissioner of General Diaz. What is needed in that army division..........................	34
47	Same to same...	Aug. 19...	General Baranda, Commissioner of Alexdro Garcia. What is wanted in the eastern division of the Mexican Republic...	35
48	Same to same...	Aug. 19...	Enclosing order to Corlies & Co. to deliver $100,000 in Mexican bonds..........	35
49	Same to same...	Aug. 19...	The subject of the interviews of the day before. Bonds to be placed at Sturm's disposal for purchases, with instructions.......................	35

NO.	FROM WHOM AND TO WHOM.	DATE.	SUBJECT.	PAGE.
		1866.		
50	Mr. Stocking to Gen. Sturm.	Aug. 13...	The revolution in Matamoras. Deposition of Gen. Carvajal. The cargo of the Everman...	37
51	Gen. Sturm to Mr. Stocking.	Aug. 22...	Instructions relative to cargo of Everman..	38
52	Gen. Sturm to Gen. Carvajal.	Aug. 22...	Duplicate receipts requested for goods sent to his consignment......................	39
53	Gen. Sturm to Mr. Romero.	Aug. 22...	Alterations of instructions in letter of the 19th inst. requested, with reasons therefor...	39
54	Mr. Romero to Gen. Sturm.	Aug. 23...	Alterations of instructions granted........-	41
55	Same to same...	Aug. 24...	Desirable to send arms to Pacific coast. Gov. Baz will say what is needed in that region..	42
56	Gen. Sturm to Mr. Romero.	Aug. 25...	Dispatches from the Rio Grande. Complications in consequence. Requests letter approving contracts made under Carvajal's authority..............................	43
57	Mr. Romero to Gen. Sturm.	Aug. 26...	Views of the affair at Matamoras. Authorises the statement requested by Gen. Sturm. Contracts under Carvajal's authority will be carried out....................	44
58	Same to same...	Aug. 27...	Governor Baz sent to consult with Gen. Sturm with reference to arms for the southern part of Mexico.........................	44
59	Gen. Sturm to Mr. Romero.	Sept. 3....	Wishes Mr. Navarro to sign arrangements made..	45
60	Mr. Romero to Gen. Sturm.	Sept. 4....	Letters of instructions of August last to be shown to Mr. Navarro.....................	45
61	Same to same...	Sept. 7....	Expects to be in Washington next week..	45
62	Gen. Sturm to Mr. Romero.	Sept. 10...	Has made contracts to supply Gen. Baranda and Sr. Benitez. Mr. Navarro has not approved them. Mr. Woodhouse's operations. Operations of parties interested in the Ochoa bonds..........	45
63	Mr. Romero to Gen. Sturm.	Sept. 10...	Encloses copy of note from Sr. Lerdo, stating that the impeachment of Gen. Carvajal has been ordered. Purchases to be suspended until further instructions of government are received........	47
64	....	Aug. 6.....	Translation of instructions from Sr. Lerdo..	48
65	Mr. Romero to Gen. Sturm.	Sept. 11...	Gen. Tapia to supersede Gen. Carvajal as Governor of Tamaulipas.................	49
66	Same to same...	Sept. 11...	Instructions to Mr. Navarro to approve contracts to be made. Approval of contracts with Fitch, Burbridge & Dunlap.	49
67	Gen. Sturm to Mr. Romero.	Sept. 12...	The instructions of Sr. Lerdo received, and will be observed........................	50
68	Mr. Romero to Gen. Sturm.	Sept. 12...	Relative to torpedoes ordered by Gen. Carvajal...	50
69	Same to same...	Sept. 12...	Not well enough to answer letter of 10th inst..	51
70	Same to same...	Sept. 13...	The goods in Matamoras to be delivered to Gen. Tapia..	51

Index. 633

NO.	FROM WHOM AND TO WHOM.	DATE.	SUBJECT.	PAGE.
		1866.		
71	Mr. Romero to Gen. Sturm.	Sept. 13..	Contracts about coal and rations to be kept in abeyance. The Sheridan to be provisioned..	52
72	Same to same...	Sept. 19..	Authorized to purchase goods for Mr. Baz—list enclosed...............................	52
73	Same to same...	Sept. 20..	All will be right when Tapia assumes command in Matamoras.........................	52
74	Gen. Sturm to Mr. Romero.	ept. 21..	Copy of letter from Dr. Hadden enclosed. Mr. Stocking's conduct in protecting goods during the revolution.................	53
75	Dr. Hadden to Gen. Sturm.	Sept. 20..	Dr. Hadden's statement........................	53
76	W. C. Peckham to Gen. Sturm.	Sept. 22..	Mr. Peckham's statement as to occurences in Matamoras................................	55
77	Gen. Sturm to Mr. Stocking.	Sept. 19..	Relative to disposition of goods saved in Matamoras...	57
78	Fitch and others to Gen. Sturm.	Sept. 19..	Representing their inability to carry out their contract on account of delays, approval of the same............................	57
79	....	Sept. 23..	Memorandum of interview between Mr Romero and Gen. Sturm.........................	59
80	Gen. Sturm to Mr. Romero.	Sept. 24..	Effect of difficulties in Matamoras. Asks authority to purchase goods in open market. List furnished..........................	60
81	Mr. Romero to Gen. Sturm.	Sept. 21..	Hopes contract with Mr. Campbell will be concluded..	61
82	Gen. Sturm to Mr. Romero.	Sept. 25..	Relative to contract with Mr. Campbell.	62
83	Mr. Romero to Gen. Sturm.	Sept. 25..	News from Matamoras. Worse than anticipated..	62
84	Gen. Sturm to Mr. Romero.	Sept. 26..	Urges every effort to obtain arms. Wants arrangements to be made with Corlies & Co. to enable him to pay for purchases..	63
85	Mr. Romero to Gen. Sturm.	Sept. 27...	Contract with Mr. Campbell approved...	63
86	Same to same...	Sept. 27.-	$108,000 in bonds to be deposited to Mr Campbell's order..	64
87	Gen. Sturm to Mr. Romero.	Sept. 28...	Mr. Campbell ordered to ship arms to New York...	64
88	Same to same...	Sept. 29...	Bonds for Mr. Campbell deposited.........	64
89	Same to same...	Sept. 29...	Reports arms purchased of American Arms Co...	65
90	Mr. Romero to Gen. Sturm.	Sept. 30...	Explains why he has not sent the instructions desired...	65
91	Gen. Sturm to Mr. Romero.	Oct. 2.....	Enclosing bills of purchases made and paid. Reports amount of bonds sent to Mr. Stocking to pay necessary expenses..	66
92	Same to same...	Oct. 2.....	Cargo of Everman discharged. Disbursement of passage money by Capt. Tuttle.	66
93	Same to same...	Oct. 2.....	Asks payment of bill of American Arms Co. Santa Anna enlisting men.............	67
94	Mr. Romero to Gen. Sturm.	Oct. 2.....	Information wanted before granting authority asked in note of 24th Sept.......	68

NO.	FROM WHOM AND TO WHOM.	DATE.	SUBJECT.	PAGE.
		1866.		
95	Mr. Romero to Gen. Sturm.	Oct. 2.....	Encloses order to Corlies & Co. for the delivery of $100,000 in bonds to make payment for arms..........................	68
96	Same to same...	Oct. 2.....	Proposes to send order to pay for torpedo...	69
97	Gen. Sturm to Mr. Romero.	Oct. 3.....	Statement of articles referred to in letter of Sept. 24, to be forwarded..............	69
98	Same to same...	Oct. 3.....	Dr. Ramsay's torpedo boat..................	69
99	Same to same...	Oct. 3.....	Deficit of bonds to pay for carbines bought...................................	70
100	Mr. Romero to Gen. Sturm.	Oct. 3.....	Relative to accounts and vouchers of Wm. Taylor and Henry Simons for goods bought of them. The $20,000 in bonds remitted to Mr. Stocking............	70
101	Same to same...	Oct. 3.....	Wants information of movements of Santa Anna...................................	71
102	Same to same...	Oct. 3.....	Communicates orders relative to steamer Everman.................................	71
103	Gen. Sturm to Mr. Romero.	Oct. 4.....	Further information as to movements of Santa Anna................................	72
104	Same to same...	Oct. 5.....	Expects to be charged with the $20,000 bonds to Mr. Stocking. Barandas Expedition...............................	73
105	Same to same...	Oct. 5.....	Steamer Everman to be discharged........	73
106	Same to same...	Oct. 5.....	Promises to send Vouchers. Will close a purchase of twenty or thirty thousand Enfield rifles.........................	73
107	Mr. Romero to Gen. Sturm.	Oct. 5.....	Opinions of Santa Anna's movements...	74
108	Same to same...	Oct. 5.....	Encloses order for bonds to pay Mr. Ramsay.................................	75
109	Gen. Sturm to Mr. Romero.	Oct. 6.....	Transmits copy of instructions for discharge of Everman........................	75
110	Same to same...	Oct. 6.....	Receipt of instructions in regard to Dr. Ramsay, and order on J. W. Corlies & Co. acknowledged.........................	75
111	Same to same...	Oct. 6.....	Reports receipt of arms from American Arms Co................................	76
112	Same to same...	Oct. 6.....	Santa Anna. Contract with the New York Mail Steamship Co.....................	76
113	Mr. Romero to Gen. Sturm.	Oct. 6.....	Bonds to be made ready for contracts about to be concluded....................	77
114	Same to same...	Oct. 8.....	Acknowledges receipt of four notes.......	77
115	Same to same...	Oct. 9.....	Information wanted of Messrs. Quintard, Sawyer and Ward......................	78
116	Gen. Sturm to Mr. Romero...	Oct. 10...	Bonds wanted to close contract for $20,000. Enfield Rifles. Complains of Ortega and Santa Anna......................	78
117	Same to same...	Oct. 10...	Quintard, Sawyer and Ward...............	79
118	Same to same...	Oct. 11...	Partial arrangements for 20,000 Enfield rifles, etc., completed. Represents the difficulty of his position.................	79
119	Same to same...	Oct. 12...	Bill of American Arms Co. transmitted, with receipt for bonds....................	79

Index.

NO.	FROM WHOM AND TO WHOM.	DATE.	SUBJECT.	PAGE.
		1866.		
120	Gen. Sturm to Mr. Romero.	Oct. 12...	A fund of $150,000 made up to send supplies to President Juarez. Arrangement broken up by Ortega. Bonds offered by Ochoa in Boston and elsewhere...............	80
121	Mr. Romero to Gen. Sturm.	Oct. 12...	Coal contract with Messrs. Quintard & Ward. Order for $20,000 bonds enclosed...........	81
122	Gen. Sturm to Mr. Romero.	Oct. 13...	Order for $20,000 bonds honored by Corlies & Co........	82
123	Same to same...	Oct. 13...	Relative to contract with Lawrie & Co...	82
124	Same to same...	Oct. 13...	Explanation of contract with Quintard, Sawyer & Co. Urges arrangement by which he can pay for goods at once......	82
125	Mr. Romero to Gen. Sturm.	Oct. 14...	$50,000 bonds enclosed for deposit with Mr. Fuentes............	84
126	Same to same...	Oct. 14...	Draft on Corlies & Co. for $50,000 bonds	84
127	Gen. Sturm to Mr. Romero.	Oct. 15...	Receipt of order for $50,000 bonds acknowledged.............	85
128	Same to same...	Oct. 15...	Asks for news, if any from Brownsville, Texas...........	85
129	Mr. Romero to Gen. Sturm.	Oct. 15...	Receipt of letters about contracts with Quintard & Co. acknowledged...........	85
130	Gen. Sturm to Mr. Romero.	Oct. 16...	Dupont de Nemours & Co. willing to sell powder..........	86
131	Mr. Romero to Gen. Sturm.	Oct. 17...	Claim of Nemours & Co.................	86
132	Same to same...	Oct. 18...	Escobedo reported negotiating for cargo of Everman. Settlement deferred for information.............	86
133	Mr. Mariscal to Gen. Sturm.	Oct. 18...	Introductory of M. C. A. Borchert.........	87
134	Gen. Sturm to Mr. Romero.	Oct. 19...	Dupont agrees to sell Gen. Sturm powder. Papers relating to old claim enclosed..........	87
135	Same to same...	Oct. 20...	Proposition from Dupont & Co. Delivery of rations by Lawrie & Co.........	88
136	Mr. Romero to Gen. Sturm...	Oct. 22...	Old claim of Dupont & Co. Authority to buy 200 barrels powder from Company. Contract with Lawrie & Co. disapproved........	88
137	Romero to Kemble & Warner.	Oct. 22...	Referred to Gen. Sturm for information about claim of Nemours & Co............	89
138	Mr. Romero to McDonald.	Oct. 23...	Referred to Gen. Sturm about proposed sale of Enfield rifles............	89
139	Gen. Sturm to Mr. Romero.	Oct. 25...	Contract with Mr. Cory for 20,000 Springfield rifles, 25,000 new Enfield rifles, etc., closed..........	90
140	Mr. Romero to Gen. Sturm.	Oct. 26...	Orders for bonds to meet Cory contract to be sent........	90
141	Gen. Sturm to Mr. Romero.	Oct. 28...	Encloses communication from Mr. Stocking............	90
142	Mr. Romero to Gen. Sturm.	Oct. 30...	$2,000,000 bonds needed on the Cory contract. Orders for amounts to be sent as needed............	91

NO.	FROM WHOM AND TO WHOM.	DATE.	SUBJECT.	PAGE.
		1866.		
143	Mr. Romero to Gen. Sturm.	Oct. 30...	Guns yet in possession of Mr. Stocking.	91
144	Gen. Sturm to Mr. Romero.	Nov. 3.....	$2,000,000 bonds should be ready when needed..................................	91
145	Mr. Romero to Gen. Sturm.	Nov. 5.....	Directions as to deposit of bonds on Cory contract...............................	92
146	Gen. Sturm to Mr. Romero.	Nov. 6.....	Navarro declines to approve contract for charter of steamer for Baranda's expedition............................	92
147	Mr. Romero to Gen. Sturm.	Nov. 6.....	Answer to confidential letter of 3d inst..	93
148	Gen. Sturm to Mr. Romero.	Nov. 7.....	Enclosing letter from Mr. Stocking.......	93
149	Same to same...	Nov. 7.....	Undertaking of Messrs. Schuyler, Hartley & Graham to furnish goods. Cory's failure..................................	93
150	Mr. Romero to Gen. Sturm.	Nov. 7.....	Instructions sent to Mr. Navarro about chartering steamer......................	94
151	Gen. Sturm to Mr. Romero.	Nov. 8.....	Explanation of contract for charter of vessel..................................	94
152	Mr. Romero to Gen. Sturm.	Nov. 8.....	Shipments. Contract with Schuyler, Hartley & Graham. Instructions as to Cory's contract........................	95
153	Same to same...	Nov. 8.....	Mr. Stocking's letter...................	96
154	Same to same...	Nov. 9.....	Dr. Navarro fully authorized to approve charter of steamer Vixen................	96
155	Gen. Sturm to Mr. Romero.	Nov. 10...	$159,000 paid out. $250,000 more needed..................................	97
156	Mr. Romero to Gen. Sturm.	Nov. 11...	Draft promised. Account of stores sent by steamer Vixen wanted..............	97
157	Same to same...	Nov. 11...	Order for $250,000 bonds remitted.........	97
158	Gen. Sturm to Mr. Romero.	Nov. 14...	Not enough bonds signed. Instructions to Mr. Fuentes asked.................	98
159	Same to same...	Nov. 14...	The Vixen sailed with cargo. Robert C. Sturm, supercargo. His instructions...	98
160	Same to same...	Nov. 15...	Arms bought of Schuyler, Bartley & Graham for Gen. Baranda................	99
161	Mr. Romero to Gen. Sturm.	Nov. 16...	Relative to steamer Vixen...............	100
162	Mr. Mariscal to Gen. Sturm.	Nov. 16...	Explanation wanted as to purchase of Schuyler & Co........................	100
163	Gen. Sturm to Mr. Romero.	Nov. 17...	Explanation given......................	101
164	Same to same...	Nov. 17...	The Vixen and her sea worthiness.........	102
165	Same to same...	Nov. 17...	The charter of the Vixen again. Combination in New York against him and the Mexican government. Labors required. To obviate difficulties urges the purchase of one or two steamers. Is not working for mere pay, or for speculation. Has not made a cent yet, but borrowed from friends. Unless some arrangements can be made to do things more expeditiously, he must resign his position. Will not be able to	

NO.	FROM WHOM AND TO WHOM.	DATE.	SUBJECT.	PAGE.
		1866.		
166	Gen. Sturm to Mr. Romero...	Nov. 17...	continue his efforts under present arrangements longer than to expedite Gov. Baz, and settle accounts.............	102
167	Same to same...	Nov. 18...	The Vixen driven into Norfolk by storm.	104
168	Mr. Romero to Gen. Sturm.	Nov. 19...	Combinations to defeat President Juarez and elevate Ortega. The collection in depot of a quantity of arms, etc., to be kept on hand for transportation. Suggestion of Baranda and Benitez to send clothing	104
169	Same to same...	Nov. 20...	Is fully aware of Gen. Sturm's energy and activity, and is persuaded that without him arms and ammunition could not have been sent home. Satisfied of his integrity also. Gen. Wallace in Chihuahua. Hopes that will be occasion for the sending of instructions. Not prepared to approve plan proposed in letter of 17th inst................	106
170	Gen. Sturm to Mr. Romero.	Nov. 22...	Introduction of Senor Don F. Ferrer, commissioner from the Governor of the State of Puebla............................	107 107
171	Same to same...	Nov. 22...	Order for $100,000 bonds wanted...........	
172	Same to same...	Nov. 22...	Statement of property on board Gov. Baz's steamer..................................	107 108
173	Same to same...	Nov. 22...	A battery not attainable for Mr. Ferrer.	
174	Mr. Romero to Gen. Sturm.	Nov. 22...	Statement enclosed of bonds received and expended, and of purchases made. Is doing the work of two men·............	108 109
175	Gen. Sturm to Mr. Romero.	Nov. 23...	Order for $100,000 bonds remitted.........	
176	Mr. Romero to Gen. Sturm.	Nov. 23...	Encloses receipt of Schuyler, Hartley & Graham. Vixen left Norfolk............	109
177	Same to same...	Nov. 25...	Instructions as to shipments for Gov. Baz and Mr. Ferrer.........................	109 110
178	Gen. Sturm to Mr. Romero.	Nov. 28...	Instructions as to sending torpedo........	110
179	Mr. Romero to Gen. Sturm.	Nov. 29...	Sailing of the Suwanee announced.........	
180	....	Dec. 2.....	Directs suspension for the present of purchases. Grant's general account of purchases made and arrearages on them.	111
181	Gen. Sturm to Mr. Romero.	Dec. 3.....	Memorandum of interview between Mr. Romero and Gen. Sturm on the subject of his agency............................	111
182	Same to same...	Dec. 3.....	$500,000 bonds needed to pay for articles purchased. Also $100,000 bonds to pay clerk hire, inspection, drayage and other incidental expenses..................	115
			A number of influential men conclude to sell to the Mexican government arms and munitions of war. Asks authority to avail himself of the good feeling. Renews proposal to collect stores in depots, and purchase two steamers......	115

22

NO.	FROM WHOM AND TO WHOM.	DATE.	SUBJECT.	PAGE.
		1866.		
183	Mr. Romero to Gen. Sturm.	Dec. 4.....	Not proper to adopt proposal until instructed on the subject by his government. Would authorize negotiations with Ames family............................	116
184	Same to same...	Dec. 4.....	The goods sent by the Everman ought not to be paid until it is known that they have been duly delivered. Order for $220.000 bonds enclosed..................	116
185	Gen. Sturm to Mr. Romero.	Dec. 5.....	Receipt of order for bonds acknowledged.	117
186	Mr. Romero to Gen. Sturm.	Dec. 7.....	The sinking of the Suwanee. The reasons given. Cannot authorize the purchase of anything else....................	117
187	Gen. Sturm to Mr. Romero.	Dec. 8.....	Not blamable for disaster to Suwanee, and other misfortunes.....................	118
188	Same to same...	Dec. 10...	Encloses certificate of Government Inspector as to sea worthiness of the Suwanee. Other evidence of like effect. Not customary to insure cargos of war material...............................	116
189	Same to same...	Dec. 10...	Receipt of Schuyler & Co. for $150,000 remitted.....................................	120
190	Mr. Romero to Gen. Sturm.	Dec. 12...	Has not charged Gen. Sturm with fault in connection with Suwanee, and is convinced of his earnestness in saving the government of Mexico..................	120
191	Gen. Sturm to Mr. Romero.	Dec. 13...	The greater the difficulty and trouble, the more ready he is to work. Schemes on foot against the Mexican government.	121
192	Mr. Romero to Gen. Sturm.	Dec. 17...	Mr. W. L. Hanscom's proposal to construct monitors for the Mexican government..................................	122
193	Same to same...	Dec. 17...	Mexican Secretary of War directs stoppage of all contracts.........................	122
194	Gen. Sturm to Mr. Romero.	Dec. 18...	There being no further need of his services, proposes to go home soon as possible. Goods on hand, and unsettled business, and his cash expenses Statement to be at once made. Wishes bonds *as his own property*, for services rendered. Urges continuance of purchases..	122
195	Mr. Romero to Gen. Sturm.	Dec. 19...	President Juarez has decided to stop all purchases. Will notify Gen. Sturm of instructions on the subject. Will try to have all settled before Gen. Sturm goes home. Wants to know *confidentially* how much compensation Gen. Sturm thinks he is entitled to in bonds..........	123
196	Gen. Sturm to Mr. Romero.	Dec. 23...	Balance of goods on hand for Gov. Baz, Gen. Baranda and Mr. Benitez purchased under previous orders. Contracts void, such as those with Fitch & Cory. Preparing to go home............	124

NO.	FROM WHOM AND TO WHOM.	DATE.	SUBJECT.	PAGE.
		1866.		
197	Gen. Sturm to Mr. Romero	Dec. 23...	Letter from Mr. Simons as to the Everman, and answer thereto enclosed. Receipt of Mr. Saavedra, agent of Gen. Escobedo, for a portion of the goods at Brazos to be remitted.............................	125
198	Same to same...	Dec. 27...	Further about the delivery to Gen. Escobedo of the Everman cargo. Advises settlement of the claim of Mr. Simons.	125
199	Same to same...	Dec. 27...	Saavedra's receipt transmitted..............	126
200	Mr. Romero to Gen. Sturm.	Dec. 28...	Order to discharge the Vixen................	126
201	Gen. Sturm to Mr. Romero.	Dec. 29...	Account for the Vixen to be settled, with a deduction..	127
202	Mr. Romero to Gen. Sturm.	Dec. 29...	$129,150 in bonds to be delivered on account for the Everman. Also amount to pay charters of the Vixen................	127
203	....	Dec. 31...	Memorandum of interview between Mr. Romero and Gen. Sturm. Settlement and payment for Everman and her cargo urged. Mr. Romero proposes payment in bonds to Gen. Sturm for his services. Gen. Sturm defers the matter until the war is over. Gen. Sturm has arranged with parties to send arms, etc., to Mexico, to be sold there for cash, if Mr. Romero and his government provide protection and freedom from charges. Mr. Romero assents.....	128
204	Gen. Sturm to Mr. Romero.	Dec. 31...	Submits bill for charter of Vixen...........	128
205	Mr. Romero to Gen. Sturm.	Dec. 31... 1867.	Order for $196,400 bonds to cover account of John T. Wright, etc........................	129
206	Same to same...	Jan. 3.....	Tents on hand not to be sold.................	129
207	Same to same...	Jan. 3.....	Declines to order $134,750 bonds to pay for charter of Everman. Reasons therefor...	129
208	Gen. Sturm to Mr. Romero.	Jan. 4.....	Receipt of orders for bonds acknowledged, with statement of parties to be paid...	130
209	Same to same...	Jan. 4.....	Order not to sell tents received.............	131
210	Same to same...	Jan. 5.....	Opinions upon the merits of claims against the government in connection with the cargo of the Everman............	·131
211	Same to same...	Jan. 5.....	Statement concerning the employment of the Everman and seizure of her cargo at Matamoras.................................	132
212	Same to same...	Jan. 5.....	The bill of Dupont de Nemours & Co. for powder, and payment thereof..........	133
213	Mr. Romero to Gen. Sturm.	Jan. 6.....	Mr. Lerdo de Tejada's order to make no further purchases for bonds. Contracts already made...	133
214	Same to same...	Jan. 6.....	$33,500 bonds to settle certain accounts of Dupont & Co..................................	134
215	Same to same...	Jan. 8.....	Statement wanted of contracts that can not be conveniently abandoned............	134
216	Same to same...	Jan. 9.....	Cannot pay the charter money of the Everman without further information...	134

NO.	FROM WHOM AND TO WHOM.	DATE.	SUBJECT.	PAGE.
		1867.		
217	Mr. Romero to Gen. Sturm.	Jan. 9.....	Regrets Gen. Sturm's belief that owners of the Everman have a righteous claim for damages...	135
218	Gen. Sturm to Mr. Romero.	Jan. 10...	Receipt of bonds for Dupont & Co. acknowledged	135
219	Same to same...	Jan. 14...	Payments made to David Smith, Dewhurst & Emerson, and for charter of Vixen	136
220	Mr. Romero to Gen. Sturm.	Jan. 18...	Receipt by Gen. Escobedo of goods at Brownsville and Roma. The vouchers wanted...	136
221	Gen. Sturm to Mr. Romero.	Jan. 19...	Vessel to ply between New Orleans and Mexican ports obtained. Requests letters to officers of Mexican ports...........	137
222	Same to same...	Jan. 19...	Sale of stores left over after discharge of Vixen	138
223	Same to same...	Jan. 19...	Receipts for bonds by Merritt, Walcott & Co., Dewhurst & Emerson, and David Smith transmitted........................	139
224	Same to same...	Jan. 19...	Attachment by Dupont & Co. of powder on hand...	139
225	Mr. Romero to Gen. Sturm.	Jan. 21...	Acknowledgment of receipts from Mr. Wright for the Vixen and stores sold to him...	140
226	Same to same...	Jan. 21...	Like acknowledgment as to David Smith, Merrit, Walcott & Co., and Dewhurst & Emerson	140
227	Gen. Sturm to Mr. Romero.	Jan. 22...	Statement of articles already purchased, by whom, and amount due therefor......	141
228	Same to same...	Jan. 22...	The vouchers called for from Mr. Stocking..	141
229	Mr. Romero to Gen. Sturm.	Jan. 22...	The proposed line of steamers between New Orleans and Mexican ports. Defers talk upon the subject	142
230	Same to same...	Jan. 22...	The claim of Dupont & Co. referred to this government.................................	142
231	Gen. Sturm to Mr. Romero.	Jan. 23...	Relative to vouchers of Merritt, Walcott & Co., and others.................................	142
232	Same to same...	Jan. 25...	Will make personal arrangements with Dupont & Co. Cannot leave New York at present...	143
233	Mr. Romero to Gen. Sturm.	Jan. 25...	Woodhouse's bonds offered for almost nothing...	144
234	Gen. Sturm to Mr. Romero.	Jan. 28...	The Woodhouse Bonds........................	144
235	Mr. Romero to Gen. Sturm.	Feb. 1.....	Written statement of proposition about steamer wanted..................................	144
236	Gen. Sturm to Mr. Romero.	Feb. 4.....	Proposal to run steamer to Mexico if inducements are conceded.........................	145
237	Mr. Romero to Gen. Sturm.	Feb. 7.....	Mr. Cattel's bills for the Suwanee. Explanations of them asked......................	146
238	Same to same...	Feb. 8.....	Further about the charter of the Suwanee.	147
239	Same to same...	Feb. 9.....	Gen. Sturm must apply to government for exemption of duties and port charges. Arrangement for the first trip possible...	148

NO.	FROM WHOM AND TO WHOM.	DATE.	SUBJECT.	PAGE.
		1867		
240	Mr. Romero to Gen. Sturm.	Feb. 10...	Mr. Stocking's report of disposition of the cargo of the Everman. Certain of the goods Mr. Romero will pay for.......	148
241	Gen. Sturm to Mr. Romero.	Feb. 11...	Reasons for signing the two certificates for charter of the Suwanee. The contract made with Mr. Romero's cognizance. Copies of the two accounts.....	148
242	Same to same...	Feb. 11...	Mr. Ames anxious to have his accounts settled........................	151
243	Same to same...	Feb. 12...	Further about the certificates for the Suwanee. Wants his position distinctly defined.............	152
244	Mr. Romero to Gen. Sturm...	Feb. 12...	Contract for the Suwanee unknown to him. What is said in conversation, cannot be taken as approbation of a fact........................	153
245	Same to same...	Feb. 14...	An interview requested. Asks for copies of orders given by Gen. Carvajal..........	154
246	Same to same...	Feb. 16...	Further explanation asked about charter money of the Everman......................	154
247	Gen. Sturm to Mr. Romero.	Feb. 16...	The goods sent to Matamoras by order of Gen. Carvajal. Position of the venders in demand for settlement............	155
248	Same to same...	Feb. 16...	Urges settlement with Mr. Ames and his friends. Copies of the powers conferred by Gen. Carvajal to be transmitted......................	155
249	Mr. Romero to Gen. Sturm.	Feb. 18...	Introductory of Col. Enrique A. Mexia, Commissioner from Gen. Pavon, commander of the Northern Line of Vera Cruz State...................	156
250	Same to same...	Feb. 18...	Inquiry about a box of musket rifles......	156
251	Gen. Sturm to Mr. Romero.	Feb. 20...	Goods for Gen. Baranda left behind......	157
252	Same to same...	Feb. 20...	Copies of powers conferred by General Carvajal enclosed.............................	157
253	Mr. Romero to Gen. Sturm.	Feb. 21...	Acknowledging receipt of copies of powers conferred by Gen. Carvajal. Asking for instructions of the Government to Gen. Carvajal............................	157
254	....	Feb. 24...	Memorandum of interview between Gen. Sturm and Mr. Romero touching accounts of Dupont & Co., and Messrs. Simons, Cattell and others............	158
255	Gen. Sturm to Mr. Romero.	Feb. 24...	Transmittal of bill of Dupont & Co	158
256	Mr. Romero to Gen. Sturm.	Feb. 25...	Agreement to pay for goods taken by the revolutionists in Matamoras. Instructions for payment of rest of goods.......	159
257	Same to same...	Feb. 25...	Purchase of Percussian caps authorized.	159
258	Gen. Sturm to Mr. Romero.	Mar. 3...	Transmits vouchers for goods shipped to Minititlan per steamer Vixen.............	160
259	Same to same...	Mar. 3...	Reports proposition of settlement made to Mr. Gilson, agent, etc.....................	160

NO.	FROM WHOM AND TO WHOM.	DATE.	SUBJECT.	PAGE.
		1867.		
260	Gen. Sturm to Mr. Romero.	Mar. 4....	Encloses copy of account of goods purchased of Ames and friends...............	162
261	Same to same...	Mar. 4.....	Will see and report what can be got for Col. ejia.......................................	163
262	Same to same...	Mar. 5.....	Instructions asked about supplies for Col. Mejia...................................	164
263	Same to same...	Mar. 4.....	Remits copies of four accounts of goods purchased with approval of Dr. Navarro............................	165
264	Same to same...	Mar. 6.....	Efforts to settle old accounts, and obtain goods for Col. Mejia. Charges of insurance, etc., of Mr. Gilson...............	166
265	Mr. Romero to Gen. Sturm.	Mar. 6.....	Conditions upon which he will settle for goods bought before order to stop purchasing..................................	167
266	Same to same...	Mar. 6.....	What goods shipped by the Everman he is ready to pay for. About the claim for insurance............................	167
267	Same to same...	Mar. 6.....	Acknowledges receipt of vouchers relative to the Vixen. Mr. Cushing's opinion about the Everman not yet to hand.	168
268	Gen. Sturm to Mr. Romero.	Mar 7.....	Claim for inspection, insurance, etc., paid by Mr. Gilson previously reported.	168
269	Mr. Romero to Gen. Sturm.	Mar. 7.....	Col. Mexia to receive nothing except of goods on hand. What may be given him..	169
270	Gen. Sturm to Mr. Romero.	Mar. 8.....	Transmits powers of Gen. Carvajal from his Government, etc........................	170
271	Mr. Romero to Gen. Sturm.	Mar. 8.....	Order for $382,450 bonds to pay account of Ames and others.......................	170
272	W. F. Stocking to Mr. Romero.	Mar. 8.....	Efforts of Gen. Sturm to pacify parties interested in cargo of the Everman.....	170
273	Mr. Romero to Gen. Sturm	Mar. 12...	Mr. Cushing's opinion received. Mr. Cattell not entitled to anything...........	171
274	Same to same...	Mar. 14...	Efforts to obtain goods for Gen. Diaz to be abandoned.....................................	171
275	Gen. Sturm to Mr. Romero.	Mar. 16...	Encloses list of goods to be sent to Tampico on private account, with statement by whom sent. Asks that he may send the goods free of charge, get money out free, and obtain such assistance in and about same as can be consistently granted. Sends receipt for the goods at Roma..	170
276	Gen. Sturm to Mr. Romero.	Mar. 16...	Encloses original authority of Mr. Laing to receive goods at Roma, and Mr. Laing's receipt for same. Asks decision about settlement for cargo of Everman...	172
277	Mr. Romero to Gen. Sturm.	Mar. 17...	Transmits copy of Mr. Cushing's opinion about charter of Suwanee.............	173
278	Gen. Sturm to Mr. Romero.	Mar. 18...	Failure to obtain money to pay interest due on April coupons. Protests against Mr. Cushing's opinion........................	173
279	Same to same...	Mar. 21...	Receipt of Messrs. Hall and Ruckel for bonds paid for medical stores...............	174

Index. 343

NO.	FROM WHOM AND TO WHOM.	DATE.	SUBJECT.	PAGE.
		1867		
280	Mr. Romero to Gen. Sturm.	Mar. 22...	Is resolved to pay at once two-thirds of the amount due for cargo of the Everman, if agreeable to Mr. Simons.	174
281	Same to same...	Mar. 22...	Bonds ordered to make part payment for rifles shipped on Everman.	174
282	Same to same...	Mar. 26...	Goods to be put at disposal of Col. Mejia.	175
283	Same to same...	Mar. 23...	Encloses letter for Gen. A. Gomez, and another for Mr. Chase, to enable Mr. Stocking's business. Suggestions as to place of disposal of goods. Declines to furnish official copy of Mr. Cushing's opinion.	175
284	Mr. Romero to Gen. A. Gomez.	Mar. 23...	Asking facilities of sale for Mr. Stocking.	176
285	Gen. Sturm to Mr. Romero.	Mar. 31...	Transmits vouchers from Ames, Gaylord, Mass. Arms Co., and C. W. Mitchell.	177
286	Mr. Romero to Gen. Sturm.	April 8...	The disposition of the goods purchased of Mr. Ames. The return of the Sheridan, if it can be done.	177
287	Gen. Sturm to Mr. Romero.	April 9...	Settlement with Mr. Simons for Everman. The Woodhouse statement.	178
288	Mr. Romero to Gen. Sturm.	April 10..	Order for $89,130 bonds to settle with Mr. Simons.	179
289	Gen. Sturm to Mr. Romero.	April 12..	What portion of the goods on hand are to be sent to Matamoras.	179
290	Same to same...	April 12..	Encloses receipt of Mr. Dewhurst, $15,950.	179
291	Mr. Romero to Gen. Sturm.	April 15..	Statement of goods to be sent to Matamoras.	180
292	Same to same...	April 17..	Statement of goods to be sent to Vera Cruz.	180
293	Gen. Sturm to Mr. Romero.	April 18..	Copies of the Woodhouse report forwarded. The steamer Sheridan.	181
294	Same to same...	April 26..	Reports settlement with Mr. Dewhurst for goods sold at Tampico.	182
295	Mr. Romero to Gen. Sturm.	April 28..	Wants report from Gen. Wallace on Woodhouse case.	182
296	Gen. Sturm to Mr. Romero.	April 30...	Freight to Gen. Berriozabal and invoice thereof.	183
297	Same to same...	April 30..	The revolt in Tampico. Gen. Gomez and the steamer McCallum.	183
298	Same to same...	May 1.....	Insurance of cargo not obtainable with bonds.	184
299	Mr. Romero to Gen. Sturm.	May 1.....	Encloses letter to Gen. Berriozabal Gen. Wallace's report on Woodhouse affair.	184
300	Same to same...	May 2......	Sorry about the difficulty at Tampico.	185
301	Same to same...	May 10.....	Promissory note for gold advanced to Mr. Macin.	185
302	Same to same...	May 23....	The bonds for Mr. Simons.	186
303	Gen. Sturm to Mr. Romero.	May 24....	Mr. Simons has not called for his bonds.	186
304	Same to same...	May 24....	Wants old matters definitely settled in some way.	186

NO.	FROM WHOM AND TO WHOM.	DATE.	SUBJECT.	PAGE.
		1867.		
305	Mr. Romero to Gen. Sturm.	May 25...	20,000 carbine cartridges for Gen. Pavon.	187
306	Same to same...	June 4....	Objections to Gen. S.'s remarks in Herald. They embarrass him very much...	187
307	Same to same...	June 4....	Questions to be answered in connection with the remarks in the Herald...........	187
308	Gen. Sturm to Mr. Romero.	June 6....	The remarks in the Herald. Answer to questions...	188
309	Mr. Romero to Gen. Sturm.	June 7....	The remarks in the Herald...................	189
310	Gen. Sturm to Mr. Romero.	June 11...	Encloses receipt of Mr. Simons............	190
311	Mr. Romero to Gen. Sturm.	June 11...	The Sheridan received by authorities. Order for $146,650 bonds to pay for her.	190
312	Same to same...	June 12...	Interest on the bonds to Mr. Simons....	191
313	Gen. Sturm to Mr. Romero.	June 14 ..	The payment to Mr. Simons..................	191
314	Same to same...	June 17...	Points insisted on by Mr. Simons...........	192
315	Same to same...	July 9.....	The delivery of the bonds to Mr. Simons	192
316	Mr. Romero to Gen. Sturm.	July 10...	War material on hand to be sent to Vera Cruz..	193
......	....	July 11...	Memorandum of interview between Mr Romero and Gen. Sturm as to unsettled accounts. Goods for Gen. Diaz. Mr. R. going to Mexico in a few weeks......	193
317	....	July 12...	Memorandum of second interview. Settlement of Gen. S.'s account. Gen. S.'s summary of his services, and what he wanted..	193
318	Gen. Sturm to Mr. Romero.	July 13...	Fillibustering schemes against Mexico...	196
319	Mr. Romero to Gen. Sturm.	July 15...	Revocation of order prohibiting exportation of arms..	197
320	Gen. Sturm to Mr. Romero.	July 17...	Difficulties of getting more arms for Mexico..	198
321	Mr. Romero to Gen. Sturm.	July 18...	No danger in sending arms to Vera Cruz	198
322	Gen. Sturm to Mr. Romero.	July 23...	Offer by Mr. Woodhouse to transport arms...	199
323	Mr. Romero to Gen. Sturm.	July 23...	Dreamy Fillibusters, and port charges on other than government goods in Vera Cruz..	199
324	Gen. Sturm to Mr. Romero.	July 25...	Offers in regard to freight to Vera Cruz.	200
325	Same to same...	July 27...	Same subject continued.........................	200
326	Same to same...	July 27...	Alexandre & Sons' offer for freight accepted..	201
327	Mr. Romero to Gen. Sturm.	July 31...	A poor Mexican wishes to go home........	201
328	Gen. Sturm to Mr. Romero.	Aug. 2....	Will send the man without charge to Vera Cruz...	202
329	Same to same...	Aug. 10...	The shipment per barque Zingarella to Vera Cruz...	202
330	Same to same...	Aug. 23...	Cash received and expended on account of purchase and shipments for Mexican Government..	202

NO.	FROM WHOM AND TO WHOM.	DATE.	SUBJECT.	PAGE.
		1867		
331	Mr. Romero to Gen. Sturm.	Aug. 24...	Account for cash expenses to be submitted to government. Return to Mexico.	203
332	Same to same...	Aug. 26...	Explanation wanted of logs of mahogany	203
333	Gen. Sturm to Mr. Romero.	Aug. 27...	The mahogany explained.....................	203
334	Mr. Romero to Gen. Grant.	Sept. 4.....	Statement of Gen. S.'s services, bargains, etc., approved, and to be transmitted to government...	205
335	....	Nov. 21...	Extract of a publication in the Diario Official of Mexico, signed by M. Romero..	205
336	Gen. Sturm to Mr. Romero.	Dec. 5.....	The cargo of the Gen. McCallum...........	212
337	Gen. Mejia to Gen. Sturm.	Dec. 18...	Declines to buy certain arms................	213
338	Gen. Sturm to Mr. Romero.	Dec. 22...	Will communicate to Mr. Lerdo in writing...	213
339	Gen. Sturm to Sr. D. S. Lerdo.	Dec. 24...	Represents his services and wishes........	214
		1868		
340	Gen. Sturm to Mr. Romero.	Jan. 16...	Arms on personal account to be left in Mexico. Wants definite arrangement in regard to privileges the government has to grant him...................................	215
341	Mr. Romero to Gen. Sturm.	Jan. 20....	The President's answer to letter of 16th inst...	216
342	Gen. Sturm to Mr. Romero.	Feb. 7.....	Certain requests to be made to Mr. Lerdo. Draft of Placido Vega................	217
343	Gen. Sturm to Senor Lerdo.	Feb. 7.....	Information wanted concerning draft of Vega. Settlements of accounts for the Suwanee, Everman, Sheridan, etc......	218
344	Senor Lerdo to Gen. Sturm.	Feb. 9.....	Requests interview at writer's house......	218
345	Same to same...	Feb. 8.....	Placido Vega's draft repudiated. Will settle the accounts with persons authorized to settle......................................	219
346	Same to same...	Feb. 8.....	Cabinet view of Gen. Sturm's claim for services. Basis of settlement............	219
347	Gen. Sturm to Senor Lerdo.	Feb. 10...	Accepts tender of $11,000 on account....	221
348	Mr. Romero to Gen. Sturm.	Feb. 11...	Appointment for interview.....................	222
349	....	Feb. 12...	Memorandum of interview between Mr. Romero and Gen. Sturm. Mr. R. proposes an amendment to Gen. S.'s letter to Senor Lerdo. Earnest conversation about it. An amendment added. Question of compensation left to generosity of the government.................................	222
350	....	Feb. 12...	Copy of memorandum handed to Gen. Sturm by Mr. Romero.......................	223
351	Gen. Sturm to Senor Lerdo.	Feb. 10...	Statement of payments to date............	224
352	Lerdo de Tejada to Gen. Sturm.	Feb. 12...	Transmits order on Secretary of Treasury for payment.................................	224
353	Mr. Romero to Gen. Sturm.	Mar. 8.....	Attacks of newspapers on Sturm. Will defend Sturm...................................	225

NO.	FROM WHOM AND TO WHOM.	DATE.	SUBJECT.	PAGE.
		1868.		
354	Mr. Romero to Gen. Sturm.	Aug. 10...	Will not forget a conversation had with Gen. Sturm..	226
355	Gen. Sturm to Mr. Romero.	Aug. 25...	Policy to settle all claims by a commission..	226
356	Same to same...	Sept. 28...	Sturm may come to Mexico.................	232
357	Same to same...	Oct. 1......	Proposes plan to settle with bondholders	232
358	Same to same...	Oct. 15...	Will arrive at Vera Cruz in November...	233
359	Same to same...	Oct. 28...	Insurance on Keese. Requests Romero to inform Mr. Gamboa about particulars of Gen. Sturm's shipment to Mexico...	234
360	Mr. Romero to Gen. Sturm.	Oct. 24...	About settlement of claims, etc. The treaty made is almost the same suggested by Gen. Sturm...............................	235
361	Same to same...	Nov. 10...	Acknowledges receipt of documents. Will advise Gamboa. Passage of law to export gold and silver ore free.........	236
362	Same to same...	Dec. 12...	Settlement of claims	226
363	Garcia to Romero	Dec. 12...	Gen. Sturm's claim a just one. Has drawn on Vera Cruz for a small amount	237
364	Mr. Romero to Gen. Sturm.	Dec. 15....	Encloses letter of Governor Garcia.........	237
365	Gen. Sturm to Mr. Romero.	Dec. 16...	Has no faith in the promises of Governor Garcia...	238
366	Ritter to Holder, Boker & Co.,	Dec. 17...	No order on the Custom House at Vera Cruz to deliver money...........................	238
367	Sturm to Lerdo de Tejada.	Dec. 24...	Request payment of $2,500 on account...	239
368	Same to same...	Dec. 26...	Same subject...	239
369	Lerdo de Tejada to Sturm.	Dec. 26...	Same subject..	239
370	Sturm to Lerdo de Tejada.	Dec. 26...	Acknowledges receipt of order for $2,500 on account of services. Will accept whatever the Government may see fit to pay in addition as a settlement in full......	240
371	Mr. Romero to Gen. Sturm.	Dec. 27...	Encloses Lerdo's answer to Gen. Sturm, with copy of order on Treasury............	241
372	Lerdo de Tejada to Sturm.	Dec. 27...	Encloses copy of order on the Treasury for $2,500, to be paid to Gen. Sturm on account of services. Wants an immediate decision from Gen. Sturm regarding his remuneration for his services...	241
373	Gen. Sturm to Mr. Romero...	Dec. 28...	Proposes to accept $2,500 additional as payment in full, if the Government will take the arms, and to satisfy, and do justice, his friends will sacrifice and lose all...	242
374	Mr. Romero to Gen. Sturm.	Dec. 29...	Knows Gen. Sturm's services, and will do what he can to compensate them. Proposition to settle with Dewhurst & Emerson	242
		1869.		
375	Gen. Sturm to Mr. Romero	Jan. 5....	Is anxious that others be satisfied. Does not believe D. & E. will accept Mr. Romero's proposition................................	243

NO.	FROM WHOM AND TO WHOM.	DATE.	SUBJECT.	PAGE.
		1869		
376	Mr. Romero to Gen. Sturm.	Jan. 21...	Same subject...	244
377	Gen. Sturm to Mr. Romero.	Feb. 3.....	Settlement with Dewhurst & Emerson. Advisability to include all claims under the treaty...	244
378	Same to same...	Feb. 3.....	About the nefarious proceedings of an Agent of the Insurance Companies......	245
379	Mr. Romero to Gen. Sturm.	Feb. 9.....	Mutiny at Puebla. Negrete took Gen. Sturm's arms..	246
380	Same to same...:	Feb. 27...	Defeat of Negrete. All the material of war he had was captured by the Government troops..................................	247
381	Mr. Romero to Gen. Sturm.	Feb. 27...	Encloses copy of letter to Dewhurst & Emerson..	247
382	Same to same...	March 5..	Agrees to the proposition of extending treaty to all claims between Mexico and the United States................................	248
383	Same to same...	March 29..	About settlement with Dewhurst & Emerson. Instructions to Dr. Navarro........	248
384	Same to same...	April 28..	State of affairs in Mexico......................	249
385	Same to same...	June 21...	Encloses a slip from a newspaper regarding an Insurance affair......................	249
386	Gen. Sturm to Mr. Romero.	July 22...	Same subject..	250
387	Mr. Romero to Gen. Sturm.	Aug. 11..	Same subject..	252
388	Gen. Sturm to Mr. Romero.	Sept. 25..	Same subject, and requests Mr. Romero to urge the Government to relieve Gen. Sturm from his embarrassing position, and repeats his former offers of settlement...	252
389	Gen. Sturm to Mr. Mariscal.	Nov. 23...	Is willing to withhold the publication of the Pamphlet he is about publishing for fifty days...	255
390	Mr. Mariscal to Gen. Sturm.	Nov. 23...	Same subject, and promises to communicate with his Government, with a view to a settlement....................................	255
391	Gen. Sturm to Mr. Mariscal.	Nov. 25..	Same subject..	256
392	Same to same.	Nov. 26..	Transmits a statement of his claims......	256
393	Mr. Mariscal to Gen. Sturm.	Nov. 30..	Same subject..	258
394			Deposition of William H. H. Terrell......	259
395			Deposition of John Hayden..................	261
396			Deposition of Thomas B. McCarty..........	262
397			Deposition of Charles A. Ray................	263
398			Deposition of William R. Holloway........	265
399			Deposition of Isaac L. Gibbs.................	266
400			Deposition of William H. Sanders..........	267

NO.	FROM WHOM AND TO WHOM.	DATE.	SUBJECT.	PAGE.
401			Deposition of Alexander H. Conner.	269
402			Deposition of Samuel M. Douglass.	270
403			Deposition of William Francis Elston.	271
404			Deposition of Herman Funke.	272
405			Deposition of John C. New.	274
406			Deposition of Adolphus Abromet.	276
407			Deposition of John A. Bridgeland.	277
408			Deposition of Maj. Gen. Lewis Wallace.	278
409			Deposition of Norman L. Latson.	280
410			Deposition of Jonathan N. Tifft.	287
411			Deposition of William C. Peckham.	289
412			Deposition of Marcellus Hartley.	290
413			Certificate of Jose M. J. Carvajal.	291
414			Deposition of Char'es E. Capehart.	292
415			Deposition of Richard M. Hall.	293
416			Deposition of Godlove S. Orth.	294
417			Deposition of Fred. P. Stanton.	295
418			Deposition of Walter Hawkes.	296
419			Deposition of O. H. Burbridge.	297
420			Deposition of B. Sellick Osbon.	300
421			Deposition of W. P. Dole.	302
422			Deposition of William J. Taylor.	304
423			Deposition of Wilbur F. Stocking.	307
424			Deposition of D. Willard Bliss.	310
425			Deposition of W. H. Farrar.	314

NO.	FROM WHOM AND TO WHOM.	DATE.	SUBJECT.	PAGE.
426	Gen. Sturm to Mr. Romero.	1867. April 10..	Gen. Sturm's report on the Woodhouse contract...	315
427	Gen. Sturm to Mr. Romero.	Aug. 23..	Gen. Sturm's Report to Mr. Romero regarding services rendered the Mexican government...	319

Lightning Source UK Ltd.
Milton Keynes UK
UKHW012150201118
332686UK00007B/362/P

9 780331 518429